831-2636

THE CLOCKWORK MUSE

THE
CLOCKWORK
MUSE

The Predictability of
Artistic Change

COLIN MARTINDALE

BasicBooks
A Division of HarperCollins*Publishers*

The author gratefully acknowledges permission to quote the following poetry:

"Crise de vers," in *Mallarmé*, trans. by Anthony Hartley (Penguin Books, 1965), © Anthony Hartley, 1965, pp. 166, 171, 174

Lettre du voyant," in *Rimbaud: Collected Poems*, trans. by Oliver Bernard (Penguin Books, 1962) © Oliver Bernard, 1962, pp. 9–11.

"Hérodiade," in *Mallarmé*, trans. by Wallace Fowlie (University of Chicago Press, 1943), p. 145.

"Un homme paisible" and "Nous sommes," in *Mid-century French Poets*, trans. by Wallace Fowlie, pp. 243 and 191–93, respectively. Copyright 1955 and reprinted with the permission of Twayne Publishers, a division of G. K. Hall & Co., Boston.

All other translations were made by the author.

Library of Congress Cataloging-in-Publication Data
Martindale, Colin.
    The clockwork muse: the predictability of artistic
change/Colin Martindale.
        p.   cm.
    Includes bibliographical references and index.
    ISBN 0–465–01186–1
    1. Arts—Psychological aspects. I. Title.
NX165.M39   1990   90–80245
700'.1'9—dc20   CIP

Contents

Contents

Contents

List of Figures and Tables

FIGURES

ix

List of Figures and Tables

List of Figures and Tables

TABLES

Acknowledgments

I N this book, I report on the results of over twenty years of research. In such a time, one accumulates a large number of intellectual and other debts. I shall note only the most important of these. Perhaps my greatest debt is to Wallace Fowlie of Duke Univeristy, who first interested me in literary history. This is really an understatement. Both through his inspired teaching and his numerous books, he led me to become fascinated with the topic. While I was at Harvard University, a number of people encouraged me in my belief that questions of art history and literary history lie within the legitimate domain of the social sciences, and offered invaluable advice and guidance on how to approach these questions: Lane Conn, David McClelland, Henry Murray, Talcott Parsons, Pitirim Sorokin, and Philip Stone. Though my approach is psychological rather than linguistic, the reader will also see the influence of Roman Jakobson. No one has had a greater influence on my thinking than D. E. Berlyne of the University of Toronto. Until his untimely death, he was a constant source of encouragement and new ideas and methods. Others who deserve special thanks for help, encouragement, and good ideas include Irvin Child of Yale University, Ravenna Helson of the University

Acknowledgments

of California, Berkeley, and Dean Keith Simonton of the University of California, Davis. A number of colleagues and graduate students at the University of Maine deserve special thanks—most notably, Nancy Hasenfus, Cynthia Kaplan, Anne Martindale, Anne Uemura, and Alan West. The research I report in this book is heavily based upon computer analyses. It could never have been done without the unlimited free computer time provided by the University of Maine. Free computer time does no good if one cannot get the computer to work. When this has been a problem, as it often has, Wayne Persons has invariably and cheerfully come to my rescue. As everyone at the University of Maine knows, if he can't fix a problem in short order, the computer must be broken beyond repair.

I thank Richard Liebmann-Smith of Basic Books, who first suggested that I write this book, and who offered invaluable help along the way. I cannot begin to express my gratitude to Phoebe Hoss of Basic Books, who helped to smooth my prose almost sentence by sentence and to rewrite initially obscure passages—there were many—that would have made sense only to those with a Ph.D. in statistics. Thanks are also due to Eva Benson, Kathy McAuliffe, and Marian Perry, who patiently typed and retyped the manuscript.

THE CLOCKWORK MUSE

CHAPTER 1

A Scientific Approach
to Art and Literature

I N proposing to apply to literature and the arts a scientific theory of
change, I am well aware that I am flying in the faces of the majority
of historians. A theory delineates the working of natural laws, and most
historians hold that art history—any history for that matter—does not
follow laws that can be discovered and codified. Scientists think quite
otherwise. Astrophysicists at Columbia University, for example, have
hooked together the equivalent of 576 Cray supercomputers to do simulation studies of the evolution of entire galaxies composed of billions of stars
(Peterson 1989). Because galaxies evolve on an extremely slow time scale,
we do not really have a shred of first-hand evidence concerning their
historical development. Yet this tremendously costly project seems completely reasonable to scientists, because they *assume* that everything in
the universe is governed by deterministic laws. It is their passion to find
out what these laws are.

As a scientist, I feel that if everything in the universe is governed by
laws, then art history must be as well. Up until the seventeenth century,
scientists debated about which part of the universe is random and which
part lawful. The debate was pretty much settled by the end of the seven-

teenth century and has not been much discussed since then. The solution was to assume that absolutely everything is lawful and nothing is random. This heuristic assumption has worked very well. Nothing is gained by disputes over what is lawful and what is not.

Most art and literary historians deny that there are universal laws of art history (Elliott 1988) on several grounds. First, historical events do not seem to be repetitive or periodic. In fact, as I shall show, historical trends in literary and artistic style are extremely regular and periodic at the right level of analysis. Most art historians operate on the worst possible level of analysis. Far too particularistic and caught up in details, they can't see the forest for the trees. Of course, Mallarmé only lived once. You cannot see regularities if you are wrapped up with individual creators and the exact details of what they created. The regularities become clear, however, if you back up and do "history without names."

A second reason that literary and other historians tend not to believe in historical laws is that seemingly chance or contingent events can have a profound influence on history. *Seemingly* is the key word here. It has always been known that many physical phenomena seem to be random and contingent. The most obvious ones concern turbulence, whether in the flow of water in rivers or in boiling pots or weather patterns. Historically, physicists assumed that turbulence is not in fact random, and that the laws governing it would eventually be discovered; in the meanwhile, they dealt with more tractable problems. Recently, progress has been made in explaining turbulent phenomena. Mathematical chaos theory shows that certain types of completely deterministic laws interacting with one another can produce time series that seem to be—but are not in fact—random (see Gleick 1987). Chaos theory is now being applied profitably (at least in the scientific sense) to other seemingly random time series such as stock and bond prices. History may sometimes verge on being chaotic in the mathematical sense of this term, but it is certainly not random.

A third problem besetting historians is their initial assumptions. For reasons I do not fully understand, they often adopt a completely nihilistic foundation built by idealistic philosophers such as R. G. Collingwood (1946) and hermeneutic philosophers such as Wilhelm Dilthey (1894). Such philosophers more or less say that we cannot really know anything or understand anything about history. As if this weren't bad enough, literary historians have lately become infected with deconstructionist notions that we can't know anything about anything at all (Derrida 1967). If this were true, it is unclear why anyone would want to study history. This approach is unproductive. If you assume that you can't know something, then you aren't likely to discover it. You most certainly can't discover it if you get mired down writing books and articles explaining the details of exactly how and why you can't know anything. If science is always positivistic at least in the attitudinal sense (Martindale 1988*b*), we might say that humanism tends to be negativistic, pessimistic, and melancholic. If for no other reason than this, I urge historians to follow the scientific path. For whatever reason, scientists seem to be a far happier lot than humanists. We know things, and there is great joy in discovery.

To discover the laws of art history, we need a viable discovery method. Since the only useful or productive discovery method we have is science, we need a science of aesthetic history. Thus, we must begin by assuming that art history is a completely deterministic process. Our job is to find the laws governing art history and ultimately to express them in mathematical equations embedded in an objective theory. Science is not concerned with meanings or essences. Astronomers do not, for example, spend their time asking such questions as "What is the meaning of the solar system?" By the same token, scientific history is concerned not with meanings or essences but with discovering reliable relationships and regularities. As such, it has no need for hermeneutics, deconstructionism, and similar schools of thought. Whatever their merits, these approaches are irrelevant to a scientific approach to literature and art.

THE SCIENTIFIC APPROACH

Science has certain useful assumptions, which have arisen for sound pragmatic reasons. I have already mentioned the initial assumption of complete determinism: everything is caused, and nothing is random. We shall never know whether this assumption is correct, but it is useful to believe it and utterly profitless to doubt it. Like other scientific assumptions, it is not open to debate. If you want to debate it, you are doing philosophy—

and thus doing something scientists tend to ignore, as they do other disciplines they consider irrelevant.

A second scientific assumption concerns the uniformity of nature: that is, we assume—unless there is a strong reason not to—that people are always and everywhere about the same. This assumption should cause no great problem on the level of basic processes, and it is basic processes with which I shall deal. There is no reason to think that John Donne's reaction to a brick falling on his foot would be any different than yours or mine. If anyone doubts this, the burden of proof is on the critic. In general, aside from cultural differences, if we don't find a historical figure's behavior completely baffling and incomprehensible, we should assume that the uniformity principle holds. Those who take a hermeneutic approach to history do not accept the uniformity principle. They spend whole careers trying to think themselves into the heads of people who were probably about the same as people are today.

The scientific principle of parsimony dictates that we should accept the simplest explanation that accounts for all of the facts. In the case of art or literary history, parsimony dictates that we ascribe aesthetic change to purely aesthetic causes if possible. The reason is that aesthetic causes are more proximal than extra-aesthetic ones. The doctrine of parsimony puts reflectionist explanations of literary change or art change at a disadvantage when they are pitted against endogenous explanations: the former are seldom as simple as the latter. Humanistic scholars seldom complain about this aspect of the scientific approach. They do, however, often complain about the inherent reductionism of science. I assume that art changes because of basic laws governing human behavior: that is, aesthetics can in principle be reduced to basic behavioral sciences.

Perhaps the biggest difference between scientific and humanistic inquiry concerns level of abstraction. Humanistic inquiry is often maddeningly particularistic, usually seeking to understand specific texts or specific artists and failing to see the forest for the trees. Given this specificity and particularism, it is hardly surprising that humanistic scholars have discovered no general laws of art history. This is not their real aim, and they have no methods for discovering or testing such laws. On the other hand, science involves an attempt to formulate laws that are extremely abstract and general. For example, the law of gravity applies to everything from planets to apples. It has nothing special to tell us about any one particular apple. In the physical sciences, this distinction causes few problems, because no one takes any special interest in specific apples. Things are far different in art history. Scientific art history at its best is aimed at discovering general laws that may tell us nothing special about individual creators—an approach that bothers some humanistic scholars, who think that great men and women should somehow receive special treatment or get exemptions from natural laws. That Goethe was a great poet did not exempt him from the law of gravity, any more than it did from the laws of literary history.

The most important principle of science is that it is empirical, forbidding statements that cannot at least indirectly or in principle be tested. Empirical tests are not necessarily quantitative. The data of literary history—mainly texts and texts about these texts—are, however, so massive that it is difficult to imagine empirical hypothesis testing that does not involve some quantification. Quantification is also generally needed to satisfy the rule that scientific observations be objective rather than subjective.

What, then, is the goal of this scientific history? First, it is to describe what in fact happened in artistic and literary traditions, how the content and the style of the artifacts arising out of them changed over time. Then, it is to explain why this rather than something else *had* to happen in terms of the simplest and most comprehensive possible theory. Conventional art history, on the other hand, often takes the form of a chronicle interspersed with comments on extra-artistic history, sentimental effusions, interpretations of texts, and what the literary theorist Jurij Lotman (1970) has called "literary chit-chat." Such material complements rather than conflicts with scientific history.

Although my methods may be new, I am of the old school when it comes to writing any sort of history. Scientific history is well over one hundred years old. Its first goal is to find out "what really happened" (Ranke 1906 [1835]). I have no truck with idealistic notions that scientific history is impossible, that history is a fantasy story made up to serve as political propaganda (Collingwood 1946; Rusch 1985). As Hippolyte Taine put it, "there are facts here, as everywhere else" (1875, p.40). You *can* write art history so that it serves as propaganda—but only if you are willing to distort the facts, and you will eventually be found out. If your thesis is that democratic or egalitarian politics has had a long-lasting influence on British poetry, you are in trouble from the start. You have to leave out almost all of the early poets, who were aristocrats. You will get bogged down in the seventeenth century: the royalists have to be left out; extra puritans need to be pulled from obscurity and put in. Then you simply have to lie. The puritans helped the royalists escape punishment, and vice versa, depending upon which side was in power. Poetry was more important than politics for many of these poets, after all. Then you have to invent. Politics usually has rather little to do with poetic content. Facts have to be completely distorted if you wish to say otherwise.

Scientific and humanistic inquiry operate at completely different levels of abstraction. Consider a mountain, any mountain. A geologist will explain that the mountain will eventually be transformed from towering stone to level soil. Raindrops will accomplish this process. Blowing sand will help. This *will* happen. It *must* happen. It is guaranteed to do so by the second law of thermodynamics. A humanistic scholar may complain that the geologist overlooks everything special and unique about the mountain. The mountain has beautiful trees, perhaps the very cedars of Lebanon. This is of no consequence. The cedars of Lebanon are what is in statistics called *error variance*. If they are cut down, the mountain may come down a bit faster or a bit slower—but its decomposition takes eons. The influence of the trees is small. What they are called does not matter at all.

Societies come down just as do mountains. The details vary but the laws do not. As Alexis de Tocqueville (1956 [1835]) remarked, the force that brought down kings will not stop when it reaches shopkeepers' doors. It never has before. It never will in future. Revolutions occur in many circumstances that differ only on the surface. On an abstract level, the same sequence of events always happens (Brinton 1960 [1949]). One could say that it is inconsequential whether the hero is named Washington or Lenin, or the place is Russia or America. The outcome is going to be similar.

Revolutions occur in the arts just as in politics. We have every reason to want to know the exact details; and it is the job of the humanistically oriented historian to tell us about them. As a scientific historian, I aim to look at the forest rather than at the trees. This is history without names, history where exactly what John Donne said, or even the fact that he rather than someone else said it, is of little interest. This approach does not necessarily contradict traditional history. To understand John Donne's place in the history of English literature, we must know the general trends in order to see what is peculiar to Donne himself as opposed to what characterizes all British poets writing in the early seventeenth century or all British poets in general. If this contention needs any support beyond that of common sense, I have this writ from Ezra Pound: "The proper METHOD for studying poetry and good letters is the method of contemporary biologists, that is careful, first-hand examination of the matter, and continual COMPARISON of one 'slide' or specimen with another" (1934, p.17).

The characteristics of Donne's style differentiate him from other poets. We cannot understand the metaphysical style unless we compute how metaphysical poets differ from other poets. We cannot understand Donne's style unless we compute how he differs from the metaphysical poets. Although this computation does not have to be quantitative, it will not be very precise unless it is. To understand Donne, we need literally to compare his poetry with all other British poetry—a task that would overwhelm the capacity of the human brain. Now we can examine the history of British poetry in many volumes, as did William Courthope (1906–10), for example—or, as I do here, sum it up in equations and graphs. Depending upon what we want to understand, one or the other approach may be more useful.

THE LAW OF NOVELTY

We live in a predictable world. Never, Salvador Dali once complained, had he ordered lobster in a restaurant and been served a baked telephone. Indeed not! In our everyday world, there is a numbing sameness. Every morning we are bombarded with automatic "Good mornings" and routine inquiries about how we are. Our days are full of pat questions and equally pat replies. Imagine what would happen, however, if some of us, tiring of this state of affairs, decide to do something about it. Decide, indeed, to outlaw any and all repetition. Once something has been said, it can never be said again. Once something has been done, it cannot be done again. This requires no act of Congress. We can implement it ourselves.

We can, as well, impose a sanction more severe than the death penalty. Anyone who says something that has already been said, or does something that has already been done, will simply be ignored. Someone who persists in the crime of repetition will find that he or she ceases to exist. No one will pay the slightest attention to the person.

Enthusiasm for this brave new world would, of course, vary. Strictly construed, our new law changes nothing. "Good morning" is never said with exactly the same intonation in exactly the same place to exactly the same person. Even if it is, the person is a day older than he or she was yesterday. Well, we shall have none of this legalistic nit picking. If we are going to make the world a better place, we should first follow Shakespeare's wisdom: "The first thing we do, let's kill all the lawyers" (*Henry VI* II.4.1.86). Lawyers will no longer be needed anyway. Laws require that we do some things and refrain from doing others. If things have already been done, it would be passé to do them again. It is against the novelty rule to obey the laws. It is against the law to break them, too. Unless a law has never been broken before, it is immoral to break it again.

It would hardly do for a business person to ask about yesterday's profits. After all, profits have already been asked about. However, no one has ever asked, "What were our profits on September 1, 1989?" Is such a question worthy of a response? It is novel, but is it novel enough? I think not. It is rather too close to questions that have been asked countless times before. Other people may disagree. An executive might get a response. A response would be more likely if the question were rephrased. For example, "without recourse to the calculus, can you tell me how many porkbelly futures we could have purchased yesterday if we subtracted our costs from our receipts and used the entire difference to buy the aforesaid futures?" This question would hardly do the next day. By then, executives might be asking about buying jelly beans in the morning with Swiss francs and inquiring about the combined weight of the company's jelly beans and deutschemarks in the evening.

Note that our new law has forced discourse to be *concrete* and specific. Specific statements are more likely to be novel than abstract ones. In fact, abstract statements are downright dangerous: in subsuming a large number of specific utterances, they pre-empt them. Asking about profits in the old days has made it difficult to ask about profits now. If only our ancestors had not asked such abstract questions. For all we know, the new order may last a thousand years. It would be wise not to rule out statements we might need later. It would be wise to avoid abstractions.

Consider a salesperson in our strange new world. The stock phrase, "May I help you," is obviously illegal. "May I help you on this day of September 1, 1989," may work—but only once. The second customer must receive a different greeting. "Perhaps you who stand imperiously before me holds in his heart the desire to purchase an eggbeater" would do. But it, too, cannot be used again. A salesperson could begin with, "You who stand there eyes lost in paradise remembering my milk drunk long ago," and hope to goodness that the customer has not read Mallarmé. This is downright cheating. Though less eloquent, longer and longer greetings might serve. Our new law is driving us to *circumlocution.* Longer and more indirect statements are more likely to be novel ones. Circumlocution alone will not do for long. Our salesman may string together more and more epithets. This will not work for long either. The strange and effusive greetings will all begin to sound more or less the same.

If a customer has come to purchase a toaster, she must somehow get to wherever toasters are without asking directly. Once there, it is obviously impossible to negotiate in the normal manner—as that, too, has already been *done.* Rather than saying, "This is our newest model," something such as "This is the rising sun of the destroyers of leavened moisture," is called for. The rule has got people speaking in metaphors. What is the customer to make of this statement? Is it a toaster from Japan? Is it a new model? The rule has rendered discourse *ambiguous.*

Thus far, I have dealt with speech. But our new law covers everything. If our customer buys the toaster, she cannot take it home. She can't take it to her home at any rate. She has already gone home. She must go somewhere else. She will not go to that place with a toaster, though. The toasters she has been shown are unworthy of attention. They look exactly like toasters she has already seen. Wherever she goes, she would not clutter up the place with such a visual cliché. No more toasters will be sold until toasters that do not look like toasters are manufactured. Each one must, of course, be unique.

On the face of it, our new law is unlikely to last for more than a few minutes. This would not be a thousand-year Reich, but a twelve-minute one. Any longer, and society would collapse into chaos. As with any revolution, there would be a conservative backlash. People do not want this much novelty. Even if they did, most people would find that they could not follow the new law even if they wanted to. They would quickly run out of new things to say and do. My hypothetical salesman is an anomaly. He can think of clever things to say. In the world we live in, such silver-tongued salespeople are likely to find themselves out of jobs. Customers who come for a toaster do not really want to leave with a refrigerator retrofitted with a hibachi. They want to take it to their own home, not to a random house. One would not expect to be served baked telephones at restaurants for long. All in all, we should rather have the lobster.

Novelty and Immortality

Rather than describing a revolution, I have magnified the world we live in. We like a bit of novelty occasionally, but not much. We do not care for people who repeat themselves endlessly. We prefer those who say or do somewhat novel things. Anyone who says or does something too novel, though, is ignored or put away. The novelty rule seems to work in reverse. It is the poets and artists who are ignored. As Wordsworth said in "The World Is Too Much With Us," "getting and spending, we lay waste our souls." Well, we apparently *want* to lay them waste. The novelty rule in its pure form is confined to the arts. Painters cannot copy old paintings. Exact replication is not allowed in any of the arts. If it were, we should make no distinction between typesetters and poets, between musical performers and composers. The notion of art forgery would make no sense at all.

We generally set the novelty rule aside so that we can go about our practical affairs. We do so to our own detriment. We *do* live by the rules I have described. So long as we live, we are not ignored—but, as has been unkindly pointed out, "in the long run, we are all dead." When we die, the novelty rule takes effect with an exceptionless brutality. It is then that we begin to be ignored. Only poets and artists escape this fate. In the long run, we *are* ignored and forgotten if in life we evaded the prescription for novelty. Our names are duly inscribed on gravestones. Wind and weather efface these names, usually long after all minds have forgotten us. We read in Ecclesiasticus (44.9), "And some there be who have no memorial, who are perished as though they had never been, and are become as though they had not been born." These "some" are all who have broken the law of novelty.

Poets do not always write with an eye toward immortality. If they are original enough, that is their reward. They may confer a second-rate immortality on others. We know the names of pharaohs because artists put their cartouches somewhere on their handiwork. We know of King Arthur because poets sang of him; for all we know, they invented him. But who ruled Rome when Horace said, "I have built a monument more lasting than bronze" (*Exigi monumentum aerae perennius; Odes* III. 30.1)? Which pope commissioned Michelangelo to paint the ceiling of the Sistine Chapel? Who was president of the United States when Edgar Allan Poe wrote "The Fall of the House of Usher"? The Duke of Gloucester will live on only in an obscure footnote because he touched the life of the still-remembered Sir Edward Gibbon and happened to say something worth quoting: "Scribble, scribble, scribble, eh, Mr. Gibbon?"

Novelty and Habituation

Need for novelty is built into the definition of being an artist, whatever other laws govern art at any point in time. This is a very odd rule: that rules must be broken, that laws must be disobeyed. Neoclassic poets and artists occasionally deny that this rule exists. It is well to keep in mind Plato's reminder that poets lie. In due course, I shall look at what neoclassic poets actually do. The data are clear: they obey the one rule of novelty. Although pressure for novelty often seems a modern requirement, it has burdened artists since the dawn of time. Novelty has been valued to differing degrees at different times; and even when not positively valued, it holds indirect sway. It does so because of *habituation,* the gradual loss of interest in repeated stimuli. Habituation is a universal property of all nervous tissue. We find it in sea slugs. We find it in rats. We find it, of course, in the human brain. It is never absent. It is the single force that has pushed art always in a consistent direction ever since the first work of art was made.

The many forces that influence art at one period or another push it in random and contradictory directions and over the centuries cancel one another out. That leaves only the pressure for novelty, a pressure as inexorable and as unidirectional as gravity. Is the history of art, then, random save for a small tendency toward more originality or surprisingness? Not at all. Pressure for novel discourse produces a special kind of novel discourse: poetry. That is, the pressure is likely to make discourse distinctly concrete, ornate, ambiguous, indirect, and metaphorical—all fundamental characteristics of poetry. Pressure for novelty of movement produces dance. Pressure for novelty of depiction produces painting. In short, pressure for novelty produces art. This is not all that the pressure for novelty does. In the next chapter, where I investigate how mind produces novelty, we shall see that pressure for novelty has got to produce systematic changes in the content and in the form of poetry and all of the other arts. These changes turn out to be exactly the changes that occur in the history of art forms.

It is not that artists are governed only by need for novelty, or their audiences only by habituation. With a few exceptions, artists treat the constraint for originality as a nuisance. It is a cost of doing business but seldom the primary goal. The poet may seek to woo her lover by speaking of the radiance of his eyes. The poet may wish to communicate a profound insight into the human condition. She may wish to play with words and show us kinships of sound hidden by disparities of meaning. But the requirement to speak in a new way is always present. As often as not, the originality constraint is satisfied according to the principle of least effort. Originality is obtained in the least troublesome way. George Kingsley Zipf (1972 [1949]) has produced impressive evidence that the principle of least effort is a universal human tendency.

Thus, two minor forces operate against each other. Habituation forces the poet to express himself or herself in new ways. The principle of least effort leads one to do this in the least bothersome way, and prevents explosive increases in novelty. These contrary forces lead to orderly change in poetry and in all other arts as well. Indeed, art history is extremely orderly and predictable.

Though I speak of these forces as minor, their importance lies in their consistency. However strong they may be, other forces that are inconsistent cannot in principle explain historical trends. Shelley loved freedom. So did Swinburne, but his real passion was for submission. Ezra Pound loved fascism. There is no consistency here, nor is the case unique. Poets are not consistent in their other attitudes any more than they are in their political beliefs. They are not consistent in what they believe poetry to be or in what they write about. We may find interludes of consistency where there is some consensus. There is never total agreement. Writers may take one side or the other in the class struggle (Plekhanov 1936 [1913]), in the struggle to oppress women or to liberate them (Millett 1978), or in the struggle to support or destroy the so-called Great Tradition of Western literature (Eliot 1932)—but these are forces that cancel rather than compound. They cannot account for long-term trends, and the history of art is long indeed.

MEANING IN ART HISTORY

Although most people consider meaning the most important aspect of art and literature, *meaning* is a vague and slippery term and thus a bad foundation upon which to build a theory of art history. First of all, we must ask about meaning for whom. We may find many things in a poem. We may find inspiration or insight in a poem by Donne. The meaning for us has nothing at all to do with the history of poetry. The poem was not written for us. Donne wrote his poems for a small circle of other poets (Williamson 1958 [1930]) and did not even intend them for publication. Donne's poetry had its main effects upon his contemporaries and successors. This is not particular only to Donne. Walter Benjamin (1968) goes so far as to say that *no* poem was ever written for an audience. However extreme this judgment, poems are often more like reveries than acts of communication.

Trying to figure out what an author meant by a poem has long been out of fashion in literary circles. The author's intention is not especially relevant to literary history—fortunately, because poets often do not know what their poetry means. As Plato put it in the "Apology," poets are like "soothsayers who say many fine things, but do not understand the meaning of them" (Jowett 1937, p.405). The meaning of a poem must certainly come into play when we examine how one poet has influenced another. The meaning for the influenced poet must be crucial. Perhaps. Contemporary critics are fond of pointing out that poetry—or any other art work—does not have a single meaning (for example, Fish 1980; Miller 1979). There are as many meanings as there are readers. Harold Bloom (1973, 1975) argues that later poets systematically misread and misunderstand earlier poets in order to avoid being influenced, in order to avoid copying. It is not meaning that is crucial. It is difference that is crucial. One must say something different—precisely as I have argued.

So far as the engines of history are concerned, meaning does not matter. In principle, one could study the history of a literary tradition without ever reading any of the literature. When I speak to an audience of literary critics, I make sure to point out that the main virtue of the computerized content analytic methods I use is that they save one from actually having to read the literature. I say this to discover whether anyone in the audience has a sense of humor and so to anger any opponents as to make their attacks incoherent. Though I do in fact read the literature, I would not really have to. One could study the history of any artistic tradition—at least in principle—without even knowing what the art form is, without knowing whether it is Chinese music or Greek vases. This statement will, I hope, be more plausible at the end of this book than it is now. I have proposed doing art history without names. The idea of history without names is not new. Am I not going a bit far to propose an art history that neglects meaning and does not even bother with the sort of art being studied? However odd in the present context, these proposals are far from new. If meaning is indeterminate, we cannot say what it is. What is the meaning of the tree outside my window? That is a silly question. The tree has no intrinsic meaning. Why should we expect a painting of the tree to have meaning? Why expect a poem about the tree to have meaning?

Could we study art history without even asking what an art form is? Certainly, but it would be a nuisance. One would have to go to silly extremes to avoid finding out what one was studying. If we look to other areas of science, the reason we could is clear. If you drop an object in a vacuum, a physicist can tell you where the object is, what its velocity is, and what its acceleration is if you provide but one piece of information: *when* you dropped the object. So long as you can assure the physicist that the vacuum is a perfect one, he or she will not bother to ask you what the object is. If you provide this information, it will be ignored as not relevant. The analogy is a good one. Much art—including art convention-

14

ally thought to be heavily influenced by audience pressures—is created in a virtual social vacuum. As for history, the whole point of universal history is to find general laws that apply no matter what nations are involved or at what time. Because the topic is complex, these laws seem less deterministic than those governing objects falling in vacuums. History is, however, not completely chaotic and unpredictable. Just as in chemistry, certain combinations in certain situations will explode. Just as in physics, certain configurations in certain places will collapse.

DEFINING A WORK OF ART

Meaning does not make a text literary. The linguist Roman Jakobson (1960, 1981) asks us to discriminate between the poetic function of language and its referential or communicative function. A recipe communicates something, but it is not a work of literature. It serves merely to communicate information. It could be paraphrased. So long as the paraphrase did not alter its meaning, no one would complain. According to Jakobson, the poetic function of language calls attention to itself; in a sense, it refers only to itself. Consider Edward Gibbon's *Decline and Fall of the Roman Empire.* It serves two functions. On the communicative level, it is a recipe for the collapse of a civilization. What Gibbon had to say about this could be rephrased and said in another way with no loss of information. In fact, the work would profit. We could get rid of Gibbon's ornate and beautiful way of putting things. Doing so, however, would destroy the literary value of the text. *What* Gibbon said is nonliterary or communicative use of language. *How* he said it is literary use of language. It is not what Gibbon said—it is not meaning—that makes *The Decline and Fall of the Roman Empire* a work of literature. It is how he said what he had to say that makes it literature.

Any text has both poetic and communicative aspects. The poetic aspect of a recipe is about zero; it is not literature. A literary text may certainly seek to communicate something—but it is not thereby literature. In other words, the meaning of a text is not really relevant to literature. Aesop's *Fables* are literary not because of their meaning, but because of how this meaning is conveyed. The same is true of any literary text. If we extract one hundred coherent meanings or interpretations of *Hamlet,* we may not have discovered a thing about *Hamlet* as literature.

A similar argument can be made concerning the other arts. The art historian George Kubler (1962) defined art as useless artifacts or the useless aspects of useful artifacts. Art is not utilitarian. There is no real use for a painting or a piece of music. Of course, they may give us pleasure, but pleasure can be gotten in many ways. A chair or a vase has an obvious function. The artistic aspects of a chair or a vase have nothing to do with their functions. The artistic aspects are decorative and, from a purely utilitarian perspective, could be dispensed with. So far as art is concerned, function is not relevant. So far as a historian of decorative art is concerned, the function of a chair is not relevant; it may not even be mentioned.

People who are not artists are often uncomfortable with Jakobson and Kubler's definitions: A work of art or literature is something that is useless and meaningless. The definitions sit better with poets and artists. Those who create so-called high art are often explicit that it is useless. It is precisely this uselessness that makes it high, not popular, art. If you create something that can be used, you are an artisan rather than an artist. In the world of art, the more useless the product, the higher the artist's status. The same is true in science. In the world of science, pure scientists have higher status than applied scientists. Pure mathematicians are on the top of the heap. What they do is completely useless and applies to absolutely nothing. They are, in fact, often disappointed when someone finds an application for their equations. One who creates useless things cannot be used. The artist is free in a way that few of us are. If you do something useful, you can be used by other people. And you will be. You become a tool yourself.

There are two reasons not to define art and literature as Kubler and Jakobson have. The first is practical. The definitions do not sit well with many people. It will not serve my purposes if the reader is annoyed from the outset with how I have defined my subject matter. The second is substantive. The definitions require us to define meaning and utility in restrictive ways. Jakobson's definition, though working fairly well for lyric poetry, runs into difficulties with forms such as the novel. The novelist, manipulating meanings by devices such as suspense and surprise, works on both the linguistic and the semantic levels. We should have to tear

16

apart form and content in an odd and arbitrary way to make our subject matter fit the definition. This is not necessary.

The consensus of most aestheticians is that art cannot be defined by the presence or the absence of a specific list of features (Dickie 1971; Peckham 1965). Art is whatever *you* say it is. It is whatever is treated as art. A rock or a piece of driftwood can be turned into art merely by putting it on display. In the hands of an artist, just about anything can be transmuted into art—a toilet seat, a canvas at which paint has been randomly flung, a picture of a Campbell's soup can, a canvas with no paint at all on it. There is simply no list of features that defines what art is.

Art is not unique in this respect. Artificial or scientific categories are defined by lists of features. Natural categories are not (Rosch 1975; Wittgenstein 1953). Wittgenstein asks us to consider what features define a game. We can find no features common to all games. For any proposed feature, we can find games that do not possess it. There is usually a winner and a loser, but not always. Witness solitaire. Games are not necessarily fun. Most of us would find little enjoyment in trying to play professional football. Many of us do not enjoy playing bridge with people who treat every hand as if it had the significance of the Battle of Hastings.

The psychologist Eleanor Rosch (1975) has shown that the members of natural categories share virtually no common characteristics. What characterizes furniture? Nothing much besides the common name. Pieces of furniture share family resemblances, just as members of the same family. Two relatives will share some features and differ on others. Taken pairwise, we find many common features. Taken on the whole, no one feature is possessed by all of the members of the family. The same is true of any other natural category. The same is true of art and literature. Works of art show family resemblances rather than being defined by an exhaustive list of features.

AESTHETIC GENEALOGY

If we want to know where the family resemblances of a human family came from, we turn to genealogy and genetics. If we can gather enough information, we can account for the resemblances. The laws of genetics will also allow us to account for the differences. We can do the same in the case of art and literature. As the geneticist Theodosius Dobzhansky remarked, "Nothing in biology makes sense except in the light of evolution" (1973, p.125). It could just as well be said that nothing in art or literature makes sense except in the light of evolution. At any one time, works of art in the same medium tend to show marked family resemblances. Without much training, we can recognize that a piece of music belongs to the baroque "family," or style. With a bit more training, we can enumerate features that allow us to make this determination. No piece of baroque music has all of these features; just a few will do. Literature and the arts show such profound historical changes, however, that it is often impossible to find any common features shared by works in the same medium produced during different eras. What, if anything, does a Bach fugue have in common with John Cage's "4'33"? Because the latter consists of 4 minutes and 33 seconds of complete silence, the two works do not even share the feature of being composed of a series of sounds. The only common feature—beyond the silence Cage's work shares with the pauses in a fugue—is that both are labeled "music." Music from Bach to Cage, has, however, changed in a series of small steps from Bach's style toward Cage's. Only if we are aware of this history does Cage's composition make any sense. I shall argue that we can explain or understand this historical progression with a theory that is altogether analogous to Darwin's theory of biological evolution. Only within the context of such a theory can we understand *either* Bach's or Cage's work. Each evolved in a lawful way from prior composers' works.

Change is equally drastic in all of the arts. Compare, for example, a painting by Poussin with one by Picasso. Both are on canvas. Paint was used to create both. Beyond that, the paintings are not markedly similar. Yet Picasso is a lawful "descendant" of Poussin. Though you do not look much like your ancestors of three hundred years ago, good portraits of everyone in your family line would clearly show why you look the way you do. In the same way, artists between Poussin and Picasso left portraits of their artistic styles. Or, take Swift's *Gulliver's Travels* and Samuel Beckett's *The Unnameable*. The latter novel does have a hero—a dried-up piece of flesh. If it has a plot, no one has yet succeeded in discovering it. Both works are certainly novels; but in reality, *Gulliver's Travels* probably shares more features with, say, a nonliterary history of the Thirty Year's

War than with *The Unnameable*. Still, a look at the novels produced between Swift and Beckett reveals the gradual transmutation between one and the other.

EXPLAINING ARTISTIC CHANGE

Although a theory is supposed to explain the relevant facts about a phenomenon, in art or literary history there is no real consensus about these facts. Narrative historians present us with a congeries of facts and dates and speculations. Because such historians do not usually admit that they have a theory, they do not need to tell us why they are presenting these data. If one did not have at least an implicit theory to write history, one would be confronted with pure chaos (Lévi-Strauss 1962), ignorant of what to report and what to leave out.

Since some histories of French literature tell us Mallarmé's street address, but others do not, the exact address must not be relevant. If we read enough narrative histories, we can extrapolate some of the relevant data—or, more precisely, what is supposed to be explained. But one learns quickly that it is impossible to learn much about history by reading history books. The history of art and literature are regular and lawful processes. Why was this not clear centuries ago? One reason is that historians have botched the story. Perhaps considering it their job to report details, they have omitted mention of obvious regularities. Worse, gaps are left in the story. It is not unusual to find whole centuries skipped over in histories of literature, music, and painting. What happened during these centuries provides the continuity that makes artistic trends blatantly obvious. It is hard to see a trend in French poetry if a historian skips from Ronsard (*c.* 1600) to Chénier (*c.* 1800). It is hard to see a trend in English poetry if an author devotes one hundred pages to Shakespeare and Milton and makes up for it by skipping the early eighteenth century. If we are to find trends, we must be more even-handed.

We can, nonetheless, get some notion of what is to be explained if we look at enough narrative histories. In any artistic tradition, there is a sequence of styles, which must be explained: that is, whether they succeed each other precipitately or gradually, and why. Styles going by different names show obvious similarities: for example, eighteenth-century neoclassicism and fifteenth-century renaissance style, and fourteenth-century gothicism and nineteenth-century romanticism. Though the earlier style did not directly cause the later style, we must explain the similarities. Perhaps art oscillates along a continuum so that such similarities are inevitable. If so, we must explain why it oscillates, and why along that continuum rather than along some other one. Of course, we must explain what the continuum is and why it exists.

Within any artistic style, there seems to be movement along this same continuum. Earlier works tend to be simpler or more classic. Later works tend to be more contorted or gothic. We see this in the gothic style itself. Early gothic cathedrals are certainly not classic in their lines, but they tend to be simple and symmetrical. We cannot even find the lines in late gothic cathedrals. The building is lost in sinuous curves. Decoration is not just pasted on; everything is decoration. Early renaissance painting resembles idealized photographs. Late renaissance, or mannerist, painting depicts figures in postures so twisted or contorted as to be humanly impossible. We must find out whether this is generally true of styles; and, if so, explain why.

Over long periods, in accordance with the law of novelty, works in an artistic tradition tend to become unpredictable or surprising. Consider the following excerpts from French poetry:

Beneath your fair head, a white delicate neck
Inclines and would outshine the brightness of snow.
(Chénier, "Les Colombes")

This evening a done-for sun lies on the top of the hill
. . . .
And he lies there, like a gland torn out of a neck.
(Laforgue, "L'Hiver qui vient")

I love you opposite the seas
Red like the egg when it is green.
(Breton, "Tiki")

The lines by André Chénier, written in the late eighteenth century, are perfectly understandable. There is no question what color these doves *(colombes)* are. Chénier tells us three times that they are white, and implies it a fourth time, apparently wanting no mistake about the matter. There is a metaphor of sorts here, but it comes down to saying that white is like white. The simile in the excerpt from Laforgue, who wrote in the late nineteenth century, is much more remote than Chénier's metaphor. A setting sun is like a bleeding gland. This is hardly, though, the first analogy to the sun that leaps to mind. Poets have talked about the setting sun for centuries. The earlier ones had an easy time of it, finding the obvious things to say. Once said, these things could not be said again. Breton's incongruous simile, written in the early twentieth century, violates conventional logic. These are not the words of a desperate man driven to madness because all the reasonable similes about the sea had already been used; these are the words of a free man. In or around 1900, poets separately and together conspired to abrogate the rule that similes must join together similar things, in an attempt to create more novel similes than had been created before.

In many poetic traditions, there has been a historical movement of similes and metaphors away from consistency toward remoteness and incongruity. Similar historical trends can be discovered in the other arts. Once European painters got the hang of how to render a two-dimensional representation of reality, they set about figuring out how to paint ever more distorted representations of reality. In fact, old-fashioned painters have always done representations that look fine to nonpainters. Every innovation has been a distortion. Correct rendition of perspective was itself seen as a distortion: important figures in the background were smaller than unimportant ones in the foreground. In the eyes of contemporary viewers, Western painting has been plunging into chaos ever since Giotto and Cimabue.

It is generally agreed that Western music has been becoming more dissonant for centuries. At least in private, most of us would agree that contemporary classical music sounds awful. It is dissonant; there is no detectable melody. But people have been saying the same thing about contemporary music for centuries. The major thirds (for example, C to E), which used to be considered dissonant, now sound perfectly consonant. A long time ago, there were few consonant chords; now there are many. Every time composers began using a new chord, it sounded awful. If we want to appear cultured, we can't admit that we don't like opera. Outside of Italy, few people have ever liked opera. When opera was first introduced, the cultural élite thought it an abomination. The poetry ruined the music and vice versa. Few people liked Beethoven's Moonlight Sonata when it was first played: it broke too many rules. If we dislike it today, it is for an opposite reason: it doesn't break any rules at all. What has caused the trends toward increasing dissonance, distortion, and incongruity?

Before I propose my theory about these trends, let me say what is wrong with competing theories. In the case of current art and literary history, the main problem is that there are no competing theories, especially for art history. E. H. Gombrich (1969), himself an art historian, points out that there have been—for the last fifty years or so—no general theories of art history. This discipline seems to have lost all confidence. Grand theories of art history have been rejected without being replaced. Part of the reason for this situation is that, before it can produce theories, a discipline needs to get its facts straight. On the other hand, without a theory, one does not know which facts to get straight—or even what counts as a fact (Comte 1830). Lacking a guiding general theory, art historians tend to focus on extremely specific topics. They produce a lot of details about these topics, but it is often not clear whether the details are relevant to much of anything. There is, however, not a complete absence of theory in the field of art history. In the following sections, I describe the most prevalent approaches to the question of change in literature and the arts: the "great tradition" non-explanation; extrinsic, or reflectionist, theories; intrinsic theories; and evolutionary theories.

The "Great Tradition" Non-Explanation

One view of trends such as I have mentioned is that they simply do not exist. Cleanth Brooks (1947), for example, held that there is no historical "progress" in literature, that all writers—regardless of when they write—are contributing to one "great tradition." This literary critic argued that they are writing on the same topics. They may do so in different ways. However, manner and topic vary randomly across time.

Furthermore, one could argue that, while modern poetic metaphors are remote or bizarre, equally strange metaphors can be found in earlier poetry. Gesualdo's early seventeenth-century compositions are as dissonant as many twentieth-century musical works. Brooks's contention that there is no systematic historical change in literature and the arts is apparently based upon the misguided "proof by example" method too often used in the humanities. When I say that there is a trend in the remoteness of poetic similes, I mean not that *every* twentieth-century simile is more incongruous than *every* nineteenth-century simile, and so on; but that there is a general movement in this direction. We can use statistics to prove that the "great tradition" hypothesis is simply incorrect.

Extrinsic, or Reflectionist, Theories

Some theorists say that since art is a reflection of society, artistic change must be a reflection of social change. As Sir Leslie Stephen put it, "Literature is the noise of the wheels of history." Such theories can be traced to Madame de Staël's (1964 [1800]) notion that literature is the reflection of society. This approach, actually rare on the level of systematic theory, is extremely common as an implicit assumption among those, such as compilers of college textbooks on art history or of literary anthologies, who have not really thought much about aesthetic theory. To those who take it as axiomatic that art tells us something about the Zeitgeist, or "spirit of the age," in which it was created, it seems reasonable to ascribe changes in art to changes in the spirit of an age; but this view is poorly supported. As the art historians E. H. Gombrich (1969) and Michael Podro (1982) have pointed out, reflectionist theorists—whether they admit it or not—can trace their lineage back to Hegel (1920 [1835]). Hegel clearly saw everything in culture, from economics through art to theology, as a manifestation of the same Absolute Spirit and thus as intimately related. In fact, it is an empirical question whether all aspects of culture and society are closely related; and Pitirim Sorokin (1937), among other sociologists, has provided evidence suggesting that they are not. While Hegel had a vague explanation for Absolute Spirit's developing or unfolding across time more or less as an acorn develops into an oak tree, it is not at all clear what he meant by Absolute Spirit. Thus, later theorists have concretized the term into *Zeitgeist,* or the way individual people tended to think and feel during a given era.

A long line of art historians have treated art as reflecting this vaguely defined spirit of the age. Anti-Hegelians from Jacob Burckhardt (1950 [1860]) through Johan Huizinga (1924) and Erwin Panofsky (1924–25) did so. Heinrich Wölfflin's (1964 [1888]) early theory and Alois Riegl's (1927 [1901]) late theory are explicit in holding that art reflects the world view of its age. Panofsky (1924–25) explains phenomena as diverse as perspective and gothic architecture as reflecting current world views. As Arnold Hauser (1963 [1958]) and Gombrich (1969) have noted, such theories—having discarded their Hegelian basis—cannot account for why the Zeitgeist changes. Thus, they cannot really explain why art changes. If changes in art derive from changes in the Zeitgeist, one has to explain why the latter changes if one wants to provide a satisfactory explanation of why art changes. The problem cannot be referred to specialists in such matters. There are no such specialists among modern historians. General historians, just like art historians, have not proposed grand theories lately. Thus, one has to be satisfied with older explanations such as the historian Oswald Spengler's (1926–28): the Zeitgeist changed because of "destiny." This is no more enlightening than Hegel's original explanation. One of the reasons general theories of art history have been out of fashion for the last half-century (Gombrich 1969; Munro 1963) is that they have no foundation once their Hegelian basis is removed.

Marxist theory does provide an explanation of why the Zeitgeist changes. Marx, of course, argued that the explanation of history lies not in changes in an abstract Absolute Spirit but in inevitable changes due to class struggles. The class that controls the infrastructure (the economy or means of production) sets up an ideology that conditions the superstructure (art, law, science, and so on). Because of changes in the infrastructure, the superstructure changes. Whether one agrees with it or not, Marxist theory gives a possible explanation of why ideology changes and, thus, of why art changes. To use Marxist terms, the cultural superstructure must rest upon the economic base. A concrete example shows that we all agree with this: you can't build a gothic cathedral unless you can afford to buy the materials and hire the help. However, from Marx and Engels (1947) on, mainstream Marxist theorists have been explicit that art is extremely independent of the infrastructure (Eagleton 1976) and, thus, largely follows its own laws. What these laws are, the Marxist theorists do not tell us. As the literary critic Terry Eagleton remarked, Marxism is not really a reflectionist theory at all: art reflects society more or less in "the way in which a car reproduces the materials of which it is built" (1976, p.51).

Though a few Marxist theorists (such as Caudwell 1937 and Hauser 1951) have proposed reflectionistic theories of art history, much of Marxist theory about art and literature is prescriptive rather than descriptive or explanatory. Confusion has arisen because Marxist theorists (for example, Plekhanov 1936 [1913]; Trotsky 1968 [1925]) often argue that it is unfortunate that art is autonomous. Read closely, they actually assert that art *is* autonomous and follows its own intrinsic laws of development, but that art and literature *ought* to be instruments of class warfare. In earlier eras, they could not be. When poetry was written by courtiers for other courtiers, it was not used for class warfare. It was not shown to the masses, who couldn't read anyway. Thus, poetry was a pretty ineffective weapon. In discussing nineteenth-century literature, Georgi Plekhanov is not at all enlightening; he is merely petulant. European writers *should*, he says, have been helping in the class struggle. They hated the bourgeoisie more than the proletariat did, but they preferred to strike aristocratic poses and spend their time creating *l'art pour l'art*. This made them decadent. Perhaps so, but saying what should have happened sheds no light on what did happen. As for why poets hated bourgeois values, Plekhanov does not even give a plausible Marxist explanation: they hated bourgeois values because such values were in fact bad. This leaves us at something of a loss when it comes to explaining why decadent poets happened to notice this supposedly obvious fact, but the middle class thought its values were just fine.

At first glance, it may seem obvious that art reflects society. For example, a portrait painting almost always depicts a person dressed in the style of his or her day and perhaps surrounded by the furnishings of the time. A moment's thought reveals that such a painting "reflects" not society but other art forms—fashion and furniture. Of course, art may "reflect" non-artistic aspects of society. There are no medieval war stories in which atomic weapons are resorted to, and no literary depictions of the events of the Second World War in which battles are settled by jousts between mounted knights. Reflectionist theorists are not, however, concerned with such surface details. Rather, they aim to explain the "deep structure" of art: for example, that gothic cathedrals reflect the supposedly soaring and spiritual character of the medieval mind.

There are at least four problems with reflectionist theories. First, they are often not testable. The social factors that art supposedly reflects are often inferred from art in the first place. As the sociologist Levin L. Schücking pointed out, "the spirit of the Gothic period . . . is first deduced from its art and then rediscovered in its art" (1966 [1923], p.6). Public opinion polls weren't conducted in the Middle Ages. No one went about knocking on doors and asking how soaring the spirit of the household was. In respect to the distant past, reflectionist theories are completely untestable. About all that survives in the long run is art. A number of years ago, I discussed an early version of my theory of aesthetic evolution with the psychologist Henry Murray. He asked me what characterized the history of Western civilization since the Middle Ages. Not realizing that this was a rhetorical question, I answered it. My answer had something to do with Faustian striving and a spirit of conquest. Murray replied that his answer was just the opposite—decay, degeneration, and collapse. If that were the answer, then one could say that the history of art reflected this decay. We agreed, though, that both answers were only opinions. There was no clear way to find a definitive answer to the question.

A second problem is that no age has ever had a unitary spirit. One of the bases of Marxist theory is that different social classes have different and contradictory ideologies (Hauser 1963 [1958]). A related difficulty is that the arts themselves are often contradictory. None of us needs a study to know that contemporary art does not reflect society or its values. Consider American art of the 1950s. Abstract expressionist painting was chaotic. Functionalist architecture was severe and classical. The arts were contradictory. They couldn't have been reflecting the same thing. To argue that they reflected alienation or depersonalization is a desperate attempt to save a theory that is simply wrong. The average American was not alienated. He or she did not feel depersonalized. Average people were too busy enjoying themselves and saving money to buy a rococo Cadillac. They did agree on one thing: nobody liked modern art. They wanted buildings with some decoration. They wanted paintings that were paintings of *something*—a duck, a tree, anything. If art reflects the spirit of a people, you might expect that at least some of these people would like it. This little technicality seems not to have occurred to reflectionist theorists.

A third problem with reflectionist theories is that there is no good reason for art to reflect society. As Heinrich Wölfflin put it, reflectionist theories do not show us "the path from the scholar's cell to the mason's yard" (1964 [1888], p.77). The sociologist Vytautas Kavolis (1968), in attempting to find a reason for reflection in the psychological need for consistency, overlooked the facts that artists' attitudes and values are often at extreme variance with the general attitudes and values of the society in which they live (Plekhanov 1936 [1913]), and that the individuals recruited as artists are not greatly motivated by a need for consistency (Martindale, Abrams, and Hines 1974). As Gombrich remarked, such "sociological explanations really turn out to be psychological fallacies" (1953, p.82). American artists may have been alienated in the 1950s, and their art may reflect that. But this line of thought does reflectionist theory no good. If art reflects the attitudes of the artistic circles of society, we are faced with a tautology: Art reflects art. Art is art. Obviously, this explains nothing at all.

Marxist theorists explicitly stress that the artistic motive of *deformation* prevents art from giving a straightforward reflection of social reality (Machery 1966; Trotsky 1968 [1925]). Though the artist may attempt to depict prototypical situations or characters, these do not directly reflect social reality but present an idealized average. Since such art is not usually very interesting, the artist is led to deformation: to be of interest, the world presented by art has to be different—either for better or for worse— from reality. This is explicit Marxist theory, not a distorted interpretation of it. My point is that mainstream Marxist theory is about as reflectionist as the theory presented in this book. Neither theory says that art is completely unrelated to the external society—but neither says that the relationship is close.

A fourth problem is that reflectionist theories are not parsimonious. Often a sufficient explanation for aesthetic trends is to be found on the level of purely artistic causes, making it superfluous to search for more remote causes. People want to believe that art gives them profound insights into social reality. They want art to reflect society. They want it to tell them about the human condition, whatever that is. This desire may grow desperate. Philippe Ariès (1981) seriously attempted to draw conclusions about eighteenth-century attitudes toward death from the writings of the Marquis de Sade. Technically, the "divine marquis" was human. Not so his attitudes, which had little to do with the attitudes of his own, or of any other, time. Reading the Marquis de Sade tells us about as much about everyday attitudes in eighteenth-century France as about quantum physics. People used to want the sun to go around the earth rather than vice versa. We can't have everything we want. The artist can create a separate reality. The rest of us have got to accept the brute facts. Art is not a mirror. No one expects mathematics to reflect society. The fact seems to be that poetry and mathematics reflect society to about the same degree. I do not expect you to accept this statement merely on my word. I expect you to accept it after I have provided the relevant data in the chapters to come.

Reflectionist theories seek a one-to-one mirroring of society in art. Relational theories argue that there is connection between social change and artistic change, but that it need not be direct. As I have implied, mainstream Marxism is really a theory of this sort. There is no doubt that art and society are related in some ways. For example, the psychologists Dean Keith Simonton (1984a) and Karen Cerulo (1984) have shown that the originality of musical compositions is lower during times of civil war and higher during times of international war. Why should this be? Melodic originality does not directly reflect anything. There is no obvious relationship between originality and war, riots, and rebellions. The relationship must be mediated by some third factor, which I shall discuss later.

A problem with reflectionist theories is that they do not provide a plausible mechanism that would cause art to reflect society. Relational theories often are able to delineate such mechanisms. For example, in 1721, the British Parliament passed a law that allowed importation of mahogany at reasonable prices. Parliament passed the law for the benefit of the shipbuilding trade, but furniture makers took advantage of it. Mahogany is strong and dense. It can be carved more intricately than oak or walnut. The law accidentally facilitated the production of elaborate rococo furniture in the later part of the eighteenth century. Without the law, the furniture could not have been quite so fancy. The law did not *cause* the rococo style. The rococo style did not *reflect* the law. The law merely facilitated something that was going to happen anyway.

Intrinsic Theories

One of the most common topics for a Ph.D. dissertation in literary studies concerns the influence of one writer upon another. The implicit theory behind studies of influence is that one author has tried to imitate, or has been inspired by, another author. While this certainly does happen, Harold Bloom (1973, 1975) has argued, as I have mentioned, for an "anxiety of influence" whereby an imitator distorts or misinterprets an original work so as to *avoid* influence. Even if this were not the case, explanations of imitation are only explanations of the diffusion of innovation (compare Findlay and Lumsden 1988; Martindale 1988*a*); and as such, they only explain how innovations come to be adopted by later artists. They shed no light at all upon the central question of how innovation occurs in the first place. Unless we can answer this question, we can explain no more than how an innovation is accepted or elaborated by other artists. As André Gide remarked somewhere, "influence creates nothing; it awakens something." This will do us little good. If we assume that an innovation has been accepted by all artists in a tradition, influence theories cannot tell us what will happen next. They can provide an explanation of the history of art forms only across short time spans.

Several theorists (Chambers 1928; Deonna 1912; Kroeber 1944; Michaud 1950) have proposed cyclical theories of art history in which artistic styles are seen as following an internally determined pattern of growth, flowering, and decay. The biologist Ernst Haeckel's famous maxim (1899) is inverted: phylogeny recapitulates ontogeny. Such theorists claim that, unless violently disrupted by external factors, any artistic tradition approximates such cycles. None of these theorists provides a valid explanation of *why* this should or must be the case. Such theories based upon qualitative cycles of growth, flowering, and decay are made suspect by the tendency to rehabilitate styles that have fallen from grace. For example, the rediscovery of beauty in baroque style in the 1920s or in mannerist style in the 1950s suggests that aesthetic quality is not a stable basis for theory building. Gerald Reitlinger's (1961, 1965) studies of the wild historical fluctuations in the prices of paintings and *objets d'art* drive this point home: what is seen as a practically worthless product of decadence in one generation may by the next be viewed as a consummate and expensive expression of a style. The cycles of quality are not like hills and valleys. They are like ripples on a pond, continually changing their locations. I believe that this approach—in which the tastes of the present create a pleasing past—is not history at all. The facts are what we need for a valid history.

A related theory is based upon the idea that there is a parallel between the historical growth of either the artist's or humankind's powers of perception or abstraction and that of the individual person. Erich Neumann (1954), a Jungian analyst, explains changes in mythic content while Erich Kahler (1968), a literary historian, explains changes in European narrative in terms of humanity's increasing powers of abstraction and analysis. These changes are seen as paralleling mental changes as an individual grows from infancy to adulthood. Although these authors make a fascinating and internally consistent case for their theories, their only evidence is the changes in art they set out to explain in the first place. That is, they provide no independent evidence that human powers of abstraction actually increased across the time span they studied. In studying early myths, Neumann faced the archeologist's dilemma: since almost all that survives from ancient times is art and myth, his theory is untestable. Kahler, dealing with more recent narratives, theorizes that the human powers of abstraction have changed massively across the last several centuries. There is no evidence at all for this assumption. Art has changed massively. There is no reason to believe that people's mental abilities have changed in any way over the last several centuries.

More recently, the scholars Suzi Gablik (1976) and Sidney Blatt (1984) have proposed that the history of European painting from the Middle Ages to the twentieth century parallels the development of the individual's mental powers from infancy to adulthood. Taken at face value, these theories are implausible. Though there is a vague resemblance between some aspects of a medieval painting and the drawings of a young child, are we to believe that Giotto and his contemporaries had a mental age of three years? I think not. Perspective and related techniques have been discovered several times in the history of painting. Each attempt took hundreds of years. A child left completely to its own devices would never get much beyond the scrawls it makes at two or three years of age (Alland 1983). There is a parallel between the history of painting and a child's progress in drawing. The reason is not far to find. Adults teach the child techniques of perspective, shading, and so on, that it took artists hundreds of years to perfect. The easier techniques were discovered first. They are also taught to children first. This and nothing more is needed to account for the parallels. In any event, Gablik and Blatt seem to have gotten things completely backward. In art history, facts are vague enough that the wrong theory can not merely distort them but invert them altogether. As we shall see, the historical trend in all of the arts more closely parallels a regression from adult to infantile perception and cognition. It is Picasso and Pollock—not Giotto or Cimabue—who paint like children. Such a historical retrogression was postulated some years ago by the psychoanalyst Anton Ehrenzweig (1954). Be this as it may, neither Ehrenzweig nor Gablik and Blatt were able to explain *why* there should be any relationship at all between "ontogeny" and "phylogeny."

To explain the tendency of art forms to change gradually and systematically over time, Kubler (1962) proposed a "rule of series" whereby certain forms logically depend upon others. To draw an example from technology, invention of the locomotive could not possibly precede invention of the steam engine. Earlier versions of this sort of theory were proposed by art historians such as Henri Focillon (1942) and Konrad Fiedler (1949). Theories of the working out of inherent possibilities of forms, of an inner logic to historical succession, are weak in that the force causing change is not clearly specified. This inner logic cannot be specified because the psychological mechanisms mediating the changes are not made explicit. Forms do not change by themselves. They change because of the operation of psychological laws governing their producers. Unless these psychological laws are known, one cannot explicate the so-called inner logic.

Evolutionary Theories

Theories concerning an inner logic driving change in the arts were anticipated by Herbert Spencer's quasi-Darwinian theory. This English philosopher, in his major statement on art (1910 [1892]), set forth the principle that art, like everything else, moves from simple to complex. By complex, he meant more differentiated and hierarchically integrated. The anthropologist Alfred Kroeber (1956) followed Spencer in proposing such a simple-to-complex law, as did Kubler (1962). It certainly seems to be the case that *if* something—whether a biological organism or a civilization—evolves, it usually follows this path. But it does not follow it forever. Species become extinct. Civilizations eventually collapse. Again, we must ask of these theorists *why* this is the case. We must also inquire why this evolution occurs in some cases (such as human beings or modern artistic genres) but only slightly in others (sharks or ancient Egyptian painting). Spencer, Kroeber, and Kubler give us no answer to either of these questions.

Whether art invariably does become more complex depends upon how complexity is defined. An abstract-expressionist painting is complex in the sense of being complicated and chaotic. It is not at all complex in the sense that Spencer was using the term, because it is not hierarchically integrated. There is some evidence that artistic genres have evolved in the way specified by Spencer. At first, there was primordial verbal art. Then there was differentiation into genres. There is some hierarchical integration in the sense that some forms are based upon or derived from others. If we look at specific genres, though, there is a lot of evidence that Spencer had things backward. The proper analogy is not biological evolution but physical evolution. There is only one long-term law of physical evolution: the second law of thermodynamics, whereby evolution is from order to disorder, entropy, or randomness. Unless people or other animals intervene, a physical object must go from complex to random. If we do intervene, we can increase order in part of the world—but only by creating more disorder in another part of the world. Total entropy or disorder must increase. It can never decrease. The second law has a special status in physics. It is the one law that can never be evaded. We can evade the laws of gravity with rockets. We can never evade the second law. It may well be that art can never evade it either.

Taine (1875) proposed a Darwinian theory of evolution of art forms. At any point in time, he held, art is a product of race, environment, and moment. By moment, Taine meant the currently prevailing Zeitgeist as well as what had already been done within a given art form. This theory was, of course, an anticipation of the inner-logic theories I have discussed. By environment, Taine meant both the physical and the cultural environments. In terms of the latter, he was explicit in arguing that certain art forms may be selected over others because of the "moral temperature" of the moment—the analogue of Darwinian fitness. I shall argue later that moral temperature is not constant enough across time to bring about systematic evolution in the arts.

Explicitly evolutionary theories of sociocultural change have recently been proposed (Campbell 1974; Cavalli-Sforza and Feldman 1981; Findlay and Lumsden 1988; Pulliam and Dunford 1980). The psychologist D. T. Campbell (1965) argues for direct application of the principles of Darwinian evolution to change in cultural systems and products. Sociocultural change, he says, is a product of "blind" variation and selective retention. The three necessities for evolution of any sort are: presence of variations, consistent selection criteria that favor some variants over others, and mechanisms for preserving the selected variants. At any time, a number of variants of a given object are produced, and the most useful, pleasing, or rewarding are chosen for retention. Then, at the next point in time, there is variation of the new form, and the process continues. Though such theories provide a general framework for thinking about aesthetic evolution, they do not tell us why aesthetic variation exists in the first place, nor were they proposed to do so.

In chapter 2, I describe a theory based upon evolutionary principles, which predicts extremely regular historical trends in the history of art and literature. In the rest of the book, I use quantitative evidence to show that their muse—and, indeed, that of music and even New England gravestones—operates almost like clockwork.

CHAPTER 2

A Psychological Theory
of Aesthetic Evolution

I F we follow D. T. Campbell's (1965, 1974) general model, a theory of aesthetic evolution must explain at least three things: the reasons for variation, the selection criteria, and the mechanisms of retention. These are only preliminary and trivial questions, however, unless the theory, in answering them, also provides an explanation of the main trends in the history of art. If, as I argued earlier, nothing in art makes sense except in the light of evolution, then a theory of aesthetic evolution must shed at least some light on everything worth explaining about art.

If you drop an object in a vacuum, gravitation will cause it to move in a specific direction at a specific rate. Just so, if art were created in a social vacuum, pressure for novelty would cause it to evolve in a specific manner. The empirical evidence suggests that art tends in fact to evolve in a social vacuum, and that non-evolutionary factors are comparatively negligible. Though art is not produced in a complete social vacuum, I believe there to be more of a social vacuum than is commonly thought. Furthermore, social forces are analogous to *friction*, in that they impede or slow down the progress of an artistic tradition. They do not cause change in art: they distort it. Of course, this is contrary to the common reflectionist view of things.

So far as the theory of gravitation is concerned, an object's mass, size, shape, and color are not relevant; they have no effect upon an object moving in a vacuum. Size, mass, and shape may affect how fast a stone rolls down a mountainside, but—given enough time—the stone will always end up at the bottom of the mountain. By the same token, many factors often thought relevant to art history (the Zeitgeist; political, economic, and other social events) are irrelevant or contribute only random "noise" in my theory of aesthetic evolution.

It is conventional to think of a work of art as a communication between an artist and an audience. This approach presupposes the existence of a distinct audience that can exert some control on the artist. For many forms of high—as opposed to popular—art, there is really no audience aside from other artists. With a few exceptions, poetry has always been written for other poets. Painters really paint for each other. Modern American painting is a small closed system located in New York City (Wolfe 1975). There is an external audience of consumers, which is very small, very rich, and completely powerless. The status of the artist is extremely high, and has been since the renaissance. A customer cannot go to an artist and order a picture of a tree. One has to accept whatever the artist feels like painting. There is a sociological catch-22. An artist who paints what the customer tells him or her to is no longer a true artist. One falls to the level of those who do paintings on black velvet. Do that, and you forfeit your claim on immortality. The audience can escape from the system. No one forces them to buy modern art. But they escape into oblivion, their only claim to immortality being their contact with the artists. If you want to say that modern American painting reflects or comments upon modern America, ignore what artists and critics say and look at the social facts. If the artists and their audience all sneaked off to Mongolia, no one would notice. If they took the poets and composers with them, no one would notice that, either.

RETENTION MECHANISMS

Obviously, mechanisms for the retention of selected art objects exist. If they did not, we should have no art history to explain in the first place. Some artifacts—such as architecture and sculpture—do a good job of retaining themselves. In literature, mechanisms for the retention of selected variants are oral traditions and written or printed copies. Analogous retention mechanisms exist in all other art forms. The question of retention cannot be answered fully until we answer the question of selection. Selection criteria determine what will be retained. Works of art are usually in great peril at some point after they have been produced. Styles change. The old begins to look ugly. Many nineteenth-century academic paintings that would today be worth a million dollars or so were simply tossed in the trash. In 1888 Sir Lawrence Alma-Tadema's *The Roses of Elagabalus* was sold for several hundred thousand dollars (in current dollars); in 1960, it was sold for a couple of hundred dollars (Reitlinger 1961). Other paintings by Alma-Tadema have simply vanished. Some are in attics. Many were just thrown away. This situation is not unique. Rembrandts have met the same fate. If the past is even a vague guide, it is possible that the same will happen to paintings by Picasso. At some point in the future, they will be seen as so ugly, and their value will be so low, that no one will want them. Retention is not always due to aesthetic reasons. Paintings are now used rather like soybeans. They have become investment commodities. Antique furniture is preserved by people who are really fighting *against* aesthetic evolution. It is bought and kept by people who do not like modern furniture.

Actual retention of artifacts in this sense is not necessary for evolution. It merely makes aesthetic evolution far easier to study than biological evolution. Our collection of aesthetic "fossils" is much more complete. In fact, retention of old works of art shows that need for novelty is a *weak* force. If it were a strong force, all the old books and paintings would have been burned, all the old buildings torn down. As I have said, need for novelty is, though weak, very, very persistent. Once an animal has bred or passed on its genes, nature wants it to die. Evolution feeds upon itself in biology as in fashion. Organisms are built to self-destruct just as are cars and clothes. Once a work of art has had its influence, it can be tossed out or not, its contribution to history largely finished. A work of art can, however, procreate posthumously. John Donne, say, can rise from the grave and have a direct influence on a modern poet—and was, in fact, exhumed, along with other metaphysical poets, by T. S. Eliot precisely for such aesthetic intercourse.

In the case of biological evolution, selected variations are, of course, encoded in the "memory" of DNA configurations. We may assume that more important or more complex DNA configurations are "forgotten" less quickly than less complex ones. The analogue is most certainly the case in the arts. If for no other reason than our educational system, the average reader of a contemporary British poet has some rudimentary "memory" of the poet's predecessors at least back to the time of Chaucer. In comparison, the average person who purchases clothing has a poor memory for prior styles of fashion. As likely as not, such a person knows little about the styles of even thirty or forty years ago. The better "memory" of the poetic system leads us to expect that it should change in a different manner than fashion. In the latter, novelty seems often to be obtained by reviving a forgotten style, an option not as available to the poet.

Two things should be explained: why old works of art are retained at all, and why we take any pleasure in them. These are different aspects of the same question. Though the question is not really a problem, people do not generally like to hear the answer. The evolution of art has about as much to do with you or with me as the evolution of kangaroos. We can certainly study the evolution of kangaroos. We can watch kangaroos breed. We are only observers. We do not take part in the process. We can fiddle around with the evolution of domestic animals. We can breed dogs so that they look different. We can't, though, turn a dog into a cat. By the same token, we can have some influence on artifacts produced for us. We can boycott Edsels, and they will become extinct. But the high arts are like wild species. We have no say in the matter. If we domesticate a wild species, it is no longer wild. If we domesticate a high art, it is no longer a high art.

Shakespeare did not write for us. He did not write for humanity. He took some note of the tastes of his contemporary audience. John Donne most certainly did not write for us. He wrote for himself and a few friends. Beethoven was explicit about the matter. When a friend told him that no one liked the *Moonlight Sonata,* he did not understand why the person was bothering with such chitchat. It did not concern Beethoven what people thought of that sonata. He did not write it for others. He wrote it for himself, and he liked it. As I have said, the notion that an artist is trying to communicate with an audience is misleading. It leads to an "audience-centric" confusion.

There may be an audience that influences high art, but it is unlikely that you are in it. The audience usually consists only of the artist. It may include a few other artists. So far as high art is concerned, we are observers rather than audience. If poets wanted to reach a mass audience, they would certainly write differently. In one sense or another, they hold such a mass audience in complete contempt. They may say that they love the masses or that they hate them. In either case, they do not bother to write anything the masses like or understand. Whether one says that Mallarmé boycotted the world or vice versa is immaterial. Mallarmé and humanity were not on speaking terms, since they spoke different languages.

Great poetry can be read in a number of ways. As time passes, it can profitably be read in new ways. When this ceases to be the case, it stops being called great poetry. The point, though, is that a modern reading of past poetry is not relevant to aesthetic evolution. The aesthetic "intercourse" took place in the past. The evolution of poetry today has to do with a very few contemporary poets. Only a reader who happens to be one of these poets is a participant in this contemporary change. Whether we read or do not read this poetry is of no relevance. The fact that people in general take pleasure in old art is not relevant to aesthetic evolution. It is the tastes of the artists that are crucial in explaining art history.

MECHANISMS OF SELECTION

Darwin (1859, 1896 [1871]) proposed two types of biological selection. *Natural selection* is based upon fitness for survival in a given environment. *Sexual selection* refers to differential mating success based upon hedonic factors. Here I describe these and indicate how Darwin's concepts can be modified to apply to the cultural rather than to the biological realm.

Natural Selection

Natural selection or fitness refers to the differential survival of organisms that are more or less adapted to the environment in which they live. Across time, organisms with more adaptive traits are more likely to survive and reproduce. Thus, their numbers increase, speciation in different environmental niches occurs, and so on. Most theorists (for example, Findlay and Lumsden 1988; Rindos 1985) who have attempted to extrapolate from biological to cultural evolution have drawn analogies with natural selection. As I have pointed out elsewhere (Martindale 1986b, 1988a), natural selection cannot be the proximal cause of cultural (or even biological) evolution. To say that an organism makes choices based upon natural selection leaves completely unexplained how the choices were made in the first place. It is only the much later consequences of these choices that influence survival. Animals obviously do not mate to maximize the fitness of their offspring—a purpose they would have to understand Darwin's theory to aim for.

May not some analogue of natural selection operate in artistic change? Although Taine (1875) argued that art works may be selected according to whether they match the "moral temperature" of the times, moral temperature seems to fluctuate too much to serve as a consistent basis for selection. In order to cause evolution, a selection criterion must be stable and long-lasting. Some evidence suggests that artists may even have developed devices to *avoid* selection on this basis. Several theorists have noted that the arts seem to have lost meaning across the last several centuries. Whereas earlier painters wanted to depict great and important subjects, later painters have tended to concentrate on form. As Ehrenzweig (1954) put it, it makes no difference to a modern artist whether he paints the king of France or a sack of potatoes. Perhaps this increasing concentration on form has an analogue in the evolution of protective coloration in animals: it makes the artist less subject to social control. It is easy to tell whether the meaning or content of a poem or painting is consistent with current social values and attitudes. It is much more difficult to determine whether formal variables are. Is iambic or trochaic meter more consistent with Marxist ideology? How can we discriminate between a Republican and a Democratic still-life?

Subtraction of meaning can, of course, backfire if current social attitudes include the belief that art *should* have meaning. Political institutions can intervene in aesthetic evolution by brute force. Nonrepresentational painters found themselves in trouble in Nazi Germany and in Russia after the October Revolution: they had subtracted too much meaning. Painters of landscapes have always been fairly safe. It is impossible to determine the political affiliation of a tree. A related device is stabilization of meaning. If all painters paint the Crucifixion, the Church is satisfied. The real business of art can than continue on the level of stylistic variables, whose relevance to religious ideology is not readily apparent.

The popular art of the 1930s was similar in America, Russia, and Germany. In retrospect, we can see that these Art Deco artists were almost contemptuous of both politicians and public. German artists put a swastika in a picture; Russians, a hammer and sickle. Take these emblems away, and it is difficult to distinguish this art from the work of Americans engaged in Roosevelt's WPA projects. Given their choice, many of these artists had little interest in depicting farmers or laborers. But the subject matter was secondary anyway. Form was what really interested them.

Hedonic Selection

If it has done nothing else, twentieth-century psychology has produced literally thousands of experiments demonstrating what has always been at least intuitively known: people prefer stimuli that give them pleasure and dislike stimuli that give them displeasure. So far as we know, the same is also true of all other organisms as well. If we know what causes pleasure and displeasure, then we shall be in a position to explain why one thing is chosen over another. In order to explain phenomena (for example, the brilliant plumage of birds such as peacocks, pheasants, and birds of paradise) that could not possibly be due to natural selection, Darwin (1896 [1871]) postulated a second criterion of sexual selection. So far as it concerns us, sexual selection might better be called hedonic or aesthetic selection: In some species, females select their mates on aesthetic grounds. The more aesthetically pleasing the male, the more likely he is to be chosen as a mate. Thus, there is a selection pressure toward increasing degrees of beauty in the eyes of the female of the species. This selection criterion can be applied immediately to cultural evolution: human beings choose the most pleasing or rewarding of the alternatives presented to them. To determine the selection criterion in the arts, then, we must first know what brings aesthetic pleasure.

The selection criterion in aesthetic evolution must be equivalent to Darwin's sexual selection or hedonic selection rather than to his more well-known selection criterion of "fitness" to the environment. While both selection criteria may operate on artistic products, their effects are different. Selection on the basis of preference has presumably been present ever since works of art were first produced. Thus, hedonic selection has exerted a constant pressure in the same direction throughout human history. On the other hand, "fitness" has tended to vary wildly across time. Pornography has low fitness in a puritanical society; moralistic literature, in a licentious society; and so on. What is fit in one epoch may not be so in another. Thus, fitness cannot be seen as exerting a consistent, undirectional pressure on works of art. I assume that morals evolve just as do the arts. The two seem, however, to evolve independently. Swings in moral style and artistic style are not synchronized. There is sometimes a relationship. Women's high fashion around 1800 tended to leave little to the imagination, fitting well enough with the licentious morality of the period. High art tends to be beyond such mundane matters. By the end of the century, supposedly staid Victorians prominently displayed in their parlors paintings that we would call pornographic (Gombrich 1956).

Determinants of Aesthetic Preference

According to the psychologist Daniel E. Berlyne (1971), one's liking or preference for a stimulus is determined by the arousal potential of that stimulus. So far as poetry is concerned, Emily Dickinson defined *arousal potential* better than I ever could: "If I read a book and it makes my whole body so cold no fire can ever warm me, I know *that* is poetry. If I feel physically as if the top of my head were taken off, I know *that* is poetry. These are the only ways I know it. Is there any other way?" (1924 [1870], p.276). I think not, but we can try to see what gives something this impact. The arousal potential of a stimulus is determined by what Berlyne called *collative properties* (such as novelty, complexity, surprisingness, unpredictability), ecological properties (signal value or meaning), and psychophysical characteristics (pitch, hue, intensity). A good deal of evidence supports the contention that people prefer stimuli with a medium degree of arousal potential and do not like stimuli with either an extremely high or low arousal potential. This relationship, described by the *Wundt curve* (see figure 2.1), is borne out by several general studies reviewed by Theodore Schneirla (1959) and Berlyne (1967) as well as by studies of aesthetic stimuli per se. The effect has been found with both literary (Evans 1969; Kamann 1963) and visual (Day 1967; Vitz 1966) stimuli. There is some question about the shape of the Wundt curve (Martindale et al. 1990), but there is no question that people do like some degree of intensity, complexity, and so on. Meaning certainly does not have an inverted-U relationship with preference. The relationship is usually *monotonic:* that is, the more meaningful something is, the better people like it. At least for artistically naïve observers, meaning is by far the most important determinant of preference (Martindale, Moore, and West

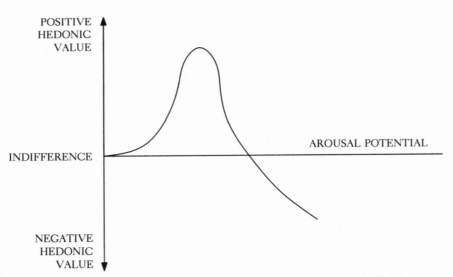

Figure 2.1 Hedonic tone and arousal potential. According to Berlyne (1971), hedonic tone is related to the arousal potential of a stimulus by what is called the Wundt curve: stimuli with low arousal potential elicit indifference, stimuli with medium arousal potential elicit maximal pleasure, and stimuli with high levels of arousal potential elicit displeasure.

1987). Artists tend not to try, however, to manipulate arousal potential by manipulating meaning, as I shall discuss. Before considering arousal potential further, let us look into why art is variable. Without variation, there is no way for evolution to work. There must be variants for any selection to take place.

THE PRODUCTION AND SELECTION OF VARIATION

There are two sources of variation in art forms. One source, which was pointed out by several early theorists—such as Henry Balfour (1893) and Alfred Haddon (1907)—is based upon the difficulty of exact replication or copying. Experiments on serial reproduction of visual designs (Balfour 1893; Ward 1949) and of verbal narratives (Bartlett 1932) show that variations always arise from copying even when people are intent upon producing an exact copy (See chapter 10 for examples of the results of serial reproduction). Similar findings have emerged from studies of rumor (Allport and Postman 1947; Rosnow and Fine 1976). Three types of trend are found in studies where people are asked to make exact copies: an occasional movement toward complexity, a much more usual movement toward simplification, and a movement toward amplification and special-ization of some details at the expense of others. Haddon (1907) concludes that the last is the most common. This usually also involves an overall simplification. Such changes arise from limitations of both technical skill and memory. In skilled artists, the first factor is negligible. Artists who, however, do not work in the presence of the model they have chosen, could be expected to have variation due to the schematizing and simplify-ing properties of memory. Memory for the salient aspects of visual scenes is quite good (Shepard 1967), but memory for details is abysmally poor (Mandler and Ritchey 1977). Verbatim memory for verbal material is almost uniformly extremely poor. People remember the gist of what they have heard, but forget the exact phrasing almost immediately (Bransford and Franks 1971). As a general rule, perception involves a good deal of simplification; and memory, much more (see Martindale 1981).

Difficulty in copying cannot, however, be the main cause of aesthetic variation, because most artists have no interest in producing exact copies of previous works in the first place. This holds for primitive societies as well as advanced ones (Brett-Smith 1984). The role definition of artist almost always calls for the creation of new, different, or original products. A person who produces exact copies of already-existing art works is usually not even considered to be an artist: we make a fundamental distinction between a typesetter and a poet.

Across the past several centuries, there has emerged a consensus that "multaneity in unity," "ordered disorder," or "unity in variety" is central to art (Gilbert and Kuhn 1939). Art is characterized by variety, incongruity, novelty, and such collative variables within the context of an overall unity. There is agreement on this point by most approaches to art and literature—French structuralism (for example, Lévi-Strauss 1963 [1958]), transformationalist approaches (Cohen 1966), Russian semiotics (Lotman 1970), psychoanalytic theory (Kris 1952), the psychobiological approach (Berlyne 1971), new criticism (Empson 1930), and cognitive approaches (de Beaugrande 1980).

Many theorists have pointed out that if art is characterized by novelty or disruption of expectation, a necessity for change is built into it. If a work of art must be novel, then each successive work of art must be different from prior works or it will not even qualify as a work of art. The Russian and Czech formalists argued that poetic devices involve "estrangement" or "deformation." What gives poetry its effect is the use of words in unusual or unexpected ways. The deformed word usage of poetry intensifies perception or grasps attention. In both everyday language and in poetic language, linguistic elements gradually become "automatized" (Tynjanov 1965 [1924]): that is, they lose their impact. Several formalist theorists (Shklovsky 1972 [1919]; Tynjanov 1967 [1929]; Mukařovský 1976 [1940]) derived from this formulation the hypothesis that literature must evolve. Because aesthetic effects arise from deformation, and because deformations gradually become automatized, there must be a constant pressure on successive artists to produce new deformations. Similar evolutionary theories have been independently formulated by James Laver (1950), Leonard Meyer (1956), Morse Peckham (1965), and Jean Cohen (1966).

As a matter of fact, the philosopher Thomas Hobbes clearly pointed out this evolutionary force several centuries ago:

For the phrases of poesy, as the airs of music, with often hearing become insipid; the reader having no more sense of their force, than our flesh is sensible of the bones that sustain it. As the sense we have of bodies, consisteth in change and variety of impression, so also does the sense of language in the variety and changeable use of words. I mean not in the affectation of words newly brought home from travel, but in new, and withal significant, translation to our purposes, of those that be already received; and in far fetched, but withal, apt, instructive, and comely similitudes.

(1840 [1650], p.455)

Habituation

These theories have usually been based upon intuitive and common-sense psychological assumptions. A more comprehensive formulation can be derived from scientific psychological theory. Without knowing it, the theorists were talking about a psychological process that has received a great deal of experimental attention. *Habituation* refers to the phenomenon whereby repetitions of a stimulus are accompanied by decreases in physiological reactivity to it. The psychological concomitant is becoming used to or bored with the stimulus. Habituation is not merely the polar opposite of need for novelty. *Avoiding* boredom is not necessarily the equivalent of *approaching* novelty. People who habituate quickly to stimuli do not necessarily have a high need for novelty (McClelland 1951). In fact, creative people like novelty but habituate more slowly than do uncreative people (Rosen, Moore, and Martindale 1983). Because of this fact and because habituation seems to be a universal property of nervous tissue (Thompson et al. 1979), it is worth discussing separately.

There is good evidence that a work of art—or any stimulus for that matter—gradually loses its arousal potential with repetition (Berlyne 1970; Skaife 1967). It follows that if a series of artists were to continue producing the same work of art or similar works of art, liking—on the part of both artists and their audience—for their productions would decrease over time. To compensate for such habituation, it is necessary for successive works of art to have more and more arousal potential.

In principle, this could be accomplished by increasing any of the components of arousal potential. Successive composers could create ever louder musical compositions, or successive painters could produce ever larger paintings. There are, however, practical limits to how loud a piece of music can be or to the size of a painting. Increasing intensity to gain arousal potential has, in fact, been used in music. Contemporary popular music has, for example, been played over the last several decades at ever louder levels in live performances. This is obvious to anyone over the age of thirty or forty who has made the mistake of wandering into a discothèque. There were no discothèques in the 1950s, but rock music was played in bars at levels that were not noxiously loud. It is now commonly played at levels as high as 100 to 110 decibels. This trick will no longer work: if the music is played any louder, it will produce pain. Over a longer term, the same trick has been used in classical music. Harpsichords are not loud and have no dynamic range; their intensity level is constant. They were driven out by pianos. Piano music is louder, and its intensity can be varied. The size of symphony orchestras has gradually gotten larger. This increase is, though, limited by economic factors; also, the larger the orchestra, the more difficult it is to keep all the players together. Paintings run into literal ceiling effects: if the thing is too large, it will not fit into a room. The painter also faces inverse economies of scale. It is no longer "legal" for painters to use apprentices, and it simply takes too long to paint a large painting by oneself. Not enough people can afford to buy it. A painter is better off doing a number of smaller paintings. In the medium of poetry, it is essentially impossible to compensate for habituation of arousal potential by increasing stimulus intensity.

Arousal potential could also be increased by increasing the meaningfulness of art works. There are several problems with this technique. First, people vary about what they see as meaningful. One cannot be sure that what is meaningful for oneself will be also meaningful to one's audience. Second, there is the problem of ceiling effects. In a religious epoch, where all painters are already painting the Crucifixion and other religious scenes, the maximum amount of meaningfulness has already been attained. Third, art is supposed to have multiple meanings. It is self-defeating to increase one aspect of meaning. The more a single meaning dominates a work, the less it is a work of art. Something that has one and only one meaning—no matter how interesting or important that meaning is—is no longer a work of art (Schmidt 1982). It may be a stop sign or a philosophical treatise, but it is not art. If, on the other hand, one adds more layers of meaning, that increases the work's ambiguity. Ambiguity is a collative variable. Collative properties such as novelty or unpredictability can vary much more freely than meaning in all of the arts. One soon finds that to increase the arousal potential of aesthetic products over time, one must increase ambiguity, novelty, incongruity, and other collative properties. This is the reason for my theoretical emphasis on collative properties rather than upon other components of arousal potential.

My argument is similar to the "exhaustion" theories of aesthetic change proposed by art historians such as Adolf Göller (1888) and Carl Lange (1903). These theories traced artistic change to what Göller termed *Formermüdung,* or "form fatigue." Göller argued that pleasure arises from the mental effort of what we would today call assimilation of perceptions to mental schemata. If this assimilation becomes too easy because of familiarity, then pleasure decreases and one looks for new forms. This theory makes perfect sense in light of modern theories about arousal. For example, E. N. Sokolov (1963) argues that arousal is caused by a lack of fit between mental schemata or expectations and perceptual inputs. It follows that a close fit between expectations and percept should yield little arousal and, therefore, little pleasure. A somewhat less close fit would produce more arousal and, hence, more pleasure (see figure 2.1).

Peak Shift

Peak shift is a well-established behavioral phenomenon (Hanson 1959). Consider an animal that is rewarded if it responds to one stimulus (such as a 200-Hz tone) and not rewarded if it responds to another stimulus (a 180-Hz tone). After training, the animal will exhibit maximal responsivity at a point *beyond* which it was rewarded and in a direction away from the unrewarded stimulus (a 220-Hz tone). J.E.R. Staddon (1975) argues that peak shift serves as the force behind sexual selection in biological evolution. Because of peak shift, female birds that prefer to mate with males with bright rather than dull plumage will show even greater preference for males with supernormal or above-average brightness. As a result, such males will mate more often and produce more offspring. As a further result, and because peak shift operates during every generation, the brightness of male plumage in the species will increase across generations.

The same considerations apply to human beings and their preferences. Preference—and thus selection and retention—will gradually shift away from what one likes to a point beyond what one maximally liked previously. For example, if an audience dislikes paintings with pale colors and likes paintings with bright colors, paintings would be likely to become brighter and brighter across time. Of course, the reverse could also occur if the initial preference were for pale colors. Peak shift does not imply a unidirectional pressure as does the need for novelty and habituation. These unidirectional pressures have already determined the direction in which art will change, and peak shift serves to keep change gradual and orderly: stimuli that are only slightly rather than vastly supernormal are preferred.

Autonomy and Least Effort

If there is a constant pressure for change in art, there are also countervailing pressures against it. On the sociological level, I have argued (1975) that the rate of change in a poetic tradition is a function of the value placed upon novelty by the poetry-producing system, and that this value is a function of the system's autonomy from its audience. The reason is that many poetic values competitive with novelty (such as beauty, appropriate subject matter, proper syntax) are ultimately determined by the need to communicate with an external audience. There really is no external audience for high art. Thus, poetic values that could hold pursuit of novelty in check are weak. High art probably changes more rapidly than popular art. However, all art-producing systems are a lot more autonomous than is commonly thought, and much more autonomous than I thought in 1975. British poets are probably about as autonomous from an external audience now as they were in 1300; their autonomy has probably not increased or decreased appreciably. On the psychological level, habituation occurs gradually, and the need for novelty is held in check by the peak-shift effect. Thus, an audience should reject not only works of art with insufficient arousal potential but also those having too much. Finally, the principle of least effort assures us that artists will increase arousal potential by the minimal amount needed to offset habituation. The opposing pressures should lead to gradual and orderly change in the arts.

Habituation Across the Generations

The exhaustion theory of Göller and others has been criticized as involving a logical error (Hauser 1963 [1958]; Wundt 1904). The theory shares with my theory the idea that the effects of exhaustion or habituation are transferred from one generation to the next. Critics have argued that this involves an improper application of an individual process to a series of individuals. Given that one generation has become bored with something, why should this have the slightest effect on the next generation? There is no reason to think that it should—if generations really existed.

Consider the audience for French poetry on 1 January of, say, 1650: it consisted of a group of people varying in age, not of a cadre that could in any sense be considered as constituting a generation. Consider the same audience on 2 January 1650. Perhaps several members had died, but they had probably been replaced by several new members. The vast majority of the audience remained the same. Whatever habituation occurred for *them* on 1 January continued on 2 January. New members had either to catch up with, or be dragged along, by this process. They were in such a minority that they could not influence taste in the slightest. The same situation has existed on every day since 1 January of 1650 to today. The audience may have grown or shrunk, but at any moment in time those already in the audience have constituted the overwhelming majority. It is this majority that transfers habituation across the "generations."

RATE OF AESTHETIC CHANGE

Jurij Tynjanov and Roman Jakobson (1971 [1928]) and Jan Mukařovský (1976 [1940]) admitted that their formalist theories could explain not the rate of aesthetic change but only the fact that such change must occur. Several factors allow us, however, to predict rate of change from the psychological theory: the average chronic and acute level of arousal of an audience, the amount of exposure of the audience to art, and the source of arousal potential in particular artistic media.

Background and Basal Arousal

There is evidence that preference for aesthetic stimuli is a function not only of the arousal potential of the stimulus itself but also of the arousal potential of "background" stimuli: that is, the arousal potential of the aesthetic stimulus is pooled with that of other stimuli in the surrounding environment. D. E. Berlyne and John Crozier (1971) allowed subjects to look at either simple or complex designs: more preference for the complex designs was found when the prestimulus environment was dark than when it was enriched. Similar findings with rats have been reported (Berlyne, Koenig, and Hirota 1966). Sensory deprivation has also been shown to increase preference for complex, unpredictable stimuli (Jones, Wilkinson, and Braden 1961). It would seem to be the case that if the arousal potential of the environment is high, aesthetic stimuli with lower arousal potential are preferred; whereas if the arousal potential of the environment is low, stimuli with greater arousal potential are preferred (Berlyne 1971).

There is some reason to believe that chronic—as opposed to acute—high-arousal states leads to the establishment of an adaptation level that requires more arousal potential or more novelty to induce pleasure. Berlyne (1971) proposed such an explanation for the consistent finding (Fischer 1961; Kavolis 1968; Lomax 1968, 1972) that more complex art is preferred and produced in complex societies than in primitive societies. A complex society subjects its members to more information input on several levels, leading to a higher arousal baseline. Stimuli with complexity sufficient to induce moderate increases in arousal from this basal level of arousal will necessarily be more complex than those sufficient to induce moderate increases from the lower baseline of individuals in primitive societies. It is not really surprising that high art is centered in cities such as New York. Because of chronic high arousal, only striking things attract notice—things that would be too striking in more serene surroundings. They wouldn't play well in Peoria.

Given these considerations, it would follow that chronically high arousal states in the artistic subculture and/or audience should lead to rapid rates of artistic change; momentary high-arousal states should retard such change. Berlyne's (1971) hypothesis that social complexity produces chronically higher arousal states is consistent with the apparently more rapid rates of aesthetic change in such societies as compared with primitive societies. Other factors that might be expected to produce chronic high arousal states would be sustained rapid social change, an urban as opposed to a rural environment, and much social mobility. Rapid momentary increases in arousal could result from wars, depressions, and revolutions. Such events could retard artistic change.

It is possible that all of these phenomena exert their effect via attention rather than via physiological arousal. Because arousal is the physiological basis of attention, the distinction is not especially crucial for our concerns. A child or a dripping faucet distract attention as well as increase arousal. One can write a poem any time, but an interesting revolution does not come along every day. Baudelaire loved the revolution of 1848: he had little real sympathy with the revolutionaries, but thought that they staged a most interesting show. Verlaine was even more enthusiastic about the Paris commune of 1871, claiming that it was a wonderful idea.

These and other examples show that the larger society can influence the art world by diverting the attention, or changing the acute or chronic level of arousal, of artists and their audience. Indeed, Dean Keith Simonton (1984a, 1986a) has produced quantitative evidence that civil disturbances have deleterious effects on artistic creativity. It is interesting to speculate that the relationship between art and society may usually be mediated by changes in arousal or attention. If this be the case, then the influence of society upon art would of necessity be diffuse and nonspecific, because focus of attention or level of arousal can influence only the overall arousal potential or impact value of works of art. Neither has a clear relationship with specific artistic content. Perhaps, then, society can influence only the rate of aesthetic evolution but not the direction this evolution takes.

Amount of Exposure

Creative people prefer more complex, novel, and surprising stimuli than do uncreative people (Barron and Welsh 1952; Houston and Mednick 1963). If we assume that the average level of creativity is higher among artists than among their audience, higher rates of change should be found with more autonomy of the art-producing system. As autonomy increases, artists come more and more to ignore the preferences of the audience and to create only for their fellow artists. Moreover, regardless of autonomy, familiarity with and exposure to art should always be greater for artists than for the external audience. Thus, artists will at any time have undergone more habituation trials. Because artists are exposed to art more or less continually, they are always ahead of whatever audience they do have. Artistic innovations are almost always met with some shock, outrage, and resistance. As I have noted, the audience may slow down change, but it cannot stop it.

Berlyne (1971) pointed out that the evolutionary theory has difficulty in explaining cases such as Egyptian art that show extremely slow rates of change. Yet, though much Egyptian painting was sealed in tombs—hardly a place to bring about speedy habituation—it did evolve as predicted by the theory (see pages 212–19). In general, the more an audience is exposed to a type of art, the faster the art should change. This assumption leads to specific predictions: we should find higher rates of change in living room furniture than in bedroom furniture, in everyday dress than in formal dress, and so on.

Components of Arousal Potential

The arousal potential of a work of art is a positive function of its psychophysical, ecological, and collative properties and a negative function of its *time-in-series,* or how often it or similar works have been repeated. Rate of change in collative properties must be influenced by the other factors determining arousal potential. Habituation seems to occur more rapidly for collative variables than for psychophysical or ecological variables. For example, we tire more quickly of a meaningless complex design than of something—our profession, say, or our children—that is very meaningful to us. Works having high arousal potential because of their psychophysical characteristics should be less likely to exhibit high levels of collative properties or high rates of change in these properties because these in combination with the psychophysical properties would make total arousal potential too high and cause negative hedonic tone. Thus, more incongruity, novelty, and surprise, and faster rates of change in these variables, should be found in small than in large works and in works composed of weak rather than intense stimuli. For example, the design of large public buildings should change more slowly than that of smaller private residences.

In the case of ecological characteristics, similar trade-offs should occur. Works depicting highly meaningful contents should change slowly and exhibit low levels of collative variables. For the believer, sacred art has high arousal potential because of its connection to his or her religion. Meaningfulness habituates slowly. Thus, it is unnecessary and counterproductive to increase arousal potential by increasing, say, incongruity. Added arousal due to incongruity would push affect into the negative range. Paintings of nudes induce some degree of sexual arousal and thus leave less room for variation in collative properties. Thus, nude painting should change more slowly than paintings of still-lifes. Nonrepresentative painting should change more rapidly than representative painting because the former has little or no intrinsic meaning.

Decline in Arousal Potential

If arousal potential could only increase and never decrease, all art everywhere should be extremely complex by now, and there should be no historical declines in complexity. Neither is the case. If high-arousal states are extreme and long-lasting enough, they are likely to retard artistic change and lead to historical declines in arousal potential. Such states are most likely to occur in situations of social chaos. Even if the art-producing system remains intact, arousal potential may decline.

Politicians can in some situations exert direct control over artists. If the politicians in question do not like art with high arousal potential, they can certainly decrease it. An obvious example is Nazi Germany, where artists producing unacceptable work were forced into exile or even killed; the remaining artists were controlled and censored in their work. Even in this extreme case, however, all that the Nazis could do was to pick one—Art Deco—of the already existing styles and destroy the others. They were not able to establish a completely new style. In order to do that, they would have had to create the art themselves.

However much artists tend to ignore their audience, they do not do so altogether. If an art form suddenly gains in popularity, the expanded audience may bring about a decline in arousal potential. This will occur if artists are "seduced" into creating *for* an audience. Such seduction seems likely if artists can make money without in their own eyes compromising their work. Something of this sort may have happened to Italian music in the nineteenth century, when opera caught on with the public, and what had been an élite art became a popular art.

If enough artists with the requisite talent cannot be recruited by a given tradition, then arousal potential will decline. This can occur for a variety of reasons. In fact, it is likely to occur if the population from which artists are recruited is small. Genius is an extremely rare trait. The small population of most primitive societies may be one of the major reasons primitive art often does not seem to show the sustained and regular sort of aesthetic evolution found in developed societies. Even developed nations with small populations may not produce enough capable artists for evolution to occur. There are just not enough people in Luxembourg to produce enough artists. A country such as the Netherlands may be on the margin as far as population is concerned: Dutch painting evolves, but there seem to be definite gaps in the record. The number of eminently creative individuals varies widely from one generation to another in any nation (Simonton 1984a). This can create problems in small nations. Once population is large enough, the supply of artists seems to be sufficient even if large numbers of them are removed. If we looked only at poetic trends, we would never guess that England lost any poets in the First or Second World War.

There are misleading cases where arousal potential has apparently shown long-lasting historical declines. The clearest example may be in women's fashion. Although the clothing worn by upper-class women has certainly become simpler across the last several hundred years, the relevant stimulus is not the clothing in isolation but the clothing plus the woman wearing it. The simpler the clothing, the more of the woman it tends to reveal. Thus, the decreased arousal potential of the clothing is more than offset by arousal potential produced by the wearer. Interested observers of sufficient age no doubt recall having observed many women wearing miniskirts: the often vivid memories of such observations are usually sketchy as to the texture, pattern, or even color of the garment, because one's attention was focused on the wearer rather than upon the miniskirt itself. It is well established that we recall only things upon which our attention was once focused. Though dresses may be simpler at present than in the eighteenth century, a woman today has a larger wardrobe. Thus, increased variety also offsets decreased complexity.

A simpler explanation is that clothing can lose some of its aesthetic qualities because of functional reasons. Fashion is not a high art. There is a pressure to increase arousal potential, but other pressures can add so much noise that the theory of aesthetic evolution is only marginally—rather than continually—applicable. Consumers can retard change by passive resistance. They can extinguish styles altogether by boycott. Walking sticks and hats are more or less extinct. The audience did this. This fact does not refute the theory of aesthetic evolution. Evolution can occur only when the environment permits it. If a politician kills all the poets, poetic evolution obviously ceases. If poets had to make a living by writing poetry, there would be no poetry; it would have gone the way of the scarlet waistcoat. On the other side of the coin, if the makers of scarlet waistcoats had not held to the silly notion that the only thing they are good for is to wear, there would still be plenty of them, and they would be quite fancy. Their functional aspect put all kinds of constraints on what they could look like. Recall Kubler's definition that if something has a use, it is not art. If something has a use, people want it to work. That gets in the way of its aesthetic aspects. If something has a use, people can stop using it and destroy its aesthetic aspects altogether. Being useless has distinct advantages. Paintings don't come with warranties. Customers can't return them and say they don't work—or that they have suddenly started to work. Customers can't say anything, really. If something is useless, it doesn't make any sense to say how long it will remain useless or to quibble about exactly how it should be useless.

THE DIRECTION OF AESTHETIC EVOLUTION

The exhaustion theories of Göller and others have been criticized because they do not provide an explanation of the direction of aesthetic evolution (Hauser 1963 [1958]; Kautzsch 1917; Wölfflin 1964 [1888]). They explain, that is, only why art changes but not the character of this change—not the way in which a specific style or the content of art changes over time. The formalist theorists (Tynjanov and Jakobson 1971 [1928]; Mukařovský 1976 [1940]) themselves uniformly agreed that their evolutionary theory could not explain the direction of aesthetic change, that it was necessary to look to extra-aesthetic social or cultural forces for an explanation of such changes. By the same token, the theories of Peckham (1965), Meyer (1956), and Cohen (1966) are mute concerning the specific direction that changes in aesthetic content will take. The main merit of the psychological theory I propose here is that it does specifically predict the sequence of contents and styles that can be expected to occur in any aesthetic tradition.

Psychological Means of Production

These predictions arise from a consideration of the psychological means by which works of continually increasing arousal potential can be produced. How can successive poets, for example, produce poetry that continues to become more and more novel, original, or incongruous over time? To answer this question, we must ask how novel works of art are produced in the first place. According to the psychoanalyst Ernst Kris (1952), novel or original ideas arise from a biphasic process: an initial inspirational stage involving "regression" is followed by a subsequent stage of elaboration involving a less regressed mode of thought. *Regression* denotes a movement away from secondary-process thinking toward primary-process thought. The secondary-process versus primary-process continuum is hypothetically the fundamental axis along which states of consciousness and types of thought vary (Fromm 1978). *Secondary-process cognition* is abstract, logical, and reality-oriented. It is the thought of everyday, waking reality. It is concerned with problem solving, logical deduction and induction, and so on. *Primary-process cognition* is free-associative, concrete, irrational, and autistic. It is the thought of dreams and reveries. In more extreme forms, it is the thought of psychosis and delirium. Jung (1963) used the terms *logos* versus *eros* to describe this continuum. *Logos* is the principle of analysis, logic, and differentiation; it is analogous to what Freud called secondary-process thinking. *Eros* has to do with synthesis, intuition, and discovery of similarity; it is analogous to what Freud called primary-process thinking. Nietzsche's (1927 [1872]) distinction between apollinean versus dionysian thought is closely related. Freud's (1938 [1900]) description of this continuum of types of thought was perceptive and illuminating. Although in my previous work I used Freud's terms *primary process* and *secondary process* as purely descriptive labels, the theory I am proposing has nothing at all to do with classical psychoanalytic theory. To avoid such confusion, I shall use the term *primordial* for primary process and *conceptual* for secondary process. It would have been equally accurate to have used other terms such as Heinz Werner's (1948) *dedifferentiated* versus *differentiated,* Jung's (1963) *eros* versus *logos,* Peter McKellar's (1957) "A-thinking" versus "R-thinking," Berlyne's (1965) "autistic" versus "directed" thinking, or Wilhelm Wundt's (1896) "associationistic" versus "intellectual" thought. All of these dichotomies are isomorphic. The reason to make up new terms is to avoid even further confusion. Just as I don't agree with everything Freud said, so I don't with everything Werner, Jung, and the others said. Thought or consciousness varies along one main axis, as is obvious to anyone who studies the topic. What the axis is called is the only thing that varies. I'll use the terms *primordial* versus *conceptual* as purely descriptive terms subsuming the dichotomies I have enumerated. The primordial-versus-conceptual axis is the main dimension along which consciousness varies. At any point in time, our thoughts lie somewhere along this axis. When I speak of variation along the axis, I don't necessarily mean extreme variation. Any time you make a distinction, your thought is relatively conceptual. Any time you see a similarity, your thought is relatively primordial.

Conceptual thought cannot produce novel ideas. It is aimed at analysis and discrimination. Deductive logic is its purest expression; and, of course, we can find from logic only what we, at least implicitly, knew in the first place. On the other hand, as Jung (1963) has well pointed out, the basic principle of primordial thought is equation and discovery of similarity. Primordial thought, being free-associative and undirected, increases the probability of novel combinations of mental elements. Such combinations form the raw material for the work of art. Once discovered, this raw material must be put into final form (for example, made to conform to current stylistic rules) in a conceptual state of mind. Kris did not discover the nature of the creative process. Virtually all eminently creative people who have reported upon how they created have said something similar. The American poet Brewster Ghiselin (1964 [1952]) provides a valuable compilation of such self-reports. It is no surprise, then, that other major theories of creativity are really identical to Kris's theory but use different theoretical vocabularies (see Martindale 1981).

Novel ideas can emerge in two ways from the inspiration-elaboration process. Holding the amount of elaboration or "revision" constant, deeper regression (movement toward more primordial cognition) should lead to more free-associative thought and therefore increase the probability of original or remote combinations of mental elements. In other words, to produce a novel idea, one must regress to a primordial state of consciousness. To produce an even more novel idea, one must regress to an even more primordial level. One might think of conceptual thought as crystalline. All of the mental elements are neatly arrayed like atoms in a crystal. But a crystal is static: the atoms don't move around and make contact with distant ones. If we increase temperature, however, the crystal will melt into a liquid, and the probability of an atom hooking up with a remote one is increased. Just so, the probability of remote mental elements colliding is greater if we increase mental "temperature"—that is, if we move toward more primordial cognition. In the mental system, as in the physical, the higher the temperature, the greater the probability of any one element colliding with another. Of course, primordial cognition alone is not enough for innovation. One needs to have a lot of mental elements, and they should be as diverse as possible (Martindale 1988a; Simonton 1984a).

Generally, elaboration is carried out in a conceptual state of mind. It consists of seeing whether an idea is in accord with current stylistic rules. For a poet, this might mean making sure that one has written sense rather than nonsense; that rhyme, meter, and syntax are acceptable; and so on. Holding degree of regression constant, decreasing the amount of elaboration (that is, elaborating less or in a more primordial state of mind) should lead to statements that are original by virtue of being nonsensical or nonsyntactic in varying degrees. Productions of the latter sort are usually more improbable than those of the former type. A statement composed of close associates but with little elaboration (such as "chairs the fooding tabler") is less probable than the most far-fetched metaphor concerning a table that is elaborated into a syntactically or semantically meaningful form. Similar considerations apply to the other arts as well.

Primordial Content and Stylistic Change

The amount of an artist's regression during the creation of an art work should leave its mark on the work: that is, the greater the regression during inspiration, the more the resulting work should reflect primordial thought. This fact allows us to predict the historical direction of changes in artistic content. Primordial states of mind are often marked by a timeless, dream-like quality:

> I saw Eternity the other night
> Like a great *Ring* of pure and endless light
> All calm, as it was bright.
> (Vaughan, "The World")

> A great black sleep
> Falls over my life:
> . . . .
> I am a cradle
> That a hand rocks
> In the hollow of a vault. . . .
> Silence, silence!
> (Verlaine, "Sagesse")

References to infantile oral and and anal themes are also common:

> If you see me, eyes lost in paradise,
> It is when I am remembering your milk drunk long
> ago.
> (Mallarmé, "Hérodiade")

> Upwards thou dost weepe,
> Heav'ns bosome drinkes the gentle streame,
> Where the milky Rivers creepe

Thine floats above and is the creame.
(Crashaw, "The Weeper")

I advance to the attack, and I climb to the assault
Like a choir of worms after a cadavre.
(Baudelaire, "Je t'adore a l'égal de la voûte
nocturne")

And only maggots bloom
In the rotten sides of women who are dead.
(Verhaeren, "La Bêche")

Physiognomic or animistic perception (attributing emotion to inanimate objects) and synesthesia (a sensation produced in one modality when a stimulus is applied to another, as when a sound induces a sensation of color) are also marks of primoridal cognition:

The distant forest, whose edge is dark,
Sleeps over there, motionlessly, in heavy repose.
(Leconte de Lisle, "Midi")

There are some fragrances cool like the flesh of children,
Sweet as oboes and green like meadows.
(Baudelaire, "Correspondances")

(See chapter 3 for more examples of primordial content.) Primordial cognition is also marked by what it lacks: abstract concepts, purposeful actions, restraint, and moral imperatives are all absent.

Primordial content can be painted as well as spoken of. The painting in figure 2.2A is realistic; conceptual thought has no problem grasping it. The painting in figure 2.2B represents something, but it is mysterious. A sense of mystery or awe is a sure sign that one is confronting something that has sprung from a primordial state of mind. The painting in figures 2.2C and 2.2D do not really represent anything besides themselves. They are even more primordial in their content than the first two paintings.

Because increasing novelty by decreasing level of elaboration is more drastic than increasing depth of regression during inspiration, artists may

Figure 2.2   Paintings with increasing amounts of primordial content.
(A) Jean Baptiste Greuze. *The Village Bride,* 1761, is photographic and realistic (Musée
du Louvre, Paris)

favor the latter method. If possible, successive artists should engage in deeper and deeper regression while maintaining the same level of elaboration. Each artist or poet must regress further in search of usable combinations of ideas or images not already used by his or her predecessors. We should expect the increasing remoteness or strangeness of similes, metaphors, images, and so on to be accompanied by *content* reflecting the increasingly deeper regression toward primordial cognition required to produce them. Across the time a given style is in effect, we should expect works of art to have content that becomes increasingly more and more dreamlike, unrealistic, and bizarre.

Eventually, a turning point to this movement toward primordial thought during inspiration will be reached. At that time, increases in novelty would be more profitably attained by decreasing elaboration—by loosening the stylistic rules that govern the production of art works—than

Figure 2.2B Gustave Moreau. *Oedipus and the Sphinx*, 1864, is photo-graphic but not realistic (The Metropolitan Museum of Art, New York. Bequest of William H. Herriman, 1921, 21.134.1)

Figure 2.2C   Yves Tanguy. *Mama, Papa Is Wounded!* 1927. is even less realistic. Oil on canvas, 36¼ × 28¾". (Collection, The Museum of Modern Art, New York. Purchase)

Figure 2.2D   Jackson Pollock. *Autumn Rhythm,* 1950, is neither photographic nor realistic (The Metropolitan Museum of Art, New York. George A. Hearn Fund, 1957, 57.92)

by attempts at deeper regression. This turning point corresponds to a major stylistic change. Changes in stylistic rules allow increased arousal potential in two ways. In either case, arousal potential can be increased in a way that requires *less* primordial thought than was required by the previous style. Thus, amount of primordial content should *decline* when stylistic change occurs. One type of style change involves allowing new elements to enter the artistic lexicon. Because the elements themselves are new, even the most obvious similes and metaphors concerning them will be new by default. This requires no great regression, because these obvious combinations come readily to mind. Once poets have said all they can think of about great men, they will be tempted to begin writing about lesser ones. Wordsworth, in his poem "The Leech Gatherer," showed definitively that it is not even necessary to say anything novel or of the slightest interest about leech gatherers when they are first introduced into the poetic realm. Just mentioning them is quite enough.

In the second type of stylistic change, the rules governing artistic style are loosened, allowing an increase in arousal potential at a cost of *less* regression than was previously necessary. Perhaps the clearest example of this type of change can be found in French poetry. Until 1900, French poets accepted the rule that the word *like* had to join like words. If a poet wanted to compose a simile, "A is like B," then "A" and "B" had in fact to be alike by some wild stretch of the imagination. By the 1890s, French poets were desperate. A lot of people had been writing a lot of French poetry for a lot of centuries. Paul Valéry was a great poet in the nineteenth century and again in the twentieth. However, these were intolerable working conditions even for a poet. Valéry simply called it quits and wrote no poetry for twenty years. He began again because working conditions had improved. If you own the store and there are no customers, the rules are whatever you say they are. Around 1900, the similarity rule was explicitly abrogated. It became acceptable to combine completely unlike words with the word *like*. Paul Eluard's image "the earth is blue like an orange" was perfectly acceptable. Surreal images are composed of easily accessible word associates such as *blue* and *orange*. No great regression is needed to think of *orange* given the word *blue*. Primordial content should decline with the introduction of a new style. Once the stylistic change has taken place, it should begin to rise again. After the obvious combinations of mental elements have been discovered, more regression will be required to think of the less obvious ones.

Specificity of Aesthetic Evolution

The evolutionary theory applies only to a series of artists working within the same tradition. Just as biological evolution is species-specific, aesthetic evolution is tradition-specific. An evolutionary change in elephants has no direct implications for kangaroos. However, traditions are not as clearly demarcated as species. What, exactly, is supposed to be evolving? It is left as an empirical question whether it is a specific tradition within a specific medium, the entire medium, or all artistic media together. If the last possibility is the case, then we should expect to find the primordial content cycles in different artistic media to be in synchrony. If the first or second possibility is correct, we should expect the cycles to be more or less randomly related. The question is of interest, because historians of art and literature have been debating for several centuries whether the arts move in synchrony. Probably because of the lack of quantitative methods, several centuries of humanistic investigation have produced no answer to this question. For purposes of suspense, I shall not answer this question until chapter 7.

Misreading and the Anxiety of Influence

It will not have escaped some readers that the evolutionary theory is similar to the theory of literary history proposed by Harold Bloom (1975). Because Bloom and I have a somewhat different style of writing, occasionally use different theoretical terms, and tend to prefer hyperboles—albeit in opposite directions—it may not be clear that our theories are even more similar than might appear at first glance. Bloom had the fortune or misfortune to teach at Yale. Though we were interested in the same things, for a long time I didn't bother to read anything he wrote, on the assumption that everyone there was a deconstructionist and didn't make any sense.

I'm glad I didn't read Bloom earlier. I would have been too influenced. That's what he is all about. His point is that poets do not want to be influenced. They do not want to be followers. But they—except for Homer—come too *late*. They have to say something different and better than those who come earlier. Bloom claims no credit for this insight. He quotes the passage from Hobbes (1840 [1650]) that I quoted earlier. Bloom doesn't mention Jakobson or Tynjanov. Why should he? They were *late*. Hobbes had already made the same point. In poetics as in poetry, it does you no credit to repeat what has already been said.

As I mentioned in the last chapter, literary critics should have seen that there are profound regularities in literary history. They should, too, have seen that these regularities were caused by the pressure for novelty. So far as I can see, though, only Bloom has seen the necessary connection between the pressure for novelty and the direction of change in literary content. In order to be novel, poets must—as Bloom puts it—"misread" earlier poets. Let us say that you see a tree and want to write a poem about it. Your poem is not really going to be as much about the specific tree as it will be about earlier poems about trees and—by extension—about all prior poems that you know. It is beyond conception that you would even think of writing a poem about the tree unless you had behind you the entire cultural conception of poetry, nature poetry, and so on.

Now Bloom is a bit extreme in saying that your poem is only a poem about other poems. If we "misread" him and say that your poem is mainly a response to prior tree poems and only minimally a response to this particular tree, he is no doubt quite right. Because you have just now seen it, many less mental elements must have to do with this particular tree than with your knowledge of poetry. Some of us had to learn a silly poem by Joyce Kilmer that had something to do with the supposition that fools could make poems about trees but only God could make a real tree. If I ever think to make a poem about a tree, I cannot make a poem about that tree proper. As a mental reflex, I also think of Kilmer's poem. That, in turn, makes me think, on the one hand, of war (Kilmer was killed in the First World War) and, on the other, of Spenser's Bower of Bliss in the *Faerie Queen* (it had trees). These in turn bring to mind other memories. We need no numbers to tell us that poems are about other poems and memories, not about whatever tree we happened to see. Did Proust write 5 volumes about a little piece of cake or 4.999 volumes about other novels? The latter, of course. Proust's *madeleine* elicited a mass of ideas the vast majority of which had nothing to do with that little piece of cake.

To avoid influence, Bloom says that later poets misread earlier ones. To do so, they use what he calls "revisionary ratios." He uncomfortably equates the latter with Freudian defense mechanisms and easily equates them with rhetorical tropes or figures of speech. Freudian defense mechanisms implicitly require a homunculus that checks what can come out of "the unconscious" into the consciousness. As both I (Martindale 1976a) and modern psychoanalytic theorists (such as Peterfreund 1971) have indicated, such a homunculus is implausible. Bloom (1975) raised similar objections.

Bloom argues that later poets use various "revisionary ratios" and "defense mechanisms" to avoid influence by earlier poets. The implication of defense mechanisms or misreading is that something is done purposely. I don't think that this is the case. Let's look at the revisionary ratios and tropes. They are all well-known traits of primordial cognition: that is, they need have nothing to do with defense mechanisms. These tropes are merely the ways of primordial cognition as seen by Freud (1938 [1900]) in what he called the dream work. The *dream work* is, according to Freud, an operation of what I have called primordial cognition. Here are the main tropes:

1. *Irony:* Asserting one thing while meaning the opposite; this is Freud's (1959 [1910]) primordial use of the same word to indicate opposite qualities.

2. *Synecdoche:* Part-for-whole or whole-for-part symbolism; an explicit primary-process mechanism (Freud 1938 [1900]; Matte-Blanco 1959).
3. *Metonymy:* The use of an associatively connected word or concept for another (as in "The White House says" for "The president says"); this is what Freud (1938 [1900]) called "displacement."
4. *Litotes:* The expression of an affinity by negating the contrary (as in "a man of no mean city"); clearly related to the equation of opposite meanings (1).
5. *Hyperbole:* The expression of a concept by a more extreme one; this can be due to displacement (3) or metaphor (6).
6. *Metaphor:* Equation on the basis of similar attributes; this is the basis of so-called Freudian symbolism (as in snake = penis) and of schizophrenic predicate logic (as in the psychiatrist Eugen Bleuler's "Switzerland loves Freedom; I love Freedom; Therefore, I am Switzerland" (1966 [1911]).
7. *Metalepsis:* The use of any combination of the preceding tropes; clearly explicit in Freud's (1938 [1900]) comments on the dream work.

Quite clearly, these tropes are mechanisms of primordial cognition. Bloom is reluctant to equate them with defense mechanisms. So am I. However, we both argue that they are consequences of the pressure for novelty. If I read him right, Bloom says that they are more consciously employed in order to *avoid* influence; whereas I say that they are automatically employed in order to *seek* novelty.

There are other differences as well. Bloom uses the term *regression* to refer to a Freudian defense mechanism; I, to refer to a movement from conceptual toward primordial cognition having nothing to do with defense mechanisms. Bloom seems to restrict his theory to what he calls "strong" poets, whereas I apply the evolutionary theory to all poets. Whereas I argue that there are systematic oscillations in primordial cognition across time, Bloom does not make such an argument. Nonetheless, the main gist of both theories is similar.

GENERAL PREDICTIONS

If the evolutionary theory is valid, several general predictions may be made about any series of artistic products produced within a given tradition: Measures of arousal potential such as novelty, complexity, and variability should increase monotonically over time. Measures of primordial content should exhibit cycles of increasing and decreasing density of words or images or sounds indicative of primordial thought. Periods when primordial content decreases should coincide with periods of stylistic change. Across very long periods of time, primordial content should increase. (I diagram these predictions in figure 2.3.) These predictions hold only if the autonomy of the artistic subculture and the chronic arousal level of a society have remained relatively constant. There are certainly cases where indices of arousal potential and primordial content have exhibited erratic trends. These should be cases where autonomy and chronic or acute levels of arousal have not remained relatively constant.

The evolutionary theory can be construed in two ways. The weak version is that the theory explains a bit, but perhaps not much, about art history. The strong version is that the theory explains the main trends in art history. Because the main axes of artistic style—classic versus romantic, simple versus complex—are isomorphic with the main theoretical axes—conceptual versus primordial content, low versus high arousal potential—it is not unreasonable to think that the strong version may be true.

ART HISTORY VERSUS INDIVIDUAL ARTIST

Humanistic scholars have complained that the evolutionary theory is cold and abstract. Of course, it is. This is the nature of scientific theories. These scholars have also complained that it tells them nothing about the work of individual artists. Here, I must disagree. As I argued in the first chapter, we cannot understand what an artist does unless we understand either the evolutionary process that has brought one to deviate from one's predecessors in a predetermined way, or how one deviates

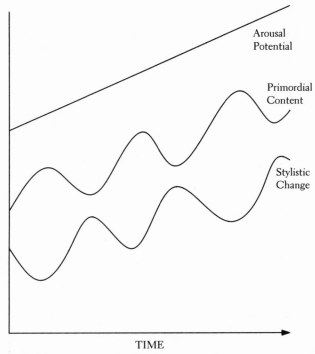

TIME

Figure 2.3 Graphic summary of theoretical predictions: in cases to which the theory applies, arousal potential should increase across time; primordial content and stylistic change should show long-term increases with superimposed oscillations. Note that primordial content and stylistic change should be out of phase: that is, the former should increase when the latter decreases, and vice versa.

from one's contemporaries. Indeed, these deviations have been taken by many as defining the style of an artist. We cannot compute these deviations unless we have first computed measures such as those described later in this book.

In any event, the theory *does* apply to individual artists. An artist cannot keep producing copies of the same work of art. Artists must outdo themselves as well as prior artists. They commonly become depressed if they think that they have failed to do so. It is more difficult to outdo oneself than to outdo those who have come before. Not all artists succeed. Before presenting quantitative evidence that artists do tend to succeed at this task, I shall return to my analogy with gravitation. Gravity explains more than why apples fall to the earth. It explains why there is an earth in the first place. Gravity accreted particles to form the earth. Without gravity, the earth would break up and disperse. Gravity gives the earth its coherence. Evolutionary pressures give an artist's career its plan. Without these pressures, there would be no coherence to an artist's work. One would produce works in a random variety of styles, which would have nothing to do with one another. We would have chaos rather than a discernible progression of styles.

Those concerned with an individual artist are often interested in the surface structure of his or her work—the specific ideas, colors, words, chords, and so on that it contains. On the other hand, any theory of art history, whether evolutionary or not, is concerned with deep structure as opposed to such particular individual differences. A general theory of art history is analogous to asking what happens if we drop an object in a perfect vacuum. Humanistic inquiry is analogous to inquiring about a particular stone rolled down a particular mountainside. No one asks about such a stone in the natural sciences. If they did, however, they could not explain its behavior without recourse to the theory of gravity. The question might be asked if the stone were a gigantic diamond that one had no little interest in finding. This is really the sort of question asked in the humanities. We rightly want to know every detail we can about Goethe and Shakespeare, since they stand far above the rest of humanity. Although the evolutionary theory does, indeed, tell us little about these details, the details cannot be placed in their proper perspective without recourse to such a theory.

Another humanistic complaint about evolutionary theory is that it reduces art history to a meaningless quest for novelty. This is rather like rejecting Darwinian theory because it reduces human history to a meaningless struggle for survival. Darwin never denied that people have done all sorts of interesting things while they struggled to survive. Had humanity not survived, however, we should not be here to ask about what these things were. The theory of aesthetic evolution involves no assertion that artists are motivated solely by a quest for novelty. Artists are interested in accomplishing many other things besides making their works novel. What these other things are varies unsystematically, whereas the pressure for novelty is constant and consistent. Thus, only it can produce systematic trends in artistic form and content. This is true even if need for novelty is a comparatively *unimportant* motive for any given artist. Even if artists were solely interested in novelty for its own sake, this would not render their work pointless. Wordsworth noted that "the introduction of a new element into the intellectual universe" must always lead to "widening the sphere of human sensibility." As William James (1961 [1902]) pointed out, the manner in which such an idea was conceived does not determine its value. If an artist says or does something of interest, the motive is not relevant. It may have been need for novelty. It may have been desire to make some money. To say something interesting, one does not need to be motivated solely by the desire to do so.

APPLYING STATISTICS TO ART

In the rest of this book, I present quantitative evidence supportive of the theory outlined in this chapter. In chapters 3 to 5, I deal with French, British, and American literature. The evidence presented in these chapters was derived mainly from computerized content analyses, which involves using computer programs to count words of different sorts. When one deals with huge numbers of texts, such a quantitative approach is needed if for no other reason than as a mnemonic device. In chapter 3, I deal further with why computerized content analysis is desirable and how it is done. In that chapter, I also attempt to show that—so long as one is dealing with a manageable number of texts—quantitative content analysis and a qualitative or literary critical approach yield comparable or complementary results.

In chapter 6, I describe data concerning the history of music and the visual arts. Most of the data in this chapter are derived from ratings by naïve observers in order to ensure objectivity. Since I rather like my own theory, it would not do for me simply to give you my own impressions of what happened in the history of art. I would have an unconscious tendency to twist the data to fit the theory. Unfortunately, most art historians, though well aware that this sort of distortion is a danger, do nothing to avoid it. In chapter 7, I deal, again in a quantitative manner, with the question of whether the arts evolve in synchrony. The evolutionary theory involves the assertion that the main forces of aesthetic evolution are intra-artistic, that art does not reflect society to any appreciable extent. In chapter 8, I examine the evidence for this assertion. I ascribe a good bit of art history to the direct and indirect effects of a continual pressure for novelty—a pressure that operates on individual artists as well as across great stretches of time. In chapter 9, I examine how pressure for novelty shapes individual artistic careers and even trends within the course of individual works of art.

As may be inferred from the mere fact that I have written this book, the evidence I present is generally supportive of the evolutionary theory. To the extent that the evidence does support the theory, I argue that this or that aspect of literary history or art history has been explained. Humanistic scholars are often uncomfortable with this claim for several reasons. For one thing, they use the term *explanation* in a different sense from the way scientists do. Humanists often use the term to mean "have a subjective sense of understanding," often of one specific poem or other work of art. We, of course, want such a subjective sense of understanding in science, too. However, the term *explanation* means something different. Science searches for abstract regularities or laws. Once found, these regularities are expressed in mathematical equations in order to describe the regularity exactly. If you drop something, it will fall. That is a regularity, but it is much more enlightening to know the specifics: for example, it will fall at a rate of 32 feet/second^2 in a vacuum on earth. A theory of gravitation provides an explanation of why this has to be the exact rate. Since we are so used to this sort of statement in physics, it doesn't occur to anyone to complain that the explanation doesn't account for why the item dropped happened to be purple or iridescent or whatever—or that it doesn't tell us anything about Shakespeare's sonnets.

It bothers some people no end when I take an exactly analogous approach to poetry. For example, I argue that the impact value or arousal potential of poetry increases across time because of need for novelty. To find out, I construct measures of arousal potential and apply them to series of poetic texts. Then I want to know the exact rate of increase. If I want to know it at all precisely, I need to fit an equation to the data points. To the extent that the equation fits the data, I say that I have explained such-and-such percentage of overall variability in arousal potential. I can make this claim because my theory predicted the increase. (Of course, someone may in future come up with a simpler or more compelling explanation.) In this process, the work of a poet is reduced to a "data point." However "unpoetic" such terminology may seem, taking such measurements by no means destroys or damages the work of the poet. It is just one way of looking at one aspect of it. More seriously, to complain that the equation does not help us understand the meaning of such and such a poem, or that it does not deepen our understanding of the poet's "fundamental mission" or some such thing, is true but silly. Since I haven't undertaken to explain such things in the first place, it makes no more sense to criticize my theory for not explaining them than it does to criticize Kepler's laws of planetary motion for not explaining why the sky is blue or why Jupiter has a red spot. Poetic word usage shows extremely regular historical changes—as I demonstrate quantitatively and explain. It makes no sense to criticize this explanation because it does not apply to some other phenomenon in which the reader happens to be interested.

Be this as it may, the goal of a scientific approach to literary history is ultimately both a set of equations that describe the main trends and an explanation of why these equations rather than others were found. Unless we gather quantitative data and then reduce these to specific equations, what we can say will be so vague as to be not worth saying. The point of statistics and equations is to simplify things, not to complicate them—a result possible, though, only if the reader understands the statistics. Thus, I have tried to explain, in what I hope is plain English, what the statistics tell us. Furthermore, the next chapter—where I apply statistics to French poetry and address it in terms of equations and graphs as well as qualitatively—will provide a framework for the rest of the book.

For those unfamiliar with statistics I should at this point explain the general rationale and basic procedures of the statistical approach I have taken throughout. If all poets wrote exactly the same poems, there would obviously be no variability in the content of their works, and we would have nothing to explain. This is obviously far from the case, though. The amount of arousal potential, for example, in works of different poets shows a good bit of variability. To have any idea at all of how much variability there is, we need to measure arousal potential in a quantitative manner. This is the point of some of the computerized content-analysis measures I describe in the next several chapters. If we were dealing with only a couple of poets, we could just read their works and decide which had more arousal potential. If we were dealing with hundreds of poets and want to rank-order their work in respect to amount of arousal potential, we should get hopelessly confused unless we took a quantitative approach. I argue that part of this variation is due to a historical increase. To find out whether this is true, we can graph amount of arousal potential by when poets wrote. If an increasing trend is there, we shall see it in the graph. Then we want to fit a line or curve described by an equation to this trend. One of the goals of science is to describe results in terms of mathematical equations: fitting the equation to the data allows us to find out how much overall variation it accounts for. If all of the data points fall on the line described by the equation, then we have accounted for 100 percent of the variation. If the data points are not all on the curve, statistical procedures allow us to say what percentage of variation can be accounted for by the equation. This percentage tells us how much of the variation can be explained by my theory—which predicts historical increases—and how much remains to be explained by other causes. You can fit any sort of curve you want to a set of data, but if the curve accounts for, say, only 1 percent of overall variance, it obviously doesn't account for much of anything. Tests of statistical significance also help. They tell us the probability of the data's being close to the curve merely by chance.

In the case of arousal potential, the theory says that it should increase monotonically across time. *Monotonic* means that, as time goes on, arousal potential increases without any declines. A linear increase (see, for example, figure 3.1 on page 89) means a constant rate of increase across time. A *correlation coefficient* can be used to describe linear increases: a correlation of 1.00, for example, is found if all of the points lie exactly on a straight line. An exponential increase (see, for example, figure 4.1 on page 123) means an accelerating increase. In the case of primordial content, the theory predicts historical oscillations. How many oscillations we find will depend upon how long a period of time we examine. There are several ways of finding out whether there are oscillations in a historical time series. The most obvious is to make a graph of the data and look at it. If one can't see any oscillations, it is—at least in our case—best to stop at this point. Occasionally I deal with data that are "noisy": that is, one can see the oscillations, but there are a lot of random zigs and zags superimposed on them. This effect is likely if one is trying to infer from a very small sample to a large population—as if one were listening to a Texas radio station in New York, when a good bit of noise or static is likely to obscure the signal. In such cases, smoothing or taking a running average makes the oscillations clearer: that is, we average together the values for successive points in time, with the goal of getting rid of the extraneous noise.

If we can see oscillations, we then want to know how much of the variability they account for. We can use several procedures to do this. Spectral analysis tells one what sorts of oscillations or periodicies are present in a set of data and how important they are. To be used effectively, spectral analysis usually needs a lot more data points than those I deal with in this book. Polynomial equations can also be used to describe data showing oscillations. A second-order, or quadratic, polynomial has one inflection or bend: for example, primordial content decreases and then increases in a U-shaped fashion, or it increases and then decreases in an inverted-U-shaped fashion. There are two inflections in a third-order, or cubic, polynomial (see, for example, figure 5.3 on page 159). In general, there is one less inflection than the order of the polynomial. Thus, for example, a fifth-order, or quintic, polynomial has four inflection points. Polynomial equations just describe oscillatory curves but don't give any more information. Oscillations can be produced by certain types of autoregressive equations. An *autoregressive equation* is one in which the value of primordial content, for example, for a given point in time is predicted from prior values of primordial content. Since I argue that the main cause of change in an art-producing system is the prior history of that system, I try to fit autoregressive equations to the data when there is enough data to allow this. I mention a number of other statistical techniques in this book. Rather than burden the reader at this point, I shall describe them as we encounter them in the following chapters.

CHAPTER 3

Crucible in a Tower of Ivory

Modern French Poetry

O N the whole, nineteenth-century French poets tended to be an ar-
rogant lot. They were geniuses, and they knew it. They spoke for
God. If God were dead, then it was their right to usurp His place. So
far as many of them saw it, their status was divine. It was certainly
they who should assume the role of the aristocracy defeated in the
Revolution. Victor Hugo was puzzled that the people of France did
not see that he, rather than Napoleon III, should rule. But then, as
Jean Cocteau much later remarked, "Victor Hugo was a madman who
thought he was Victor Hugo." Baudelaire had a similar delusion: he
thought he was Baudelaire. Rimbaud was "he who would be God."
This was not idle chitchat. He was a sorcerer, after all—at least with
words; and the goal may have been within his grasp. Conventional
diagnoses do not fit these poets. Just as biological evolution creates
such impossibly fanciful creatures as birds of paradise, aesthetic evolution creates such beautifully depraved creatures as decadent poets. This
is, indeed, a good place to begin our inquiry.

There are several reasons to begin with the history of French poetry since 1800. Nineteenth-century French poetry, written in the romantic style, exhibited what I have called a "romantic progression" (Martindale 1975). Romanticism was carried to its logical—or illogical—extreme across the course of the century. Around 1900, there was an extreme stylistic change. Our predictions are clear. Primordial content should increase across the course of the nineteenth century and begin to decline around 1900. The increase in arousal potential, predicted by the theory, from 1800 to the present is easy to see—and to measure—because the main method of increasing arousal potential was to increase the remoteness of the elements joined in metaphors and similes.

If all this is clear, why do we need to bother with quantitative measurements? In a sense, we don't. I could merely take a poll of experts on French poetry, explain the theory, and ask them whether it was right. Most, but not all, would probably respond in the affirmative. Some would raise valid objections. Consider the hypothesis that metaphors and similes became more incongruous, as they seem to have done. Still, the fact that such striking images stick in one's mind may have led me to overlook metaphors and similes that do not fit the prediction. Maybe a few of these images have distorted my vision of what happened. How are we to find out? We have got to read the poetry with a less biased eye. But we are talking about thousands and thousands of pages of poetry. I could read it all, but I could not remember it all unless I were allowed to take notes. What would I do with my notes? I could use them to write a narrative account. The account would be very long. Because I am biased, we still could not be sure that I had not inadvertently overlooked similes that did not fit the hypothesis. Only a reader who was already an expert on French poetry could be asked to judge this. Thus, it comes down to a question of counting—something I should not do lest any unconscious bias of mine lead me to include poets who fit the theory. Objections from literary critics themselves suggest that the hypotheses be tested in a quantitative way.

THE QUANTITATIVE APPROACH

Here, briefly, is what I did. First of all, the population must be defined. I was conventional and used the most eminent French poets to be sure I could talk about the same people as do other literary historians. Dividing the span from 1770 to 1909 into consecutive twenty-year periods, I used for each period the three poets with the most pages in the *Oxford Book of French Verse* edited by St. John Lucas and P. Mansell Jones (1957) (see table 3.1). There are some deviations from the expected because I had to use poets for whom I could obtain fairly complete English translations. Thus, I include Chénier even though he was born in 1762. I used Nerval rather than Alfred de Vigny because there was no adequate translation for the latter. I translated Millevoye and Musset myself, because there was nobody reasonable to substitute for them. Birth date is the only fact that we can usually be sure of. It is difficult to seriate poets by *when* they wrote. In any event, as we shall see, the content of most poets' verse does not change massively across the course of a lifetime.

I had no particular reason for using Lucas and Jones as the basis for my choice of French poets. One would get about the same set of poets no matter how eminence is defined. The crucial factor is the objective selection of poets. Lucas and Jones certainly used their taste and judgment in making their selection, but they didn't make it with any bias either for or against the evolutionary theory because it didn't exist in 1957. Also, I had no compelling theoretical reason for dividing the time into twenty-year periods. Shorter periods might have made for too fine-grained sampling, leaving us with some obscure poets. Longer periods would have made too coarse a sampling.

Once I had my sample of poets, I had to decide who would do the counting. Human raters are not accurate, as the statisticians Frederick Mosteller and David Wallace discovered when trying to do content analysis: "People can't count, at least not very high" (1964, p.7). People also disagree. People are slow. And people want to be paid a lot of money for their slow and sloppy work. Computers have a lot of advantages. They are fast. They delight in drudgery. They are stupid. They don't read things

TABLE 3.1
Modern French Poets
(1770–1909)

Period F1 (Born 1770–89)
1. André Chénier 2. Pierre-Jean de Béranger 3. Charles-Hubert Millevoye
Period F2 (born 1790–1809)
4. Alphonse de Lamartine 5. Victor Hugo 6. Gérard de Nerval
Period F3 (born 1810–29)
7. Alfred de Musset 8. Théophile Gautier 9. Charles Baudelaire
Period F4 (born 1830–49)
10. Stéphane Mallarmé 11. Paul Verlaine 12. Tristan Corbière
Period F5 (born 1850–1869)
13. Jean-Arthur Rimbaud 14. Emile Verhaeren 15. Jules Laforgue
Period F6 (born 1870–89)
16. Paul Valéry 17. Guillaume Apollinaire 18. Jules Supervielle
Period F7 (born 1890–1909)
19. Paul Eluard 20. Henri Michaux 21. René Char

into a text. They can make stupid mistakes, but only if a programmer has given them the wrong instructions.

It was not necessary to put the complete works of each poet into computer-readable form. I used a random sample to get an idea of the characteristics of the entire population. If I put in the sections of each poet's work that I thought were best or most interesting, the entire procedure would have been a waste of time, biasing the sample. In the classic example of such flawed random sampling—the 1936 *Literary Digest* prediction that the Republican candidate, Alfred Landon, would win the presidential election by a landslide ("Topics of the Day," pp.5–6)—the population was drawn from telephone books. In the midst of the Great Depression, a lot of people could not afford a telephone, and virtually none of them were going to vote for a Republican. Another reason for random sampling is that it would cost too much to put everything in, and would be wasteful even if one could afford it. Statisticians have figured out how big a random sample needs to be in order to be a valid representative of a population. The samples I used are adequate.

For this study, 50 page numbers were drawn at random from the most recent and most complete edition of each poet's works, and the first 8 lines were used. If the eighth line did not end with a phrase delimiter (:, ;, ., !, or ?), the sample was continued until one was encountered. This produced samples of about 3,000 words per poet. In this—as well as in all my other studies of poetry—translations and verse dramas were not included. For purposes of computer analysis, all contractions were spelled out and archaic spellings were modernized. In cases where a poet did not use punctuation (Apollinaire was the main culprit), it was added by an assistant who did not know the purposes of the study. (Further details are given in Martindale 1975.)

The fact that English translations of the French poetry were analyzed makes little difference for my purposes. In content analysis, one "translates" everything into a small number of mega-words or categories. A content-analysis category such as *aggression* equates everything from "miff" to "kill." Unless a translator has altogether botched the job, the translated word will be correctly categorized. I took care to use only literal translations. The content-analysis categories used to measure primordial content have been translated into French and German. One gets about the same results if one analyzes, say, a German text with the German version or a translated text with the English version (Delphendahl and Martindale 1985; Hogenraad and Orianne 1986; van Eeckhoudt 1981).

AROUSAL POTENTIAL

We can assess the arousal potential, or poetic power, of poetic texts in a subjective, qualitative manner or in an objective, quantitative manner. I shall present some qualitative evidence first and then turn to the quantitative.

Qualitative Evidence

Unless the arousal potential of French poetry increased from around 1800 to the present, we have nothing to explain, and the theory would not apply. Let me first examine a series of examples that do suggest an increase. I quoted earlier these lines from "Les Colombes" by André Chénier, a pre-romantic poet:

> Beneath your fair head, a white delicate neck
> Inclines and would outshine the brightness of snow.

There is no incongruity to speak of in this image. It gives us a sort of absolute zero for metaphor distance. By *metaphor distance,* I mean the remoteness of the things compared in a metaphor or simile. Compare Chénier's lines with these from "L'Expiation" by Victor Hugo, an early romantic poet:

> Waterloo! Waterloo! Waterloo! bleak plain!
> Like a wave which boils in an urn too full,
> In your arena of woods, of hills, of valleys,
> Pale death mingled the dark battalions.

The opening is repetitious, making it clear that Hugo wants to say something about Waterloo. What he says about it, though, is incongruous. It is a bleak plain—as is literally true of parts of the battlefield. Note what Hugo does: he compares the bleak plain to a wave, and the wave, to boiling water. A bleak plain brings to mind flatness and motionlessness, which are just the opposite of a churning wave or boiling water. By the third line, the bleak plain has got hills, valleys, and woods. A real plain has none of these things and is, furthermore, not like an urn or an arena. It is flat. A valley is like an urn or an arena, but the supposed plain has got both hills and valleys. In the last line, we have a contrast between "pale" and "dark." In context, the words do not clash, but their connotations do. We are so used to reading poetry that we may miss some of the beauty of the last line. Hugo has got things completely backward—on purpose, of course. Death did not mingle the battalions. The battalions mingled with each other and thus caused death. There is much more incongruity to be found in the lines. It is the incongruity and deviation from strict denotative meaning that gives these lines their poetic power. Poetic power *is* arousal potential.

If you don't read them closely, Hugo's lines are not striking. The stakes have been upped since his time. Let us look at some later nineteenth century poetry. This image from Baudelaire's "A une dame créole" offers a good comparison with Chénier's image:

> Her complexion is pale and warm; the dark enchantress
> Holds her neck with a nobly affected air.

Where clearly Chénier is talking about white doves, Baudelaire leaves us in no little confusion. He is talking about a creole woman. We suppose that her complexion might be dark. Baudelaire says it is pale. It is both pale and warm. Connotatively, that is incongruous. "Pale" and "cold," rather than "warm," go together. Recall Hugo's unsurprising "pale death." In any event, the woman is pale for only half a line. By the end of the line, she is "dark." I like this verse, and I am not criticizing it when I point out that we would have trouble picking out this woman in a line-up. There is also some incongruity we may miss. Nineteenth-century French society was racist: Baudelaire is elevating or ennobling a woman of low status.

Here is an example whose incongruity cannot be missed:

> The violin quivers like an afflicted heart;
> Melancholy waltz and languid vertigo!

. . . .
The sun is drowned in its clotted blood.
(Baudelaire, "Harmonie du soir")

The analogy in the first line, though remote, makes sense. The second line would give any neoclassic critic an attack of (lascivious?) apoplexy. Waltzes are not usually melancholy but tend to be light-hearted. But what is "languid vertigo"? I don't feel languid when I have vertigo. Far from it. Baudelaire has gone beyond what the ordinary person is likely to see any sense in. You can see the sense in the last line, but note the incongruity: The sun is drowning. A sunset is red. Blood is red. If we imagine that clotted blood refers to clouds of a certain sort, we are reading this idea in. Baudelaire would probably tell us that the line doesn't refer to anything except itself. Several decades earlier, Gautier (1955 [1835]) specifically said that a poem is *not* a message: it is an object; it just *is*. Baudelaire agreed with him.

The setting sun gave later poets no end of trouble, as in these lines from Laforgue:

> This evening a done-for sun lies on the top of the hill,
> Lies on its side, in the straw, on its overcoat.
> A sun white as a gob of spit in a tavern
> On a litter of yellow straw,
> Of yellow autumn straw.
>
> ("L'Hiver qui vient")

Compared with this, Baudelaire seems trite. And Laforgue made it terribly difficult for later poets to say anything new about the setting sun.

Mallarmé is a difficult poet. I could take an example at random and be fairly sure of finding considerable incongruity. Here is a passage from "Hérodiade" that is, I think, quite beautiful:

> Yes, it is for me, for me, that I flower, alone!
> You know it, amethyst gardens, buried
> Endlessly in learned dazzling abysses,
> Hidden golds, keeping your ancient light

> Under the sombre sleep of a primordial earth,
> You stones wherein my eyes like pure jewels
> Borrow their melodious light, and you
> Metals which give to my young hair
> A fatal splendour and its massive form!
> (Fowlie 1953, p.145)

Exactly what "amethyst gardens, buried endlessly" means is not obvious. It is more clear, though, than what a "learned abyss" is. Be careful with the next lines: the gold is not under the earth but, impossibly, under the *sleep*. Hérodiade's eyes borrow their light *within,* not from, the stones— again, literally impossible. If Mallarmé had meant that the gold is under the earth rather than under the sleep of the earth, he would have said so. If he had said so, this would not be good poetry. To say that there is gold under the earth is neither interesting nor novel.

One does not have to be so careful with twentieth-century French poetry, whose incongruity is blatant. Consider these examples:

> I love you opposite the seas
> Red like the egg when it is green
> You move me into a clearing
> Gentle with hands like a quail
> (Breton, "Tiki")

> You see the bare plain on the side of the dragging sky
> The snow high as the sea
> And the sea high in the blue
> . . . .
> Foolish my true gold standards
> Plains my good adventures
> Useful verdure delicate cities
> . . . .
> I see men true sensitive good useful
> Throw away a burden slighter than death
> And sleep joyfully in the noise of the sun
> (Eluard, "Nous sommes" [Fowlie 1955, pp.191–93])

85

I do not need to point out the incongruities. You can find meaning in this surreal poetry; what it is is more or less up to you. My concern is not with meaning per se (read literally, the excerpts have less and less meaning over time) but with differences between meaning, or incongruity.

Quantitative Evidence

I chose my examples because they are both striking and also representative. We need no numbers to establish that there are no surreal metaphors in Chénier or Hugo. But how regular was the trend? Was Mallarmé's poetry really more incongruous than Baudelaire's? Here we need quantitative evidence. In 1966, Jean Cohen looked at textual samples from French classical, romantic, and symbolist poets. Although only three poets represented each era, the results are strong. Cohen measured the frequency of what he called "impertinent epithets," or syntactically inappropriate ways of modifying a term. For example, Victor Hugo's "He climbed the bitter stairs" is not grammatical, in that an inanimate noun is modified by an animate adjective. This is a rule poets break a lot. How much? Cohen collected figures to tell us: 3.6 percent of the time in classical poetry, 23.6 percent in romantic poetry, and 46.3 percent in symbolist poetry. Cohen also counted incongruous use of color terms—as in Mallarmé's "white agony" or Rimbaud's "black perfumes." Classic poets didn't use enough color terms to allow a count. That tells us something itself: their poetry was abstract and conceptual. Romantic poets used color terms "inappropriately" 4.3 percent of the time; symbolist poets, 42 percent of the time. The more poetry violates the conventional rules of grammar, the more impact value, or arousal potential, it has. Clearly arousal potential increased across time.

Cohen also found evidence for incongruity between sound and sense. *Enjambment* refers to the lack of punctuation at the end of a line of poetry, so that its sense runs over to the next line. When French poetry is read aloud, you are supposed to pause at the end of each line whether or not the end of the line coincides with a grammatical pause. English poetry always has a brief pause, but it is not supposed to be there. The pause is longer in French poetry, and it *is* supposed to be there. In enjambed lines, this leads to pauses that conflict with meaning. How frequent are enjambed lines? Cohen found 11 percent for classical poetry, 19 percent for romantic poetry, and 39 percent for symbolist poetry. Words that rhyme in poetry are at least implicitly equated (Jakobson 1960). There is less incongruity in equating words from the same grammatical class than in noncategorical rhymes (for example, rhyming a noun with a verb). Cohen found 18.6 percent noncategorical rhymes in classical poetry, 28.6 percent in romantic poetry, and 30.6 percent in symbolist poetry.

Unless otherwise specified, the quantitative results I mention in this book are statistically significant and thus unlikely to have arisen by chance. By convention, a result is usually accepted as significant if it could have arisen by chance less than 5 times out of 100; and a lot of the results are much more significant than this. (Readers who want more statistical details than I give here may consult the original sources.)

How can we measure metaphor distance? A computer program can find some similes. The word *like* in poetry almost always signifies a simile. It almost never means affection. Poets are extreme. They *love* and they *adore*, but they almost never *like*. But similes are also signified by "as," and metaphors are just stated. It would be easier to hand-score a text than to write a program that could accurately locate metaphors. Trying a gross measure, I wrote a program that looked for co-occurrence within the same sentence of four sets of polar-opposite categories: Strong and Weak, Good and Bad, Active and Passive, and Approach and Avoidance. Of course, this measure is indirect. Although the logic is that a poet who persistently puts incongruous words in the same sentence is trying to be incongruous, the measure tells only whether a poet is using words of opposite connotations in the same sentence. The measure can fail in two ways: it can score incongruity where none is present (as in "The strong father rescued the weak child"), and it can also miss subtle incongruities. If the measure fails too much in these ways, it won't yield meaningful results. I took the radical—for psychology—approach of actually reading the texts and noting what was getting scored as incongruous, in order to assure myself that the measure was really getting at what it was supposed to. The categories, the subcategories, and some sample words in each category follow:

Strong	Weak
Strong: god, could, king, power, father.	Weak: child, little, lose, poor, cannot.
Hard: rock, stone, hard, glass, iron.	Soft: soft, gentle, tender, murmur, whisper.
Glory: great, gold, golden, pride, divine.	Anxiety: fear, tremble, dread, terror, blush.
	Sadness: tears, sad, pain, weep, woe.

Good	Bad
Good: good, home, church, worth, fine.	Bad: bad, crime, shame, wrong, false.
Angelic: white, pure, pale, sacred, angel.	Diabolic: black, dark, fate, curse, hell.
Moral imperatives: should, right, virtue, honor, law.	Anality: sweat, rot, dirty, disgust, filth.

Active	Passive
Active: wind, spirit, run, free, storm.	Passive: lie, death, dead, die, bed.
Random movement: wave, roll, spread, swell, shake.	
Ascend: rise, fly, throw, flight, leap.	

Approach	Avoidance
Love: love, friend, dear, kind, pity.	Aggression: break, war, beat, strike, wound.
Social behavior: say, tell, call, speak, meet.	

For each sentence in each text, the program computed whether any of these incongruous juxtapositions occurred. If a text uses a lot of Strong and Weak words, some may end up in the same sentence just by chance. To correct for this possibility, I divided the observed percentage of juxtapositions by the percentage expected by chance for all four types of juxtaposition. Then, all four types of juxtaposition were standardized, or given equal weight, and added up. The measure of metaphor distance is related to the number of sentences in a text: the reason is that if two texts have the same number of words but one has 100 sentences and the other had 1,000, the second has an unfair advantage. Thus, I equated number of sentences statistically to achieve the final measure, as in figure 3.1. The best-fitting trend line is also shown. (The *best-fitting line* is the one that comes closest to going through a set of points: that is, the distance of the points from the line is minimal.) As you can see, the trend is straight up, as predicted. The measure is correlated .53 with birth date, a result that supports the prediction. Figure 3.1 shows that the measure of incongruous

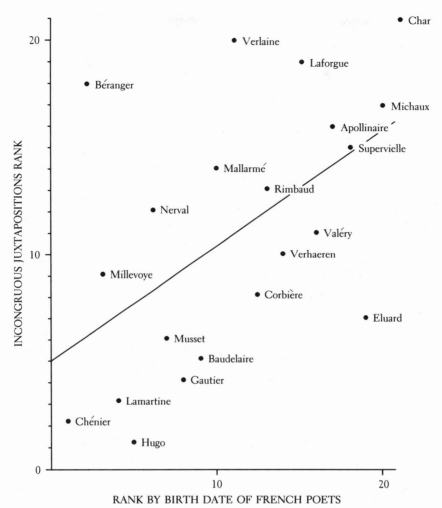

Figure 3.1   Amount of incongruous juxtapositions in texts by twenty-one French poets born between 1790 and 1909 graphed by birth-date rank. Incongruous juxtapositions increased across time. The best-fitting trend line describing this increase is shown.

juxtapositions failed miserably in two cases: it did not pick up Eluard's extreme—but subtle—incongruities and fooled the computer with Béranger's fairly trite poetry—that is, with such apparent incongruities as "the strong father loved his weak child." If these poets are omitted, the correlation rises from .53 to .71. Verlaine's score is also somewhat too high for the same reason that Béranger's score is elevated. Nonetheless, the predicted overall trend is clearly present.

We can also measure arousal potential in other ways. When we get to British poetry (see chapter 4), I present a powerful general measure which is based on linguistic variables such as word length. It is known that such variables get distorted in translation (Herdan 1966). The number of word associations elicited by a word in a fixed amount of time is in part a measure of ambiguity. Number of associations is also related to word frequency and other variables, so it is not a perfect measure of ambiguity. Allan Paivio, John Yuille, and Stephen Madigan (1968) got normative data on number of associations elicited by 925 nouns. I wrote a program, called SEMIS, to apply such norms. The program computes, for any text, the average number of associations for the text words that were found in the dictionary. In this case, the dictionary is the list of 925 nouns and the average number of word associations elicited by each noun. If a text word is not in the dictionary, we don't know its association value, so it is not included in the tally. The logic is different from that in straightforward content analysis, in which, if a text word is not in the dictionary, it is tallied as a zero rather than ignored. The correlation between average number of associates and birth date is .46. If we take number of associates to be a measure of ambiguity, this is more evidence in favor of the theoretical prediction.

One of the poets in my sample suggested that what I have called arousal potential can be achieved by intermixing ambiguous and unambiguous words:

> . . . you must not
> Choose your words without some obscurity:
> Nothing more dear than the gray song
> Where the Vague joins the Precise.
> (Verlaine, "Art poétique")

We can easily find out whether poets followed Verlaine's advice by examining trends in the variability of the ambiguity measure. A poet who mixes vague and precise words will cause a large standard deviation in the ambiguity measure, because the standard deviation is a statistical measure of variability. Indeed, I found that the standard deviation increases across time. The correlation is .43.

My measures and Cohen's measures all tell us the same thing: the arousal potential of French poetry has increased since 1800. The examples I gave were, in fact, representative. For all the effort I have gone to, I deserve to give a bit of a sermon. For those of a scientific bent, the sermon is brief: one can establish something without counting. In the present instance, the trend in French poetry is obvious. If you read enough of the poetry, you will see the trend. For those of a humanistic bent, the sermon is longer: you can't establish *much* without counting. So far I have not done anything radically different from what a literary theorist would do. I read the relevant texts. I abstracted a trend. My quantitative measures are crude. A critic could make more refined judgments, but they wouldn't do any good unless they were quantified. I can say that the correlation between birth date and incongruous juxtapositions is about .53. Unless the critic quantifies, he or she can't say this. In due course, the advantages of being able to say this sort of thing will become clear.

PRIMORDIAL CONTENT AND STYLISTIC CHANGE

My theory says that French poets increased arousal potential either by increasing depth of regression or by stylistic change. I have already noted that they engaged in deeper and deeper regression until 1900, a process that should have resulted in increases in primordial content. Around 1900, there should have been a decrease in primordial content coincident with stylistic change. Though I shall again make my case on two levels of evidence—qualitative and quantitative—I shall here invert the order and look at the quantitative evidence straightaway.

Quantitative Evidence

To have any evidence to look at, we need a measure of primordial content. I constructed such a measure by searching the theoretical litera-ture for attributes of primordial content that could reasonably be measured by counting individual words (Martindale 1969, 1975). The attributes were taken mainly from the work of Heinz Werner (1948), Freud (1938 [1900]), and Jung (1959). Though Freud and Jung were good observers of primordial cognition, some of their *explanations* of such cognition are not compelling, at least not to me. In looking for attributes, I treated them as purely descriptive theorists. For example, Freud said that oral, anal, and sexual content are associated with primordial cognition—a conclusion based on his observations of the verbalizations of people in primordial states of mind. His explanation of *why* such content is associated with primordial cognition need not concern us. After finding a number of attributes that should measure primordial cognition, I attempted to find as many words as possible that would unambiguously measure each attribute. I came up with a list of about 3,000 words divided into 29 categories. The categories and examples of the words in each follow:

Drives

1. Oral: breast, drink, lip
2. Anal: sweat, rot, dirty
3. Sex: kiss, naked, caress

Perceptual Disinhibition

1. Random movement: wave, roll, spread
2. Diffusion: shade, shadow, cloud
3. Passivity: die, lie, bed
4. Voyage: wander, desert, beyond
5. Chaos: wild, crowd, ruin

Sensation

1. Hard: rock, stone, hard
2. Cold: cold, winter, snow

3. Vision: see, look, green
4. Touch: touch, thick, stroke
5. Soft: soft, gentle, tender
6. Taste: sweet, taste, bitter
7. Sound: hear, voice, sound
8. General sensation: fair, charm, beauty
9. Odor: breath, perfume, scent

Regressive Cognition

1. Narcissism: eye, heart, hand
2. Concreteness: at, where, over
3. Brink passage: road, wall, door
4. Timelessness: eternal, forever, immortal
5. Unknown: secret, strange, unknown
6. Consciousness alteration: dream, sleep, wake

Icarian Imagery

1. Fire: sun, fire, flame
2. Height: up, sky, high
3. Water: sea, water, stream
4. Ascend: rise, fly, throw
5. Descend: fall, drop, sink
6. Depth: down, deep, under

A set of seven categories measuring the inverse of primordial thought—analytic or conceptual thought—were also drawn up:

1. Temporal references: when, now, then
2. Moral imperatives: should, virtue, law
3. Instrumental behavior: assemble, cure, forge
4. Social behavior: tell, speak, meet
5. Abstraction: know, thought, think

6. Restraint: must, stop, bind
7. Order: measure, array, divide

As a summary measure of primordial content, I tallied the percentage of words in the primordial-content categories and subtracted the percentage of words in the conceptual-content categories. (In general, it is a waste of time to go through various statistical machinations to give equal weight to each of the categories; one gets about the same thing if the simple or the complicated method is used.) Primordial cognition is not emotional. Emotional content is not really related to the conceptual-primordial axis. In other words, an emotional state of mind lies midway between the conceptual and the primordial states. Since I wanted to discuss the emotional content of literature, I constructed a set of categories to measure such content. Exactly what we call the categories is not crucial. What we want is an exhaustive list of words with emotional connotations of any sort:

1. Expressive behavior: cry, sing, art
2. Glory: gold, great, pride
3. Aggression: break, war, strike
4. Love: love, friend, kind
5. Sadness: sad, pain, weep
6. Anxiety: fear, tremble, dread
7. Positive emotion: smile, joy, happy

The content categories were applied to the texts with a program called COUNT (Martindale, 1973*a*). Such a program looks up each text word in the dictionary of words assigned to each category, and keeps a tally; then it reports that such-and-such a text had, say, 18.2 percent primordial-content words. This is easier said than done. The program removes suffixes so it can match text words with root forms in the dictionary, thus solving the problem of having to enter every possible form of the target words in the dictionary. There is then, however, the problem of possible mismatches: for example, removing a final *e* equates "hope" and "hop," which is not desirable. Obviously, the program has to be written so as to avoid this sort of thing (for further details, see Martindale 1975 or Stone et al. 1966).

How do we know that my measure of primordial content measures what it is supposed to measure? This is the question of validity. There are several sorts of validity. The measure has *face validity:* that is, it looks reasonable. It has internal consistency: when applied to texts, the categories correlate the way that they should. The primordial-content categories are all correlated with one another and negatively correlated with the conceptual-content categories. *Construct validity* refers to whether the measure works as it is theoretically supposed to work. Across the years, I and other researchers have collected a good bit of evidence that it does. Significantly more primordial content has been found in the poetry of poets exhibiting signs of psychopathology than in that of poets not exhibiting such signs (Martindale 1975); in the verbalizations of psychotic as opposed to nonpsychotic patients (West and Martindale 1988); in psychoanalytic sessions exhibiting therapeutic "work" as opposed to those marked by resistance and defensiveness (Reynes, Martindale, and Dahl 1984); in sentences containing verbal tics as compared with asymptomatic sentences (Martindale 1977*a*); in texts composed by a subject under the influence of psilocybin as contrasted with texts composed before and after the drug experience (Martindale and Fischer 1977); in fantasy stories written by people under the influence of marijuana as opposed to stories written by people given a placebo (West et al. 1983); in fantasy stories told by younger as opposed to older children (West, Martindale, and Sutton-Smith 1985); in written fantasy stories of subjects with more right-hemisphere electroencephalographic activity (Martindale, Covello, and West 1986); in fantasy stories of hypnotized as compared with unhypnotized subjects (Comeau and Farthing 1985); and in folktales of more primitive as opposed to more socioculturally complex preliterate societies (Martindale 1976*b*).

Another way of measuring primordial cognition is to assess concreteness of vocabulary. This, though a rather insensitive measure, is of some use. Primordial cognition, in tending to involve concrete objects, should be expressed with a concrete vocabulary. Conceptual cognition, operating on abstract concepts, should be expressed with a less concrete, more abstract vocabulary. Concreteness of vocabulary is not an infallible measure of primordial versus conceptual thinking. "I *threw* my *hat* on the *table*" is concrete but does not suggest much primordial cognition. "I *imagined* an *ineffable eternity*" is abstract but does suggest primordial cognition. Several investigators have collected good norms for concreteness of vocabulary. The program SEMIS provided me with the average concreteness of the words used in poetic texts. Several measures of concreteness were used:

General concreteness: Michael Toglia and William Battig (1978) collected ratings of concreteness for 2,854 frequent English words belonging to all grammatical classes.

Noun concreteness: Allan Paivio, John Yuille, and Stephen Madigan (1968) collected ratings for 925 frequent English nouns.

Verb concreteness: Hilary Klee and David Legge (1976) gathered concreteness ratings for 200 English transitive verbs.

Adjective imagery: There are no norms for adjective concreteness, but imagery value is closely related. Raymond Berrian et al. (1979) collected ratings for 328 frequent English adjectives.

In figure 3.2, the data for primordial content show the predicted trend. We may supplement these data with measures of concreteness of vocabulary. Overall concreteness also rises to a peak and declines. The peak is in period 4 rather than period 5, but the slight difference between the two periods is of no significance. Noun concreteness shows a similar trend, as does the imagery value of adjectives. Verb concreteness does not change at all. This finding is consistent with the fact that the poetry we are considering is phrasal rather than clausal (Miles 1964): that is, it aims to achieve its effect by manipulation of nouns and adjectives rather than of verbs. What the literary critic Josephine Miles calls clausal poetry is action-oriented. As we shall see, the poetry I am considering has little, if anything, to do with action.

Primordial content does reach a peak in period 5 and declines thereafter. What assures us that the decline coincides with a stylistic change? Humanistic readers familiar with French poetry may not see the sense of this question. It is blatantly obvious that a massive style change occurred around 1900. It is not obvious if one hasn't read the poetry. Even if one has, he or she may have misread it. Though there are several ways to show that a style change did occur, this style change is quite obvious, so I shall take the simple way out. (As I shall argue in the next chapter, there is a more objective way of measuring stylistic change—but one that, to be effective, requires more poets than we have in the present case.)

The romantic-symbolist style of the nineteenth century can be called

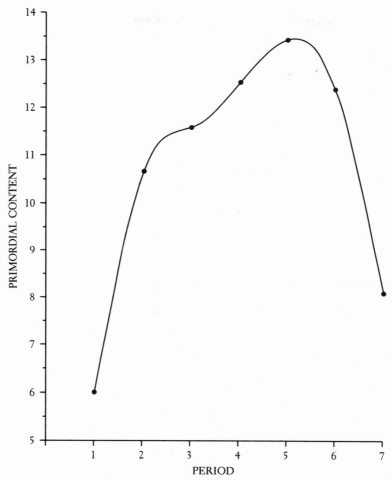

Figure 3.2   Average percentage of primordial content in the poetry of twenty-one French poets born during seven consecutive twenty-year periods from 1790 through 1909. Primordial content increased and then decreased in an inverted-U fashion. The initial increase coincided with the working out of the romantic style. The decrease coincided with a stylistic change culminating in surrealism.

analogical: similes predominate. The post-1900 style is not so tentative: words get equated rather than compared; this style can be called *equational.* I created two categories, Analogy and Being. Analogy is composed of seven words *(as, like, same, seems, alike, resembles).* Being contains present tense forms of *to be (is, be, are, am, being).* The category Being is always much more frequent than Analogy. Once the categories have been made comparable statistically, Analogy should be higher than Being when the analogical style is in force—as it is. Being should be higher than Analogy when the equational style is in force: in periods 6 and 7, Being is higher than Analogy, as expected.

In respect to emotion, as figure 3.3 shows, emotional terms have been consistently dropped from French poetry across the entire time span—as has occurred also in British poetry (see chapter 4). To say that poetry is concerned with the expression of emotion is simply wrong. It used to be, but it has not been focally concerned with emotion for the last several hundred years.

Qualitative Evidence

A qualitative examination shows that the computer has not misread the poetry. Early nineteenth-century French poetry is romantic. W. T. Jones (1961) enumerates six "axes of bias" that differentiate the eighteenth-century enlightenment syndrome from what he calls the romantic syndrome (the romantic biases are italicized):

1. Order versus *Disorder:* System, clarity, structure, analysis versus complexity, fluidity, disorder, novelty, chance, and indeterminacy.
2. Static versus *Dynamic:* Calm versus change and frenzy.
3. Discreteness versus *Continuity:* Either-or division and pluralism versus unity, synthesis, inclusion, pantheism, and monism.
4. Outer versus *Inner:* Objectivity versus experience.
5. Sharp-Focus versus *Soft-Focus:* Clarity and distinctness versus threshold phenomena and the ineffable.
6. This-World versus *Other-World:* The here-and-now versus spatial, temporal, or fantasy escape.

This list makes it clear that the enlightenment syndrome corresponds to conceptual thought, and the romantic syndrome to primordial thought. Hugo's (1963 [1827]) preface to his drama *Cromwell* may be taken as a manifesto of French romanticism. Where classicism stressed universal human traits, romanticism stressed the individual poet's personality—that

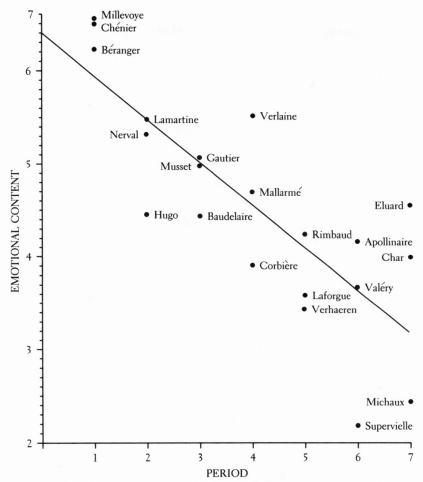

Figure 3.3 Percentage of emotional content in the poetry of twenty-one French poets born during seven consecutive twenty-year periods from 1790 through 1909. Emotional content decreased drastically across time. The best-fitting trend line describing this decrease is shown.

is, inspiration and original genius. Rather than classic balance and order, Hugo called for a synthesis of the beautiful and the grotesque in order to achieve the sublime; for a loosening of stylistic rules and restrictions; and for an emphasis on content rather than on form. New content was to be allowed into poetry. The commonplace and the humble as well as the idiosyncratic and exotic constituted acceptable content. Such topics were disallowed in purely classical poetry, which restricted content to the exalted and noble and to universal or prototypical characters and actions.

Classical poetry focused on human interaction. Though romantic poetry did not neglect this, the focus moved toward nature, which tended to be apprehended in animistic or physiognomic terms. John Ruskin (1844) calls this the *pathetic fallacy,* or the attribution of emotion to inanimate nature. No matter what we call it, it is a mark of primordial cognition (Werner 1948). Lamartine provides a good example of early romantic poetry:

> Thus, always pushed towards new shores,
> Carried forever into eternal night,
> Can we never on the ocean of the ages,
>   Cast anchor a single day?
> . . . .
> O time, suspend your flight! and you, propitious hours,
>   Suspend your course!
> Let us relish the swift delights
>   Of the most beautiful of our days!
> . . . .
> O lake! mute rocks! caves! dark forest!
> You whom time spares or that it can rejuvenate,
> Keep of that night, keep, beautiful nature,
>   At least the memory!
> . . . .
> Let it be in your repose, let it be in your storms,
> Beautiful lake, and in the sight of your laughing hills,
> And in these black firs, and in these savage rocks
>   Which hang over your waters!
>   ("Le Lac")

These lines give evidence of primordial thought, but to no extreme degree. There is animistic perception. There is a concern with timelessness, but not timelessness per se. The text is rhetorical and sentimental. It is oriented—as is most early romantic poetry—toward communication.

Compare Lamartine's animistic perception with that of Nerval, a post-romantic poet:

Man, free thinker! do you believe that only you think
In this world where life explodes in everything?
Your liberty disposes the forces that you have,
But the universe is absent from all your councils.

Respect in the beast of active spirit:
Every flower is a soul unfolded to Nature;
A mystery of love sleeps in metal;
"Everything is sentient!" And everything has power over your being.

Fear, in the blind wall, a gaze that watches you;
A word is connected even with matter. . . .
Do not make it serve some impious purpose!

Often in the humble being lives a hidden God;
And, like an eye born covered by its lids,
A pure spirit grows beneath the rind of stones!

("Vers dorés")

Lamartine's "laughing hillsides" do not seem particularly primordial, but Nerval's eyes in stones do. Indeed, a clinical psychologist might wonder whether this poem was written by a schizophrenic. It was.

The poet Leconte de Lisle (1818–94) was not schizophrenic, but his work shows a good deal of primordial content:

Noon, king of summers, spread out on the plain,
Falls in sheets of silver from the heights of the blue sky.
Everything is quiet. The air flames and burns breathlessly;
Earth dozes in its dress of fire.

The expanse is vast, the fields have no shade at all,
And the spring where the flocks drank is dried up;
The distant forest, whose edge is dark,
Sleeps over there, motionlessly, in heavy repose.

Only the great ripe cornfields, like a gilded sea,
Roll into the distance disdaining sleep;

As peaceful children of the sacred earth,
Fearlessly they drain the sun's cup.

Sometimes, like a sigh from their burning soul,
From the bosom of the heavy ears which murmur among themselves,
A majestic and slow undulation
Awakens, and goes to die on the dusty horizon.
. . . .
Man, if, heart full of joy or of bitterness,
Toward noon you passed into the radiant fields,
Flee! nature is empty and the sun devours:
Nothing is alive here, nothing is sad or joyous.

("Midi")

There is no conceptual thought in these lines. This is a poem about pure
sensation. Human emotion is mentioned in the last stanza; but, at least,
metaphorically, the audience is told to go away. Compare these lines with
those of Lamartine: here the rhetoric and sentimentality have been ban-
ished.

In the preface to his novel *Mademoiselle de Maupin*, Gautier (1955
[1835]) called for such a banishment. Art should *not* communicate, he
said. The poem should be an object, rather than a message. This was the
beginning of *l'art pour l'art*, or art for art's sake. Gautier was explicit in
rejecting romantic concerns with cognition, emotion, humanitarianism,
and rhetoric. He was equally explicit in saying that poetry should focus
on raw sensation. In our terms, this is a clear call to move from conceptual
toward primordial cognition. Other postromantic poets agreed with Gautier. Later poets, however, said he had not gone far enough—as later poets
always say about earlier poets writing in the same style.

Baudelaire called for even deeper regression. "Language and writing,"
he argued, should be "taken as magical operations, evocatory sorcery"
(1961 [1855–62], p.1256). His poetry shows synesthesia rather than ani-
mism:

Nature is a temple where living pillars
Sometimes let confused words escape;

Man passes there through forests of symbols
Which observe him with familiar gazes.

Like long echoes which mingle far away
Into a deep and dark unity,
Vast like night and like light,
Scents, colors, and sounds answer one another.

There are some fragrances cool like the flesh of children,
Sweet as oboes and green like meadows,
—And others corrupt, rich, and triumphant,

Having the expansion of infinite things,
Like amber, musk, benzoin, and incense,
Which sing the raptures of the mind and of the senses.

("Correspondances")

He mixes mysticism with a lascivious quality:

> A room which resembles a reverie, a veritably spiritual room, where the stagnant atmosphere is lightly tinted with rose and blue.
>
> The soul takes a bath of sloth there, flavored by regret and desire. —It is something twilight-like, bluish and rosy; a dream of delight during an eclipse.
>
> The furniture has stretched out, prostrate, languorous forms. The furniture has the air of dreaming; one would say it was endowed with a sleep-walking life, like the vegetable and the mineral. The fabrics speak a mute language, like flowers, like skies, like setting suns. . . .
>
> To what benevolent demon do I owe thus being encircled by mystery, by silence, by peace and by perfumes? O beatitude! what we generally call life, even in its happiest expansion, has nothing in common with this supreme life which I now know and that I savor minute by minute, second by second!
>
> No! there are no more minutes, there are no more seconds! Time has disappeared; it is Eternity which reigns, an eternity of delights.

("La Chambre double")

At least metaphorically, Baudelaire is explicit in stating the reason for regression:

We wish, so much this fire burns our brains,
To plunge to the depths of the abyss, Hell or Heaven, what
   difference?
To the depths of the Unknown to find something *new!*
                                        ("Le Voyage")

This is a metaphorical statement of my theory: one must regress in order
to find novelty.

Baudelaire ushered in symbolism and decadence. He was a difficult
poet to outdo, but the symbolists accomplished the feat. We find a great
deal of oral content and content evocative of infancy—themes that,
psychoanalysts argue, indicate deep regression:

> I am a cradle
> That a hand rocks
> In the hollow of a vault. . . .
> Silence, silence!
> (Verlaine, "Sagesse," II, 5)

Narcissism, or turning inward upon the self, also indicates extreme primordial thought:

> I love the horror of being a virgin and I wish
> To live in the terror which my hair gives me
> So that at evening, lying on my bed, inviolate
> Reptile, I may feel in my vain flesh
> The cold scintillation of your pale light,
> You who die, you who burn with chastity,
> White night of icicles and cruel snow!
> (Mallarmé, "Hérodiade" [Fowlie 1953, p.145])

Narcissism is accompanied by a withdrawal of interest from the outside
world. All life is within. The world is dead:

> Mourning turns in the depths of the sky, like millstones,
> Its black suns;

And only maggots bloom
In the rotten sides of women who are dead.

To the east of the meadow, in the rough soil,
On the scattered corpse of old ploughlands,
Rules there, and forever,
Plate of bright steel, lath of cold wood,
The spade.

(Verhaeren, "La Bêche")

Jung (1963) noted that the black sun seems to be an archetypal index of extremely primordial thought. A Freudian would label as anal-regressive content the maggots blooming in the rotten sides of dead women. Anyone who gave such a stomach-turning response to the Rorschach test would be likely to end up with a diagnosis of schizophrenia. Indeed, Verhaeren, though never officially diagnosed as schizophrenic, was a bit odd: for example, he had to have his doorbell disconnected because its ringing caused him physical pain.

The early romantic poets were more than poets. Chateaubriand and Lamartine both served in the French foreign ministry. Hugo and Béranger were elected to parliament. Alfred de Vigny (1797–1863) marked a turning point. As a young man, he dreamed of military glory, but there were no wars to fight. A bit later, calling—as Sainte-Beuve put it (1837)—for the poet to retreat into a "tower of ivory," he literally retreated into his manor house in the west of France. In order to achieve the deep regression needed to write late nineteenth-century French poetry, one had to withdraw. Withdrawal facilitates regression, as does psychopathology. The later writers did tend to withdraw, some almost into a self-imposed sensory deprivation. Flaubert went for months without leaving his house, as did Verhaeren. These were hardly men of action. The journals of Baudelaire and Flaubert are filled with complaints of lassitude and abulia, or lack of will. Getting out of bed in the morning was to them a Herculean task. Nerval was psychotic. Verhaeren was at least on the fringes of psychosis. Mallarmé, an anxious man literally terrified of his students, had to make his living as a high-school teacher. Baudelaire could not handle his own, rather simple finances. As a result of his ill-conceived experiment to contract syphilis deliberately and not have it treated, he died of general paresis of the insane. Verlaine's verse is often cheerful, but he was easily annoyed—as witnessed by his attempts to murder several people, including his mother. Fortunately he was an incompetent murderer and muffed the attempts, but not for want of trying. Being a chronic alcoholic, he was usually too drunk to murder well. Nervous breakdowns of one sort or another were commonplace. Although the psychiatrist Cesare Lombroso (1895) and Max Nordau (1895) have gotten a bad reputation for their arguments that creative genius is a form of degeneration or psychopathology, they were focusing on such creators as those in my sample. Some of these poets were mad. Others tried to drive themselves mad. They had to.

The symbolist poets knew what they were about. They were straining to achieve an extremely primordial state of mind. Mallarmé called for a descent into the self. Rimbaud and Valéry wrote seriously about their desire to be God. Mallarmé hinted at the same goal. What does it mean to be God? This is really the goal of all mystics—the desire for a merging of self and world—and is as primordial as consciousness can become. Rimbaud, in his "Lettre du Voyant," provided instructions:

> For *I* is someone else. If brass wakes up a trumpet, it is not its fault. To me this is obvious: I witness the unfolding of my own thought: I watch it, I listen to it: I make a stroke of the bow: the symphony begins to stir in the depths, or springs on to the stage. . . .
>
> I say that one must be a *seer*, make oneself a *seer*.
>
> The poet makes himself a *seer* by a long, prodigious, and rational *disordering* of *all the senses*. Every form of love, of suffering, of madness; he searches himself, he consumes all the poisons in him and keeps only their quintessences. This is an unspeakable torture during which he needs all his faith and superhuman strength, and during which he becomes the great patient, the great criminal, the great accursed—and the great learned one!—among men. —For he arrives at the *unknown!* Because he has cultivated his own soul—which was rich to begin with—more than any other man!
>
> (1871, pp.270–71 [Bernard 1966, pp.9–11])

The idea of poetry as object rather than message is carried to its logical extreme with symbolism. Verlaine is fairly explicit:

Music before everything.
And for that prefer the Uneven
More vague and more soluble in the air
With nothing heavy or stationary in it.

Flee as far as possible from the murderous Epigram,
Cruel Wit, and lewd Laughter
That make the eyes of the Azure weep
And all that common kitchen garlic!

Take eloquence and wring its neck!
                              ("Art poétique")

He rejects everything connected with communication: epigrams, wit, eloquence, direct statements.

Mallarmé was more obscure:

Diction is too weak to express objects by touches corresponding to them in color or in motion. . . . Beside *ombre*, which is opaque, *ténèbres* is not very dark; what a disappointment in face of the perversity that gives to *jour* and to *nuit* contradictorily, dark tones for the former and bright ones for the latter. . . .

The pure work implies the elocutory disappearance of the poet, who abandons the initiative to words mobilized by the shock of their inequality; they light one another up with mutual reflections like a virtual trail of fire upon precious stones, replacing the breathing perceptible in the old lyrical blast. . . .

I say: a flower! and, out of the forgetfulness where my voice banishes any contour, inasmuch as it is something other than known calyxes, musically arises, an idea itself and fragrant, the one [flower] absent from all bouquets.
                    ("Crise de vers" [Hartley 1965, pp.166, 171, 174])

In the first passage he—like Verlaine—focuses on the sound of words rather than their meaning. Words are taken as concrete objects—a clear mark of primordial thought (Freud 1938 [1900]). Schizophrenics, like symbolist poets, treat words as concrete things (Fenichel 1945). In the second passage, Mallarmé is really saying that poetry should be free association. The poet does not create the poem: it creates itself. Compare Rimbaud's comment "I am present at the breaking forth of my thoughts" (1966 [1871], p.270). Poetry is not communication. It refers to nothing but itself. The third passage suggests that poetry is a magical incantation, created not by the poet but by the words themselves. This makes sense only in a primordial state of mind. Another indication of such a state is Mallarmé's virtual "phobia" against direct naming (Fowlie 1953). The quotation from Verlaine shows a milder form of this phobia. Schizophrenics show a similar phobia of names and a tendency toward elliptical reference (Mednick 1958), though neither Mallarmé nor Verlaine were schizophrenic. My point is that avoidance of direct naming is a general trait of primordial thought.

There is a limit to primordial thought. The symbolists ran up against the same problem that confronts the mystic. Words cannot describe the experience of extremely primordial states of consciousness, but words are the very stuff of poetry. Symbolism is romanticism taken as far as it can go. A style change was needed, or poetry would end. Marcel Raymond (1963 [1940]) describes the confusion that resulted from this need for a stylistic change. The return to classicism Jean Moréas (1856–1910) called for would not do: his verse was not novel and today is only of historical interest. Francis Jammes (1868–1938) and other poets attempted to return to sentimental romanticism with updated content:

> I love in the past Clara d'Ellebeuse,
> the pupil of old boarding schools,
> who went, on warm evenings, beneath the linden trees
> to read the *magazines* of other days.

> I love only her, and I feel on my heart
> the blue light of her white throat.
> Where is she? Where was that happiness then?
> Into her bright room some branches came.
>   (Jammes, "J'aime dans les temps")

Compare the freshness of these lines with Verhaeren's blooming maggots. Clara d'Ellebeuse is not intimidating and awesome like Mallarmé's icy, crystalline Hérodiade. Jammes's lines are cute. Cuteness does not have enough impact value.

The poets Raymond (1963 [1940]) calls the *fantaisistes*—Guillaume Apollinaire, André Salmon, Pierre Reverdy, and Max Jacob—called for a stylistic change that would allow arousal potential to increase at the cost of less regression. They were aware that novelty must increase rather than decrease: *"Surprise is the greatest source of what is new. It is by surprise, by the important position that has been given to surprise, that the new spirit distinguishes itself from all the literary and artistic movements which have preceded it"* (Apollinaire, 1948 [1918], p.233). The *fantaisistes* brought new content into poetry:

> It is Christ who ascends into the sky better than the aviators
> He holds the world's altitude record
> . . . .
>
> And everything eagle phoenix and Chinese pihis [birds]
> Fraternize with the flying machine
>
> Now you walk through Paris all alone amid the crowd
> Herds of bellowing busses roll by near you
> $\qquad\qquad\qquad\qquad\qquad$ (Apollinaire, "Zone")

More important, metaphors and similes were allowed to join things that are not really alike:

> I stop to watch
> Upon the incandescent grass
> A serpent wander it is myself
> Who am the flute which I play
> And the whip which chastises the others.
> $\qquad\qquad$ (Apollinaire, "Les Collines")

In this string of metaphors, Apollinaire is a serpent which is a flute which is a whip. How did he come up with this? He is combining close associates. He is in contiguity with the snake. Therefore, he *is* the snake. Snakes, flutes, and whips are all long, so they get equated—an equation disallowed by previous stylistic rules because the things equated are not similar enough. The *fantaisistes* still demanded some similarity, as indicated by Reverdy's rules concerning the poetic image:

> The image is a pure creation of the spirit. It is not born of a comparison, but from the joining of two realities, more or less distant. . . . An image is not good because it is brutal or fantastic, but because the association of the ideas is distant and just, . . . spontaneously bringing together without comparison two distant realities of which the mind alone has seized the connections.
>
> (1918, pp.32–34)

The surrealists carried the stylistic revolution one step further. André Breton remarked that "the best [simile] is the one that presents the greatest degree of arbitrariness" (1963 [1924], p.52). Eluard agreed: "If judgment approves the image, however little, it kills it" (quoted by Raymond 1963 [1940], p.286). The content of surreal poetry is not primordial. These poets combined close associates readily available to conceptual thought. The old rules did not allow such close word associates to be combined in similes or metaphors because the things they denote are not similar. *Blue* and *orange* are close associates. The earth viewed from outer space is blue. Thus, Eluard's image, "the earth is blue like an orange." *Voilà.*

In general, surrealist similes combine close associates with the word *like* even if the things the words refer to are not alike. This was perfectly legal. The rules of writing poetry had been changed. It was easy, too. Deep regression is not needed to do this. And there is little primordial content in surrealist poetry, as in this example:

> Stretching his hands out of the bed, Plume was amazed at not touching the wall. "Well," he thought, "the ants must have eaten it, . . ." and he went back to sleep.
>
> Soon after, his wife took hold of him and shook him: "Good-for-nothing," she said, "Look! while you were busy sleeping, they stole our house from us." It was true. Wherever he looked, he saw the sky. "Bah! it's done now," he thought.

Soon after, he heard a noise. It was a train rushing at them. "With all that haste," he thought, "it will certainly get there before us," and he went back to sleep.

(Michaux, "Un Homme paisible" [Fowlie 1955, p.243])

APPLYING THE EVOLUTIONARY THEORY

Though they use far different terms, I think that most literary critics would agree that the trends in primordial content and incongruous juxtaposition are the main ones in modern French poetry. Aside from appealing to authority, however, I computed for myself how much the two theoretical variables accounted for the overall variability among the twenty-one French poets. I had first to compute how much overall variability there was.

The Harvard III Psychosociological Dictionary (Stone et al. 1966) is a general set of content categories. If function words are ignored, it categorizes about 80 percent to 90 percent of the words in a text, and thus is likely to pick up any historical trends not subsumed by the theoretical measures. Since I shall refer to these categories later, I list them here with sample words for each:

SOCIAL REALM

Persons

Self: *I, me, mine*
Selves: *we, us, ours*
Other: *you, yours, they* (including *thy,* and so on)

Roles

Male role: *actor, boy, brother*
Female role: *actress, aunt, bride*
Neuter role: *baby, American, anybody*
Job role: *agent, author, captain*

Collectivities
  Small group: *agency, band, board*
  Large group: *administration, army, church*

CULTURAL REALM

Cultural Objects
  Food: *bean, beer, candy*
  Clothing: *button, dress, fur*
  Tools: *bag, automobile, ambulance*

Cultural Settings
  Social place: *abroad, America, bedroom*

Cultural Patterns
  Ideal value: *ability, able, beauty*
  Deviation: *abnormal, blind, crazy*
  Action norm: *agreement, business, commission*
  Message form: *art, book, cash*
  Thought form: *abstraction, basic, contrast*
  Nonspecific objects: *affair, aspect, capital*

Natural Realm
  Body part: *arm, body, brain*
  Natural object: *plant, animal, mineral*
  Natural world: *air, beach, gulf*

QUALIFIERS
  Sensory reference: *aloud, black, fresh*
  Time reference: *after, again, began*
  Quantity reference: *add, any, big*
  Space reference: *about, ahead, back*

PSYCHOLOGICAL PROCESSES

Emotions
  Arousal: *attitude, awaken, felt*
  Urge: *dream, eager, incentive*
  Affection: *admire, affection, charm*

Pleasure: *cheer, delight, funny*
Distress: *afraid, alarm, break*
Anger: *angry, boil, burn*

Thought
Sense: *appear, attend, aware*
Think: *assume, choice, doubt*
If: *almost, chance, else*
Equal: *alike, same, consist*
Not: *cannot, not, differ*
Cause: *affect, cause, result*

Evaluation
Good: *admirable, clean, fair*
Bad: *awful, bitter, cheap*
Ought: *duty, ought, proper*

BEHAVIORAL PROCESSES

Social-Emotional Actions
Communicate: *address, admit, answer*
Approach: *arrive, attach, bring*
Guide: *aid, allow, benefit*
Control: *appoint, arrest, bind*
Attack: *annoy, attack, beat*
Avoid: *abandon, absent, conceal*
Follow: *agree, apology, consent*

Instrumental Actions
Attempt: *aim, apply, bid*
Work: *adjust, construct, cook*
Get: *afford, attain, beg*
Possess: *belong, occupy, lock*
Expel: *blew, cast, defecate*
Move: *pull, put, run*

On the basis of their scores on each of these categories, we can compute correlations among the poets in our sample. The more similar the profiles of two poets, the higher the correlations between them will be. If all poets

used exactly the same words, their profiles would all be perfectly correlated. If the words used by each poet were completely unrelated to the
words used by other poets, all of the correlations would be zero. We know
that the truth must lie somewhere between these two extremes: that is,
we know that poets cluster together into groups—for example, some tend
to write lyrical poetry, whereas others write epic poetry. We want to know
how many dimensions are needed to account for the similarities among
poets. Fortunately, once we have correlated all of the poets with one
another, a procedure called multidimensional scaling will tell us just this.*
Multidimensional scaling tells us that the twenty-one French poets differ
along three main dimensions. These three dimensions account for 94
percent of the similarity matrix. We assume that the remaining 6 percent
is due to random error.

We can picture the twenty-one poets as occupying points in a three-
dimensional space. The more similar two poets are in word usage, the
closer their points are in this space. The more dissimilar they are, the more
remote are their points. To what extent can we explain their location in
this space with the two main theoretical variables, primordial content and
incongruous juxtapositions? To answer this question, we compute canonical correlations and then what is called redundancy (Stewart and Love
1968). The details of these procedures need not concern us. It is the result
with which we are concerned. The two evolutionary theory variables
account for about 43 percent of the overall variation among the twenty-
one poets. The rest of the variation is due to other causes including, I
would expect, a good bit of random error of measurement. Primordial
content is highly correlated with one of the dimensions but not with the
other two. The second dimension is related to reference to male figures
and, to some extent, reference to social action. The third dimension has
to do with female figures and emotion. In other words, the evolutionary
theory—which explains variations in primordial content—accounts for
one of the three main dimensions along which the sample of poets varies.
Variation along the other two dimensions is not accounted for by evolutionary forces, at least not those described by my theory. I leave to future
theorists the task of explaining variation along these other two dimen-

---

*Since the details of this procedure are rather technical, the interested reader should consult Kruskal
and Wish 1978; Martindale, 1984a; Young, Lewyckyj, and Takane 1983).

sions. It might be due to personality or to external social forces, to name but two of many possibilities. I am quite pleased to be able to offer an account for 43 percent of overall variation.

Since our qualitative examination backed up the quantitative results, the question arises why we need any numbers if we can find out what happened merely by doing some reading. In the present case, the numbers kept me from making a serious error. Initially, based on my qualitative reading of surrealist and earlier French literature, I expected only a slight dip in primordial content in period 6, and that period 7 would show a lot of primordial content (Martindale 1969). Though they use different terms, critics far more conversant with the texts than I imply at least that primordial content might have risen across the entire time span we have studied (Fowlie 1967; Raymond 1963 [1940]). One reason is that some surrealist painting (such as Salvador Dali and Max Ernst) certainly looks primordial and dreamlike. Furthermore, what the surrealist poets said they were doing leads us to misread much of their poetry. We must always keep in mind Plato's reminder that poets lie. A lot of what the surrealist poets said they were doing makes it sound like primordial thought. Consider Breton's definition of surrealism:

> Pure psychic automatism by which one proposes to express whether verbally, or in writing, or by any other means, the real functioning of thought. Dictated by thought, in the absence of all control exercised by reason, beyond all aesthetic or moral preoccupation.
>
> Surrealism rests on the belief in the superior reality of certain forms of associations neglected until now, in the all-powerfulness of the dream, of the disinterested play of thought. It tends to destroy definitively all other psychic mechanisms and to substitute these for them in the resolution of the principal problems of life.
>
> (1963 [1924], p.37)

This seems like a direct call for primordial thought—as does Breton's later comment:

> Everything leads me to believe that there exists a certain point in the mind where life and death, real and imaginary, past and future, communicable and uncommunicable, high and low, cease to be perceived contradictorily.

Now, it is in vain that one would seek in surrealist activity any other motive than the hope of determining this point.

(1963 [1929], pp.76–77)

Opposites are equated only in primordial thought—but the content of surreal poetry is not noticeably primordial. Thus, we need to assess Breton's last sentence carefully: the ultimate *aim* of surrealism may be *toward* primordial thought. Surrealism was not based on primordial thought, though ultimately it headed in that direction. But all styles head in that direction, as I shall further discuss in the following chapters.

CHAPTER 4

Centuries of British Poetry

I AM told that a recurrent nightmare of literary scholars is that someone will feed all the poetry through a computer and come up with an
equation that explains everything. It is rather too bad that computers are
banal blue and gray boxes tended by kids in tennis shoes. It would be a
far better nightmare if they were dead black and bore the dreaded runes,
if they were tended by brutes in jackboots, if they were "dark, satanic
mills" that destroyed and devoured anything they were fed. That would
fit better, too, with the violence that Timothy Reiss (1982) sees beneath
the sterile veneer of science. Computer analysis is, however, completely
nondestructive. It will extract some information from *Paradise Lost* but
will not, in so doing, shred and destroy the poem. Perhaps this chapter
will allow literary scholars to sleep a bit easier. One equation can't possibly
capture the rich complexity of six hundred fifty years of British poetry.
Five or six equations are probably needed, and I have approximated only
a couple of them.

FROM CHAUCER TO THE MODERN POETS

My goal is to explain the history of British poetry from Chaucer to the present. The first step toward this goal is to explain how the words used in British poetry have changed. We have the texts, and we can objectively tabulate changes in word usage. Once we have done so, we can sum up our results in an equation. The equation is just a shorthand, or succinct, way of describing the changes we have found. We can describe the changes in words, but words aren't usually as precise as numbers. We seek the laws governing these changes. Even if we were completely successful at finding these laws, there would still be much to do. Explaining why word usage changed does not necessarily explain changes in meaning—in the ideas the words were used to convey. Though literary theorists seem in general to disagree, it seems to me that we should not quibble over meaning until we have a persuasive description and explanation of basic facts that are more objectively measurable.

Our first task is to decide exactly what constitutes British poetry: whether all poetry ever written in Britain, or the accepted canon of British poetry. Literary theorists are spending a good bit of time arguing whether a stable canon really exists. Feminist critics, for example, argue that women writers have been unfairly excluded. From the point of view of evolutionary theory, it really doesn't make much difference how we define the population of British poets. Any reasonable definition will get us a historical series of several hundred poets who were subject to the same evolutionary laws.

The epoch from 1290 to 1949 was divided into thirty-three successive twenty-year periods. I ranked the poets born during each of these periods on the basis of number of pages devoted to them in the relevant Oxford anthology of English verse (Chambers 1932; Grierson and Bullough 1934; Hayward 1964; Larkin 1973; Sisam and Sisam 1970; Smith 1926; Yeats 1936). For the last twenty periods—1550 to 1949—the seven poets assigned the most pages were included in the sample. The period 1530–49 provided only six poets. The list of 170 poets in table 4.1 probably includes all the British poets you have heard of as well as some unfamiliar ones. For only a couple of the periods are poets of much worth excluded. For most periods, some poets of little worth are included. Although it might

TABLE 4.1
British Poets (1290–1949)

Period (According to Birthdate)	Poets
1 (1290–1309)	Richard Rolle, Laurence Minot
2 (1310–29)	John Gower, John Barbour
3 (1330–49)	Geoffrey Chaucer, William Langland
4 (1350–69)	Thomas Hoccleve, Andrew of Wyntoun
5 (1370–89)	John Lydgate, John Hardyng
6 (1390–1409)	James I (king of Scotland), Charles of Orleans
7 (1410–29)	Robert Henryson, Benedict Burgh
8 (1430–49)	Thomas Norton, Blind Hary
9 (1450–69)	John Skelton, William Dunbar
10 (1470–89)	Sir Thomas More, Steven Hawes
11 (1490–1504)	Sir Thomas Wyatt, John Heywood
12 (1510–29)	Henry Howard (Earl of Surrey); Thomas, Lord Vaux
13 (1530–49)	Thomas Sackville (Earl of Dorset), Nicholas Breton, Sir Edward Dyer, George Turberville, George Gascoigne, Giles Fletcher the elder
14 (1550–69)	Edmund Spenser, William Shakespeare, Samuel Daniel, Michael Drayton, Sir John Davies, Sir Walter Ralegh, Sir Philip Sidney
15 (1570–89)	John Donne; Ben Jonson; William Drummond of Hawthornden; George Wither; Edward, Lord Herbert; Phineas Fletcher; Francis Beaumont
16 (1590–1609)	John Milton, Robert Herrick, George Herbert, Thomas Carew, Francis Quarles, Edmund Waller, Sir John Suckling
17 (1610–29)	Richard Crashaw, Andrew Marvell, Henry Vaughan, Abraham Cowley, Richard Lovelace, Joseph Beaumont
18 (1630–49)	John Dryden, Thomas Traherne, John Wilmot (Earl of Rochester), Charles Cotton, Sir Charles Sedley, Charles Sackville (Earl of Dorset), Katherine Philips
19 (1650–69)	Jonathan Swift, Matthew Prior, John Pomfret, Anne Finch (Countess of Winchelsea), Daniel Defoe, William Walsh, John Oldham
20 (1670–89)	Alexander Pope, John Gay, Isaac Watts, Thomas Tickell, Joseph Addison, Nicholas Rowe, Thomas Parnell
21 (1690–1709)	James Thomson, John Byrom, John Dyer, Samuel Johnson, Charles Wesley, William Hamilton of Bangour, Matthew Green
22 (1710–29)	Thomas Gray, Christopher Smart, William Collins, Oliver Goldsmith, Mark Akenside, William Shenstone, William Whitehead
23 (1730–49)	William Cowper, William Mickle, Charles Churchill, James Beattie, John Langhorne, John Wolcot (Peter Pindar), Erasmus Darwin
24 (1750–69)	Robert Burns, Thomas Chatterton, William Blake, George Crabbe, Sir John Henry Moore, Thomas Russell, William L. Bowles
25 (1770–89)	William Wordsworth, George Gordon (Lord Byron), Samuel Taylor Coleridge, Sir Walter Scott, Thomas Moore, Walter Savage Landor, Thomas Campbell
26 (1790–1809)	Alfred, Lord Tennyson; John Keats, Percy Bysshe Shelley, John Clare, George Darley, J. H. Reynolds, Thomas Hood
27 (1810–29)	Robert Browning, Matthew Arnold, George Meredith, Dante Gabriel Rossetti, Sidney Dobell, Emily Brontë, A. H. Clough

TABLE 4.1 *(Continued)*

Period (According to Birthdate)	Poets
28 (1830–49)	Algernon Charles Swinburne, Thomas Hardy, William Morris, Gerard Manley Hopkins, James Thomson, Christina Rossetti, Robert Bridges
29 (1850–69)	Laurence Binyon, William Butler Yeats, Francis Thompson, Oscar Wilde, Lionel Johnson, Ernest Dowson, George William Russell (A.E.)
30 (1870–89)	T. S. Eliot, D. H. Lawrence, Sir John Squire, Ralph Hodgson, Edith Sitwell, Rupert Brooke, John Masefield
31 (1890–1909)	W. H. Auden, Sir John Betjeman, Basil Bunting, Louis MacNeice, Robert Graves, Wilfred Owen, Hugh MacDiarmid
32 (1910–29)	Dylan Thomas, John Wain, Philip Larkin, John Heath-Stubbs, Donald Davie, Kingsley Amis, Roy Fuller
33 (1930–49)	Derek Walcott, Ted Hughes, Anthony Thwaite, Peter Redgrove, George Macbeth, Brian Patten, Alan Brownjohn

have been preferable to select poets on the basis of their contemporary rather than their present-day fame, there is no objective method of determining contemporary fame, nor is it a reliable guide to importance. An artist's perceived merit seems to fluctuate for a few decades after his or her death and then, contrary to popular belief, tends to settle down to a fairly stable value (Reitlinger 1961; Simonton 1984a). The list is not perfect in other ways. John Cleveland or Edward Benlowes could well be on the list because of their importance in the development of English poetry. Thomas Traherne is on the list but probably should not be: he is a good poet, but since his works were discovered only recently he did not influence his contemporaries or poets who wrote soon after him. Since the Oxford anthologies include poets born in Great Britain who subsequently migrated as well as poets born elsewhere who wrote for long periods of time in Great Britain, such poets (for example, T. S. Eliot in the latter category) were included in our list. A few exclusions were necessary: poets whose birth dates are unknown, given the method of assigning poets to periods; a few poets (such as Henry VIII) who did not write much poetry; and Lewis Carroll, on the assumption that the computer would make no sense of his nonsense verse.

For periods 1 to 12, only two poets per period could be found, even when I went beyond the Oxford anthologies and also consulted Henry Bennett (1947), Eleanor Hammond (1927), William Renwick and Harold Orton (1939), and George Watson (1974). For these early periods, birth dates are questionable—even for several of the poets included—or little of their poetry remains. Thus, the results for the early periods must be much more tentative than those for the later ones. Furthermore, although during the early periods English and Scottish poetic traditions were fairly distinct, to get enough poets we must mingle together English and Scottish poets. Finally, since early poetry was written in Middle English and Middle Scots, it had to be translated into modern English. Sampling and preparation of texts was done in the same way as for the study of French poetry. (Further details and results of earlier studies of this series when it contained a smaller number of poets may be found in Martindale 1969, 1975, 1978a, 1984a.) The sample totaled 521,566 words.

Arousal Potential

The first question of interest concerns the prediction that the arousal potential of poetry has increased over time. I constructed the Composite Variability Index to measure the collative properties of texts (Martindale 1978a): that is, their complexity, surprisingness, incongruity, ambiguity, and variability. This is a more general measure than that used in the study of French poetry. The index is composed of the following measures:

1. *Polarity* (a measure of semantic intensity or strikingness).
2. Number of *word associates* (a measure of use of words with multiple meanings, and thus, more potential ambiguity).
3. *Hapax legomena* percentage (percentage of words occurring only once in a document: an index of complexity or difficulty). (In order to compute this and the following measures, I wrote a program called LEXSTAT [Martindale 1974a].)
4. *Mean word length* (a measure of complexity or difficulty).
5. *Coefficient of variation of word frequency* (a measure of variability or unpredictability). The coefficient of variation is the variance divided by the mean. If a poet used each of his or her words exactly twice, average word frequency would be 2, but the coefficient of variation would be 0. To get a high score on this measure, some words have to be used a lot and some infrequently. This seems to be a poetic rather than a normal pattern of using words.
6. *Coefficient of variation of word length* (another measure of variability). This is a measure of tendency to intermix long and short words.
7. *Coefficient or variation of phrase length* (yet another measure of variability).

This is a measure of unpredictability of phrase length, a *phrase* being a sentence or a string of words terminated by a colon or semicolon.

The Composite Variability Index is for the most part a measure of unpredictability or entropy. A text that is unpredictable should be surprising. The more unpredictable a poem is, the less certain we are what the poet is going to say next. The Composite Variability Index gets at unpredictability on a basic linguistic level. Most readers may, of course, not pay a lot of attention to whether, say, a poet is intermixing long and short words. Although, as Jakobson (1973) notes, poetic language attempts to call attention to itself, it is not always successful. One can read poetry as if it were prose, and miss the interplay of words. Though linguistic variability is not the main aspect of poetry, it certainly is the easiest to measure.

The Composite Variability Index varies across periods in a highly significant way. Analysis of variance shows that differences among periods are much greater than differences within them. *Analysis of variance* is a statistical procedure that partitions, or divides up, the variability in a set of data. In our case it tells us that 71 percent of variation in the index is due to differences among periods—and that these differences are due to an uptrend over time (see figure 4.1). The equation for the trend is:

$$AP = 10 + \frac{1}{-10.23 + 10.41e^{-.00036P}},$$

where e is the base of the natural logarithms, and P is period. The equation accounts for 76.5 percent of variation in the mean values. Almost as good a fit (74 percent) is obtained with a simpler exponential equation:

$$AP = 10 + 4.74e^{.035P}$$

As is obvious from the figure, the rate of change in arousal potential has accelerated across time. Indeed, arousal potential has been changing and accelerating, according to the preceding equations, since before Chaucer. It is speeding up its rate of change, as it has always been doing.

The figure shows that means for the early periods vary a lot around the trend line. Arousal potential does not increase as smoothly from period to period as it does in later centuries. Some of this variability arises because it is difficult to apply the Composite Variability Index to these texts. For example, since punctuation in Middle English was capricious and incon-

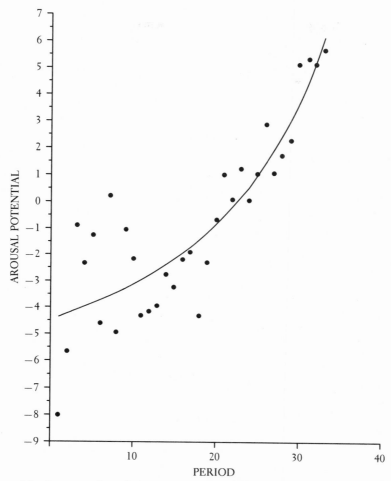

Figure 4.1 Average value of the Composite Variability Index (a measure of arousal potential) in texts from 170 British poets born in thirty-three consecutive twenty-year periods from 1290 through 1949. The best-fitting trend line, also shown, indicates an accelerating rate of increase in arousal potential.

sistent by modern standards, and several poets did not use it at all, we had to guess at it in what was probably a too conservative fashion. Also, with only two poets per period, the averages are less stable than those for later periods. I expect that some of the variability is real. When a poetic tradition is first coalescing, poets are less sure of the rules of the game and of who else is playing. They are likely as a consequence to overshoot and undershoot the mark—that is, to produce too much or too little variability. If we disregard the first ten periods because of the uncertainties just mentioned, we find that the rate of change in the variability or impact value of British poetry has not appreciably increased or decreased across the last four hundred fifty years or so.

Some of the components of the Composite Variability Index do not go straight up across time, but all of them also show highly significant long-term increases. Poets of different periods prefer to obtain arousal potential in different ways. In some periods, poets emphasize long words and lots of infrequent words; whereas in others, poets use words of high polarity.

An obvious objection to a theory that takes a quest for novelty and variability as the basis for literary history is the existence of movements such as neoclassicism that ostensibly call for simplicity, order, symmetry, and balance. The English neoclassical poets occupy periods 18 to 21. The Composite Variability Index continued to rise across these periods. An examination of the component indices shows that some of them, such as polarity, did decrease. These decreases were, however, more than offset by increases in other measures—such as the percentage of words that occurred but once in a document, and mean word length (see figure 4.2). In other words, the neoclassic poets more than compensated for decreases in some of the components by increasing others. These results suggest that the popular view of the neoclassical style as a reversion to order following seventeenth-century excess is incorrect. On the contrary, it would seem that the neoclassic style shift was in the service of *increased* arousal potential or variability. These poets' rhetoric concerning order with regard to some aspects of poetic practice has obscured their pursuit of disorder in other aspects.

Primordial Content

While primordial content rose over time, a cyclical or oscillatory trend is superimposed on the uptrend (see figure 4.3). Statistical analysis shows that 62 percent of the variance in primordial content is accounted for by interperiod differences; the remaining 38 percent, by individual differences among the poets within periods. For the means in figure 4.3, 70

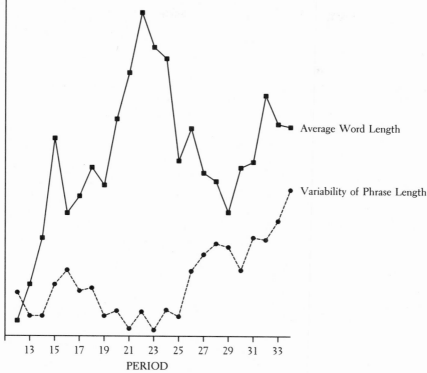

Figure 4.2 Illustration of trade-off among components of the Composite Variability Index: As average word length increased from period 15 to period 21, there was a decrease in variability of phrase length. As word length decreased from period 21 to period 28, there was an increase in variability of phrase length. Although the overall arousal potential of British poetry has increased across time, there have occasionally been simplifications of one aspect of poetic practice (for example, average word length) which have been compensated for by complication of other aspects of poetic practice (for example, variability of phrase length).

percent of the variation is due to a monotonic uptrend. This trend is purely linear: it does not accelerate or decelerate across time. However, as may be seen in the graph, the means do not all fall on a straight line; the other 30 percent of variation is due to the quasiperiodic oscillations around the trend line. Presumably, the linear uptrend has occurred because poets needed more and more primordial cognition to think of useful word combinations. Theoretically, the oscillations indicate stylistic changes. Thus, in British poetry, primordial content does tend to decline

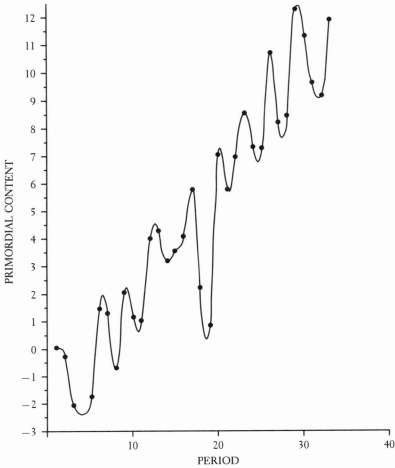

Figure 4.3 Average amount of primordial content in texts from 170 British poets born in thirty-three consecutive twenty-year periods from 1290 through 1949. As predicted, primordial content increased across time with superimposed quasiperiodic oscillations.

during periods commonly seen as involving initiation of new styles—Chaucerian, Skeltonic, Tudor, Jacobean, neoclassic, preromantic, romantic, postromantic, and modern—and to rise once a new style is established.

Spectral analysis of the means shown in figure 4.3 shows several peaks indicating the existence of superimposed cycles between 3 and 4 periods in length. Of course, we can tell that by just looking at the graph. Stylistic change allows primordial cognition to decline. Once the stylistic change is completed, primordial content begins to increase again. It has to, because poets have to engage in more primordial cognition to find the increasingly rare useful word combinations allowed by a style. How far primordial content falls, or how long a cycle in primordial content is, will depend upon how extreme a style change is and how much useful poetry it produces. Cycles of exactly the same duration and amplitude would occur only if all style changes were equally fruitful. This situation is hardly likely, if for no other reason that the poets who begin a stylistic change cannot know ahead of time how fruitful it is going to be. To know this would mean that they knew all of the useful similes and poetic devices implicit in the style. If they knew this, they would themselves have used all of them.

To sum up our results in an equation, an *autoregressive statistical analysis* is most appropriate. In such an analysis, one attempts to predict the mean score for one period from the mean scores for prior periods. Of course, this is consistent with the evolutionary theory, which asserts that the main cause of poetic content in any period is the poetic content of prior periods. Cycles of the sort observed can arise from what is called a *second-order autoregressive process:* that is, the mean value for a given period is determined by the values for the prior two periods. Before we can test whether this is the case, the data have to be *detrended:* that is, the linear increase has to be statistically removed; then we can look just at the oscillations. Autocorrelation analysis of detrended average primordial content scores for the thirty-three periods supports this notion. We find the pattern expected with a second-order autoregressive process. A completely different pattern of autocorrelations would be found if reflectionist theory (primordial content in a given period is due to extraliterary "shocks" in the current and/or prior periods) were true. (Details about how the analysis allows me to draw these conclusions are given in Gottman 1981.)

The best autoregressive model for primordial content in a given period (PC_t) is $PC_t = -.368PC_{t-2}$: that is, amount of primordial content in the poetry of a given period is a function of primordial content two periods earlier. Primordial content scores correlate significantly with this model. Since only 16 percent of the oscillation in primordial content is explained by autoregression, other factors are causing most of the oscillation. Theoretically, the cycles are caused primarily by stylistic changes and should, as I just argued, vary in their amplitude and duration as a function of how extreme these stylistic changes were.

The measures of concreteness of vocabulary all increase at a highly significant level across time. Correlations with period range from .44 for concreteness of verbs to .57 for adjective imagery. The concreteness measures do not show the sort of periodic oscillation exhibited by primordial content. Primordial cognition does tend to operate on concrete rather than abstract mental elements. However, concreteness of vocabulary has causes other than such cognition. As I mentioned in the first chapter, poetic statements about abstractions are dangerous: once one has been made, it rules out a large number of statements. Statements about concrete particulars are not so lethal. If stylistic change involves adding and dropping words, abstract words seem to be the ones at risk of being dropped, and concrete words have the best chance of being added.

The historical trend in use of words describing emotions is consistent with theoretical expectations. References to emotion show an inverted-U trend: emotional words rose from 3 percent or 4 percent in most of the early periods to 6.2 percent in period 20 and then fell to 2.6 percent by period 33. If emotional states represent a point midway between the primordial cognition and the conceptual cognition poles, this pattern makes sense: with movement from the conceptual pole toward the primordial pole, there should be an initial increase in the use of emotional terms as the midpoint of the continuum is reached, and then a decline with movement past this point toward the primordial end of the continuum.

Specific Trends in Poetic Language

Since it is clearly necessary to distinguish trends in poetic language from trends in language in general, for control purposes I analyzed some nonliterary texts. The *Annual Register,* a narrative description of world events for the year, has been published yearly in England since the mid-eighteenth century. There is no reason to believe that writers for the *Annual Register* have felt compelled to increase the arousal potential of their prose, their job being simply to report upon what has occurred in the past year. For the period from 1770 to 1970, I drew at random ten samples from the *Annual Register* for every tenth year (1770, 1780, and so on). The mean number of words per volume sampled was about 2,690. The total sample consists of 56,055 words. The Composite Variability Index, which was computed for each sample, showed no interperiod differences and no linear trend over time. Likewise, there were no interperiod differences for primordial content or any linear or oscillatory trends. Thus, trends found in poetry appear not to be mere reflections of general trends in the English language.

In order to obtain a longer sample of English prose, I took 5 samples of about 340 words each for every twentieth year from 1510 to 1970 from the *British Statutes* (Acts of Parliament). To avoid the highly stylized opening paragraphs of the statutes, samples were taken only from the middle and ending sections, to produce a sample of 40,789 words of legalese. This may not be the most representative English, but I cannot think of a longer series of prose that would be comparable as to subject matter, style, and so on. (The sample can't be pushed further into the past because English laws were written in French before 1500.) Again, the Composite Variability Index showed no significant variation across periods and no significant linear trend. The correlation with time was insignificant (.14).

Primordial content does show marginally significant differences among periods. Although this is not due to a linear trend (the correlation with period is −.01), there seems to be some order in the differences. Mean values of primordial content for each period look like quasiperiodic oscillations (see figure 4.4). An autoregression analysis shows an equation of exactly the same form as I found for British poetry. If the cycles in poetry and Acts of Parliament are in phase, this would be a fairly deadly blow to my entire theory, implying that both statutes and poetry reflect some common cause.

To see whether the cycles were in phase, I aligned the two series. Poets were selected according to birth dates, but the statutes were taken from specific years. On average, poets born between 1470 and 1489 would have a birthdate of 1480. They would be thirty years of age in 1510, the date of our first sample of statutes. Using this method of alignment, I found an insignificant correlation between primordial content in poetry and the statutes. If I split the poets into different birth periods, different alignments did not increase the correlation. Before correlating the two series, we should first remove the autoregressive component from each series

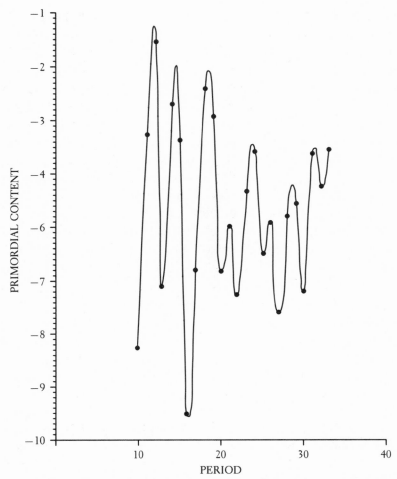

Figure 4.4   Average amount of primordial content in the British Acts of Parliament at twenty-year intervals from 1510 through 1970. The amount of primordial content is much lower than in poetry. Although there are cycles in primordial content in the Acts of Parliament, they are uncorrelated to those found in poetry.

(Haugh 1976). If we do that, the correlation between poetry and the statutes disappears almost altogether. I also tried to predict primordial content in poetry from all possible combinations of primordial content in the statutes in the same period and the prior three periods. I did the reverse to try to predict primordial content in the statutes. In neither case could a significant relationship be found. The best predictor for poetry is the content of statutes three periods earlier, but it accounts for only 7 percent of the variance and is not at all significant. The best predictor for the statutes is poetic primordial content in the prior period, which accounts for 4 percent of the variance and is completely insignificant.

If primordial content in the statutes is unrelated to primordial content in poetry, why does it oscillate at all? Perhaps the history of law is in some sense analogous to the history of literature. Maybe it, too, has styles that persist for a few decades and then give way to new styles. Members of legislative bodies certainly act as if they were under pressure to create and pass laws. Somehow, it will not do for legislators to meet and decide that no new laws are needed. Needed or not, new laws are going to be passed. Thus, legislators are really under pressure to produce new combinations of words, called laws, just as are poets. Suppose Parliament enacts a set of far-reaching new laws (initiates a new style). Subsequent Parliaments are going to have to pass laws that elaborate upon and refine the general laws. Eventually the result is going to be a set of overly specific, complicated, and contradictory laws. At this point, another stylistic change is in order: that is, a new set of general laws. These laws will also need refinement, so the whole process will begin anew. If this is at all close to capturing what legislative bodies do, then we might expect oscillations in primordial content because of oscillations in generality versus specificity of laws—an argument that cursory reading of the British statutes does support. General statutes are often followed by more concrete and specific ones that clarify the earlier statute or limit it so as to prevent unintended consequences. On the other side of the coin, a variety of specific statutes may eventually be replaced by an overarching general law. If we had a more appropriate measure of impact or complexity, we would almost certainly find that the complexity of law has increased across time. In an abstract sense, then, legal and poetic discourse are subject to evolutionary pressures that are isomorphic.

Stylistic Change

If declines in primordial content coincide with introduction of new styles, as they seem to do, we should seek some quantitative evidence to support this statement. After all, literary critics are hardly unanimous as to exactly when stylistic changes occurred in British poetry. Aside from poets' pronouncements that they have changed styles, a critic must judge whether a style is new on the basis of changes in the content of poetry. We should be able to measure such changes in an objective manner.

One of a poet's tasks is to combine words in a way that is pleasing or interesting to an audience. The latter habituates to old combinations and demands new ones. I have argued that increasing primordial cognition makes the poet more efficient at finding such new combinations—but the audience's habituation to the words themselves makes for continual pressure to change the poetic lexicon by adding new words and dropping old ones. This pressure is compounded by the fact that there is only a finite number of useful combinations—no matter how much primordial cognition one engages in—in a given set of words. Thus, the poetic lexicon should show continual change. An indicator of stylistic change may be the addition and deletion of words at an above-average rate. Of course, stylistic change also involves changes in the rules governing poetic practice: that is, the rules governing how words may be "legally" combined. This aspect of stylistic change, though, is more difficult to measure.

Josephine Miles (1964) argued that we can measure stylistic change by tabulating changes in the poetic lexicon. She claimed that the first practitioners of a new style tend to add new words to their poetic vocabulary without dropping an abnormally large number of the old words used by prior poets. Once the new style gains a foothold, the old words tend to be dropped. Although Miles presented convincing quantitative evidence for her contention, she did not do any statistical tests that would have allowed us to assess the significance of the patterns. Since the data Miles did present are not complete, I could not simply apply statistical tests to them myself—but I can certainly approach our texts in the same spirit.

If we computed how many unique words the poets in each period used, we could compute how many of these words were retained from the prior period, how many were new, and how many of the words used in the prior period had been dropped. For any period, the number of unique words (types) depended upon the total number of words (tokens) in our sample. In general, the number of types declines as the number of tokens increases (Herdan 1966). In a text composed of 10 words, each of them could be unique—as opposed to a text of 100 words, where function words (which account for about 40 percent of the words in a text) would probably be repeated. Now, with two poets per period for periods 1 to 12, six poets in period 13, and seven poets per period thereafter, our earlier samples are much shorter than our later ones. Because there is no completely satisfactory way to splice the early and late data together, I shall consider only the periods for which we have seven poets per period. Also, because we want to compute the number of word types in one period relative to the prior one, we cannot use the first period with seven poets since the prior period had only six poets. For the usable periods, the total number of words (tokens) does not differ significantly. The average number of tokens per period is 20,970, whereas the average number of types (unique words) per period is 4,814. In total, we are dealing with a sample of 398,432 tokens and 91,471 types. Because the number of tokens in each period is almost identical, it doesn't distort the number of types per period.

Our first question is how many *word types*—that is, different or unique words—the poets of each period used, regardless of whether a word was used once by one poet or a lot of times by all of the poets in the period. (I have tried various ways of weighting words by frequency of usage and invariably ended up with a complicated and confusing mess. Avoiding a confusing mess is also the reason for dealing with aggregate data rather than with data for each poet. We only have about 3,000 tokens for each poet.) If poets are aiming to produce striking word combinations, we might expect that they would probably increase the number of word types across time. Other things being equal, the probability of novel word combinations should be a function of how many different words one has to work with. As may be seen, however, number of types has fluctuated rather than increased (see figure 4.5). Apparently, other things are not equal.

Figures 4.6 through 4.8 show the percentage of word types added, kept, and dropped in each period. It is apparent that the poetic lexicon has turned over at an increasing rate across time. As time passes, an ever larger percentage of poets' vocabulary consists of new words, and an ever smaller percentage of words retained from the prior period.

Obviously, poets cannot add more than 100 percent of their vocabulary or drop more than 100 percent of the vocabulary of the previous generation. If present trends continued, poets born about one hundred years from now would exceed this addition rate. It must be, then, that the rate of addition and deletion will have to decrease as they approach the

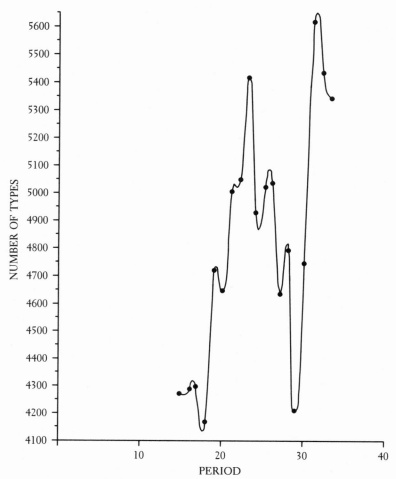

Figure 4.5 The number of word types (unique words) in texts from British poets born in twenty consecutive twenty-year periods from 1550 through 1949. The number of tokens per period (total number of words in the sample for the period) is about 21,000. In spite of this, number of word types has varied considerably.

100-percent ceiling. If poets have increased addition and deletion rate in order to increase the arousal potential of their poetry, then slowing down the rate of increase would cause arousal potential to decline. A system that thrives on change will die if change is no longer possible. A decrease in arousal potential means poetic failure. In order to compensate for such a

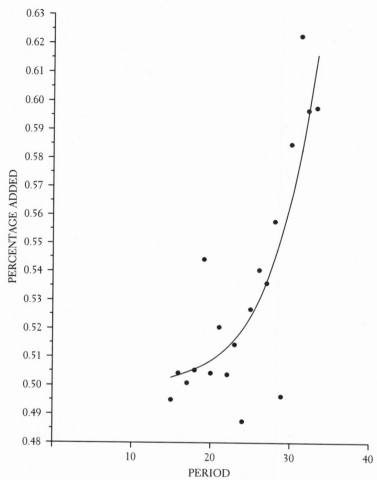

Figure 4.6 The percentage of word types added to the British poetic lexicon during each of twenty consecutive twenty-year periods (by poets born between 1550 and 1949). Words have been added at an accelerating rate, as shown by the best-fitting trend line.

decrease, poets would have to engage in further primordial cognition until this, too, reached its limit. Another strategy would be to increase the total number of word types in the poetic lexicon. There is a limit to this as well. The number of types cannot exceed the number of tokens. In a text in which the number of types was equal to the number of tokens, every word

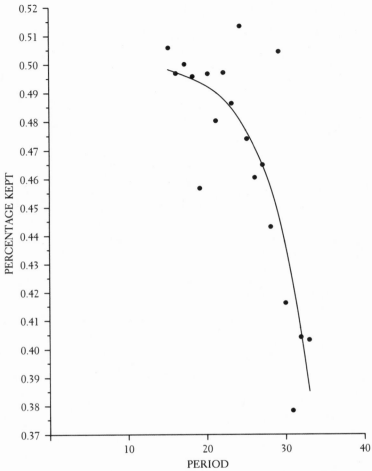

Figure 4.7 The percentage of word types in the British poetic lexicon retained from the prior period during each of twenty consecutive twenty-year periods (by poets born between 1550 and 1949). Across time, fewer and fewer words have been retained, as shown by the best-fitting trend line.

would be used only once. Such a text would be incomprehensible because it couldn't be "glued together" by function words. Of course, comprehensibility seems not to be a poet's primary aim.

I leave to future poets the solution to these problems, while I return to explaining the past. Although addition and deletion rates have in-

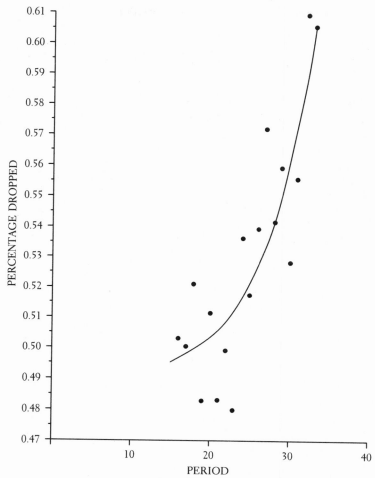

Figure 4.8 The percentage of word types dropped from the British poetic lexicon during each of twenty consecutive twenty-year periods (that is, for each period the percentage of word types in the prior period that were *not* used in that period). Across time, words have been dropped at an accelerating rate, as shown by the best-fitting trend line.

creased across time, all of the data points are not on the trend line. Perhaps the deviations have to do with stylistic changes. If Miles is correct, then either addition or deletion can indicate a stylistic change. If we add the percentage of types added together with the percentage of types deleted in each period, we have an index of stylistic change. In figure

4.9, stylistic change and primordial content are shown in standardized form so as to be comparable. The index of stylistic change looks as we would expect: it tends to increase when primordial content decreases, and vice versa.

Stylistic change and primordial content are not perfect inverses of each other, part of the reason being that neither is a perfect measure. Let us see what information we can piece together from these measures. Both have increased across time—theoretically, because of poets' efforts to counter habituation. The oscillations superimposed on these increases tend to be out of phase: poets tend to favor one or the other method of increasing arousal potential. There is, however, no iron-clad rule that a poet who adds or drops a lot of words is forbidden to engage in primordial cognition when it comes to combining the words one uses in one's poetry. There is merely a tendency for this not to be the case.

Once vocabulary has changed significantly, poets tend to slow down the rate at which they add and discard words, and focus on extracting the useful combinations present in the vocabulary at hand. As this becomes more difficult, they engage in more primordial thinking in order to discover these combinations. Now if poets had perfect knowledge and acted under no constraints, there should be no oscillations in either primordial content or stylistic change: that is, poets could "compute" how many words to add and drop so as to increase arousal potential without having to engage in a lot of primordial thought. Poets probably do not do this because they would have to add and delete words at too fast a rate. We can make computations to see whether the data show any indication that stylistic change is held in bounds.

The data support the implication that poets increase arousal potential *(AP)* by a combination of primordial cognition *(PC)* and stylistic change *(SC)*. The equation

$$AP = .58PC + .25SC$$

explains 88 percent of the variation in arousal potential (as measured by the Composite Variability Index) for the periods in question. This is the same percentage of variation explained by an equation relating arousal potential to the mere passage of time. In fact, we can explain 95 percent of the variation in arousal potential if we combine primordial content and the proportion of types added in a period *(A %)*:

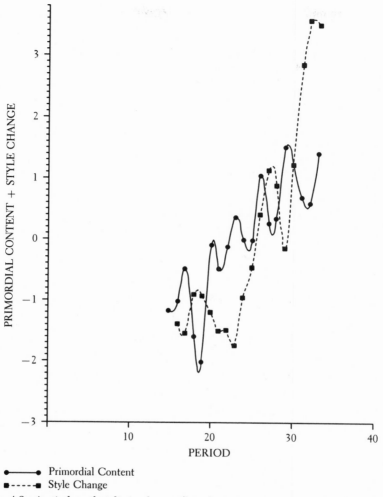

Figure 4.9 An index of stylistic change (based upon percentage of words added and dropped) and primordial content in each of twenty consecutive twenty-year periods (for poets born between 1550 and 1949). The index of stylistic change has tended to increase when primordial content decreased and vice versa, as predicted by the theory (compare figure 2.3, page 70).

$$AP = .64PC + .49A\%.$$

While deletion of words no doubt had an impact on contemporary audiences, we have no way of measuring that impact objectively.

If primordial cognition and stylistic change caused changes in arousal potential, what caused changes in these variables? Theoretically, the changes are due to habituation (passage of time) and to the effect of these variables on each other. We can try to predict primordial content (PC_t) in a given period (t) from values of primordial content in earlier periods (PC_{t-i}) and present (SC_t) and prior (SC_{t-i}) values of stylistic change.

The best prediction equation—in that we can find no better, and all predictors are statistically significant—is

$$PC_t = 12.81 + .51t - .55SC_{t-1} - .52PC_{t-1} - .56PC_{t-2}.$$

This equation explains 91 percent of the variation in primordial content. In words, all the equation says is that primordial content increases linearly with time and decreases as a function of stylistic change in the prior period and of amount of primordial content in the prior two periods.

The best equation for stylistic change (SC_t) accounts for 94 percent of the variation:

$$SC_t = -1.027 + .0094e^{.175t} + .57SC_{t-1} - .50SC_{t-2}.$$

The first two terms in the equation $(-1.027 + .0094e^{.175t})$ just tell us that stylistic change increases exponentially with time. The third term $(+.57SC_{t-1})$ shows that if the value of stylistic change in the prior period was high, the value in the current period will also be high. However, this effect is held in check by the last term $(-.50SC_{t-2})$, which tells us that stylistic change at $t-2$ (two periods previously) inhibits stylistic change in the current period. Once stylistic change begins, it tends to persist into the next period but not into the one after that.

When we put the equations together in a diagram (figure 4.10), it is not immediately apparent what the relationships in the diagram are going to cause. Since the equations explain almost all of the variation in arousal potential, stylistic change, and primordial content, they must cause some oscillation in the last two variables. Indeed, equations of this sort are likely to produce oscillations. The equation for primordial content contains several negative feedback terms: if primordial content was "too high" in

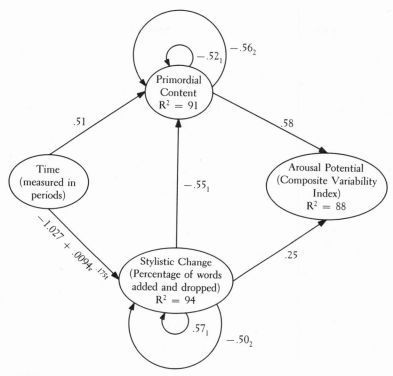

Figure 4.10 Empirical relationships among the theoretical constructs. (With the exception of the equation relating stylistic change to time, the numbers shown on the lines are correlations. Subscripts indicate lags. R^2 indicates amount of variability explained by the relationships shown.) With the passage of time, primordial content and stylistic change increased. In turn, primordial content and stylistic change brought about increases in arousal potential. Also shown are the relationships between prior values and values for a given period: The amount of primordial content in the two prior periods is negatively related to primordial content in a given period. The amount of stylistic change is positively related to stylistic change in the prior period and negatively related to stylistic change two periods earlier. These influences of the past on the present set up oscillations. Finally, as shown, stylistic change drives down the amount of primordial content in the next period.

prior periods, current poets decrease it; if too low, current poets increase it. This is what a thermostat does to temperature. Because of delay—when the thermostat turns on the furnace, there is a delay before the furnace can get the temperature to the desired level—the target temperature is continually overshot and undershot. The same overshooting and undershooting will occur with primordial content. Primordial content is also controlled by stylistic change in the prior period: if there was a lot of stylistic change in the prior period, primordial cognition is decreased. It is not necessary, because the new style sufficiently increases arousal potential. If there was little stylistic change in the prior period, primordial cognition is increased. It has to be if arousal potential is to be increased sufficiently. On the other hand, the equations don't show primordial content holding stylistic change in check. Primordial content in the same period and the prior period is, in fact, negatively correlated with stylistic change. However, the correlations are comparatively uninformative. The ones shown in figure 4.10 do a better job of explaining trends in stylistic change.

The equations describe our data well. Now, how well could a scientist who had these equations in 1650 have predicted the future course of poetry? Such a person could have had data on primordial content and stylistic change from periods 15 (1570–89) and 16 (1590–1609). Let us say that our imaginary scientist took these data, plugged them into the equations to predict values for period 17, took the results to predict values for period 18, and so on recursively. Since we know the values for periods 15 and 16, we can find out. Although our scientist's predictions would not be perfect, he would predict that primordial content would increase and also oscillate in cycles lasting three or four periods—as it has, of course, done. Even if our scientist made wild guesses about the data for the first two periods, the equations would produce cycles in this range. I have tried this procedure using a variety of essentially random numbers to start the recursive process. The general result is irregular cycles of primordial content that last for 3 or 4 periods superimposed on an uptrend.

The exponential term ($.0094e^{.175t}$) in the equation for stylistic change assures us that—at some point—it is going to take off for infinity and swamp all the other terms. As I indicated, it would eventually lead to the absurd prediction that British poets would be adding and dropping words at a rate greater than 100 percent. In the simulations I have been discussing, that point turns out to be somewhere around the present. That is, the predictions for stylistic change are well behaved until around period 34 (1950–69). Then, or soon thereafter, the predicted values for stylistic change become too large, driving the values for primordial content to levels that are too low. This outcome is consistent with my contention that the rate of additions to and deletions from the lexicon must slow down, and that the inflection point must be nearly upon us.

THE EXTINCTION OF STYLES: THE METAPHYSICAL POETS

Since poets don't do content analyses and compute how many words they and their predecessors have added and dropped, how do they decide when to stay with an old style and when to introduce a new one? I conducted a study of seventeenth-century English metaphysical poets to test three hypotheses concerning the reasons for stylistic change (Martindale 1984*b*). The question of interest was why and when poets switch from the first method of increasing arousal potential (deeper regression during inspiration) to the second method (change in elaboration). I can think of three plausible explanations why stylistic changes occur. One might be called the *least-effort hypothesis:* poets adopt a new style when it is easier or requires less effort to increase arousal potential in it than in the old style (Martindale 1975). In this view, one could successfully continue the old style only at the cost of increasing difficulty. An implication of this explanation is that both arousal potential and primordial content should continue to increase across the entire time during which the old style is used: that is, the style yields the requisite increases in arousal potential due to poetic engagement in ever deeper regression.

Another explanation is the *exhaustion hypothesis.* In this view, the late practitioners of the old style fail to increase the arousal potential of their poetry compared with that of their predecessors. Arousal potential may decline, or its rate of increase may fall below the acceptable level. As a result, new poets choose—or invent—other styles; the audience comes to prefer any new style that produces poetry with the requisite arousal potential. One problem with the least-effort hypothesis is that a new poet cannot know that the old style requires too much effort without trying to write in it. The initiators of new styles are not, however, usually defectors from a previously dominant style. Rather, they tend to begin their careers as practitioners of the new style—a likely tendency if the old style had produced actual failures, as suggested by the exhaustion hypothesis.

The most obvious possible reason for exhaustion is that, given the rules of the old style, there are no more usable combinations of ideas left. Of course, not every conceivable poem in the old style will have been written, but those remaining will be too similar to existing ones for anyone to want to write more. On the theoretical level, to say that no ideas are left implies that regression has reached its maximum depth. Had it not, even deeper regression would produce more new ideas. If this were the problem, then measures of primordial cognition should level off in the late stages of a style.

A third explanation, which can be called the *evolutionary-trap hypothesis*, is based on the strong possibility that primordial cognition and originality are in fact curvilinearly related: that is, there is a point beyond which deeper regression leads not to more originality or variability, but to just the opposite—less originality and variability. Extreme primordial cognition involves not only disorganization but also simplification of mental contents (Martindale 1981), making for fewer mental elements to combine and hence less variability or originality. In this view, the late practitioners of a style get caught in an evolutionary trap: the increased regression, which should lead to more originality, in fact does not. If this explanation is correct, then primordial content should increase across the entire time span of a style, whereas indices of arousal potential should increase at first and then decline.

While the evolutionary theory applies to any poetic style, the seventeenth-century English metaphysical style of poetry might be expected to yield particularly clear results. These poets had a high degree of autonomy from the larger society and were, for the most part, not dependent for their living upon either patrons or sales of their poetry, which often was not even published. Drayton thus called them "chamber poets." Furthermore, they usually knew one another and were familiar with, and influenced by, each other's work.

Metaphysical wit was defined by Samuel Johnson as "a combination of dissimilar images or discovery of occult resemblances in things apparently unlike." "The most heterogeneous ideas," he continued, "are yoked by violence together" (1905 [1779], p.20). The dissimilarity of images combined in metaphysical similes and metaphors, I have argued elsewhere (Martindale 1975) on qualitative grounds, tended to increase across the time that the style was in effect. The same argument has been made by other critics, such as George Williamson (1958 [1930]). While John Donne's or Henry King's similes do indeed yoke together heterogeneous images, those of later metaphysical poets, such as Edward Benlowes or John Cleveland, are—to quote Williamson—"abstruse," "grotesque" and "extravagant." Finally, there is one of the last, worst (or best, depending upon one's taste) metaphysical conceit, Marvell's

> But now the Salmon-Fishers moist
> Their Leathern Boats begin to hoist;
> And, like Antipodes in Shoes,
> Have shod their Heads in their Canoos.
> ("Appleton House")

Thus, arousal potential—or at least incongruity—seems to have increased across the course of the metaphysical style.

Qualitative evidence would also suggest an increase in primordial content. Compare, for example, the intellectual content of Donne's poetry with the voluptuous oral imagery of Crashaw or the concrete physical sensations that dominate Marvell's poetry. In comparing the early metaphysical poet George Herbert with the later Henry Vaughan, T. S. Eliot says, "The emotion of Herbert is clear, definite, mature, and sustained; whereas the emotion of Vaughan is vague, adolescent, fitful, and retrogressive" (1927, p.263). There is little value, though, in dwelling upon such qualitative evidence when quantitative methods will give us more precise answers to our questions.

On the basis of comments in Douglas Bush (1962), Robert Sharp (1940), and George Williamson (1958[1930]), I constructed a list of metaphysical poets, each called metaphysical by all three authors (see table 4.2). Selection of poets and textual sampling were done in the same

TABLE 4.2
Metaphysical Poets (1570–1629)

Period (By Birth Date)	Poets
1 (1570–84)	John Donne; Edward, Lord Herbert; Aurelian Townshend
2 (1585–99)	Sir Francis Kynaston, Henry King, George Herbert
3 (1600–1614)	Edward Benlowes, Richard Crashaw, John Cleveland
4 (1615–29)	Abraham Cowley, Andrew Marvell, Henry Vaughan

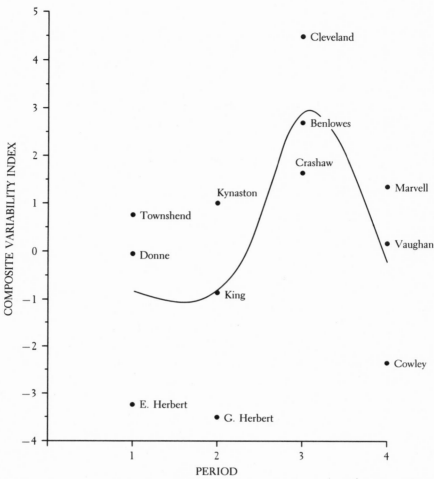

Figure 4.11   Values of the Composite Variability Index in texts of English metaphysical poets born in four consecutive fifteen-year periods from 1570 through 1629 and the best-fitting trend line describing these values. The main trend is an increase from period 1 to period 3 and a decline from period 3 to period 4. Thus, the late metaphysical poets failed to increase the arousal potential of their poetry.

manner as in the studies of French and British poets, except that here I used fifteen-year periods. The time span from 1570 to 1629 was divided into four consecutive periods, and three metaphysical poets were selected to represent each period.

Testing for trends in the Composite Variability Index, I found a signif-

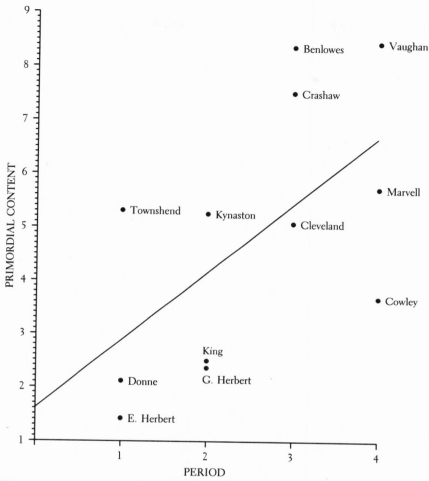

Figure 4.12 The percentage of primordial content in texts from English metaphysical poets born in four consecutive fifteen-year periods from 1570 through 1629 and the best-fitting trend line describing these values.

icant cubic trend (see figure 4.11) accounting for 71 percent of the variance: the Composite Variability Index rose from period 1 through period 3 and then declined. In other words, the late metaphysical poets failed to produce the requisite increases in arousal potential—a finding contrary to the least-effort hypothesis of stylistic change but consistent with the exhaustion and evolutionary-trap hypotheses. An examination of trends in primordial content allows us to confirm one or the other of these hypotheses.

Primordial content shows a significant linear increase across all four periods (see figure 4.12). This linear trend accounts for 59 percent of the overall variability in primordial content. There is no sign of leveling off of this trend during the later periods. The pattern of results is most consistent with the hypothesis that the late metaphysical poets were caught in an evolutionary trap: They engaged in deeper and deeper regression, but did not achieve the desired increases in arousal potential. Once entrapped, the metaphysical style perished and was replaced by the ensuing neoclassical style.

THE SOCIOMETRY OF BRITISH POETRY

Corollaries of the evolutionary-trap hypothesis are that the initiators of a new style make no attempt to write in the previously dominant style, and that those working in the old style generally do not convert to the new. The physicist Max Planck observed, "A new scientific truth does not triumph by convincing its opponents and making them see the light, but rather because its opponents eventually die, and a new generation grows up that is familiar with it" (1949, pp.33–34). Perhaps something similar happens in poetry. In a sociometric study of sixty-four of the poets included in my study of British poetry, I sought, by systematically searching reference works, to answer the question of who knew whom personally (Martindale 1977b). We would expect that personal acquaintance with another poet would make one susceptible to being influenced by that poet.

Only nineteen of the sixty-four poets (30%) knew none of the other sixty-four. Even this is an overestimate. I know from other sources that many of these poets were not, in fact, isolates, but the search procedure used did not reveal this. As often as not, the poets who were acquainted knew each other before they became known to the world at large. Thus, the interpersonal bond did not arise solely out of the obligation famous people seem to feel to call at least casually upon other famous people. A surprising number of the poets were related by blood or marriage: The Sackville family has produced eminent poets for several centuries. Heywood, More, Donne, and Cowper—though they seem to share little in style—were relatives. Dryden and Swift were cousins. Edward, Lord Herbert, and George Herbert were brothers. This close interconnectedness suggests that British poetry could be construed as having been passed on by an oral tradition as much as by a written one.

Cohesiveness varied as a function of stylistic change. Only four of the sixteen poets (25%) who wrote during periods of stylistic change (when primordial content declined from the level attained in the prior period) knew poets from prior periods. Ten of them (63%) knew one or more poets working during the same period in which they were working. In contrast, twenty-three of the forty-eight other poets in the sample (48%) knew poets from prior periods, but only fourteen (29%) were acquainted with poets born within their own period. Several poets, of course, knew both contemporary and earlier poets. We may infer that stylistic changes are initiated by cohesive groups with relatively few ties to prior generations. On the other hand, those who carry on a style have more ties to previous generations and fewer ties among themselves.

THE MAIN DIMENSIONS OF POETIC CONTENT

Trends in the categories of the Harvard III Psychosociological Dictionary are consistent with the results I have described. The picture presented by these categories is that British poetry has moved away from references to persons, roles, and human concerns on the levels of cultural patterns, emotions, social-emotional acts, instrumental acts, and thoughts. On the other hand, it has moved toward a focus on concrete objects whether culturally produced (Cultural Objects) or natural (Natural Realm). On the basis of the Harvard III Dictionary categories, we can compute correlations among the 170 poets in the sample: the more similar the profiles across the categories, the more similar any pair of poets is, and the higher the correlation will be. This similarity matrix of poets was subjected to a multidimensional scaling program, ALSCAL (Young, Lewyckyj, and Takane (1983). This is the same sort of analysis as the one reported at the end of chapter 3 (pages 111–15). The point is the same. We want to know the main dimensions along which British poets vary. Then we want to know how much of this variability can be accounted for by the evolutionary theory.

Multidimensional scaling provides a spatial representation of the similarities among the group of poets, with more similar poets being placed closer together. The question to be answered is how many dimensions are needed to represent the similarities. ALSCAL provided a four-dimensional solution, implying that the poets in the present sample differ along four basic dimensions. Indeed, 95 percent of interpoet similarities are accounted for by these four dimensions.

The question of interest is the extent to which a poet's position in this space can be predicted from his or her scores on the two main theoretical variables, primordial content and the Composite Variability Index. A measure of redundancy (Stewart and Love 1968) was computed. The measure tells us how much of the variation in one set of variables (the four multidimensional dimensions in this case) can be accounted for by another set of variables (the two theoretical variables in this case). The redundancy score, 40 percent, means that almost half of the overall variation among the poets in the sample can be accounted for by the two theoretical variables.

Rather than looking at similarity in content, we can look directly at similarity in word usage. In the process of examining how many words were added and dropped during each period, it was necessary to compute which words were used by each of the poets in the sample. Since this had to be done anyway, it cost little extra effort to compute how often each poet used each of these words. These data allow us to correlate each poet with all other poets. If two poets used exactly the same set of words at exactly the same frequencies, we would obtain a correlation of 1.00. To the extent that their word usage differed, the correlation would be lower. The correlations thus tell us how similar poets were in their word usage. As with the correlations based on the Harvard III categories, multidimensional scaling was used. In this case, it tells us that five dimensions are needed. The theoretical variables—arousal potential and primordial content—can account for 34 percent of the overall variation in this multidimensional space.

To see what the multidimensional axes are measuring, we can correlate each with our content analysis categories. Let us focus first on the content axes. The first seems to have to do with lyric poetry, being correlated with references to self and others (for example, "you"). Both of the theoretical variables are most highly correlated with this axis. The second axis gets at epic or action-oriented narrative poetry, being positively correlated with references to male roles, actions, control, and aggression. Axis 3 is correlated positively with references to emotions, ideal values, small groups, instrumental behavior, message form, various references to restraint and control, and references to selves ("we"), others ("you"); it is negatively correlated with references to self, male role, and the natural world. For want of a better term, we might say that the axis gets at the contemplative aspect of poetry. The fourth axis clearly has to do with emotion. As well as correlating with all of the emotion categories, it shows high correlations with references to women.

The first two axes of the word-frequency space correspond to the first two axes of the content space. The last three are all correlated with references to emotion. The fifth axis seems to be getting at love poetry. It is primarily correlated with female roles and affection. The third and fourth axes both are related to reference to emotions. The main difference is that the third axis shows a high correlation with references to self, whereas the fourth shows a high correlation with references to related others ("you").

The multidimensional axes do not really tell us anything startlingly new. What is surprising is that we do not need more dimensions to capture the differences among poets. Poetry is about the self and its inner life (the first axis of both spaces), action in the world (the second axis of both spaces), and emotions (the remaining axes). Poetry has not remained static on most of these dimensions. Across time, poetic content has moved along axis 1 so that it has become more and more concerned with the self and its depths. In other words, primordial content has increased more or less steadily across time. The earliest British poetry was concerned with action in the world (axis 2). This concern declined until the seventeenth century and has remained relatively stable since then. Contemplative and emotional poetry (axes 3 and 4) is mainly a phenomenon of the seventeenth and early eighteenth centuries.

As a rule of thumb, if a phenomenon varies in an N-dimensional space, one needs about N equations to describe it. Conversely, if a system is governed by, say, three equations, it can probably be "contained" in a three-dimensional abstract space (Mayer-Kress 1986). So, as I said at the beginning of the chapter, we probably do need about five equations to capture most of what has happened over the centuries with poetic word usage. We are dealing, I should note, with a very simple system. For purposes of comparison, human brain waves seem to be about fifteen-dimensional (Mayer-Kress 1986), and we haven't the slightest idea about any of the relevant equations. To say that the history of poetry is simple does not mean that the equations describing it will turn out to be simple or unimportant. While any physicist will tell you that physics deals with simple phenomena, the equations in physics are far from simple to most of us.

I have been talking, I know, in rarefied or abstract terms, our 170 poets ending by being represented by points in four- or five-dimensional hyperspaces. It is *where* they are in these abstract spaces that I have aimed to account for by four or five equations. The exciting thing is that poetry moves through these spaces in very orderly ways across the course of time, and I think we can eventually capture the beauty of this sweep of history with quite simple and beautiful equations. Of course, this is hardly the usual way of talking about the history of poetry. However, I think that it adds to or complements—rather than in any way contradicting or negating—the more usual approaches.

CHAPTER 5

On American Shores

Poetry, Fiction, and Musical Lyrics

A T this point, it may seem that I have stacked the deck in favor of the evolutionary theory. French and British poetry constitute long, strong, and unbroken traditions. Both are fairly resistant to the importation of foreign styles. To put my theory to a more rigorous test, we need a literary tradition less closed to external influences. Czech poetry would do nicely: it has its own tradition but has also been buffeted about by importations from neighboring countries (Jakobson 1981). The fact that most readers don't know a thing about Czech poetry would put me in a strong position, except that I don't know anything about it either. Fortunately, we can study the matter on the familiar ground of American poetry.

AMERICAN POETRY

After getting off to a nice start in the seventeenth century with the Massachusetts poet Anne Bradstreet, America fell mute, and virtually

nothing was written until the late eighteenth century. Poetry and literature of all types were mainly imported from England. There was no
coherent American poetic tradition to speak of until the late eighteenth
century. When it did begin in earnest, its style was based on British
models. Today, to use a genealogical analogy, American poets are not sure
who their ancestors are. Do they belong to the tradition of poetry written
in English? If so, they must compete against both prior British and
American poets. Do they belong to a distinctly American tradition? If so,
then British poetry is irrelevant. American poets cannot completely ignore
British poetry. Even if they attempt to create a distinctly American
"voice," this act of rebellion is a rebellion against something. And that
something is the British tradition. British writers don't have this problem
of double parentage. With a few exceptions, they have simply ignored
"colonial" verse until the twentieth century.

The fact that American writers aren't sure which tradition they are
writing in poses problems for the evolutionary theory. Just as biological
evolution occurs within species, literary evolution occurs only within coherent traditions. Is the American poetic tradition coherent enough to
sustain clear-cut evolution? I think so—but this is a question we wouldn't
even think to ask about British or French poetry. Another problem with
American poetry is that American poets have probably formed a less
cohesive social group than did British or French poets. Even more than
British poets, French poets tended to know each other personally. Almost
all of the French poets discussed in chapter 3 knew each other if they were
alive at the same time. They knew their comrades or competitors and their
predecessors, and thus no doubt evolution was allowed to occur in an
orderly fashion. Early American poetry was pretty much a New England
affair. Everyone knew everyone else. This situation had changed by the
late nineteenth century, when some poets lived in Boston, others in San
Francisco, and so on. Though I have not studied the matter quantitatively, it seems certain that American poets have not constituted as cohesive and interconnected a group as have French and British poets. That
their knowledge of each other has been more at second hand would have
further diluted evolutionary processes.

I found it impossible to begin my study with American poets born
before 1750. A few poets were, of course, born before then, but not
enough to make up an unbroken series. I set out to select the most

eminent poets born in successive twenty-year periods from 1750 to 1949: four poets for each of the first two periods, five for periods 3 to 7, and six for periods 8 to 10. Thus, I ensured that no important poet was left out for the early periods. For the most recent periods it is too soon in most cases to say exactly who will ultimately be regarded as important and who not. Eminence I defined as before. I began with the *New Oxford Book of American Verse* (Ellmann 1976), which provides enough poets for most periods. Owing, however, to the high standards of its editor, Richard Ellmann, this anthology doesn't include any poets at all born between 1770 and 1789. This is a reasonable omission in an anthology of good poetry, but it won't do for our purposes. I supplemented Ellmann's list by consulting the anthologies compiled by Louis Untermeyer (1931) for the early periods, Edwin Markham (1934) for the middle, and Helen Vendler (1985) for the later, and came up with the set of poets in table 5.1. Joseph Hopkinson was omitted from period 2 because he did not write enough poetry to allow his inclusion. T. S. Eliot was omitted from period 7 since he was included in the British series; if he were included, the results would not come out any differently. Bliss Carman, included in

TABLE 5.1
American Poets (1750–1949)

Period (By Birth Date)	Poets
1 (1750–69)	Joel Barlow, Philip Freneau, Phillis Wheatley, John Trumbull
2 (1770–89)	Richard Henry Wilde, John Pierpont, Samuel Woodworth, Richard Henry Dana
3 (1790–1809)	Ralph Waldo Emerson, John Greenleaf Whittier, Edgar Allan Poe, Henry Wadsworth Longfellow, William Cullen Bryant
4 (1810–29)	Walt Whitman, James Russell Lowell, Herman Melville, Jones Very, Frederick Goddard Tuckerman
5 (1830–49)	Emily Dickinson, Sidney Lanier, Ambrose Bierce, Joaquin Miller, Bret Harte
6 (1850–69)	Edward Arlington Robinson, William Vaughan Moody, Edgar Lee Masters, Edwin Markham, Bliss Carman
7 (1870–89)	Ezra Pound, William Carlos Williams, Robert Frost, Wallace Stevens, Marianne Moore
8 (1890–1909)	Hart Crane, Theodore Roethke, E. E. Cummings, Robert Penn Warren, Allen Tate, Langston Hughes
9 (1910–29)	Robert Lowell, Galway Kinnell, Denise Levertov, Charles Olson, A. R. Ammons, Randall Jarrell
10 (1930–49)	Sylvia Plath, Gary Snyder, I. A. Baraka (Leroi Jones), Charles Wright, Mark Strand, Dave Smith

period 6, was Canadian but spent most of his productive years in the United States. Sampling of texts was done as with the French and British poets. I ended up with a sample of 155,130 words.

Arousal Potential

As predicted by the theory, arousal potential increased across the time-span that I studied. The results for the Composite Variability Index are shown in figure 5.1. The best-fitting trend line, which accounts for 56 percent of interperiod variation, is the simple straight line shown in the figure. The statistics tell us to ignore the deviations in the values for period 3 (a bit high) and for period 6 (a bit low). Incongruous juxtapositions also increased in a linear fashion (see figure 5.2). In this case, the period-4 texts produce values higher than I would like, and the period-6 poets are again too low. Again, the statistical tests tell us to ignore these discrepancies and to give credence only to the overall trend. The late nineteenth century, when the period-6 poets were beginning to write, has been called an interregnum in American poetry. Longfellow and many of his generation lived long, casting a dark shadow over the end of the century. This may have led people to avoid becoming poets. The dominance of the older generation perhaps kept away those who at other times would have become great poets.

Primordial Content and Stylistic Change

Primordial content increased significantly across time—but with a clear nonlinear trend (see figure 5.3). We can capture this trend with a single cosine curve. Putting this together with the linear trend, we arrive at the equation

$$PC = 7.28 + .39P + 1.90 \cos(.83P + 4.03),$$

where P stands for Period. The trend specified by this equation is shown in the figure. It accounts for 71 percent of interperiod variation among

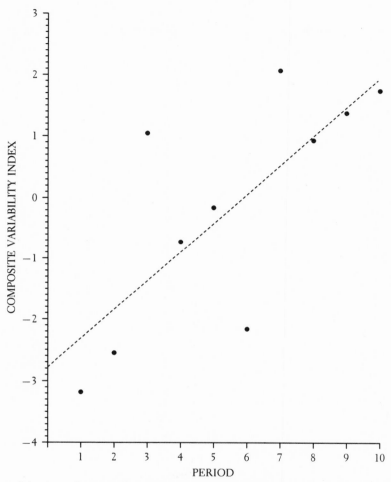

Figure 5.1 Arousal potential as measured by average values for each period of the Composite Variability Index for texts from fifty-one American poets born in ten consecutive twenty-year periods from 1750 through 1949. The best-fitting trend line indicating the linear increase across time is also shown.

the means, thus bearing out the evolutionary theory in respect to American poetry.

The data suggest a stylistic change beginning in period 4 and continuing through period 7. The upward trend in primordial content after period 7 suggests that the possibilities of this style are still being worked out. The earliest American poetry, critics agree, was written in an im-

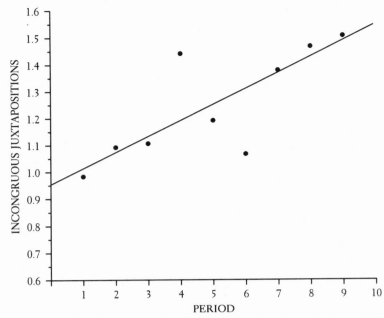

Figure 5.2 Arousal potential as measured by average values for each period of number of incongruous juxtapositions in texts from fifty-one American poets born in ten consecutive twenty-year periods from 1750 through 1949. The best-fitting trend line indicating the linear increase across time is also shown.

ported British style. The form was at first decidedly neoclassical, but the tone was—or soon became—romantic. The increase in primordial content from periods 1 to 3 suggests a working out of this style. We find a "romantic progression" toward more primordial content across the first three periods, culminating in the generation of Poe and Longfellow. You cannot take romanticism much further than Poe did—at least not in America. His descendants were the French symbolists, who literally deified him. Mallarmé wrote a beautiful sonnet that was read when a tombstone was finally put up to mark Poe's grave in 1875. "This sonnet," Mallarmé wrote, "was recited at the unveiling, at Baltimore, of a block of basalt as a monument to Poe, with which Americans weighted down the poet's light shadow, in order to make sure that it never reappeared" (Wilson 1955, p.420).

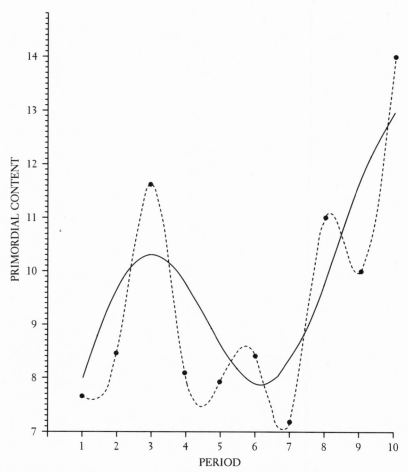

Figure 5.3   The average amount of primordial content in texts from fifty-one American poets born in ten consecutive twenty-year periods from 1750 through 1949. The solid line is the best-fitting trend line. Deviations of the points from this line should be ignored, at least from a statistical perspective.

American poetry headed in a direction opposite to that Poe had traveled. There were ideas in the American romantic style, but there was a strong emphasis on the linguistic aspect of poetry—on the music of sound patterns, of meter, and of rhyme. This is unusual only in light of what happened with later American poetry. Prose is the medium for communicating ideas. Poetry is supposed to focus more on sound patterns. There are no terribly deep ideas in the romantic poets. As the literary historian Hyatt Waggoner (1968) rather cruelly illustrates, the "message" in Longfellow's poems is literally incoherent: it usually makes no sense. Poe (1955 [1842]) pointed out that Longfellow was actually a good poet when he forgot his didactic point and wrote musically. That was really the whole point of the American romantic style. Writing musically is what Poe did best.

Poe has fared poorly with subsequent American—but not French or British—poets and critics. Perhaps the main reason is that later American poetic style up to today is neither linguisitic nor musical, but has focused on communicating *ideas* about *reality*. Our graph indicates a long-lasting stylistic change commencing after Poe. It is clear both what the change in style is, and also who started it. In the early twentieth century, poets and critics looked back to the nineteenth century and saw only Whitman. With increasing distance, it has become clear that a more towering figure stands behind Whitman, and that Whitman appears to be only one of his many mouthpieces. Indeed, in the last several decades it has become apparent that trends in American poetry after Poe make no sense at all unless we trace them back to Ralph Waldo Emerson. The critic Leslie Fiedler (1964) recognized this influence to some extent. Waggoner (1968) saw that it was more massive than Fiedler thought. More recently, the critic Harold Bloom (1975) has traced literally everything back to Emerson. Emerson, though born in period 3, was starting something new while the rest of his generation was finishing something old.

Emerson was certain what poetry should be. It should find goodness and beauty everywhere. It should do this because everything is a manifestation of God. The poet should, as he put it in "The Poet," find subject matter in common things, in "the mud and slime of things." Poe hated mundane reality. Emerson loved it. He said, in his Harvard Divinity School address, that it isn't mundane at all if you look at it right: "God IS, not WAS," and manifests Himself in everyday, common reality. Poets should believe this, experience this, and communicate their experiences. If you take this message seriously, you will end up writing odes to grocery stores and gasoline. American poets have taken it seriously, and they have ended up writing such odes. Whether they knew it or not, a good case can be made that they did so because of Emerson's influence. It is not that easy to see God in a hot-dog stand. It is not that easy to see Him anywhere. A lot of American verse has to do with despair about this fact. As Waggoner has pointed out, a lot of American poetry makes sense only if it is read as religious poetry. That focus, too, can be traced directly to Emerson.

In his own poetic practice, Emerson made clear by example that the poet should attempt above all to communicate the wisdom of his insights. The idea takes precedence. If meter or rhyme get in the way, then they should be disregarded. Emerson did use meter and rhyme, but he distorted his syntax to avoid distorting his ideas. Here is an example from "Bacchus" that is not atypical:

> Wine which is already man,
> Food which teach and reason can.

This is simply not acceptable poetry by British standards. It is neither musical nor decorous. It is not acceptable to twist around syntax just to get things to rhyme. Matthew Arnold, not knowing what to make of Emerson's poetry, concluded that it really wasn't poetry at all (1889, p.153). That is certainly a good hint that Emerson was doing something very new stylistically. Later poets developed the style. Whitman called Emerson his "Master." As he remarked to John Trowbridge, "I was simmering, simmering, simmering; Emerson brought me to a boil" (Trowbridge 1903, p.367). What did Whitman do? Exactly what Emerson said an American poet should do. Whitman took the commonplace as his subject matter. Armpits, for example. Since poetic devices got in the way of his ideas, he threw them away and wrote in free verse.

Emerson's influence didn't stop with Whitman. Jones Very was Emerson's avowed disciple. So, with some reluctance, was Emily Dickinson. So was Edward Arlington Robinson. So was Robert Frost. Indeed, anyone influenced by Whitman or any of these poets was, in fact, influenced by Emerson. But that comes down to literally all subsequent poets. Whitman was ahead of his time in the formal aspects of his style. Emerson's influence was first felt most strongly in respect to content: across the last half of the nineteenth century, the content of poetry became increasingly commonplace and ordinary. Emerson said it should be this way, and this is the way it was. Poets got their effect by bringing new subject matter into the realm of poetry. Emerson's idea was to see the transcendent in the ordinary. At worst, though, the new style just presented the ordinary.

If you get too ordinary, ordinary people may actually read your poetry. That was the sad fate of Edgar Lee Masters. His *Spoon River Anthology* (1915) became a best seller. Critics never forgave him for that. Robert Frost more or less brought this prosaic-content aspect of the Emersonian style to its logical conclusion. Most of Frost's contemporaries—Ezra Pound, T. S. Eliot, William Carlos Williams, Wallace Stevens—did not turn away altogether from the ordinary. They developed the formal aspect of what Emerson and Whitman had started. The danger in the Emersonian disregard for poetic devices is that poetry will end up sounding like prose. Pound, Eliot, and their contemporaries made sure that didn't happen. Finally, the style change was complete. The poets in our last three periods have—in the main—worked out the possibilities inherent in the style of Pound, Eliot, and Williams. But it is not really their style. It is ultimately Emerson's style.

No matter whose style it is, to work out the possibilities of a style calls for more primordial cognition—exactly as occurred across the last several generations. The subject matter remains ordinary, but the ordinary is seen in a more and more delirious and numinous fashion. Only in this recent poetry is Emerson's vision fully realized: to see the oversoul, the transcendent in the ordinary. Aside from Emily Dickinson, most nineteenth-century poets carried out only the first part of Emerson's dictum: more and more they focused on the ordinary, overlooking the extraordinary. Seeing it was left for twentieth-century poets.

Although most of these poets were not directly influenced by Emerson, Bloom and other critics have made a good case that the influence was there nonetheless. While in most cases the overt religious concerns are gone, the Emersonian goal of seeing the strange and transcendent in the familiar is clearly present. Hence, the persistent focus on "unpoetic" subject matter in American poetry and also the attempt to find some deeper meaning behind this subject matter. The latter goal is, however, really mystical or religious. Without the religious impetus—the belief that something greater *does* lie behind ordinary reality—there would be no reason for the poet to write about the mundane.

In period 9, primordial content shows a dip—important stylistically if not statistically. The dip is due mainly to Robert Lowell, A. R. Ammons, and Charles Olson, who were all attempting to innovate on the stylistic level. This is clearest with Olson. Matthew Arnold thought that Emerson's verse was interesting but not really poetry. My reaction to Olson is more extreme: what he wrote is neither interesting nor poetry; its snippets of phrases seem almost random. In doing these studies, I have read some pretty bad poetry. I know it is bad because I have the feeling that I could have written better. In the case of Olson, I speak lines like his every day but don't bother to write them down. Everybody does. How come he gets called a poet and the rest of us don't? There are plenty of bad and boring poets. Olson is the only poet who makes me angry. I suppose that there could be no surer sign that he is doing something radically new. If it is radically important only time will tell.

The measures of concreteness of vocabulary all show strong interperiod differences. The main trend in all cases is a linear increase. Correlations with period range from .38 for verb concreteness to .68 for noun concreteness. Adjective imagery and verb concreteness also exhibit some nonlinear trends, but the trend in total concreteness and noun concreteness is purely linear. Thus, as with modern British and French poetry, American poetry has moved away from abstract toward concrete content—a trend that no doubt has something to do with the movement toward primordial cognition during inspiration. Poetic vocabulary tends, however, not to move strongly toward abstract content during periods of stylistic change, when words are being added to and deleted from that vocabulary. Generally abstract words are dropped and concrete ones added—a tendency that may have to do with the principle of least effort. Statements about abstract concepts rule out a large number of other potential statements. Statements about concrete objects do not. A wise poet uses concrete words, which do not foreclose statements he or she may need in the future.

Just as in modern British and French poetry, emotional content has declined with time in American poetry, the correlation with period being −.79. In other words, across time, American poets have been less and less concerned with emotions (see figure 5.4). As I have mentioned before, the notion that poetry is concerned with human emotions is extremely misleading if it is not qualified. Poetry used to be focused on emotions, but

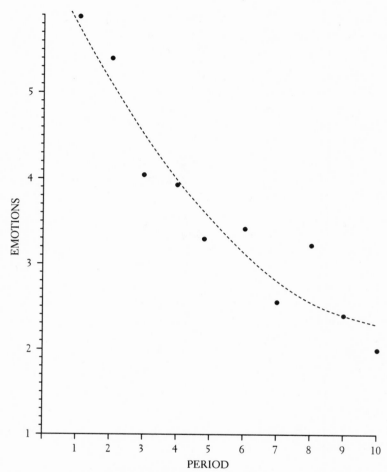

Figure 5.4   The average percentage of words referring to emotions in texts from fifty-one American poets born in ten consecutive twenty-year periods from 1750 through 1949. With the passage of time, American poets have become ever less concerned with emotions.

that was several hundred years ago. A reader may go to poetry to find out about emotion recollected in tranquillity or some such thing. If he goes to modern poetry with such a goal, he will be disappointed unless he misreads the verse. In period 1 (1750–69), 5.87 percent of poetic words are categorized as emotional. By period 10 (1930–49), the proportion has fallen to 1.96 percent—about the same amount of emotional content as can be found on the front page of the *New York Times.*

Applying the Evolutionary Theory

To see how much of the overall variability in poetic language the evolutionary theory accounts for, I followed the same procedures that were used for French and English poetry. I first intercorrelated the poets' profiles on the Harvard III categories to measure their relative similarity. Then, through multidimensional scaling, I found that four dimensions accounted for 94 percent of the variation among the poets. Correlating these dimensions with the content categories suggests that the dimensions are getting at lyric, narrative, and two sorts of emotional modes. We can account for 25 percent of variation in this space with our theoretical variables—a good bit less than the figure for French and British poetry. One reason for this discrepancy may be that the American series contains more minor poets—who may not really have a good sense of tradition— than do the French and British series. They may be perfectly fine poets, but their concerns may be tangential to those of poets writing in the focal American tradition. In fact, if we examine only the four most eminent poets for each period, 43 percent of the similarity among them can be accounted for by the theoretical variables—about the same figure as for French and British poetry.

Specific Trends in Poetic Language

To make sure that these trends are specific to poetic language, I studied trends in the content of stories on the front page of the *New York Times* from 1855 through 1985. Twelve samples—one for a randomly selected day of each month—were drawn for every tenth year beginning in 1855. About the first 20 lines from the upper right-hand column were used for each of the 168 samples, to give a total sample of 22,700 words. Analysis of this corpus shows that 2.12 percent of these words have to do with emotion. This figure has shown no temporal trends. The average value for primordial content is -2.6. Analysis of variance shows that primordial content has not significantly varied across periods. The Composite Variability Index and Incongruous Juxtapositions do not show significant inter-period variation either. Concreteness of vocabulary shows no historical trends at all.

Poetry *Magazine*

The magazine *Poetry* was founded in 1912 by Harriet Monroe and continues to be published today. Virtually all of the poets in our sample who were born in recent periods have published some of their work there. Though *Poetry* is selective in its acceptance policies, the preponderance of its material is not by extremely eminent poets. It could not be otherwise, since a journal publishing only the works of the most eminent poets would not have enough to fill its pages. I looked at trends in the texts published in *Poetry* magazine to get an idea of the extent that the evolutionary theory applies to poets in general as opposed to eminent poets.

Poetry magazine does not give a random sample of all poetry written in America, but we have to draw the line somewhere. Virtually everyone in America has at one time or another written some poetry if only to fulfill a classroom assignment. In a sense, the evolutionary theory is relevant to this vast amount of poetry. Almost all of it has become "extinct" early in the selection process, the author having rejected it as displeasing or uninteresting. Published poetry has passed not only this selection criterion but has also been selected by at least one editor. The majority of published poetry fails, however, to survive later selection: that is, it is rejected by other poets, critics, and readers in general. While the editors of *Poetry* are more exacting in their choices than the editors of many lesser known little magazines, the texts published in it should give us an idea of the workings of literary evolution at a fairly early stage in the selection process.

For every fifth year from 1915 to 1985, I selected ten pages from the magazine at random and analyzed the first sixteen lines—or a bit more if the sixteenth line did not end with a phrase delimiter; these 150 samples from fifteen time periods totaled 16,550 words altogether. The Composite Variability Index shows a marginally significant correlation of .14 with time. It does tend to increase, but there is clear variability. If we get rid of this variability and examine the trend in means for each period, the correlation is much higher—.66—and clearly significant. One of the reasons the trend in the Composite Variability Index is not stronger is that the poets in the sample have emphasized some of its components and de-emphasized others. Returning to our total sample of 150 texts, we find that Polarity has decreased significantly with time (correlation −.22). Authors have moved away from trying to produce an impact with striking words to understatement. On the other hand, they are also using longer and rarer words. The correlation between time and the hapax legomena percentage, or words that occur only once in a document, is .20; while that between time and word length is .23.

An analysis of variance of primordial content shows significant inter-period differences (see figure 5.5). Interperiod differences account for only 18 percent of overall variation among the 150 texts. Even the mean values shown in the figure are rather noisy. By "filtering" out some of this noise with the two-period moving average, also shown in the figure, we find what looks like three styles—the first culminating in the 1930s, the second in the 1950s, and the final one still under way. This trend can be partially accounted for by significant autocorrelations at lags of both one and two periods.

There is some similarity between the pattern of primordial content in *Poetry* and that in the sample of eminent poets, but the differences are more striking. The general trend for the eminent poets in periods 7 to 10 is sharply upward; the trend for the *Poetry* texts downward. For 1985, there is 6.6 percent primordial content. For the poets born in period 10, the average amount of primordial content is 14.03 percent. Whether the texts in *Poetry* indicate that their authors are on the wrong track, or ushering in a massive style change, it is too early to say. If British poetry is any guide, it would seem that American poetry is certainly due for a stylistic change fairly soon. After all, the eminent poets seem to be working out the possibilities of a stylistic change that in one sense began with the generation of Ezra Pound but in another really began long before with Emerson. If our period 10 does mark a peak in primordial content, the peak-to-peak time (period 3 to period 10) for American poetry will be around 140 years. In the British sample, peak-to-peak times were usually 60 to 80 years and never more than 100 years. Thus, it is probably a fairly safe bet that a major stylistic change is upon us.

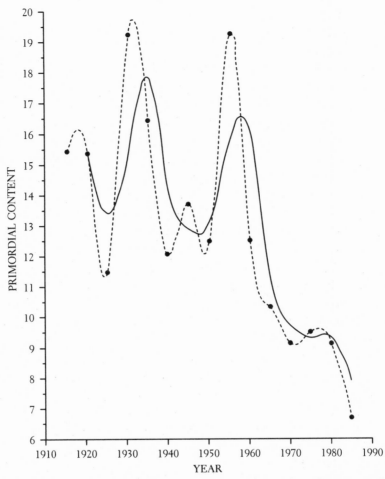

Figure 5.5   The average amount of primordial content in texts from *Poetry* magazine for every fifth year from 1915 through 1985. The solid line shows a two-point moving average that highlights the main trend in primordial content.

SHORT STORIES

Let us up the stakes again and test the robustness of the evolutionary theory on historical trends in short stories. Writers of fiction are more dependent upon an external audience than are poets. Since for all practi-

cal purposes you can't make money writing poetry, the poet has considerable freedom: nothing he or she writes is going to make money, so there
is no sense in trying. Unfortunately, the case is different with fiction. You
can make money with it, but only if a lot of people like it. Publishing firms
publish poetry for prestige, but they want to make a profit with fiction.
They resist publishing fiction that no one will buy. This situation puts
something of a non-evolutionary pressure on the writer. Even worse, the
writer may want to make money and thus write more for an external
audience and less for other artists. Of course, the external audience
habituates and wants novelty. However, it must habituate more slowly
than artists because it is exposed less frequently to literature than they.
The real problem with the external audience is that it may place all sorts
of non-aesthetic pressures on literature. If the audience takes a puritanical
turn, it won't read pornography. If it gets obsessed with abolishing slavery,
it wants Simon Legree stories. If the audience's desires get really extreme,
the environment will be distinctly unfavorable to aesthetic evolution. To
use a biological analogy, sexual selection can proceed only in a benign
environment. In an environment with a lot of predators, birds of paradise
could not have evolved, for their brilliant plumage would have attracted
those predators.

To find out whether an external audience has prevented or distorted
aesthetic evolution in the case of short stories, we divided the time span
from 1820 to 1989 into consecutive ten-year periods. Five (three for
earlier decades) American stories were selected for each decade. Stories
were selected from several anthologies (Foley 1965, 1975; Jessup 1923;
Patten 1905; and *The Best American Short Stories* 1970–85) in the order
listed until the requisite number for a decade had been obtained. If more
than the required number of stories was available, selection was random.
Only one story by any one author was included in the sample. If possible,
stories longer than thirty pages were not used. For the periods 1970–79
and 1980–89, the five authors with the most anthologized stories in *The
Best American Short Stories* were determined. (For the last period, only
the period 1980–85 was used because the study was done in 1986.) Then
one story by each was selected at random. (Details are given in Martindale
and Keeley (1988) and Martindale and Martindale 1988b.) The stories are
listed in table 5.2.

Five approximately 250-word samples were selected from each story.

TABLE 5.2
American Short Stories (1820–1985)

Period	Author	Story
1820–29	Washington Irving	"Rip van Winkle"
	William Austin	"Peter Rugg, the Missing Man"
	William Cullen Bryant	"The Indian Spring"*
1830–39	Nathaniel Hawthorne	"The Grey Champion"
	James Hall	"The Seventh Son"
	Nathaniel Parker Willis	"The Lunatic's Skate"*
1840–49	Thomas Bangs Thorpe	"The Big Bear of Arkansas"*
	Edgar Allan Poe	"The Cask of Amontillado"
	William Gilmore Simms	"Those Old Lunes! or Which Is the Madman?"
1850–59	Herman Melville	"The Town-Ho's Story"*
	Frederick J. O'Brien	"The Diamond Lens"
	Harriet Prescott Spofford	"In a Cellar"
1860–69	Bret Harte	"Tennessee's Partner"*
	Edward Everett Hale	"The Man Without a Country"
	Mark Twain	"The Celebrated Jumping Frog of Calaveras County"
1870–79	Harriet Beecher Stowe	"Captain Kidd's Money"*
	Thomas Bailey Aldrich	"Marjorie Daw"
	Bayard Taylor	"Twin-Love"
	Edward Page Mitchell	"The Tachypomp"
	George Washington Cable	"Posson Jane"
1880–89	Frank Stockton	"The Lady or the Tiger?"*
	Charles Egbert Craddock†	"Over on T'Other Mounting"
	Joel Chandler Harris	"Trouble on Lost Mountain"
	Constance Fenimore Woolson	"The South Devil"
	James Lane Allen	"The White Cowl"
1890–99	Hamlin Garland	"The Return of a Private"
	Henry James	"The Real Thing"
	Sarah Orne Jewett	"The Courting of Sister Wisbey"
	Ambrose Bierce	"One of the Missing"*
	Stephen Crane	"The Open Boat"
1900–1909	O. Henry	"The Furnished Room"
	Jack London	"To Build a Fire"
	Owen Wister	"Extra Dry"*
	Julian Hawthorne	"Lovers in Heaven"
	Silas Weir Mitchell	"The Mind-Reader"
1910–19	Sherwood Anderson	"The Strength of God and the Teacher"
	Elsie Singmaster	"The Survivors"
	Theodore Dreiser	"The Lost Phoebe"
	Irvin S. Cobb	"The Belled Buzzard"*
	Wilbur Daniel Steele	"The Woman at Seven Brothers"
1920–29	Ernest Hemingway	"My Old Man"
	Ring Lardner	"Haircut"*
	Willa Cather	"Double Birthday"
	Dorothy Parker	"A Telephone Call"
	Charles Caldwell Dobie	"All or Nothing"

TABLE 5.2 *(Continued)*

Period	Author	Story
1930–39	Erskine Caldwell	"Masses of Men"*
	William Saroyan	"The Daring Young Man on the Flying Trapeze"
	John Steinbeck	"The Leader of the People"
	Zora Neale Hurston	"The Gilded Six-Bits"
	Stephen Vincent Benét	"A Tooth for Paul Revere"
1940–49	Carson McCullers	"The Ballad of the Sad Café"
	Shirley Jackson	"The Lottery"
	James Thurber	"The Catbird Seat"*
	William Maxwell	"The Patterns of Love"
	Peter Taylor	"Rain in the Heart"
1950–59	Ray Bradbury	"February 1999: Ylla"*
	John Cheever	"The Country Husband"
	Jack Kerouac	"The Mexican Girl"
	Flannery O'Connor	"A Good Man Is Hard to Find"
	Frank Butler	"To the Wilderness I Wander"
1960–69	Joyce Carol Oates	"Where Are You Going, Where Have You Been?"
	James Baldwin	"Tell Me How Long the Train's Been Gone"
	John Updike	"Pigeon Feathers"
	Kay Boyle	"Seven Say You Can Hear Corn Grow"*
	William Eastlake	"A Long Day's Dying"
1970–79	Cynthia Ozick	"Yiddish in America"
	Ward Just	"Burns"
	Donald Barthelme	"The New Music"*
	John William Corrington	"The Actes and Monuments"
	Susan Minot	"The Tide and Isaac Bates"
1980–85	Carl Johnson	"Lemon Tree"
	Ursula LeGuin	"The Professor's Houses"
	William Morris	"Fellow-Creatures"
	Sharon Sheehe Stark	"The Johnstown Polka"
	Norman Rush	"Instruments of Seduction"*

*For the significance of the asterisks in this table, see page 174.
†Pseudonym for Mary Noailles Murfree.

The samples averaged somewhat longer than 250 words, because each sample was terminated at the first end-of-phrase delimiter (period, colon, or semicolon) at or after 250 words. For each story, the first and last 250 words were used. The other three samples were selected so that their midpoints were at three equally spaced intervals between the first and last samples. The average number of words in each of the seventy-five story samples was 1,308. The total sample was composed of 100,740 words.

Arousal Potential

According to the evolutionary theory, arousal potential should increase monotonically across time. The Composite Variability Index, based upon within-sentence variability, works well with poetry but may not be the best measure for prose. The writer of prose may seek to increase arousal potential by manipulation of units larger than the sentence. For example, the sequence of the surface structure of narratives may become increasingly disordered vis-à-vis the deep structure. It is conventional to differentiate the sequence of events in the narrative as told—what Ludomir Doležel (1972) called the *fabula sequence*—from the sequence of events as they would actually have occurred (the *plot sequence*). Across time, writers may tend more to write stories where the plot sequence does not coincide with the fabula sequence, or it may be more difficult to infer deep structure from surface structure. For the American stories, the Composite Variability Index varies significantly across periods—but not the way it is supposed to. As may be seen in figure 5.6, the index decreases throughout the nineteenth century and only then begins to increase. Over all, the Composite Variability Index shows a significant U-shaped pattern. While it has increased significantly over the twentieth century, it decreased insignificantly throughout the nineteenth century.

It makes sense to argue that twentieth-century writers have sought to increase the arousal potential of their stories by manipulating surface-structure stylistic features: they write in a poetic style. Arousal potential comes from the way in which a story is told rather than from what happens in it. Nineteenth-century writers tended to write in a prosaic style in which they sought to increase arousal potential in other ways. Many nineteenth-century stories use local color, emphasizing exotic locations, characters, and dialects. Action and plot were more important in producing an impact than was surface structure. As long as arousal potential could have been sufficiently increased in this way, surface structure devices could have been allowed to simplify. My contention is that net arousal potential probably did not decrease across the course of the nineteenth century. Declines in the Composite Variability Index were more than offset by increases in other, unmeasured, sources of arousal potential. Hypothetically, writers follow a least-effort principle in trying to increase arousal potential. They

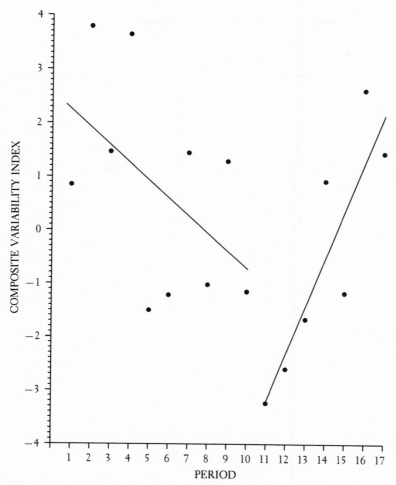

Figure 5.6   The mean values of the Composite Variability Index for seventy-five American short stories written in the seventeen decades between 1820 and 1985. As shown by the trend lines, the index declined from the 1820s to the 1910s and rose from the 1920s to the 1980s.

do not increase arousal potential maximally but only to the minimum amount necessary to satisfy themselves and their readers.

In order to test this assertion, we asked naïve readers to perform a subjective content analysis getting at other sources of arousal potential. The psychologists William Brewer and Keisuke Ohtsuka (1988) had judges read and rate a subset of the sample of twentieth-century short stories.

Their finding that rated suspense and curiosity increased across the century suggests an increase in arousal potential. Later writers apparently increased the arousal potential of their narratives by increasing suspense and ambiguity. Since Brewer and Ohtsuka's results are in conformity with predictions concerning a historical increase in arousal potential made by the evolutionary theory, we obtained ratings of a larger set of stories using some of their measures. Because of the amount of time involved in the study, only some of these stories could be included. For each of the seventeen periods, the story closest to ten pages in length was selected (denoted by asterisks in table 5.2). Each story was divided into five approximately equal parts. After reading each part, subjects were asked to fill out four 7-point rating scales (taken from Brewer and Ohtsuka 1988) indicating the amount of Suspense, Curiosity about the Past, Curiosity about the Future, and Surprise they felt at that moment. Suspense was measured by the question "At this point, to what extent do you now feel anticipation, excitement, or anxiety about events yet to come in the passage?"; curiosity about the past, by "At this point, to what extent do you now want to learn more about past events (events that already occurred in the passage up to this point, or before the passage began)?"; curiosity about the future, by "At this point, to what extent do you want to learn more about events yet to come in the passage?"; and surprise, by "In the portion just read, to what extent did you feel surprised by any information or events in the passage?" Forty male undergraduates took part in the study. Each read only one of the stories. Each story was rated by either two or three subjects.

Rated suspensefulness of the stories increased linearly across time ($r = .27$), whereas rated curiosity and surprisingness showed no trends. As for the five story segments, suspense following the first and last segment increased across time ($r = .39$, and $r = .30$, respectively). Suspense following the three middle segments showed no statistically significant temporal trends ($r = .10$, $- .04$, and $.06$). Apparently authors attempted to increase the arousal potential of the most salient or memorable parts of their stories—beginning and end—and neglected the less salient middle segments. A possible reason for this tendency is that the same amount of suspense should produce more arousal at more salient points in a narrative. If this be the case, then these findings are consistent with the least-effort hypothesis. We might also invoke the least-effort hypothesis as an explanation for why suspense but not curiosity or surprise increased across time. Induction of curiosity or surprise are active processes; an author has to do something to bring them about. On the other hand, creation of suspense is a passive endeavor: to produce suspense, the author *withholds* something from the reader; rather than telling something, one tells nothing. Because doing nothing is easier than doing something, the least-effort principle dictates that this route will be chosen.

Primordial Content

According to the evolutionary theory, primordial content should exhibit an oscillating trend across time (see figure 5.7). Interperiod differences are statistically significant. We used only the direct measures of primordial content (that is, we didn't subtract the indirect measures) since these produced a more clearcut trend. According to the evolutionary theory, literary change is in large part an autoregressive process: at any given time, the value of primordial content is determined more by its past values rather than by past or present extraliterary forces. To test this idea, an autoregressive analysis of trends in primordial content was performed: it revealed that primordial content in a given period is significantly related to primordial content in the prior two periods. The best prediction equation, which yields a significant fit with observed values accounting for 53 percent of the variance, is

$$PC_t = -.71 \ PC_{t-1} + .55 \ PC_{t-2}.$$

The pattern of autocorrelations is consistent with the hypothesis that primordial content is autoregressive rather than being due to extraliterary shocks (Gottman 1981).

The increase and decline in primordial content coincide with stylistic shifts in American fiction. Primordial content begins its decline at the beginning of the series. This decline coincides with a change from an imitation European romantic or gothic style to the native American "local color" school of the nineteenth century. Once the style is fully in effect, primordial content begins to rise. In the 1920s, the decline in primary-process content coincides with the introduction of a new, less exotic style. Settings and, especially, characters in this new style are not exotic. There is a focus on characters' thoughts and feelings as opposed to their behav-

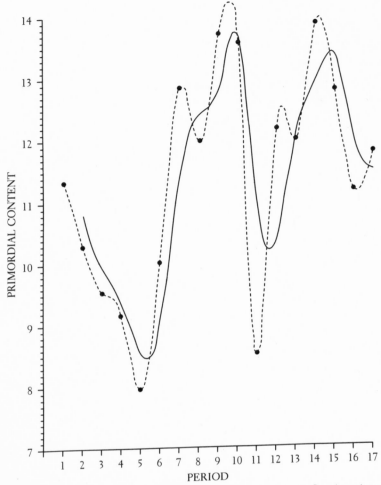

Figure 5.7 The mean percentage of primordial content in seventy-five American short stories written in the seventeen decades between 1820 and 1989. The solid line shows a two-decade moving average.

ior. The way in which a story is told becomes at least as important as what happens in it. The decline in primordial content across the last several decades apparently coincides with the introduction of a contemporary style marked by introduction of characters somewhat more exotic, deviant, or nonconforming and even more introspective than was the case with the earlier twentieth-century style.

To find out how much of the total variability in the short stories could be accounted for by the evolutionary theory, I tested them as I had poetry (see pages 111—15): that is, applied the Harvard III Dictionary and carried out multidimensional scaling. The theoretical variables—primordial content and the Composite Variability Index—accounted for 19.2 percent of the variation in the multidimensional space. This is less than the amount of variance accounted for by these variables in the case of poetry. This is in line with the contention that writers of short stories are less autonomous than are poets.

POPULAR MUSIC LYRICS

The field of popular music lyrics will, I think, stretch the evolutionary theory. I imagine that the writers and performers of popular music do operate under evolutionary pressures. However, if we study best-selling lyrics, we are by definition giving over selection of our sample to a mass audience that may be making its selections for many reasons other than habituation. That habituation does play some role is suggested by the fact that popular music does not stay popular for long. Rather, a song climbs to the top of the charts, stays there awhile, and then loses its appeal.

For the period under consideration, popular music historians argue that there are several major stylistic changes (Belz 1969; Gillett 1972). The first and most important is the emergence of rock 'n roll around 1951 to 1953. It quickly became dominant and lasted until the end of the 1950s. In the late 1950's, a variety of stylistic innovations were introduced, which culminated around 1960 in "psychedelic" rock—as typified by the Beatles and the Rolling Stones. If the historians are correct, we would expect primordial cognition to decline from 1950 until around 1952 or 1953, increase until around 1960, decline, and then begin to increase again. Across the entire epoch, we would predict an increase in arousal potential.

Cynthia Kaplan (1975) conducted an extensive study of the top ten popular songs for each of the years from 1950 through 1972. For each year, this psychologist selected the ten best-selling single records from listings given in *Cash Box* magazine. Instrumentals—that is, songs with no lyrics—were not used. The lyrics as sung were put into computer readable

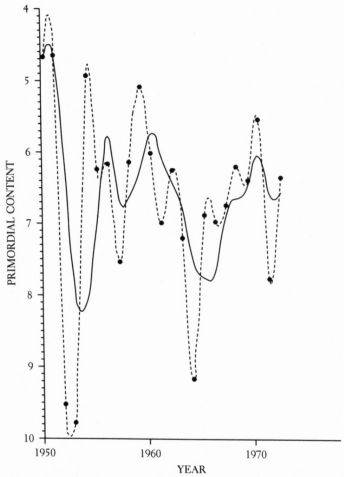

Figure 5.8 The mean yearly amount of primordial content in 230 American popular music lyrics written between 1950 and 1972. The solid line shows the three-year moving average. (Smaller numbers indicate *greater* amounts of primordial content.)

form. Thus, for example, no matter how many times a chorus was repeated, it was included that many times—to produce a sample of 48,155 words. The top-selling songs for the years 1950 to 1972 are in table 5.3.

The measure of incongruous juxtapositions used with French and American poetry increased significantly across time. Kaplan used the categories tapping conceptual content as an inverse measure of primordial

TABLE 5.3
American Popular Songs (1950–72)

1950	Gordon Jenkins	"Goodnight Irene"
1951	Patti Page	"Tennessee Waltz"
1952	Johnny Ray	"Cry"
1953	Percy Faith	"Song from Moulin Rouge"
1954	Kitty Kallen	"Little Things Mean a Lot"
1955	Bill Haley and the Comets	"Rock Around the Clock"
1956	Elvis Presley	"Don't Be Cruel"
1957	Debbie Reynolds	"Tammy"
1958	Tommy Edwards	"It's All in the Game"
1959	Bobby Darin	"Mack the Knife"
1960	Percy Faith	Theme from *A Summer Place*
1961	Shirelles	"Will You Love Me Tomorrow?"
1962	Chubby Checker	"The Twist"
1963	Chubby Checker	"Limbo Rock"
1964	Beatles	"I Want to Hold Your Hand"
1965	Supremes	"Back in My Arms"
1966	Barry Sadler	"Ballad of the Green Berets"
1967	Box Tops	"The Letter"
1968	Beatles	"Hey Jude"
1969	Archies	"Sugar"
1970	Norman Greenbaum	"Spirit in the Sky"
1971	Three Dog Night	"Joy to the World"
1972	Don McLean	"American Pie"

content. The direct measures of primordial content show similar trends but not as strongly. Analysis of variance showed highly significant variation in Kaplan's inverse measure of primordial content across years. Values for successive years are shown in figure 5.8.

Because the data are quite noisy, a three-year moving average is also shown in the figure.

As can be seen, primordial content did decrease from 1950–51 to 1952–53 as predicted. Although there are fluctuations, there was a significant increase in primordial content from 1952–53 to 1958–59. After the latter years, a period of stylistic change lasted until 1964–65; it was accompanied by a significant decrease in primordial content. Once the style was established, primordial content began to increase as the possibilities of the style were exploited. Thus, the results do in general conform with theoretical expectations.

CHAPTER 6

Taking the Measure of the
Visual Arts and Music

I N this chapter, I shall show how the evolutionary theory applies to the visual arts and music. After dealing with the history of British, French, Italian, and American painting, I shall turn to several aspects of the development of gothic architecture, which has often been seen as a prime example of the working out of evolutionary forces of the sort I have been discussing. To counter the belief that need for novelty is a modern force important only in Western art, I also examine ancient and non-Western art: Greek vases, Egyptian painting, pre-Columbian sculpture, and Japanese prints. The evolutionary theory also helps us, as I argue next, to understand the history of music. I end with a stroll through some New England graveyards, where we see that evolutionary forces guide the hand even of those who carve monuments to the dead.

Although the theory applies to all of the arts as well as to literature, testing it on paintings requires different measures of arousal potential and primordial content. After Berlyne (1974) and his colleagues showed that arousal potential can be measured by rating scales (as in Simple versus Complex, Passive versus Active), I found that primordial content can also be measured by them (as in Natural versus Unnatural, Representational versus Nonrepresentational). In a study I did with Michael Ross and Ivan Miller (1985), one group of people rated a set of paintings on such scales, whereas another group wrote stories about the same paintings. The stories were then content-analyzed with the same dictionary used to measure primordial content in poetry. There were high correlations between primordial content in the stories and the degree to which the paintings used to elicit these stories were rated as being unnatural, nonrepresentational, nonphotographic, and meaningless.

EUROPEAN PAINTING

European painting has become less representative and realistic across the last several centuries—a movement we can interpret as being toward primordial content. Was this movement in the service of increasing arousal potential? Was it accompanied by the theoretically predicted oscillations in primordial content? The best way of answering these questions is by asking naïve and impartial observers. We do not want the preconceived opinions of art critics if our goal is to test the evolutionary theory. While few people today are completely naïve about the history of painting, the amazing naïveté of the average undergraduate is fortunate for my purposes—if not for the greater scheme of things.

British and French Painting

For my study of British and French painting, I selected reproductions in an objective manner, dividing the epoch from 1590 to 1929 into seventeen consecutive twenty-year periods. The three most eminent French and British painters born during each period were selected by going through a set of reference works. Eminence was determined in several steps. First, the number of centimeters Sir John Rothenstein (1970) devoted to each artist was tabulated. An artist was counted as being British or French if he or she was born in the country or worked there for a prolonged period. Rothenstein yielded a sufficient number of artists for almost all of the French periods and for most of the British periods. This list was supplemented, if necessary, by consulting a series of other reference works in a predetermined order (for details, see Martindale 1989). Eminence was assigned in descending order according to which of the books a name appeared in. After painters had been selected, the goal was to find a color reproduction of a painting containing people (but not a portrait) by each of the painters. For painters not working in representative styles, this constraint was not imposed. Reproductions were taken from another set of standard sources, again searched in a predetermined order. The painters included in the study are listed in tables 6.1 and 6.2. As may be inferred from table 6.1, some of the early British painters were not native-born. The relative lack of constraint on subject matter puts the evolutionary theory to a severe test: that is, to use a biological analogy, we are studying a series belonging rather to the same artistic genus or family than to the same species. It is, of course, at the level of the species that evolution occurs.

Eight 7-point rating scales were used. Two ("Like" versus "Dislike" and "Interesting" versus "Uninteresting"), though not of primary relevance to testing the evolutionary theory, were included in this and most of the other studies reported in this chapter merely because I initially told

TABLE 6.1
British Painters (1590–1929)

Period	Painters
1 1590–1609	Robert Walker, Cornelius Johnson, Sir Anthony van Dyck
2 1610–29	Sir Peter Lely, William Dobson, John Michael Wright
3 1630–49	Sir Godfrey Kneller, Mary Beale, Willem van de Velde II
4 1650–69	Michael Dahl, Sebastiano Ricci, Antonio Bellucci
5 1670–89	Sir James Thornhill, Marco Ricci, Giovanni Antonio Pellegrini
6 1690–1709	William Hogarth, Joseph Highmore, Francis Hayman
7 1710–29	Sir Joshua Reynolds, Thomas Gainsborough, Richard Wilson
8 1730–49	Benjamin West, John Singleton Copley, Henry Fuseli
9 1750–69	William Blake, Sir Thomas Lawrence, Sir Henry Raeburn
10 1770–89	Joseph Turner, John Constable, David Cox
11 1790–1809	Richard Bonington, Samuel Palmer, Edward Calvert
12 1810–29	Dante Gabriel Rossetti, Sir John Everett Millais, Ford Madox Brown
13 1830–49	James Whistler, Edward Burne-Jones, Arthur Hughes
14 1850–69	Walter Sickert, Sir John Lavery, Philip Wilson Steer
15 1870–89	Sir Jacob Epstein, Percy Wyndham Lewis, Spencer Frederick Gore
16 1890–1909	Ben Nicholson, Victor Pasmore, Francis Bacon
17 1910–29	Alan Davie, Richard Hamilton, Leon Kossoff

TABLE 6.2
French Painters (1590–1929)

Period	Painters
1 1590–1609	Nicolas Poussin, Claude Lorrain, Georges de La Tour
2 1610–29	Sébastien Bourdon, Jacques Courtois, Charles Lebrun
3 1630–49	Joseph Parrocel, Charles de La Fosse, Jean Baptiste Jouvenet
4 1650–69	Nicolas de Largillière, Antoine Coypel, Alexandre-François Desportes
5 1670–89	Jean-Antoine Watteau, Jean-François de Troy, Jean-Marc Nattier
6 1690–1709	François Boucher, Jean-Baptiste-Siméon Chardin, Jean-Baptiste Pater
7 1710–29	Jean-Baptiste Greuze, Gabriel François Doyen, Louis Carmontelle
8 1730–49	Jacques-Louis David, Jean-Honoré Fragonard, Hubert Robert
9 1750–69	Pierre-Paul Prud'hon, Anne-Louis Girodet-Trioson, Jean-Baptiste Isabey
10 1770–89	Jean-Auguste-Dominique Ingres, Antoine-Jean Gros, François Gérard
11 1790–1809	Eugène Delacroix, Camille Corot, Honoré Daumier
12 1810–29	Gustave Courbet, Jean-François Millet, Pierre-Cécile Puvis de Chavannes
13 1830–49	Paul Cézanne, Paul Gauguin, Edgar Degas
14 1850–69	Georges Seurat, Henri de Toulouse-Lautrec, Henri Matisse
15 1870–89	Pablo Picasso, Georges Braque, Raoul Dufy
16 1890–1909	Jean Dubuffet, Victor de Vasarely, Yves Tanguy
17 1910–29	Alfred Manessier, Nicholas de Staël, Bernard Buffet

subjects that I was interested mainly in their preferences for works of art. Had I told them about the evolutionary theory before they made their ratings, most people would have had a tendency to tell me what they thought I wanted.

Probably the main determinant of arousal potential is the novelty evoked when a painting is first exhibited—an experience that cannot be measured by present-day raters. Impressionism, for example, is no longer shocking and novel, but familiar. On the basis of past research (Berlyne 1974), two scales—Disorderly versus Orderly and Tense versus Relaxed— were used as measures of arousal potential. On the basis of Martindale, Ross, and Miller's (1985) findings, four scales were used as measures of primordial content: Not Representative of Reality versus Representative of Reality, Not Photographic versus Photographic, Unnatural versus Natural, and Otherworldly versus This World.

Seventy-seven undergraduate women were tested in groups of thirty-one, twenty-five, and twenty-one each. Each group was shown—in a random order—one French and one English slide from each of the seventeen periods. Each slide was shown for ten seconds in a dark room. Then, dim lights were turned on, and with the slide still in view, thirty-five seconds were allowed for ratings.

I used a statistical procedure to see how well subjects agreed in these ratings. If subjects don't agree in their ratings, the ratings aren't good for much. If they do agree, one can average across subjects and get a single rating for each painting. That makes subsequent analyses a lot easier. Agreement on all rating scales and the composite scores, primordial content and arousal potential, was far greater than we would expect by chance for all three groups. The composite scores were computed by adding together the relevant scales previously described. An average score collapsing across subjects was computed for each painting for use in further analyses.

An analysis of variance of arousal potential scores showed significant differences across periods. Forty-one percent of variation in scores is due to interperiod differences, leaving 59 percent of the variance attributable to intraperiod differences. This intraperiod variation may be attributed to differences in subject matter; individual differences among painters due to personality, temperament, social class, and so on; and a fair amount of random error. Freely granting that more variance is due to these factors than to evolutionary factors, let us collapse across artists and analyze mean scores for each period.

Arousal potential shows an accelerating uptrend across time that can be described by exponential functions. For the British series,

$$AP = 6.54 \, e^{.00006 \times 1.7t},$$

where e is the base of the natural logarithms, and t is period. With this equation, we can account for 62 percent of the variance among means. For the French series, the equation

$$AP = 6.63 \, e^{.00006 \times 1.7t}$$

accounts for 48 percent of the variation. Though rate of change in arousal potential has probably accelerated across time, the present results may overstate the case. A more diverse set of measures might not show such extreme acceleration. Be that as it may, the trend in arousal potential is as predicted by the evolutionary theory.

To test the predictions of the evolutionary theory, a mean primordial content score for each period was obtained. For both series, the theory predicts a historical increase in primordial content with superimposed oscillations (see figures 6.1 and 6.2). As the graphs suggest, statistical

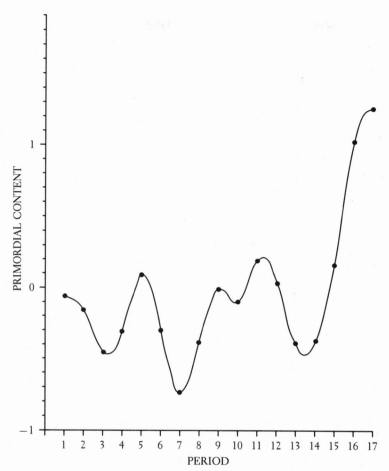

Figure 6.1 The average amount of primordial content (two-period moving averages) in fifty-one British paintings by painters born in seventeen successive twenty-year periods from 1590 through 1929.

analyses showed that there was a statistically significant increase in primordial content across time.

Autoregressive analyses of the residuals from this increasing trend showed that primordial content in two prior periods (PC_{t-1} and PC_{t-2}) significantly affect primordial content in a given period (PC_t). These autocorrelations produce the oscillations in figures 6.1 and 6.2. For the French series, the oscillations in primordial content correspond nicely

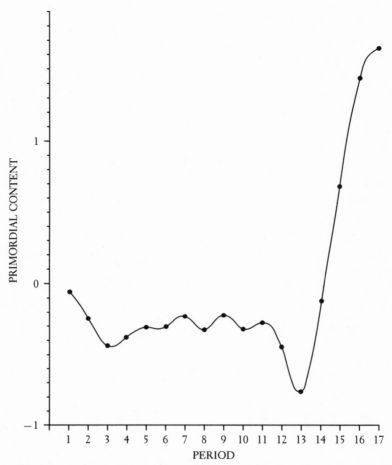

Figure 6.2 The average amount of primordial content (two-period moving averages) in fifty-one French paintings by painters born in seventeen successive twenty-year periods from 1590 through 1929.

with successive styles. The U-shaped trend from periods 2 to 7 corresponds with the baroque-rococo style; that from periods 7 to 9, with neoclassicism; that from 9 to 10, with romanticism; and that from 11 to 17 with impressionism-expressionism. For the British series, periods 2 to 5 correspond to the imported baroque style, and periods 6 to 11 with picturesque-romantic. The trend from period 12 to period 17 amalgamates an early academic-preraphaelite-impressionist style with an expressionist continuation.

Putting the autoregressive results together with the temporal increase, I obtained the following equation for the British series,

$$PC_t = .116 - .15t + .02t^2 + .65PC_{t-1} - .94PC_{t-2},$$

where t stands for "period." The highly significant fit accounts for 86 percent of the variance among the means. The equation for the French series,

$$PC_t = .33 - .17t + .01t^2 + 1.22PC_{t-1} - .95PC_{t-2},$$

is also highly significant and accounts for 93 percent of the variation. If we ascribe these results to forces specified by the evolutionary theory, they indicate that there is little left to explain: for the British series, 14 percent of the variance remains to be explained; and for the French series, only 7 percent. Since part of this discrepancy must certainly be error variance, it is likely that the effect of extra-artistic forces on British and French painting is negligible so far as primordial content is concerned. As indicated before, the law of parsimony dictates that variance be allocated to intrinsic causes before extrinsic causes are considered.

Italian Painting

Italian paintings produced between the fourteenth and the eighteenth century have also been studied (Martindale 1986a). The reasons for this choice were both theoretical and practical. On the theoretical level, where Berlyne (1971) and Gombrich (1979) have argued that pressure for novelty, and the evolutionary trends it induces, are of relatively recent origin, I wanted to show that this is not the case. On the practical level, Italian painting across the time span studied constitutes—despite some regional differences—a long and uninterrupted tradition, and large numbers of reproductions of these paintings are readily available. The theory is meant to apply only to artists working within the same tradition. Artists are theoretically in competition only with those they know and see as being their predecessors, not with all prior artists.

The epoch from 1330 to 1729 was divided into twenty consecutive twenty-year periods. For each period, the goal was to select the four most eminent Italian painters born during the period. Eminence was defined as the number of centimeters devoted to the painter in the biographical listings given by Sylvie Beguin and colleagues (1964), André Chastel (1963), and Frederick Godfrey (1965), in that order (see table 6.3). A color reproduction of a painting containing at least one person or part of a person (but not a portrait) by each painter was located by searching a set of reference works and catalogues in a predetermined order. Sketches, details, reproductions with prominent frames, collaborative works, and works of unproven authorship were excluded. If more than one suitable reproduction was found in the same source, a choice was made at random. If no suitable reproduction could be found, a work by the next most eminent painter born during the period was selected.

Twenty-four 7-point rating scales were used. Only some of these are of interest for our purposes. Because of the large number of paintings to be rated, three groups of subjects were used. Each group rated color slides of all eighty paintings, shown in a random order, on eight of the twenty-four rating scales. The eight rating scales used by each group were also chosen at random from the set of twenty-four scales. Each slide was shown for ten seconds in a darkened classroom. Then the lights were turned on; and with the slide still in view, subjects made their ratings during the next thirty seconds.

After establishing that subjects agreed in their ratings, I obtained a mean score for each painting on each of the variables by collapsing across subjects. The rating scales were subjected to *factor analysis* to see whether the scales were measuring, as hoped, a smaller number of underlying dimensions. Factor analysis, which represents similarities among scales in a multidimensional space, indicated that the scales were really measuring five axes or dimensions. It was clear that two of these factors were, as hoped, getting at the theoretical variables. One factor—referred to as arousal potential—had high loadings on the scales Active, Complex, Tense, and Disorderly. Another—referred to as primordial content—had high loadings on Not Photographic, Not Representative of Reality, Otherworldly, and Unnatural.

Analysis of variance of factor scores was used to test for the predicted trends. Arousal potential exhibited the predicted temporal increase; no significant deviations from this main trend were present (see figure 6.3).

For primordial content, linear, quartic, and cubic trends were all significant (see figure 6.4). Figure 6.4 shows the predicted oscillations. A spec-

TABLE 6.3
Italian Painters (1330–1729)

Period Birth Date	Painters
1. 1330–49	Bartolo di Fredi
	Andrea Vanni
	Spinello Aretino
	Luca di Tommè
2. 1350–69	Gentile da Fabriano
	Gherardo Starnina
	Taddeo di Bartolo
	Jacopo Avanzo
3. 1370–89	Fra Angelico da Fiesole
	Masolino da Panicale
	Stefano da Verona
	Lorenzo Monaco
4. 1390–1409	Paolo Uccello
	Antonio Pisanello
	Tommaso di Masaccio
	Domenico Veneziano
5. 1410–29	Piero della Francesca
	Andrea del Castagno
	Benozzo Gozzoli
	Gentile Bellini
6. 1430–1449	Andrea Mantegna
	Sandro Botticelli
	Giovanni Bellini
	Antonello da Messina
7. 1450–69	Leonardo da Vinci
	Vittore Carpaccio
	Luca Signorelli
	Filippino Lippi
8. 1470–89	Michelangelo Buonarroti
	Titian
	Raphael
	Giorgione
9. 1490–1509	Parmigianino
	Giulio Romano
	Bronzino
	Pontormo
10. 1510–29	Veronese
	Tintoretto
	Jacopo da Bassano
	Giorgio Vasari
11. 1530–49	Francesco Bassano
	Palma Giovane
	Alessandro Allori
	Maso di San Friano
12. 1550–69	Annibale Carracci
	Orazio Gentileschi

TABLE 6.3 *(Continued)*

Period Birth Date	Painters
13. 1570–89	Lodovico Carracci
	Agostino Carracci
	Michelangelo da Carravagio
	Guido Reni
	Carlo Saraceni
	Domenichino
14. 1590–1609	Guercino
	Pietro da Cortona
	Michelangelo Cerquozzi
	Andrea Sacchi
15. 1610–29	Giovanni Castiglione
	Mattia Preti
	Salvator Rosa
	Bernardo Cavallino
16. 1630–49	Luca Giordano
	Andrea Pozzo
	Baciccia
	Elisabetta Sirani
17. 1650–69	Alessandro Magnasco
	Sebastiano Ricci
	Giuseppe Crespi
	Francesco Solimena
18. 1670–89	Giovanni Piazzetta
	Giovanni Pittoni
	Marco Ricci
	Jacopo Amigoni
19. 1690–1709	Giovanni Battista Tiepolo
	Canaletto
	Pietro Longhi
	Giovanni Pannini
20. 1710–29	Francesco Guardi
	Giovanni Domenico Tiepolo
	Bernardo Bellotto
	Francesco Carpella

tral analysis indicates a cycle of about six twenty-year periods. As usual, I tested the evolutionary theory's prediction that the amount of primordial content in a given period is related to that in prior periods. The autoregressive analysis indicated that the best prediction equation for primordial content in period t (PC_t) was

$$PC_t = .40\ PC_{t-1} - .41\ PC_{t-3}.$$

This significant fit accounts for 54 percent of the variation, or a little over

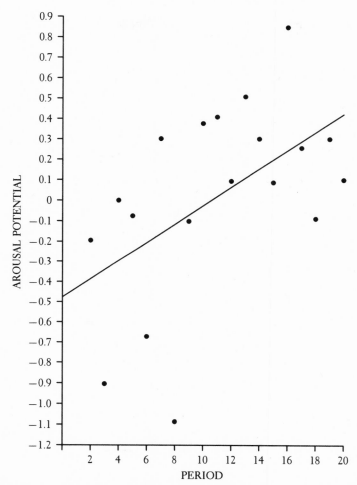

Figure 6.3 The average arousal potential (two-period moving averages) in Italian paintings done by eighty painters born in twenty consecutive twenty-year periods from 1330 through 1729. The historical increase in arousal potential is shown by the best-fitting trend line.

half of the observed interperiod variation in primordial content. The cycles coincide with generally recognized styles: late gothic (periods 1–5), renaissance–mannerist (periods 6–10), baroque (periods 11–17), and rococo (periods 18–20).

As has been found in earlier studies, the oscillations in primordial

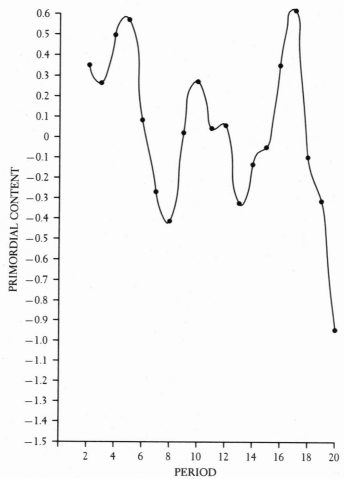

Figure 6.4 The average amount of primordial content (two-period moving averages) in Italian paintings done by eighty painters born in twenty consecutive twenty-year periods from 1330 through 1729.

content in Italian painting are smooth rather than abrupt and jagged—as is consistent with the idea that stylistic change is a gradual rather than an abrupt process. The late gothic style, for example, shades gradually into the renaissance style. It is arbitrary exactly when to start labeling paintings as being in the renaissance style. It seems as if stylistic rules change in an incremental rather than in an all-or-none fashion. If one accepts the idea that primordial content rises once a style is in effect, the present results support the idea that mannerism is the final stage of renaissance style rather than a separate style. Somewhat simplistically, one might say that mannerist painters worked with the general framework of renaissance stylistic rules. However, in order to achieve the requisite increases in arousal potential, they introduced the distortions and bizarre qualities that characterize mannerism. Theoretically, these distortions are reflective of the depth of regression toward primordial cognition to which mannerist painters were pushed in the quest for novelty. Only when further regression was impossible did baroque stylistic innovations begin to be introduced.

AMERICAN PAINTING

I did a study of American painting in which I controlled for genre and subject matter more than I had done with British, French, and Italian painting. The period from 1750 to 1929 was divided into nine consecutive twenty-year periods. I selected from Michael Zellman (1987) color reproductions of paintings by the seven most eminent painters born in each period. Eminence was defined in terms of the highest price paid for an artist's painting between 1975 and 1985. Zellman provides a tabulation of prices for each painter. However crass this way of defining eminence may seem, it provides a sample that is about the same as would be obtained if eminence had been defined in some more discrete way. Permanent expatriates were excluded from the sample, but immigrants who came to America permanently were included. I used only representative paintings with people prominent, excluding landscapes and purely abstract paintings. I took "nonrepresentative" to mean any painting in which the painting's subject wasn't immediately apparent. To control further for content, I also excluded primitive or folk art, paintings with Western or Indian themes, and hunting scenes, each of which seems to be a fairly distinct genre. To get enough paintings for the earlier periods, it was necessary to include portraits, although portrait painting is also a distinct genre (see table 6.4).

I asked twenty-five women undergraduates to rate the paintings on several theoretically relevant scales. The paintings were, of course, shown in a random order. The subjects agreed quite well on their ratings, so I obtained a mean rating for each painting. Ratings of the degree to which a painting was otherworldly, unnatural, unrealistic, and meaningless were added together to get a measure of primordial content. The arousal potential measure was the sum of ratings on the scales Tense, Strong, Complex, and Active.

Analysis of variance indicated that both measures varied significantly across periods. Arousal potential showed a linear increase across periods. There were, as predicted, no significant deviations from this trend. Means for primordial content are shown in figure 6.5. Interperiod differences were accounted for by a significant quartic, or fourth-order, trend, also shown in the figure. We want to find such a trend because the theory predicts the presence of the oscillations that it indicates.

TABLE 6.4
American Painters (1750–1929)

Period and Birth Date	Painters
1. 1750–69	Ralph Earl, William Birch, Gilbert Stuart, John Trumbull, John Brewster Jr., Charles Peale Polk, Ezra Ames
2. 1770–89	Raphaelle Peale, Rembrandt Peale, Washington Allston, John Wesley Jarvis, Zedekiah Belknap, Samuel Lovett Waldo, John Lewis Krimmel
3. 1790–1809	Samuel F. B. Morse, Robert Street, Asher Brown Durand, Henry Inman, John Quidor, Robert W. Weir, William S. Mount
4. 1810–29	George Caleb Bingham, William T. Ranney, David Gilmour Blythe, Arthur F. Tait, Thomas W. Whittredge, Lily Martin Spencer, Eastman Johnson
5. 1830–49	John LaFarge, Archibald M. Willard, Winslow Homer, Thomas Nast, Edward Lamson Henry, Thomas Eakins, William M. Chase
6. 1850–69	Robert F. Blum, Edward Henry Potthast, Maurice B. Prendergast, Childe Hassam, Edmund C. Tarbell, George B. Luks, Alfred H. Maurer
7. 1870–89	William J. Glackens, Charles Webster Hawthorne, Everett Shinn, John D. Graham, George W. Bellows, Edward Hopper, Thomas Hart Benton
8. 1890–1909	Man Ray, Norman Rockwell, Raphael Soyer, Richard Lindner, Willem de Kooning, Arshile Gorky, Fairfield Porter
9. 1910–29	John Koch, Andrew N. Wyeth, George Tooker, Richard Diebenkorn, Larry Rivers, Alex Katz, Ralph Goings

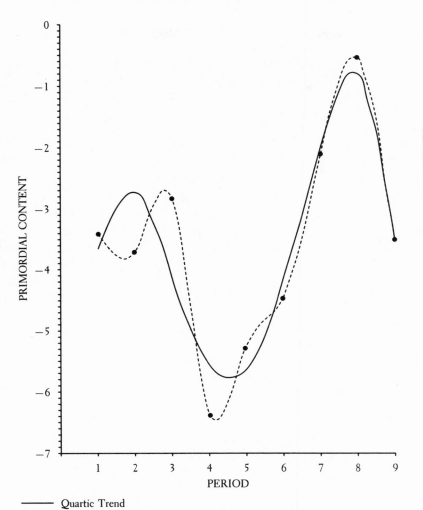

— Quartic Trend

Figure 6.5   The average amount of primordial content in seventy-two American paintings by painters born in nine consecutive twenty-year periods from 1750 through 1929. The solid line indicates the best-fitting trend line. Variations of the means from this line are statistically unimportant.

Figure 6.6 Thomas W. Whittredge, *In the Garden* (Private collection. Photo: Vose Galleries of Boston, Inc.)

Figure 6.7 Childe Hassam, *New York Street Scene*, 1900 (Private collection)

Figure 6.8 Willem de Kooning, *Woman, I,* 1950–52, 6'3 ⅞" × 58" (Collection, The Museum of Modern Art, New York. Purchase)

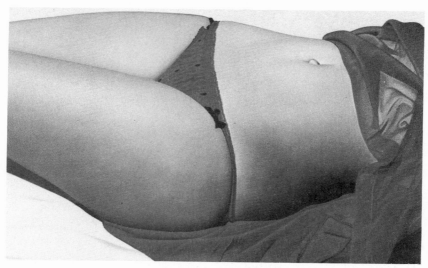

Figure 6.9   John Kacere, *Kelly* (red), 1977. Oil on canvas. (O.K. Harris Works of Art, New York)

Most, but not all, of the earlier paintings are portraits in a vaguely neo-classical style. There is a slight increase in primordial content from period 1 to period 3. The marked decline from period 3 to period 4 coincides with a shift to an American or local-color style. Once this style is in place, it seems to last for the next one hundred years. Across this time, primordial content increases, corresponding to an increasingly dreamlike or unrealistic cast to the paintings (see figures 6.6 to 6.8). Of course, we are lumping together a number of genres, and not every painting in the sample is an example of this trend. The decline of primordial content in period 9 corresponds to the introduction of the photographic realist style (see figure 6.9).

GOTHIC ARCHITECTURE

In the case of architecture, it is possible to increase arousal potential by increasing size or height. Theoretically, successive architects could increase arousal potential by simply building larger and larger buildings. Inevitably, cost would become a factor. Cost for material and labor may increase at a faster rate than size. Attempts to increase arousal potential by increasing size also run into structural problems. If a building is to be of any use, it has to have a roof. If the building is tall, it is likely to attract lightning; and until recently, a roof constructed of wood would sooner or later burn from being struck by lightning. To avoid this hazard, a stone roof is called for. Before the invention of steel beams, a stone roof could not be flat: the tensile strength of stone is low, so the roof would collapse. A domed roof is one possibility. Because a dome is a hemisphere, it has one and only one possible shape. There is thus no possibility for evolution because there is and can be no variation.

Romanesque churches were built using tunnel vaults (see figure 6.10A), where the weight of the roof does not flow straight down the walls: there is an outward or horizontal thrust, which the walls must be thick enough to contain. In consequence, the walls must be extremely thick. The taller the building, the thicker the walls must be, making large windows impossible. Thus, the interior of a romanesque building is very dark.

Gothic architecture rests upon the use of groin vaults (see figure 6.10B). Structurally, a gothic cathedral is a series of groin vaults. As shown in the figure, most of the force of the roof is brought to ground at the groins. A groin vault literally does not need walls, because the columns at the groins carry all the weight. Windows of large size can be substituted for walls. The weight of the roof is not directly down the columns supporting the groins. There is also a strong outward or horizontal thrust; hence, the flying buttresses on gothic cathedrals (Mark 1982), which carry the lateral thrust to ground. Beyond a certain height, the buttresses are unstable; and as at the cathedral at Beauvais, the buttresses themselves require buttresses.

Groin vaults offer limitless possibilities. They do not need to be quadripartite as in figure 6.10B. They can be used to span any area, no

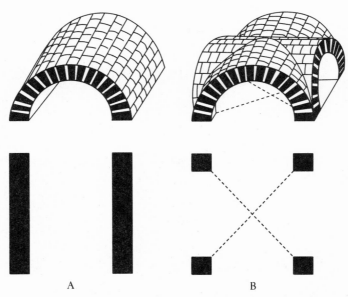

Figure 6.10 Tunnel Vault and Groined Vault In a tunnel vault *(A)*, the weight of the roof is borne all along the walls, preventing all but the smallest windows. In a groined vault *(B)*, the weight of the roof is borne only at the four corners of the vault. Because the walls bear no weight, they can be replaced by large windows.

matter how irregular its size. The problem with them is that the groin—where the stones of the roof meet—is ragged and irregular. The line of the groin is still irregular even if the stones are plastered over. The gothic solution to this was to cover the groin with a stone rib (Frankl 1962). The ribs do not play a structural role; they support nothing, as can be demonstrated by removing them (Acland 1972; Mark 1982). Nothing falls down if they are removed. After a cathedral is built, the only purpose of the ribs is aesthetic. While it is being built, the ribs—which are erected first—make the webbing (the stones making up the vault) much easier to put in place.

English Rib Vaulting

There is a difference in the ribs used in French and English cathedrals. French ribs are fairly plain and do not show much historical change. On the other hand, English ribbing techniques show extreme changes. Late English gothic vaults have almost deliriously complicated ribbing. One reason for this was probably economic. The French strove to make their cathedrals as large and high as possible, and could afford to do so. Until Beauvais Cathedral collapsed, each French city of means wanted to have a higher cathedral than all prior cathedrals. After Beauvais, they thought better of this goal, but the cathedrals were already quite high. Compared with France, England was a poor country in the Middle Ages. The English simply could not afford to build immensely high cathedrals. As a consequence, the vaults were much lower than those of French cathedrals. Being lower, the ribbing was easier to see and thus desirable to elaborate on.

Francis Bond (1913) has hypothesized that least effort also led English masons to add essentially useless ribs to cathedral vaults. The more ribs, the easier the web is to fill in with stone. A vault with many ribs is much easier to fill than a vault with quadripartite ribs (see figure 6.11A–C). Effort saved in one place is, however, lost in another. With the progression from simple quadripartite to lierne ribs, the ribs themselves become more difficult to cut, each having to be a different length and curvature. This complexity causes more impact, or arousal. It also saves trouble for those who put up the webbing, but it causes trouble for those who design and cut the ribs. A solution that minimizes effort and maximizes arousal potential is to cut all the ribs the same length and make them all have the same curvature. The result does not look simple at all. It looks amazingly ornate. The result is the culmination of English gothic vaulting: the fan vault (see figure 6.11D). There is a good reason that the fan vault marks the end of English gothic architecture. Fan vaults look not only complex, but also pretty much alike (compare Bond 1913) because all of their ribs are identical. In other words, there is no variation. Where there is no variation, there can be no evolution. Fan vaults, thus, cannot evolve. The masons had inadvertently caught themselves in an "evolutionary trap" from which there was no escape. At least in the case of English vaulting techniques, it would seem that aesthetic and adaptive selection worked in the same direction. The masons who built the cathedrals were striving for both impact value and ease of construction.

To find out whether naïve subjects would rate a series of English gothic vaults as showing increasing amounts of arousal potential and primordial

A. Ridge

B. Tierceron

C. Lierne

D. Fan

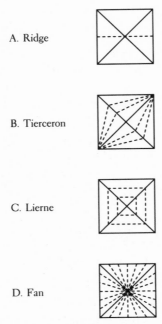

Figure 6.11   Types of ribbing in gothic vaults as elaborations on quadripartite ribbing *(shown with solid lines)*. The extra ribs *(dashed lines)* are structurally unnecessary, serving a decorative purpose and making it easier to fill the webbing of the vault. The most common elaborations are ridge *(A)*, tierceron *(B)*, lierne *(C)*, and fan *(D)* vaulting.

content, we (Martindale and Martindale 1988a), divided the period from 1150 to 1550 into four one-hundred–year periods. These periods are usually referred to as "early," "decorated," "perpendicular," and Tudor. The goal was to find five black and white photographs of cathedral vaults from each period (see figures 6.12 and 6.13 for examples of the first and last periods). Photographs of poor quality and photographs taken by pointing the camera straight up at the ceiling were excluded, as were photographs taken from very oblique angles. If possible, straight-on photographs of naves or choirs showing as much of the ceiling as possible were used. The photographs were taken from works by James Acland (1972), Herbert Felton (1957), John Harvey (1961), and Nikolaus Pevsner (1960). A slide of each was prepared.

We asked fifteen female undergraduates to look at the slides in a

Figure 6.12   Early quadripartite ribbing. Nave, looking east, Salisbury Cathedral, begun 1220 (National Trust, London/Art Resource, New York)

Figure 6.13   Late fan vaulting. Chapel, King's College, Cambridge, 1512 (Courtesy of Bettman/Hulton)

random order and to rate each on several seven-point scales designed to measure the theoretical variables. A measure of primordial content was obtained by adding together the ratings of Otherworldly, Unnatural, Meaningless, and Dreamlike. The measure of arousal potential was obtained by summing scores for Tense, Strong, Complex, and Active. The correlation between period and primordial content was .68. The correlation between arousal potential and period was .85. No significant deviations from these trends were present—exactly the desired result. Within the confines of one style, both variables should increase monotonically with time.

Someone who knows about gothic architecture may complain that we have merely demonstrated the obvious—as, indeed, we did. We did so for three reasons. First, since not everyone is an expert on gothic architecture, I hope the results will be of interest to them. Second, experts—including those on gothic architecture—have a way of losing sight of the forest for the trees. The trends are much stronger than experts may believe. Most art historians focus so much on details that they tend to miss regularities. Third, we wanted to answer the occasional complaints that the theory of aesthetic evolution is complicated or difficult to understand. So far as any one artistic style is concerned, the theory is simple, something you really knew all along.

French Cathedrals

In a related study, late romanesque and gothic cathedrals built between 1000 and 1550 were divided into five consecutive periods based on historians' (Bony 1983; Frankl 1962; Kubach 1975) divisions of the architectural styles (Martindale and Martindale 1989). The romanesque period was defined as 1000 to 1140; the early gothic period, 1140 to 1193; the high gothic, 1194 to 1230; the rayonnant, 1230 to 1400; and the flamboyant, 1400 through 1550. The reason for these specific dates has to do with when certain cathedrals definitive of each style were begun. Black-and-white slides were obtained representing each period. Two different views of the cathedrals were represented in the slides: naves (the inside, altar area) and façades. Five slides per period represented each view. Slides were selected using photographs in available books on gothic architecture that met certain criteria in a predetermined order (for example, the cathedral should not combine decorations from other styles, photographs taken from the least angled view as possible were selected before those depicted obliquely, and so on).

The raters were fifteen women undergraduates who were naïve as to the purpose of the study. Each of the slides, shown in a random order, was rated on several 7-point scales. Arousal potential and primordial content scores were calculated based on theoretical considerations and the results of prior studies. Arousal potential was computed by adding together the scales Tense, Strong, Complex, Active, and Unusual. Primordial content was computed by adding together the scales Otherworldly, Unnatural, Meaningless, and Dreamlike.

Arousal potential increased across periods; the correlation with period was .69. In further analyses, deviations from this trend were found not to be significant. Primordial content also showed a purely linear increase across periods, with a correlation of .43. These results were somewhat surprising because we had included late romanesque cathedrals in the study. Historians generally distinguish the romanesque and gothic as two distinct architectural styles. Stylistic changes are accompanied by a decrease in primordial content. However, as indicated by the linear trend, primordial content increased across all periods—the pattern expected within a particular style. This finding indicates that the romanesque and gothic styles are not perceived by naïve subjects as distinct styles, and that the romanesque may be considered to be an early form of gothic architecture. Two possible reasons for this finding come to mind. First, the differences between late romanesque and early gothic cathedrals are subtle, having to do with window shape and type of vaulting. One can question whether the transition from late romanesque to early gothic is a real stylistic change. Unless one happens to notice that the windows are curved rather than pointed at their tops, one would take the beautiful romanesque cathedral at Limburg an der Lahn as a perfect example of early gothic. Rib vaulting is not a sure sign of gothic style. It can be found in several cathedrals labeled as romanesque. Second, most romanesque cathedrals have been improperly restored. For example, interior walls have often been stripped to rough stone. Originally, they were plastered and covered with paintings. The walls of gothic cathedrals used to be plainer than those of romanesque cathedrals. The reverse is now the case.

There are regular trends in the history of gothic architecture, of which the theory of aesthetic evolution provides a simple explanation, and reflectionist theories provide very complex explanations. I think particularly of Erwin Panofsky's explanation of the structure of gothic architecture in terms of the structure of scholastic argumentation (1924–25). Very clever man, Panofsky. Very learned, too. But maybe he learned the wrong things. Art historians often overlook the principle of parsimony. So long as it accounts for all the facts, the simplest explanation is the correct one. There may or may not have been spiritual agitation in the Middle Ages. We have every reason to believe that the principles of least effort and of habituation operated then as now. These principles are quite sufficient to explain why gothic cathedrals look the way they do. An explanation ought to be like architecture. First you put up the basic structure. Only then do you add the ornamentation. Try to do it the other way around and you will end up with a pile of rubble.

ANCIENT ART

Since it is often argued that need for novelty is a pressure only on modern Western artists, I have investigated the art of other traditions, such as Greek vase painting and ancient Egyptian painting. Yet, in a broad sense, one could argue that these should be included as early examples of Western art. Accordingly, I have also studied such thoroughly non-Western traditions as pre-Columbian sculpture and Japanese *ukiyo-e* prints.

Greek Vase Painting

Ancient Greek vase painting is of interest on several counts, not the least being that several distinct stylistic changes can be observed: geometric (*c.* 1000–700 B.C.), early black-figure (*c.* 700–600 B.C.), black-figure (*c.* 600–500 B.C.), red-figure (*c.* 500–450 B.C.), and white-ground (after 450 B.C.) (Buschor 1921; Robertson 1959). Painted Greek vases served both utilitarian and artistic purposes. Some were clearly used as utensils. Others were so expensive or nonfunctional that they must have been regarded as works of art. Another indication that they were so regarded is that many were signed by both potter and painter. The best guess is that potters and painters were regarded as more than artisans but less than artists.

Vases in the geometric style employed repetitive designs in black on a red background. The early black-figure style retains geometric design, but breaks it up and uses it as a space-filling device in depictions of human figures. The latter are shown by black outlines made by thick brushstrokes on a red ground (see figure 6.14). The black-figure style is characterized by solid black-silhouette figures on a red ground. The ground is red for the simple reason that this is the color of the clay after firing. Interior features of the black figures are indicated by incised lines. Brushwork is evident only in occasional painting of accent colors (see figure 6.15). The red-figure style constitutes one of the most clear-cut stylistic changes in art history. It is a complete inversion of the black-figure style: the background is black and the figures are red (see figure 6.16). The red-figure style opened up possibilities not offered by the black-figure style. The most important of these involved depiction of interior details of figures. Rather than being indicated by incised lines, they could be painted in with shades of black. The white-ground style involved actual painting in a variety of colors on a background of white slip. Unfortunately, the colors on white-ground vases have so faded and flaked that it takes considerable effort to imagine what they looked like when first produced. In contrast, undamaged vases in earlier styles look as if they had just emerged from the kiln. For this reason, white-figure vases were not included in the study. To control for content, geometric vases—which do not usually depict people—were not included either.

Because of stylistic differences among vases made in different regions, only Athenian vases were included in the study, and only ones showing people or parts of people to keep the subject matter constant. Only details rather than pictures of entire vases were included. All color pictures in Robertson (1959) meeting these criteria were included in the study. A color slide of each of these pictures was prepared. Approximate dates (B.C.) and number of vases for each date (in parentheses) were as follows: 650 (1), 625 (2), 567 (3), 527 (5), 512 (5), 487 (4), and 462 (4).

As well as the Like-Dislike scale (which was included, but not used, in this study), I used nine scales designed as measures of arousal potential and of primordial content. Twelve undergraduate women were shown the

Figure 6.14   Early black-figure Athenian jar. Detail (Museum, Eleusis)

Figure 6.15 Black-figure Athenian hydria. Detail (Rijksmuseum van Oudheden, Leiden)

Figure 6.16   Red-figure Athenian jar. Detail (Inv. 8732, Spitzamphorades Kleophrades-Malers, Staatliche Antikensammlungen und Glyptothek, Munich)

slides in a random order and asked to rate each. As desired, subjects were naïve in respect to where the stimuli were from but agreed in their ratings. Because subjects agreed in their ratings, I was able to average across subjects to obtain a single score for each of the paintings on each of the variables.

The nine rating scales of interest were factor-analyzed to see whether the set of scales was measuring a smaller number of underlying dimensions. It was clear that the nine scales were really measuring two dimensions. Factor 1, measuring primordial content, grouped together the scales otherworldly, unnatural, not photographic, dreamlike, complex, and tense. Factor 2, measuring arousal potential, grouped together the scales meaningful, active, and strong. Thus, it seems that ancient Greek artists obtained arousal potential—at least in the eyes of modern raters—by the depiction of strong, meaningful action rather than by the depiction of tension or complexity. I would suspect a problem with the rating scales except that, as we shall see, almost exactly the same factor structure has emerged in two other studies of ancient art.

For arousal potential, the theory predicts a monotonic increase across time. I found the linear trend, but not deviations from it, to be significant. In the case of primordial content, an oscillatory pattern was predicted and, again, was found. Both quadratic and quintic trends were significant. Primordial content increased during the early black-figure style, fell precipitously with the introduction of the later black-figure style, and then began to rise again (see figure 6.17). The same pattern of decreasing and then increasing primordial content is seen with the red-figure style. This is exactly the pattern predicted by the theory.

Ancient Egyptian Painting

It does not require a quantitative study to see that ancient Egyptian painting did not evolve coherently across the three thousand years of its existence (c. 3200–333 B.C.). Its style was not static, however; rather, periods of efflorescence and development were followed by periods of relapse. So severe do these relapses appear to have been that all record of certain artistic techniques was destroyed; and later artists had to develop them all over again, rather than elaborate on those directly learned from their predecessors. This is a reasonable hypothesis in light of the more or less complete collapse of Egyptian civilization several times over this period. Thus, it is no more reasonable to expect a continuous line of artistic evolution in ancient Egypt than in, say, Italy between 1000 B.C. and the present.

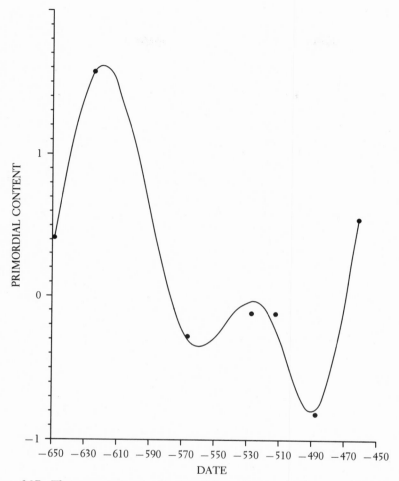

Figure 6.17 The average amount of primordial content in Athenian vase paintings done between 650 and 462 B.C.

Unfortunately, there are not enough examples of early Egyptian painting to allow one to reach any definite conclusions. It is not generally realized how few early Egyptian paintings survive. Many discussions of Egyptian art history are misleading in several respects. First, they do not make clear that there are gaps in the historical record lasting for hundreds of years. Ignoring these gaps makes as much sense as describing a "transition" from Poussin to Picasso without taking account of all intervening artists. Second, gaps are often filled in by art objects of different types. Given the genre specificity of aesthetic evolution, this makes as much sense as bridging the gap from Poussin to Picasso with a discussion of costume jewelry. I consider here wall paintings (almost all from Theban tombs) from the eighteenth and early nineteenth dynasties, as only from this brief period do we have enough precisely dated comparable examples to allow precise study. The eighteenth dynasty began around 1580 B.C. with the expulsion of the foreign Hykos rulers. The period from 1580 to 1375 B.C. saw a more or less continual expansion of Egyptian power and prosperity. The pharaoh Amenophis IV—or Akhenaten— (1375–58 B.C.) initiated profound religious reforms which, after his death, met with a violent reaction and a reinstitution of the old polytheistic religion. Along with this reaction went destruction of much of the art produced during his reign.

Egyptian paintings are generally datable only to the reign of a pharaoh. My goal was to select five color reproductions of paintings produced during the reigns of each pharaoh from Tuthmosis III through Rameses II. In order to assure comparability, I used only paintings depicting people. Painted reliefs and severely damaged paintings were not used. The reproductions were selected from Arpag Mekhitarian (1978) where possible; otherwise, from Nina Davies and Alan Gardiner (1936). The reigns of Akhenaten and Tutankhamen were combined because there are not enough surviving paintings from the former's reign. The stimuli selected consisted of five paintings each from eight successive reigns: Tuthmosis III (1501–1448 B.C.), Amenophis II (1448–22 B.C.), Tuthmosis IV (1422–11 B.C.), Amenophis III (1411–1375 B.C.), Akhenaten and Tutankhamen (1375–48 B.C.), Haremhab (1348–15 B.C.), Sethos I (1312–1298 B.C.), and Rameses II (1298–35 B.C.). The last two are pharaohs of the nineteenth dynasty.

Twenty-three undergraduate women rated the slides; rating scales and procedures were the same as in the study of Greek vases.

When the nine rating scales of interest were factor-analyzed, the results were almost identical to those in the study of Greek vases. The only difference was that Complexity had a higher loading on the arousal potential factor than on the primordial content factor. When predictions were tested, arousal potential did tend to increase over time. However, the main trend was more complex. As may be seen in figure 6.18, arousal

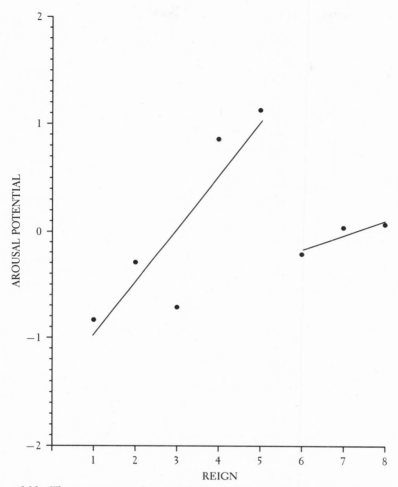

Figure 6.18   The average arousal potential of Egyptian paintings from the reigns of eight successive pharaohs (1501 to 1235 B.C.)

potential increased through the reigns of Akhenaten and Tutankhamen, declined precipitously, and then began to rise again.

The results for primordial content suggest an initial stylistic change between the time of Tuthmosis III and Amenophis II (see figure 6.19). Once this style was in place, primordial content began to rise. A second stylistic change—coinciding with the drop in arousal potential—followed the reigns of Akhenaten and Tutankhamen.

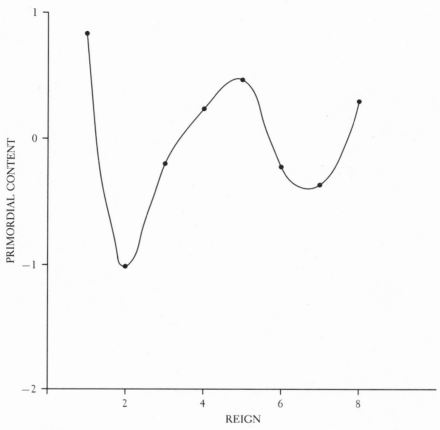

Figure 6.19 The average amount of primordial content in Egyptian paintings from the reigns of eight successive pharaohs (1501 to 1235 B.C.)

For example, a painting in the tomb of Tuthmosis III is, by the standards of either earlier or later Egyptian art, a pitiful work (figure 6.20). Not all paintings of this era were quite so bad, but they seem to have been done by poorly trained painters. This suggests that artistic institutions— and thus artistic continuity—had broken down during the prior Hyksos era. The stylistic change occurring between Tuthmosis III and Ameno- phis II can be seen as a rediscovery of standard Egyptian techniques and motifs. Once rediscovered, style did not remain static: it evolved. The trends shown in figures 6.18 and 6.19 suggest that Akhenaten did not initiate a new style; on the contrary, he reigned during the culmination

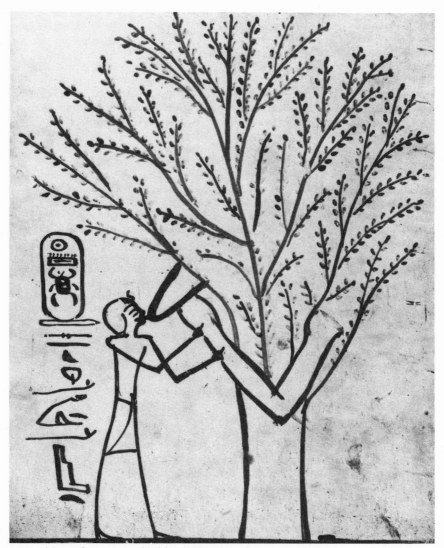

Figure 6.20 *The King Suckled by the Sycamore Goddess.* Burial chamber of Tuthmosis III, Thebes, c. 1501–1450 B.C. (Editions d'Art Albert Skira, Geneva)

of an old one. Compare figure 6.21, produced during Akhenaten's reign, with figure 6.20. Though only a little over one hundred years separate the two, the amount of change is really much *greater* than the amount of change across a typical century in modern Western painting. The first painting resembles the drawing of a child, whereas the second is a mannered and distorted arabesque—certainly a larger difference than between, say, the eighteenth-century Watteau and the nineteenth-century Delacroix.

The stylistic change and the drop in arousal potential during Haremhab's reign is easy to explain. The reactionary priestly class *forced* artists to paint in an archaic manner. Anything connected with Akhenaten was anathema, including the style that flowered during his reign. The evolutionary theory does not say that art always evolves toward greater arousal potential. Art does so only when artists have sufficient autonomy from external forces and institutions. Once the reactionary stylistic change had been forced on artists, arousal potential and primordial content began to

Figure 6.21 *The Daughters of Akhenaten.* Detail, from El-Amarna, c. 1375–58 B.C. (Ashmolean Museum, Oxford)

increase once more. If the period studied is at all representative, we might want to reassess our view of Egyptian art. Rather than being static, it appears to have been a long series of aborted examples of evolution.

Pre-Columbian Sculpture

To see how the evolutionary theory fares with non-Western art, I examined pre-Columbian Mexican art, which was produced over a long period of time by civilizations unrelated to our own. Unfortunately such a study cannot be fine-grained because most pre-Columbian art cannot be precisely dated. All we can do is try to discern long-term trends over a period of around two thousand five hundred years.

I selected for study sculpture produced in mid-Mexico between 1000 B.C. and A.D. 1521. Although this sculpture was produced by different cultures, they were interrelated with one another rather than being isolated civilizations (Alcina Franch 1983). Maya and Northwest Mexican (for example, Nayarit, Jalisco, Colima) art was not included because these represent contiguous, but almost completely unrelated, cultural traditions. Following José Alcina Franch and other experts on pre-Columbian art, the period in question was divided into three periods: preclassic (1000 B.C.–1 B.C.: Olmec), classic (A.D. 1–A.D. 1000: Teotihuacan classic, Zapotec, and Vera Cruz classic), and postclassic (A.D. 1000–A.D. 1521: Toltec, Huaxtec, Mixtec, and Aztec). Figures 6.22 and 6.23 show sculpture from the preclassical and postclassic periods.

To determine whether naïve observers would rate sculpture as increasing in arousal potential and primordial content across the time span of interest, I selected color reproductions of ten sculptures from each of the three periods. If possible, figures of stone rather than clay or other materials were selected, and pictures in which the size of the sculpture could be inferred from extraneous cues were excluded. Where possible, cultures representing each period were given approximately equal representation. In the few cases where too many examples were available, extras were excluded at random. Reproductions were selected from Alcina Franch (1983), Sir John Rothenstein (1970), and Hans Disselhoff and Sigvald Linné (1961), in that order.

The rating scales were the same as in the prior two studies except that

Figure 6.22 Colossal head, Olmec culture, c. 1500–300 B.C. (Museo Nacional de Antropologia, Mexico City)

the scale Usual–Unusual was substituted for Photographic–Not Photographic, because the latter is ambiguous when applied to sculpture. Thirteen undergraduate women rated the stimuli.

The results of a factor analysis of the nine scales of interest were almost identical with what I found for Egyptian painting. Both arousal potential and primordial content exhibited linear increases across time—both trends predicted by the theory. Across long periods of time, both arousal potential and primordial content should show upward trends. No doubt, a more fine-grained study would show that neither of these trends are smooth. As one culture replaced another, often violently, perturbations would certainly be found.

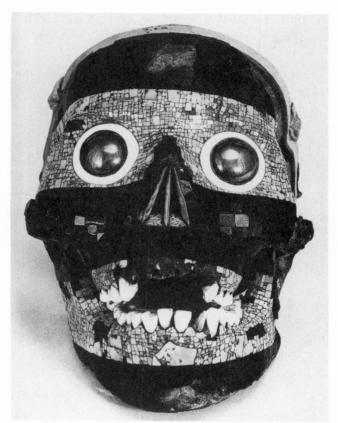

Figure 6.23 *Tezcatlipoca*, multiform god of night and protector of warriors, Aztec culture, c. 1325–1521 (By courtesy of the Trustees of the British Museum, Reg. no. St401)

JAPANESE PRINTS

The Japanese word *ukiyo-e* means "pictures of the floating world." The floating world refers to everyday pleasures, especially in the courtesan districts. Most *ukiyo-e* depict courtesans and Kabuki actors. Early *ukiyo-e* (c. 1630–80) were painted, whereas later ones (c. 1680–1909) were mass-produced as blockprints. *Ukiyo-e* are of interest for several reasons. First, throughout most of the time they were produced, Japan was isolated from the Western world. Second, they were mass-produced popular works rather than being regarded as high art. Their possessors originally treated them as "nothing more than worthless scraps of paper" (Takahashi 1972, p.174). As such, the evolutionary theory might seem less applicable to them than to Western high art.

The period from 1630 to 1909 was divided into fourteen consecutive twenty-year periods. Artists with the largest number of reproductions in Roni Neuer, Herbert Libertson, and Susugu Yoshida (1978) and Richard Lane (1962) were included in the study. One print by each artist was selected at random and assigned to the period in which it was executed. Some deviations from this procedure were required to obtain three prints for each period. In order to fill underrepresented periods, artists were removed from overrepresented periods at random, another artist was selected at random, and so on. No artist was represented by more than one print. To ensure comparability of content, several constraints were placed on the prints used. It was necessary that the print have at least partially clothed human figures in the foreground. The following types of prints were excluded: erotic prints, sumo wrestler prints, prints showing only head and shoulders, and extremely tall, narrow prints. Each of these types is a subgenre presumably with its own unique history.

The ratings were made by seventeen female undergraduates. Subjects agreed significantly on all rating scales. Average ratings were obtained for use in further analyses. A factor analysis yielded two factors: one—with high loadings on the scales Not Representative, Otherworldly, Unnatural and Not Photographic—taps primordial content; the other—with high loadings on Complex, Active, Tense, and Disorderly—taps arousal potential. Arousal potential increased linearly across time. Deviations from this trend were not significant. Primordial content showed an oscillating pattern, with linear and several higher-order trends significant (see figure 6.24).

The stylistic changes—hypothetically indicated by decreases in primordial content—correspond to generally recognized ones (Takahashi 1972). The slight downturn after period 2 corresponds to the replacement of painting by blockprinting. Early blockprints were colored in by hand; an example, from period 5, is shown in figure 6.25. The downtrend following period 5 corresponds to the introduction of blockprinting of color. Not only were more colors used, but they were more vivid than during the hand-painting era. An example, from period 7, is shown in figure 6.26. Theoretically, the new style brought about increased arousal potential by

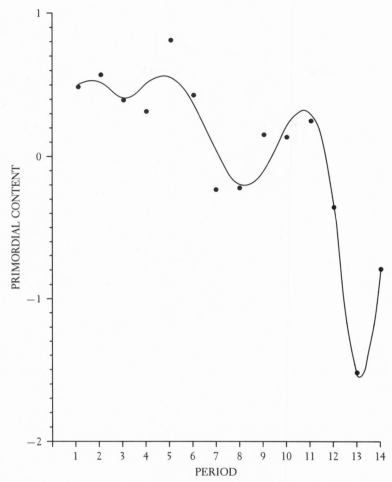

Figure 6.24 Mean amount of primordial content in Japanese *ukiyo-e* prints from fourteen consecutive twenty-year periods from 1630 through 1909.

introduction of more color and more vivid colors. To be sure, the skill of depiction has improved as well. However the audience would be expected to habituate to these factors. The stylistic change following period 11 coincides with the opening of Japan to the West. It involves introduction of Western content and, to some extent, styles. More arousal potential was to be gotten from the novelty of a brick building than from the "mannerist" distortions of the late periods of the prior style. Theoreti-

Figure 6.25 Kiyonobu, *The Actor Uemura Kichisaburo as Nyosan no Miya, c.* 1705 (Art Institute of Chicago)

Figure 6.26 Buncho, *Handayu, an Actor in a Female Role,* late 1760s. (The Metropolitan Museum of Art, New York. Bequest of Henry L. Phillips, 1940. The Henry L. Phillips Collection. JP 2729)

cally, Western influence did not *cause* the style change. Rather, a style change was needed in order to keep increasing arousal potential. If Japan had not been opened to the West, the style change would hypothetically have occurred anyway but would have involved different surface-level content and techniques.

MUSICAL EVOLUTION

We should be able to study trends in the history of music as we do those in the visual arts. A study of historical trends in the melodic originality of European classical music by Dean Keith Simonton (1980 *a*, *b*) yielded results that do not conform exactly to theoretical predictions. Melodic originality was defined as the originality or unusualness of note-to-note transitions in musical themes. Simonton found that, although melodic originality did show a strong upward trend from 1500 to 1950, several clear dips in the curve were present. Since Simonton's study included a gigantic sample of musical themes by virtually every composer whose works are included in the classical repertory, it is impossible to question its accuracy. However, melodic originality is only one method of producing arousal potential. Other methods include, for example, simultaneous and successive dissonance. In the study of the history of British poetry, it became clear that poets during a given period may allow some arousal-producing devices to decline, but offset such declines by increasing other collative variables. The net result is that a composite measure of arousal potential exhibits a monotonic increase from the fourteenth century to the present. A similar process may have occurred in the history of music. To get another measure of arousal potential, as well as to measure primordial content, people were asked to rate musical themes on a variety of scales (Martindale and Uemura 1983).

The epoch from 1490 to 1909 was divided into twenty-one consecutive twenty-year periods. For each period, the goal was, first, to select the three most eminent composers born in France, Germany, Great Britain, and Italy; and, second, to select a representative theme from the work of each composer. Robert Illing (1963) provides a chronology of European composers with each composer assigned to one of four levels of eminence, which served as the basis for selection of most of the composers. For a number of periods, however, it was necessary to consult a series of other reference works in order to find a sufficient number of composers. These works were consulted in a predetermined order, and the first composer not on the Illing list was added to our list. In order to find three composers born during each period for each nation, compromises were necessary in several cases. If not enough composers born in the nation during the period could be found, we used composers who lived for extended periods in Great Britain, but were not born there. In the case of Germany, Austrian-born composers were included; and in the case of France, Belgian and Flemish composers. This method of assigning composers to countries is only an approximation. A number of the composers in the sample spent extensive periods of time in countries other than the one where they were born. When you come down to it, there aren't that many composers. We finally found three for each period, but it wasn't as easy as one might imagine. Though Illing provides birth dates, these occasionally conflict with the dates given in most other sources. In such cases, the date given by the other sources were used.

After composers had been selected, one of their compositions was selected from a set of thematic catalogues or from a source cited by other reference works. Again, this was a lot easier said than done for the more obscure composers. Where more than one composition was available, one was selected at random. Then the theme of each work—almost always the incipit, consisting of three to six bars—was played by a professional violinist and tape-recorded. This procedure resulted in a set of 252 themes. Because of the large number of themes to be rated, three groups of raters each rated 84 themes, presented in a random order, on thirteen 7-point scales. Each group of raters heard themes from all four countries for each of the twenty-one periods.

Two factors emerged from our analysis. The first seems to measure arousal potential. Scales with high loadings on this factor were Complex, Tense, Active, and Strong—scales that have been shown to be valid indices of arousal potential in other studies. The second factor seems to tap the primordial-conceptual dimension. Scales with high loadings were Unnatural, Meaningless, and Disorderly. Simonton's (1980b) measure of melodic originality was also computed for each of the themes. Two-note transitional probabilities for the first ten notes of all 252 themes were computed. Then, melodic originality was computed for each theme by summing the probabilities of each of its two-note transitions. This measure was inverted so higher values would indicate greater originality.

Arousal Potential

The two measures of arousal potential seem to be measuring different aspects of this construct. For all 252 composers, they show a modest but significant correlation ($r = .21$). Analysis of variance showed that the factor-score measure of arousal potential varied as a function of both period and nation. German and British composers received lower ratings than did French and Italian composers. However, the interaction between period and nation was not significant. Thus, there were no significant differences in trend across the four nations. The effect for period arose mainly from an increase across periods. As predicted, there were no significant deviations from this trend. For the melodic originality scores, only the period effect was significant, with again a strong linear uptrend. However, as Simonton found, there was also a significant deviation from linearity.

To test the hypothesis that increases in other determinants of arousal potential cancel out decreases in melodic originality, a composite arousal potential score was formed by adding together standardized factor scores and melodic originality scores for each composer. Analysis of variance of these scores showed significant effects for nation and for period. As may be seen in figure 6.27, the trend for Germany and Britain is a monotonic uptrend. For France, there is a clear linear uptrend, but a slight inverted-U trend is superimposed upon it. For Italian music, there is a clear inverted-U trend. Of course, the theory predicts a consistent increase rather than such an increasing and then decreasing trend. The composite arousal potential measure for Italian music rises across the first part of the epoch under study, but clearly falls across the second part. We might suppose that later French composers may have increased simultaneous dissonance—not measured in this study—in order to offset the slight decline in the aspects of arousal potential that were measured. This seems unlikely to have occurred with Italian composers: there is too much of a decline to offset. We have come upon what may be the most striking and

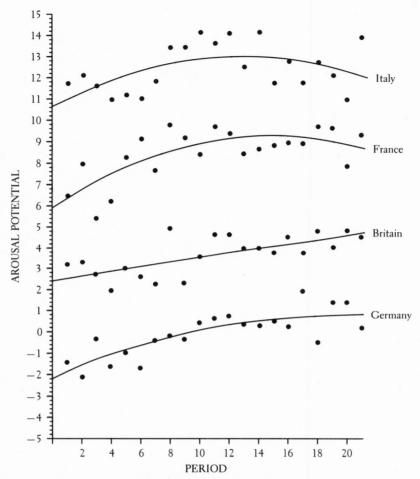

Figure 6.27   The average arousal potential of 252 European musical compositions by composers born in consecutive twenty-year periods from 1490 through 1909.

surprising discovery reported upon in this book. According to the theory, the arousal potential of music has to increase across time. Clearly, the arousal potential of so-called Italian music did not increase. The most reasonable explanation seems to me that what has heretofore been referred to as Italian music is not music at all. It is something else altogether. This is certainly more plausible than admitting that the evolutionary theory could ever be wrong. A more mundane and less interesting explanation for the decline in arousal potential is that the audience for which Italian composers wrote changed drastically across time. Many of the nineteenth-century Italian composers included in the sample wrote popular operas for a mass audience. According to the evolutionary theory, such an audience—especially if its size increased in the course of the century—could account for the observed decline in arousal potential.

Primordial Content

Scores on the second factor were used as measures of primordial content (see figure 6.28). The predicted oscillations can be seen clearly for the German and British series and somewhat less clearly for the French series. Declines in primordial content in general coincide well with stylistic changes suggested by historians of music (for example, Cannon, Johnson, and Waite 1960; Hughes 1974; Ulrich and Pisk 1963). In the figure, the generally accepted sequence of musical styles—mannerist (M), early baroque (B_1), late baroque (B_2), classical (C), early romantic (R_1), late romantic (R_2), and modern (M)—are indicated for the German, the British, and the French series. In the Italian series, there are discrepancies between declines in the curve and this series of styles. Several declines occur where no stylistic change occurred, and stylistic changes are generally held to have occurred in periods where there is no decline in primordial content. This can be attributed to several causes. The most plausible is that this stuff is not music. There are also more mundane possibilities: There were several fairly distinct intranational musical traditions (such as Roman versus Venetian). While I may be silly to say that Italian music was not music, it is not at all silly to say that it was not Italian. Since Italy did not exist as a coherent nation until the mid-nineteenth century, different styles (such as late baroque and preclassical) were probably being used simultaneously by composers in different parts of what is now Italy during the same period.

An autoregressive analysis of the means shown in figure 6.28 supports the evolutionary theory's contention that the value of primordial content in any period is caused by values of primordial content in prior periods as opposed to, say, external social, economic, or cultural factors. Because the first autoregressive parameter was not statistically significant for the

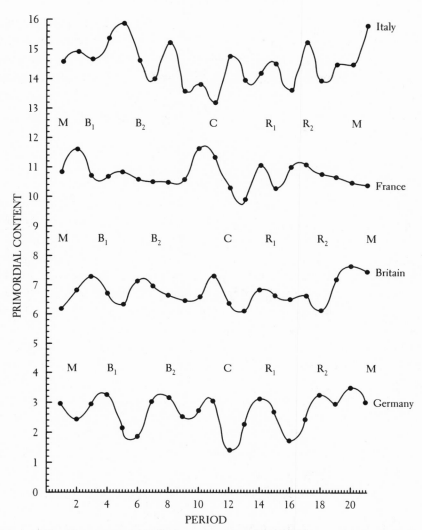

Figure 6.28 The average primordial content in 252 European musical compositions by composers born in consecutive twenty-year periods from 1490 through 1909. In most cases, primordial content declines with the introduction of new styles: M (mannerist), B_1 (early baroque), B_2 (late baroque), C (classical), R_1 (early romantic), R_2 (late romantic), and M (modern).

German series, the best prediction equation for primordial content in period t (G_t) is:

$$G_t = -.58\,G_{t-2}.$$

When actual scores are correlated with this model, a significant fit is found. The model accounts for 36 percent of the variability in actual scores.

The British series showed a pattern of results similar to the German. In this case, the best prediction equation was:

$$B_t = -.40\,B_{t-2}.$$

The model accounts for 20 percent of the variance in actual scores.

For the French series, primordial content in period F_{t-2} was again the best predictor of primordial content in period F_t. In the Gallic case, it was necessary to include scores from other periods in the model. The best-fitting model included all lagged values from periods $t-1$ through $t-5$. When actual scores were correlated with this model, a significant fit was found. The model accounts for 34 percent of the variance in observed scores. For the Italian set, no statistically significant model could be found. As I've said, this stuff may not be music, and wasn't written in Italy anyway.

NEW ENGLAND GRAVESTONES

Evidence for the theory of aesthetic evolution can be found all around us, not only in the high arts. While I could speak of changes in fashion that delight or annoy, I shall conclude instead with a somber witness to the theory.

From the late seventeenth century until the middle of the nineteenth century, New England gravestones were carved on flat slabs of native stone (usually slate, but sometimes sandstone, schist, and granite). The typical stone has an incised or relief carving at the top. Below this carving is inscribed the name of the deceased, date of death, and other personal information. On many stones an epitaph, consisting usually of a Biblical or poetic quotation, is also inscribed. The carving on seventeenth- and eighteenth-century stones usually depicts either a face or a skull, generally with wings attached (see figures 6.29A and 6.29B). Around 1780–1810, depending upon locality, there was a relatively abrupt stylistic shift to neoclassical subject matter: a willow tree and urn combination was by far the most common motif. In most graveyards, a substantial majority of eighteenth-century stones carry the winged-head design and a substantial majority of early nineteenth-century stones carry the tree-and-urn motif.

Within each general style, there is a good deal of variation in the manner in which the subject matter is executed. For example, on some stones the subject is depicted by incised lines on a flat surface, whereas on others it is depicted by relief carving with the background cut away. On relief-carved stones, the figure is sometimes modeled so as to give a three-dimensioned representation. On other stones, the relief is flat so

Figure 6.29 Evolution of gravestone motifs
(A.) An example of the winged skull gravestone motif.
(B.) An example of the winged face gravestone motif.

that the representation consists of a flat background plane and a flat foreground plane.

It could be said that the position of a work of visual art on the primordial-conceptual continuum has to do with the degree to which it corresponds to the pattern of light falling upon the retina (primordial) versus the abstract concept or idealized form of the object in question (conceptual). This is similar to what Wölfflin (n.d. [1915]) called the painterly versus linear continuum. A conceptual or linear work (such as a cartoon drawing or a painting by Botticelli) emphasizes the outlines of forms. A primordial or painterly work (such as an impressionist painting) de-emphasizes outlines and attempts to depict raw percepts rather than concepts.

Though I have done no quantitative work on the topic, I have wandered through virtually every old graveyard I have found close to hand. There is clearly a linear to painterly progression within both the skull-and-wings and the tree-and-urn styles. For example, in the Penobscot Valley of Maine, the following succession of variations on the tree-and-urn motif is distinct: early linear, 1800–1820 (see figure 6.29C); late linear, 1820s (see figure 6.29D); early painterly, 1830–40 (see figure 6.29E); and late painterly, 1840–50 (see figure 6.29F). The movement from linear to painterly is a retrogression from conceptual to primordial. Furthermore, within both the linear and the painterly styles, there is an analogous conceptual to primordial movement. It would be wrong to ascribe this stylistic progression to gradual development of skill in stonecarving. The late winged-head relief style would seem to require more rather than less skill than the early linear neoclassic style. Contemporary with the early incised linear style, one finds examples of the older winged-head style all done in relief. At least some carvers switched from this older style to the early linear style or alternated between the two (Forbes 1927; Ludwig 1966).

These trends are of interest on several counts. Graveyards are visited infrequently. When they are visited, the primary focus of attention is seldom the aesthetic properties of tombstones. Thus, we would not expect a fast rate of habituation on the part of the audience. Furthermore, people who purchase gravestones are usually in a state of bereavement (momentary or acute high arousal), which should decrease their normal desire for novelty. Since a carver of gravestones is more a craftsman than an artist, we might expect carvers to be interested more in the quality of their

Figure 6.29

(C.) The early linear style (1800–20): outlines of the tree and the urn are incised, and each individual leaf on the tree is depicted by an incision.

(D.) The late linear style (1820s): outlines of tree and urn are still incised, but groups of leaves are represented more impressionistically as long straplike incisions.

(E.) The early painterly style (1830–40): tree and urn are now represented by a flat, *raised* relief with only the interior details incised.

(F.) The late painterly style (1840–50): similar to early painterly, except that the late painterly style moves toward a contorted and arabesque representation.

workmanship as opposed to the novelty of their designs. Thus, it is gratifying that the evolutionary theory seems to work so well in this context. As I have remarked, a selection pressure has to be long-lasting but not necessarily intense in order to work its ways.

Thus, the evolutionary theory applies to the tomb painting of ancient Egypt as to the tombstones of New England. It is not a theory whose relevance is confined to high art or modern art alone. The more I investigate the question, the more I think that the evolutionary theory provides unique insight to all art no matter exactly what it is or when created.

CHAPTER 7

Cross-National, Cross-Genre, and Cross-Media Synchrony

BIOLOGICAL evolution takes place at the level of the species, because only members of the same species can breed with one another.
It is also a local affair: members of the same species remote from one
another do not have the opportunity to breed with one another. In
aesthetic evolution, however, it is not immediately apparent what the
artistic equivalent of a biological species is. Although we could say that
it is a specific genre within a specific type of art—for example, lyric poetry,
or epic poetry, or landscape or portrait painting, this doesn't seem right.
Genres are "cross-fertile": that is, epic poetry, say, seems able to influence
lyric poetry. "Cross-fertility" also seems to occur between different media:
sculpture and painting, for example, seem to exert strong influences on
each other. To confuse matters further, aesthetic evolution is not localized
to the extent that biological evolution is. French and English rabbits don't
mate with each other for the simple reason that they can't get across the
English Channel. French and English poets, though, do influence each
other at least from time to time.

Exactly what is evolving? Does the art of an entire civilization evolve together, or do individual genres in individual nations each evolve on their own? The answer almost certainly lies between these extremes. The evolutionary theory tells us that we shall find synchronous evolution only where there is long-lasting and consistent influence, but not where we shall find such consistent influence. For this empirical question there are data that should give us a general answer—if one exists—in respect to consistent influences across nations, genre, and media.

CROSS-NATIONAL SYNCHRONY

Poetry

To what extent have the British, French, and American poetic traditions influenced each other? We know from literary history that there is not one simple answer to this question. At the beginning of the nineteenth century, British romanticism was—if we are to believe poets' own reports—influential on French and, especially, American poetry. Afterward, French poetry consistently had a much bigger impact on British poetry than vice versa, and also on twentieth-century American poetry, but not on American poetry of the late nineteenth century. Aside from Edgar Allan Poe, American poetry has had essentially no influence on French poetry. British poetry until recently seems to have influenced American poetry more than the reverse. As I mentioned in chapter 5, because of the language they write in, Americans have to pay some attention to British poetry. Though critics only admit it when forced to, most nineteenth-century American poetry was relatively undistinguished and held little to interest British poets. Beginning with the generation of Ezra Pound and T. S. Eliot, the tables were turned, and American poetry did start to influence British poetry.

The correlations computed to investigate cross-national influences are not statistically significant, there being few overlapping periods. The correlations of .60 between primordial content in British and French poetry, of .45 between British and American poetry, and of −.38 between American and French poetry are potentially misleading. Since primordial content in British and American poetry both increased across the time span of interest, they will correlate with everything else that increased across time—the price of cigars, for example. By detrending all three series, I removed from them linear trends and autoregressive influences; this detrending only slightly lessened the correlations.

I tried to see whether I could predict primordial content for any one nation from detrended correlations for the current and two prior periods for the other two countries. In detrending the data, any *intra* national influence was removed. In respect to British and French poetry, no combination of values from other countries yielded a significant prediction equation. For American poetry, however, I could account for 79 percent of its variation with the equation

$$A_t = .08 - .90 \, F_{t-1},$$

where A_t stands for detrended primordial content in American poetry, and F_{t-1} stands for detrended primordial content in French poetry during the prior period. Since we had only seven periods to start with, I regard this finding as extremely tentative. In fact, I think it is fortuitous. Note the negative form of the relationship, implying that American poets do the opposite of what French poets did in the prior period. Empirically, they *did* do so across the time span studied but not *because* French poets did whatever they did. Across most of the time span for which we have data for both series, primordial content in French poetry showed an inverted-U pattern, but a U-shaped one in American poetry. I think that the cause of these patterns was mainly what had happened in prior French and American poetry, respectively: that is, that both trends were mainly caused by intranational evolution. The best way to find out whether the poetry of different nations tends *in general* to evolve in synchrony is to do more studies that cover longer time spans. At present, the evolution of poetry in different nations does not seem connected in any significant way. If it were, we should have been able to predict the poetry of any one nation from that of the others.

Painting

British and French painting appear to be closely related, their primordial content having a correlation of .84. This correlation is, however, at least partially spurious: the positively accelerated uptrend that both series share makes the two series also correlate with everything from the gross national product of Bulgaria to the population of Peru. After detrending and removing the autoregressive component, I found that the data suggest a weaker, but still significant, correlation of .50 for primordial content. As well as examining correlations between contemporaneous periods, I also examined correlations between lagged values of the two series. English painting (E) can be predicted from earlier French painting (F):

$$E_t = .41F_t + .48F_{t-2}.$$

This equation is significant and accounts for 49 percent of the variance in detrended scores. We can predict 24 percent of the variance in French painting from English painting, but the equation is not significant. When I considered only the overlapping periods for which I had data for American painting, I found the following significant equations for detrended primordial content:

$$A_t = .02 + 2.36E_t - 1.44E_{t-2}$$

$$E_t = .07 + .83F_t + .32A_{t-2}$$

$$F_t = -.03 + .31A_t.$$

This gives us a closed circle. When the longer series of French and British painting was considered, it was clear that French painting influences British painting more than vice versa. Now we see that American painting is predictable from British painting. Closing the circle, I found French poetry to be at least synchronously related to American poetry. Painting seems to be a much more international enterprise than poetry. At least for the last two centuries, British, French, and American painting appear to be closely related even when we take statistical precautions to avoid spurious findings. The Italian, British, and French series overlap for several periods. Using the preceding approach, I found no significant equations, owing either to an insufficiency of data or to less cross-national synchrony in earlier centuries.

Music

Figure 6.28 (page 231) in the last chapter does not give a clear answer to the question of how much European music evolved in synchrony. The cycles seen there are not exactly in phase. When I simply intercorrelated primordial content in the same period for British, French, German, and Italian music, I found only one marginally significant relationship—between Germany and Britain (.41). This is no surprise when we know that the English, chronically short of composers, have made up the slack by importing them from Germany. There does, however, seem to be more interrelated change than this. Trends in primordial content in German, British, and French music are described by similar autoregressive equations. If, by mere chance, they all started out at the same point, they could appear to be correlated even if they were not (see Jenkins and Watts 1968). To test for real cross-national correlations, I had first to remove from each series any secular trends and autoregressive influences in order to work with *deviation scores* (the difference between the observed score for each period and the score predicted by the polynomial and autoregressive equations for each nation) (Haugh 1976). While the German-English correlation remains after this detrending, it unveils no other hidden synchronous relationships. I then tried to relate these detrended scores for each nation to those for the other three nations for the current and prior three periods.

The best equation for primordial content in German music (G) was:

$$G_t = .05 + .64B_t + .32I_{t-1} - .64F_{t-3}.$$

This equation yields a nice fit to observed scores, accounting for 65 percent of the variation in these scores. In words, the equation indicates that primordial content in German music not accounted for by primordial content in prior German music is influenced by British music in the current period, by Italian music in the prior period, and by French music three periods earlier.

For British music (B), the best equation is:

$$B_t = -.02 + .37G_t + .59G_{t-1} + .46F_{t-3}.$$

There is again a good fit to observed scores, with 61 percent of the variance accounted for. The finding of a large German influence on British music is consistent with conclusions based upon nonquantitative methods.

In French music (F), the equation

$$F_t = -.02 + .53G_{t-1} - .71B_{t-1} + .14I_{t-2} + .45B_{t-2} + .45G_{t-3}$$

explains 85 percent of the variation in the detrended scores. French music seems to be more derivative than German or British music: all of the influence from other nations comes from prior periods. Italian music (I) is again unique. No statistically significant extranational influences are present—a finding consistent with the conventional historical wisdom that Italy has influenced other nations in musical style rather than vice versa. Trends in European music were not strictly in synchrony, but there were strong cross-national influences. Both of these facts have, of course, long been known. However, statistical procedures give us a way of precisely estimating the strength and direction of such influences.

CROSS-GENRE SYNCHRONY: SHORT STORIES AND POETRY

To investigate whether trends in American short stores and American poetry are related, I aggregated the data for short stories into twenty-year periods and aligned these data with the poetic series. The short story periods were aligned so that their midpoint would coincide, on average, with the thirtieth birth date of the poets. Thus, the short-story periods 1 to 2 (written 1820–39) coincide with the third poetry period (born 1790–1809), and so on. Although it proved impossible to predict poetry from fiction, it is possible to predict fiction from poetry. For primordial content in the short stories (SS), I found a significant relationship with primordial content in poetry (P),

$$SS = -.01 - .54P_{t-2},$$

which accounts for 69 percent of the variance and suggests that poetry and fiction may have evolved in synchrony, with poetry in the lead. The negative relationship between poetry and fiction is like what we found between American and French poetry, and may also be fortuitous. In both cases, the time series are too short for any firm conclusion to be drawn.

In the more obvious approach of aggregating the short stories by author birth date, the relationship vanishes. We cannot predict poetry from short stories or vice versa. This anomalous finding probably has to do with the nature of the short-story data, each author being represented by only one story. As I shall discuss in chapter 9, authors often change style across the course of their careers. To get enough stories for each decade, well-known authors had to be shuffled around. Poetry was sampled in a different way, with poets' ages being averaged out. Some figures I have gathered suggest that about half a poet's output is finished before age thirty (Martindale 1975). Thus, for a poet born in 1800, we can say that his poetry was "on average" written in 1830. It should, then, relate to stories written around then rather than to, say, a story written in 1870 by someone who also happened to be born in 1800.

The short stories also overlap with the series of texts from *Poetry* magazine. Here, the only reasonable way to align the texts is by when they were written. The *Poetry* sample of 1915 corresponds with short stories written during the 1910s, and so on. With only one exception, primordial content in the two series moves in exact synchrony. The rank-order correlation is .67, which is marginally significant. With only eight decades of overlap, we can't ask for more than marginal significance. It does seem that American fiction and poetry tend to evolve together.

CROSS-MEDIA SYNCHRONY

A *cross-media artistic style* is one that works of art in more than one form of art exhibit. The term *baroque,* for example, applies to music, painting, architecture, and poetry. Other common terms for cross-media styles include *romantic, gothic, rococo, renaissance, classic* or *neoclassic,* and *mannerist.*

These terms designate works of art in different media which were created during roughly the same epochs, but these epochs may be several hundred years in length. The idea of *period style* involves synchronization of styles across media during much shorter intervals of time. What we might call "second-order" cross-media styles include such polarities as ethos versus pathos (Sachs 1946), ideational versus sensate (Sorokin 1937), and my own notion of conceptual versus primordial (Martindale 1975). All of these polarities are cognate in that they refer one way or another to the distinction between cognitive and realistic versus imaginative and unrealistic. The first pole subsumes styles such as renaissance or neoclassic; and the second, styles such as gothic or mannerist. These second-order cross-media styles are not temporally bound but are held to apply across media—though works in different media will not all necessarily show the same style during the same epoch.

Cross-Media Styles

The baroque, neoclassic, and romantic painting and architecture in figures 7.1, 7.2, and 7.3 do show certain similarities. The baroque style is ornamented, "strong," and complex; whereas the classic style is simple and severe. The romantic style is picturesque. These examples alone, however, do not demonstrate that styles in painting and architecture have any real connection.

The piling up of wild and incongruous ornament allows us to call the following poem baroque:

> O thou undaunted daughter of desires!
> By all thy dower of lights and fires;
> By all the eagles in thee, all the dove;
> By all thy lives and deaths of love;
> By thy large draughts of intellectual day,
> And by the thirsts of love more large than they;
> By all thy brim-filled bowls of fierce desire,
> By all thy last morning's draught of liquid fire;
> By the full kingdom of that final kiss
> That seized thy parting soul, and sealed thee His,

Figure 7.1.   Examples of the baroque style
(A) Andrea del Pozzo, *The Entrance of Saint Ignatius into Paradise.* Ceiling fresco, Sant'
     Ignazio, Rome (Alinari/Art Resource)
(B) Johann Fischer von Erlach, Karlskirche (S. Charles Borromeo), Vienna (Marburg/Art
     Resource)

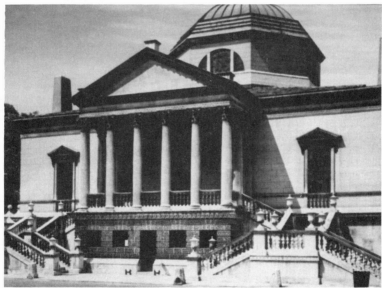

Figure 7.2. Examples of the neoclassic style
(A) Jacques-Louis David, *The Oath of the Horatii* (Musée du Louvre, Paris)
(B) Lord Burlington, Chiswick House, Middlesex, England
    (Photo: English Heritage, London)

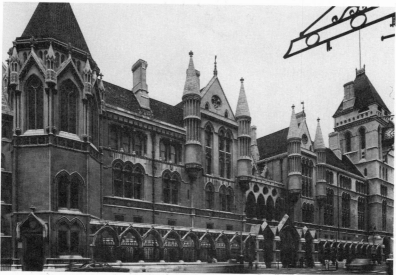

Figure 7.3. Examples of the romantic style
(A) Caspar David Friedrich, *Solitary Tree* (Nationalgalerie, Berlin)
(B) George Street, The Law Courts, London (National Trust, London/Art Resource, New York)

By all the Heavens thou hast in Him
(Fair sister of the seraphim!);
By all of Him we have in thee;
Leave nothing of my self in me.
Let me so read thy life, that I
Unto all life of mine may die!
    (Richard Crashaw, "The Flaming Heart")

The incongruity here is far more apparent if you know that this is a religious poem: its subtitle is "Upon the Book and Picture of the Seraphical Saint Teresa."

Contrast this with the calm of a neoclassic poem:

Now hardly here and there a hackney coach
Appearing, showed the ruddy morn's approach.
Now Betty from her master's bed had flown,
And softly stole to discompose her own.
The slipshod 'prentice from his master's door
Had pared the dirt and sprinkled round the floor.
Now Moll had whirled her mop with dexterous airs,
Prepared to scrub the entry and the stairs. . . .
    (Jonathan Swift, "A Description of the Morning")

Where Crashaw's whole poem whirls, here only Moll's mop whirls. Now compare "the ruddy morn's approach" with nature's in romantic poetry:

O Wild West Wind, thou breath of Autumn's being
    Thou from whose unseen pressures the leaves dead
Are driven like ghosts from an enchanter fleeing.

Yellow, and black, and pale, and hectic red,
Pestilence-stricken multitudes! O thou
    Who chariotest to their dark wintry bed

The wingèd seeds, where they lie cold and low,
    Each like a corpse within its grave until
Thine azure sister of the Spring shall blow

> Her clarion o'er the dreaming earth, and fill
> (Driving sweet birds like flocks to feed in air)
> With living hues and odours plain and hill;
>
> Wild Spirit, which art moving everywhere;
> Destroyer and preserver; hear, O hear! . . .
> (Percy Shelley, "Ode to the West Wind")

Shelley's poem has the wild spirit of Crashaw's, but the former's imagery is centered and individualistic whereas Crashaw's is decentered and unfocused. Thus, we might say that it is more similar to the romantic than to the baroque painting. Of course I have picked extreme examples, and we already know what goes with what. Would people who do not already know the answers be able to discriminate the three styles regardless of medium?

From the time of Gotthold Lessing (1962[1766]), the concept of cross-media style has been vigorously criticized. Lessing argued that, because painting is spatial whereas literature is linear, the two cannot by their very natures express the same message. The literary critics René Wellek and Austin Warren (1942) pointed out flaws in the reasoning of several cross-media theorists. They criticized attempts to find a basis for cross-media style in the mood evoked by works of art, in the intention of the artist, and in common social and cultural backgrounds. These critics claim, without empirical evidence, that the moods evoked by artworks are too idiosyncratic to serve as a basis for cross-media styles. A more telling point is that an artist's intention and the effects of social and cultural background can be translated in very different ways in different media. James Merriman noted that the evidence usually given for the existence of cross-media styles is based on "improper sampling, metaphorical transfer of terms, arbitrary conversion, sheer subjectivity and more or less free associationalism" (1972, p.156). Improper "pick and choose" sampling is rampant among cross-media theorists: parallels between the arts are "demonstrated" by choosing the two most similar works out of many thousands. An example of metaphorical transfer of terms would be calling both the sonnets and the sculptures of Michelangelo "jagged." *Free-associationalism* refers to the tendency to equate works in different media because they were created at the same time.

It is safe to say that the concept of cross-media styles is held in low regard by most humanistic scholars (Peckham 1965; Praz 1970). If one reads the works of some of the "worst offenders," it is easy to see why. Most cross-media theorists espouse a reflectionist viewpoint and seem to be desperately striving to show implausible cross-media similarities. Morse Peckham uses Wylie Sypher (1952, 1960) as an example. Sypher's work shows a virtually complete disregard for sampling in any sense of the term. At least to my mind, wild and implausible analogies abound. The reader is left with the impression that the putative cross-media similarities either exist only in the mind of the writer or would never be noticed unless they were specifically brought to a naïve observer's attention. To confirm this impression, Nancy Hasenfus and I began a series of studies (Hasenfus, Martindale, and Birnbaum 1983). What began as a simple effort to demonstrate that even the most common cross-media styles are not at all apparent to aesthetically naïve observers, ended up as an investigation of how such people are actually able to perceive both cross-media styles and period styles. Since I myself am a cross-media theorist—in having proposed a generalized primordial-versus-conceptual characterization of all the arts—I find myself in bad company. I have been put there by the facts quite against my will.

Those trained in the arts are able to label a painting and a musical composition, say, as baroque. Although there has been no systematic work on the subject, it is clear that the success of art experts at this sort of task is far from being a matter of chance. Even I can do it almost perfectly. Thus, people can certainly be trained to discriminate cross-media styles. But how does this discrimination operate? Cross-media theorists argue that it is based on the perception of similar qualities in works from different media. Those who deny this theory say that the only thing similar between, say, baroque music and painting is the stylistic name. The discrimination is, they argue, based on different qualities in the different media. For example, a fugue is called baroque, as is a painting with a lot of cupids in it, but it does not follow that fugues and cupids are similar in any way. Artistic training gives the same name to these different qualities. If this be the case, then artistically naïve subjects should show no ability to group together examples of the same style from different media. If cross-media theorists are correct, then it is reasonable that untrained people would spontaneously perceive cross-media similarities and group together instances of the same style.

According to Berlyne (1971), a work of art has three types of properties: psychophysical properties intrinsic to the stimulus (such as pitch, hue, intensity), collative properties (such as novelty, complexity, ambiguity), and ecological properties (such as denotative and connotative meaning). Berlyne held that these properties taken together determine the arousal potential of a work of art. Each of these aspects of a work of art offers several possibilities for cross-media correspondence. The psychologist S. S. Stevens (1975) showed that cross-modal matching on the intensity dimension is reliable. Another psychologist, Lawrence Marks (1975), showed that there are reliable consistencies in the matching of the brightness of colors and the "brightness" (defined by pitch and loudness) of sounds. Collative variables (such as complexity or novelty) are clearly defined across all media. Kenneth Burke (1957) argued that cross-media styles are based on two dimensions that Berlyne would call collative variables: unity and diversity. Meaning can also serve as the basis for cross-media styles—as is obvious in art forms having specific content, such as representational painting and sculpture. In terms of connotative meaning, Charles Osgood, George Suci, and Percy Tannenbaum's (1957) three factors of evaluation, potency, and activity show up in a variety of rating tasks irrespective of what is being rated. Thus, connotative meaning could serve as a basis for equating works in different media. Finally, overall arousal potential or resultant liking (see figure 2.1, page 42) could serve as a basis for cross-media styles. I have argued that it makes sense to talk about primordial content in all of the arts. The experiment I did with Ross and Miller (1985) suggests that this cross-media effect is more than giving the same name to different things. In our experiment, people wrote fantasy stories in response to paintings. Primordial content in the stories—as measured by content analysis—was correlated with primordial content—as measured by rating scales—in the paintings.

In an experiment to measure the sensitivity of artistically naïve people to cross-media styles, subjects were asked to sort reproductions of baroque, neoclassic, and romantic architecture, music, painting, and poetry on the basis of similarity. Out of these sortings, we created a similarity matrix and subjected it to multidimensional scaling. If the subjects were sensitive to cross-media styles, this would lead examples of these styles to be closer together in the resulting multidimensional space.

The experiment dealt with examples of baroque, neoclassic, and romantic styles, the three most commonly used cross-media stylistic terms. After the styles and media to be studied had been decided on, selection of stimuli involved two steps. First, we selected artists representative of each of the styles in each of the media, and then representative works by each artist. In the selection of artists, a large set of standard reference works gave us the artists most frequently referred to for each style and medium (see table 7.1). We found the best-known works by each artist by tabulating how often works had been reproduced, performed, or anthologized. For example, we searched a set of twenty-eight anthologies in selecting poems.

Ultimately we confronted sixteen subjects with a set of color pictures of paintings and architectural façades, cassettes each containing one minute from the beginning of a musical composition, and eight-line excerpts of poems typed on 5-by-8 cards. The subjects were told to arrange this material into similar groups. Specifically, the stimuli were arranged in four piles—one for each medium—before each subject. Though we didn't say so, it was clear to subjects that by "similar" we meant something other than similar art media. The subjects were told that they could make as many groups as they wanted and could rearrange their groups at any time.

Subjects could not correctly identify the artists or the titles of any of the paintings, poetry, or music. Several subjects correctly identified an architectural work (Monticello and the Houses of Parliament in all cases) or an architect (Jefferson in all cases). Since we had included reproductions of many well-known works of art, the number recognized or identified seems low. Neither during the experiment nor during extensive post-experimental questioning did anyone indicate an awareness that the stimuli could be grouped into the three styles used in the experiment. In contrast, an artistically trained man whom we pretested quickly and spontaneously remarked that he assumed we wanted to see whether he could sort the stimuli into baroque, romantic, and classical groups. That none of our subjects seemed to have the slightest notion of such a possibility further supports our belief that, as hoped, they were artistically naïve.

TABLE 7.1
Artists in the Cross-Media Style Experiment

| | Style | | |
Medium	Baroque	Neoclassical	Romantic
Painting	Sir Peter Paul Rubens	Jacques-Louis David	Joseph Turner
	Pietro Da Cortona	Joseph Vien	Caspar David Friedrich
	Andrea del Pozzo	Gavin Hamilton	Eugène Delacroix
	Bartolomé Esteban Murillo	Benjamin West	Jean Louis Théodore Géricault
	Giovanni Lanfranco	Jean-Auguste-Dominique Ingres	Moritz von Schwind
Poetry	Richard Crashaw	Alexander Pope	William Wordsworth
	John Donne	John Dryden	Samuel Coleridge
	Giambattista Marino	Jonathan Swift	George Gordon, Lord Byron
	Luis de Góngora y Argote	Samuel Johnson	Percy Bysshe Shelley
	Andreas Gryphius	Nicolas Boileau	Victor Hugo
Architecture	Gianlorenzo Bernini	Claude Nicolas Ledoux	Sir George Gilbert Scott
	Francesco Borromini	Jacques Germain Soufflot	George Street
	Sir John Vanbrugh	Richard Boyle, Lord Burlington	Sir Charles Barry
	Johann Fischer von Erlach	William Kent	Richard Upjohn
	Johann Balthasar Neumann	Thomas Jefferson	Alexander Davis
Music	Johann Sebastian Bach	Carl Philipp Emanuel Bach	Louis Hector Berlioz
	Dietrich Buxtehude	Johann Christoph Bach	Frédéric Chopin
	Georg Frederick Handel	Franz Joseph Haydn	Franz Liszt
	Antonio Vivaldi	Wolfgang Amadeus Mozart	Felix Mendelssohn
	Jean-Philippe Rameau	Luigi Boccherini	Robert Schumann

Subjects arranged the stimuli into an average of nine groups. The post-experimental questionnaire indicated that they used three main strategies. Nine people mentioned the emotion or feeling evoked, thirteen mentioned content (either real or, as in music, imagined), and nine mentioned stylistic factors (such as complex, flowery, chaotic, pretty). To see whether people agreed in their sorting of stimuli, we split them randomly into two groups. A program designed to measure agreement in sorting (Lingoes 1967) showed that agreement was extremely good. Then, multidimensional scaling was done to discover the dimensions along which subjects were discriminating the stimuli. Two dimensions were important (see figure 7.4). Statistical analysis showed that subjects were grouping together instances of the same style from different media with accuracy far beyond chance. Fifty-five percent of baroque art works, 60 percent of neoclassical art works, and 65 percent of romantic art works were correctly classified. We would expect only 33 percent in each case

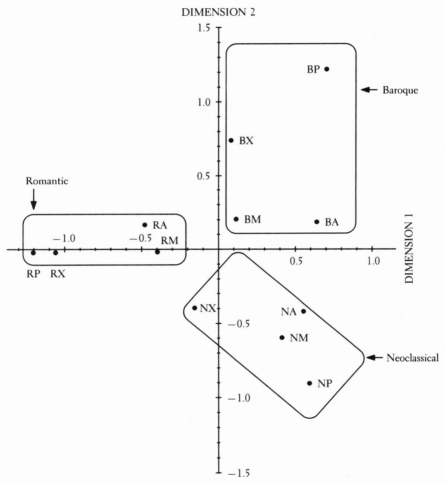

Figure 7.4 Perceived similarities among styles and media as indicated by multidimensional scaling. As shown by the boxes, people perceive examples of the same style as similar regardless of artistic medium. (Key: B = baroque, N = neoclassical, R = romantic; M = music, P = painting, X = poetry, A = architecture)

on the basis of chance. Thus, artistically untrained subjects do show a clear and significant tendency to perceive cross-media styles. Both baroque and neoclassical styles differ from the romantic style on the first dimension: that is, people see baroque and neoclassic styles as being similar to each other and dissimilar to the romantic style. Baroque and neoclassical styles do not differ significantly on this dimension. The second dimension differentiates baroque and neoclassical styles and, to a lesser extent, neoclassical and romantic styles. Baroque and romantic styles do not differ significantly on this dimension. Thus, people see baroque and romantic styles as similar to each other and dissimilar to the neoclassic style on this dimension. In summary, people perceive the three styles as varying in two fundamental ways, or along two dimensions. Unfortunately, multidimensional scaling does not tell us how to label these dimensions.

An examination of the works occupying extreme positions on the two dimensions helps to give a preliminary answer to the question of how they should be labeled. On the first axis, highest scores were obtained by Lord Burlington's Chiswick House (figure 7.2B) and C. P. E. Bach's Symphony no. 3, and lowest scores by Liszt's Symphonic Poem no. 3 and Shelley's "Ode to the West Wind"—a contrast between calm and composed works on the positive end of the axis and more frenzied ones on the negative end. The highest scores on the second axis were obtained by Crashaw's "The Flaming Heart" and Buxtehude's Chaconne for Organ in E Minor, whereas the lowest scores were obtained by Jonathan Swift's "A Description of the Morning" and Claude Ledoux's Tollhouse—a contrast between complexity and simplicity. Although the two dimensions seem to be related to primordial versus conceptual content and arousal potential, we need more information before we can be sure of this interpretation.

The results of the experiment showed that artistically naïve adults are sensitive to cross-media styles. Presumably, the basis for this sensitivity is an untrained "direct" perception of cross-media similarities in the works of art. It is, however, possible that, though the subjects seemed to have had minimal exposure to high art, they had learned something as a consequence of whatever exposure they did have. If such learning were the cause of our results, then younger subjects should show no such sensitivity to cross-media styles. Children are not sensitive to artistic styles even within a single medium. For example, the psychologist Pavel Machotka (1966) found that children younger than seven or eight years of age tend to evaluate paintings mainly on the basis of content rather than formal or stylistic characteristics. Howard Gardner (1972) found that children younger than eleven years of age sort paintings according to content rather than style unless given special training. To investigate the ability of children to discriminate cross-media artistic styles, we undertook a partial replication of our experiment with nursery school children having an average age of four years.

We used only the pictures of paintings and architecture in this study. The children could not have read the poems, and we assumed that they would not listen with any degree of concentration to the music. Since children of this age do not know what the word *similar* means, we had to teach them. Children were asked individually if they would like to accompany the experimenter to a room in order to play a game. The game consisted of sorting cards containing geometric figures into rows containing similar figures. We used a variety of synonyms for similarity (such as "look alike"). We chose for our study the sixteen children who were able to sort the geometric stimuli according to some vaguely rational criterion (such as size or shape) at or before the end of several sessions.

In our study, the children sorted the stimuli, and we did the same type of analysis as in the experiment with adults. The result was clear: the children were sorting in part according to styles apparent in several media. They correctly classified 80 percent of baroque, 40 percent of neoclassic, and 60 percent of romantic artworks. The children's sorting was more influenced by medium than was the adults', and the children used one rather than two dimensions to discriminate the styles. On this dimension, styles were arrayed from baroque through neoclassic to romantic. Nevertheless, the children did perceive statistically significant differences among the three styles. To make absolutely certain that our results are not influenced by learning, someone should repeat this experiment with Chukchee shamans, Tibetan recluses, and people of that sort. Until then I think we are safe in concluding that cross-media styles are psychologically real: that is, they exist in the stimuli and are perceived there rather than being figments of a theorist's mind.

Adults differentiate the three styles along two dimensions. The statistical procedures I have described tell us that, but they do not tell us what these dimensions are. To get a firmer idea, I had another group of subjects rate the paintings on a number of scales. When these ratings were correlated with a painting's position in the multidimensional space for adults, we found the dimensions to be what I suspected: primordial versus conceptual content and arousal potential. The first dimension is positively related to the scales Not Realistic, Unnatural, Improbable, and Otherworldly. The second dimension is positively related to the scales Complex, Unclear, Exciting, and Vibrant.

Period Styles

The results of the first set of experiments led us to wonder about the sensitivity of naïve observers to cross-media styles that last a relatively short time—that is, period styles. In order to assess the sensitivity of artistically naïve adults to period styles in British art, we used six consecutive forty-year periods, beginning with 1600. (Though the results of this study were published in 1983, it was done in the mid-1970s, before it had become clear that God divided all art forms into the twenty-year periods I have discussed up to now.) Our goal was to select two British painters, poets, architects, and composers born during each period and then to select two works by each. As usual, we selected artists who were the most referred to in standard reference works (see table 7.2) and artworks according to which were most anthologized or reproduced. The procedure was about the same as for the study of cross-media styles, the main difference being that an architect was represented by both an exterior and an interior view of the same building.

Now, this experiment is one literally destined to fail. It is not at all apparent that naïve subjects will sort the stimuli correctly. Though they might see a similarity between, say, Gainsborough and Reynolds, can we expect them to go on and put these two together with Cowper and Smart and so on? Statistically speaking, we chose a weak design: that is, the way the data have to be analyzed may indicate no result when there really is one. Since we have only two works per artist and two artists per period, it is difficult to get significant results. We were forced into this design because we wanted to be sure that the artists we used would be regarded as typical of their period by art critics and literary critics.

Our naïve subjects, who rated themselves as knowing almost nothing about art and couldn't identify any of the works of art or artists, agreed

TABLE 7.2
Artists in the Period-Style Experiment

Period	Painting	Poetry	Architecture	Music
1 (1600–1639)	Peter Lely	John Milton	Sir Roger Pratt	William Lawes
	John Michael Wright	John Dryden	Christopher Wren	Matthew Locke
2 (1640–79)	Sir Godfrey Kneller	Jonathan Swift	Nicholas Hawksmoor	John Blow
	Marcellus Laroon, the younger	Matthew Prior	Sir John Vanbrugh	Henry Purcell
3 (1680–1719)	William Hogarth	Alexander Pope	William Kent	Georg Frederick Handel
	Richard Wilson	James Thomson	James Gibbs	William Boyce
4 (1720–59)	Thomas Gainsborough	William Cowper	Robert Adam	Muzio Clementi
	Sir Joshua Reynolds	Christopher Smart	John Nash	Johann Christoph Bach
5 (1760–99)	Joseph Turner	William Wordsworth	George Basevi	Johann Cramer
	John Constable	John Keats	Sir Charles Barry	John Field
6 (1800–1839)	John Everett Millais	Alfred, Lord Tennyson	Augustus Pugin	Samuel Wesley
	Dante Gabriel Rossetti	Robert Browning	George Street	William Sterndale Bennett

very well in their sortings. On the basis of the two dimensions we found significantly related to period style, a statistical analysis correctly classified 34 percent of the stimuli. We would expect about 17 percent correct classification if people had sorted the stimuli purely on the basis of chance. People aren't as good at discriminating period styles as cross-media styles, but their performance is far beyond chance.

In further studies, we asked people to rate the stimuli on scales theoretically having to do with primordial content and arousal potential. Again, it seemed that subjects were implicitly discriminating the styles on the basis of primordial content and arousal potential. In these studies, we also asked people to estimate the date of composition of artworks and to guess the country in which they were produced. Only thirty-four of seventy-one subjects were correct about country of origin. Subjects agreed on estimated date of creation, but these estimates were uncorrelated with the actual date. Ratings of primordial content and arousal potential were significantly related to both of the crucial dimensions. Although the subjects weren't differentiating the theoretical variables as well as they had in the studies of cross-media styles, they clearly were able again to discriminate period styles at far beyond chance levels.

Regardless of medium, naïve observers do see something similar in works of art created during the same epoch. It may not be that the arts evolve together, but that all arts evolve because of the same forces. These forces across time will both cause arousal potential to increase and also tend to make primordial content increase. Thus, we could find similarity across media even if each medium were evolving completely independently.

CROSS-MEDIA EVOLUTION

For most nations, I just don't have enough data to say anything conclusive about cross-media synchronony of evolution. Our best chance of clarifying matters is with British poetry, painting, and music, where we have much longer series than elsewhere. To what extent have British poetry, music, and painting evolved together? Has British art in general evolved, or has each of the arts evolved in isolation from the other? Figure 7.5, which shows trends in primordial content in the three together, does not yield a clear answer. The cycles are not completely in phase. It is impossible for painting to be in phase with poetry and music: the latter tend to have three-period cycles, but painting has a four-period cycle. Poetry and music do move together across at least parts of the time span studied. Primordial content in poetry and music are, however, both autoregressive processes with similar parameters: if both started out by chance at the same point, they could appear to be correlated even if they were not (Haugh 1976; Jenkins and Watts 1968; Pierce 1977).

After detrending to remove such a danger, I arrived at clear results for poetry and painting. No variable or combination of variables yielded a significant correlation. The results for music were different. Music could be predicted from prior values of painting by an equation accounting for 56 percent of the variation in music scores. To have longer time

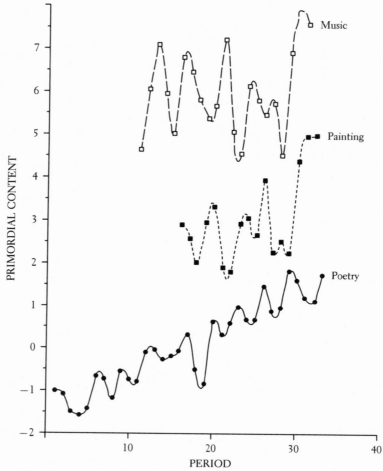

Figure 7.5 Primordial content in British poetry, painting, and music for creators born in successive twenty-year periods beginning in 1290. Values for painting and music have been shifted upward to avoid overlap of the curves.

series with which to work, primordial content in music was correlated with only primordial content in poetry. Again, it was found that music scores could be significantly predicted from poetry scores in prior periods. The equation accounts for 30 percent of the variation in music scores. On the other hand, correlating poetry scores with music scores alone yielded insignificant results. Thus, music seems to be influenced by prior developments in both poetry and painting. Music is not only influenced by poetry and painting but, as has often been suggested, tends to lag behind them: that is, earlier values of primordial content in poetry and painting are most important in determining later values of primordial content in music.

Why this pattern of results emerges is not completely obvious. It is reasonable to think, though, that it is easier to translate a theme or idea from poetry or painting to music than to perform the reverse translation. It is easier to understand what a poem or painting is about than to understand what a piece of music is about. Thus, a poet or painter has a better chance of influencing a composer than vice versa. Since, as I have noted, British poets form a remarkably interconnected series, tending to know each other personally, we can profitably think of British poetry as having been passed on as an oral tradition. British poets and composers tended not to be personally acquainted; nor were the composers in general personally acquainted with contemporary painters. Thus, a composer would more likely be influenced indirectly (as by reading) by earlier poets or painters, who had already attained fame, than by contemporaries working in comparative obscurity.

Over time, the increasing vividness of the plumage of birds of paradise and the increasing brain size of primates have nothing to do with each other aside from the fact that evolution caused both trends. Though things are not so clear in art, we can make them clearer than might at first be thought. In general, the arts tend to evolve fairly independently, but there is—at least now and then—some cross-fertilization.

CHAPTER 8

Art and Society

T HE answer to the question how art and society are related depends crucially upon what we mean by the question. We can certainly find artists who share or reflect the morals, values, and concerns of the larger society—such poets, for example, as Longfellow or Whittier. As soon as one thinks of them, though, one thinks of Poe, who had, as D. H. Lawrence remarked, "no truck with Indians" (1955[1924], p.966). Nor did Poe have anything to do with anything of his time; he has even been criticized because his work had not the slightest thing to do with the society in which he lived. Yet other poets mirror—by actually inverting—current social concerns. The French decadent poets' motto *épater la bourgeoisie* ("shock the middle class") more or less guarantees that their verse will contain some inversion of contemporary values and concerns.

The fact is that art may be related to society in different ways at different times and places. Though I have argued that art is not as closely related to society as is often thought, I do not mean that it is not related at all. The evolutionary theory explains a lot about art history, but not everything. I assume that there are many other laws that govern the historical development of artistic traditions. In this chapter, we shall investigate whether there are general regularities in how artistic content is determined by factors in the external society. Let us hope that we can find some other general laws that shed further light on the history of art.

THE IMPACT OF EXTRALITERARY FACTORS ON BRITISH POETRY

I have said that factors external to the poetic system have little effect upon poetic style and content. Each poet measures differently in respect to the Composite Variability Index. Analysis of variance tells us that 29 percent of the differences among poets on this index are attributable to factors within a period. Since all the poets in a period are subjected to pretty much the same social and cultural changes, such changes cannot be causing much of the within-period variation; some must be due to such individual factors as genre, personality, talent, and social class. The remaining 71 percent of variance attributable to interperiod differences could possibly be caused by extraliterary forces. However, the equation I gave in chapter 4 (page 122) accounts for 76.5 percent of this variation. Parsimony dictates that we give over this historical increase to the evolutionary theory since an intraliterary explanation is simpler than an extraliterary one. This leaves 23.5 percent of interperiod variation—that is, 16.7 percent of overall variation—to be explained by extraliterary factors *and* random error of measurement. In other words, extraliterary factors are fairly inconsequential.

We can apply the same line of reasoning to primordial content, where 49 percent of the variation is due to differences among poets writing during the same period and is thus not readily explained by either the evolutionary theory or by extraliterary changes. Of interperiod variation, 83.6 percent can be accounted for by the linear trend and primordial content in prior periods. This leaves only 16.4 percent of interperiod variation—or 8.4 percent of total variation—to be explained. Since a good bit of this must be error variance, it does not seem worthwhile trying to account for it.

Rather than pursuing this statistical approach any further, let us attack the problem from an empirical angle. Even if poetic content is not related to much in the external society, it must be related to something. To find out what, I correlated available time series with the content of poetry. As soon as we contemplate this approach, it becomes apparent that we are constrained to deal with aspects of society and culture that are not only measurable but have, in fact, been measured. Indeed, we have more precise long-term quantitative data on poetry than on, say, economic trends. I have gathered a large number of extraliterary time series and constructed several more summary indices. The most important of these follow:

1. *Philosophical emphasis.* Sorokin (1937, vol. II) measured sensate versus ideational emphasis in several aspects of European philosophy. By *sensate*, Sorokin meant realistic and empirical (Locke would be an example), whereas by *ideational* he meant an emphasis on the mental and a priori (Hegel would be an example). Sorokin provided figures for the number of philosophers adhering to sensate versus ideational emphasis in systems of truth, ethical systems, and first principles: temporalism versus eternalism, realism versus conceptualism, singularism versus universalism, materialism versus idealism, and indeterminism versus determinism. Measures of sensate emphasis were standardized and added to yield an index of Net Sensate Emphasis. Sorokin's measures refer to when philosophers worked rather than where they were born. In this case—and in those following—the extraliterary periods correspond to twenty-year periods centered thirty years after the birth periods. Because we cannot measure the Zeitgeist directly, Sorokin's figures give us at least an indirect measure of it.

2. *Internal disturbances.* Sorokin (1937, vol. III) has provided figures indicating the extent and severity of internal social disturbances (riots, rebellions, and so on) in Great Britain. According to the Marxist art historian Arnold Hauser (1963[1958]), such disturbances may indicate the emerging strength of a social class that would be receptive to a new artistic style.

3. *War.* Sorokin (1937, vol. III) also provides figures for the number of casualties for battles engaged in by Great Britain. At least some Marxist theorists view war as an extension of the class struggle for control of means of production.

4. *Technological innovations.* Sorokin (1937, vol. II, p.136, col. 3) provides tabulations of European technological innovations. As he (1937) has noted, Marxism ultimately attributes much social and cultural change to the emergence of new technology: technological innovations create new means of production; a class struggle ensues for control of these means of production.

5. *Prices.* E. H. Phelps Brown and Sheila Hopkins (1956) estimated a composite

index of prices for food, fuel, and textiles in England across the last seven centuries.

6. *Wages.* Phelps Brown and Hopkins (1955) tabulated figures for wages earned by British building craftsmen for the last seven centuries.

7. *Wages relative to prices.* Based on their figures for wages and prices, Phelps Brown and Hopkins (1956) computed a measure of wages relative to prices; higher numbers indicate greater purchasing power. The index can be taken as a measure of general prosperity, which should be negatively related to conflicts among social classes.

8. *Industrial productivity.* Brian Mitchell (1975) computed an index of British industrial productivity from the eighteenth century to the present. We might expect this measure to give us an idea of the vitality of the British economy.

9. *Interest rate.* The yield on consols (British government bonds) gives us an idea of interest rates back to the early eighteenth century. (For figures see Mitchell and Deane 1962 and Mitchell and Jones 1971.) In general, low interest rates foster economic development, and high ones retard it.

10. *Coal consumption.* Because general figures for industrial productivity do not go back very far, I used amount of coal imported at London as reported by John Nef (1932) and Mitchell and Deane (1962) as an indirect measure.

11. *Temperature.* D. Justin Schove (1961) gives figures for the winter temperature in northern Europe beginning in the 1100s. I have no reason to expect that temperature should correlate with literary content, but that is precisely why I included it. Large correlations would suggest that we had discovered something bizarre or—more likely—that our statistics were wanting.

12. *Illegitimacy rate.* The ratio of illegitimate to legitimate births may be a measure of moral permissiveness. It was certainly low during the puritan era (the 1650s) and comparatively high around 1600, 1800, and the 1960s—all relatively liberal eras. However, it was low throughout the Restoration (1660–1688), which was—at least for the upper class—probably the most licentious era in English history. For reasons that no one knows, the illegitimacy rate is fairly closely related to the overall fertility rate. (My figures were taken from Laslett and Oosterveen 1973, Mitchell and Deane 1962, and Mitchell and Jones 1971.)

Each extraliterary series was aggregated to describe twenty-year periods centered thirty years after the birth periods of poets. Simple correlation of these measures with our theoretical variables—primordial content and the Composite Variability Index—led to all kinds of perfectly ridiculous discoveries. The literary variables are highly correlated with wages, prices, industrial productivity, and so on. As for the external variables, pretty much everything is correlated with everything else. The reason for these correlations is not far to find. Most of the series show strong increases across time. Many of these, such as industrial productivity and the Composite Variability Index, have increased at an accelerating rate. I statistically removed these secular trends to discover the real relationships. If two series are really related, the relationship will still be there after such detrending.

I found one significant correlation between the two theoretical variables, arousal potential and primordial content (which were also detrended), and the detrended external indices. The Composite Variability Index correlated .50 with temperature—a fluke, I expect, since we had found statistically that we couldn't plausibly expect to find any correlations. Primordial content marginally correlated with both prices and wages. The Composite Variability Index also marginally negatively correlated with rate of technological innovation. To make sure nothing was being missed, I lagged the literary variables to see whether earlier values of these predict later values of the external variables, and the external variables to see whether these could predict the literary variables. One of the forty-eight lagged correlations is significant. The Composite Variability Index negatively correlated with sensate emphasis in philosophy in the following period. However, we would expect one or two out of forty-eight correlations to be significant just by chance. Considering unlagged and lagged correlations, I found two of the seventy-two correlations to be significant—less than we would expect just on the basis of chance—and concluded that the theoretical variables are in fact unrelated to the aspects of extraliterary change we have measured.

I then turned to the Harvard III categories as being more likely to produce some relationships. First I removed long-term trends from these categories and from the external series. I correlated the fifty-four categories with the twelve external series. I also lagged the categories and computed another set of correlations to see whether changes in literature could predict changes in the external variables. Then I lagged the external variables and did more correlations to see if changes in external forces could predict changes in literature. That gives us 1,944 correlations. Just by chance, we've got to find something. This is a problem. Before we look at the correlations, let's consider how many are significant. For any one of the external series at any one lag, we have fifty-four correlations, two or three of which will be significant just by chance at the .05 level. That is about the number we find for several of the series. Table 8.1 gives the number of significant correlations.

The table tells us several things. First, there is no use looking at the correlations for the last five series in the table: they only produce about the number of correlations we would expect by chance. On the other hand, the series toward the top of the table do look promising, showing far more correlations than could have arisen merely from chance. Though wages show more than the expected number of correlations, I also dropped this measure, since the correlations are fairly redundant with the wage-price ratio correlations. If we compare lagged correlations, we can get an idea of what predicts what. The economic variables and illegitimacy rate anticipate or precede changes in literature. The reverse is the case for innovations and sensate emphasis in philosophy. War is pretty much a toss-up.

Now for the correlations. Because we are dealing with a small number of periods for some of the series, I take seriously anything where the probability that the correlation is really zero is less than 1 in 10. For all

TABLE 8.1

Significant Correlations between Harvard III Categories and British Extraliterary Time Series

Series	Lag		
	−1	0	+1
Innovations	17	16	9
Sensate Emphasis in Philosophy	17	12	13
Wage-Price Ratio	1	12	12
Illegitimacy Rate	6	5	18
War	6	7	4
Industrial Productivity	1	5	5
Wages	2	6	3
Coal Consumption	2	2	3
Prices	2	3	1
Interest Rate	2	1	3
Internal Disturbances	1	3	1
Temperature	1	2	2

NOTE: A lag of −1 means the literary variables were lagged, whereas a lag of +1 means the external variables were lagged.

of the series, the correlations at different lags are almost always consistent: that is, if the series correlates significantly with a content category at one lag, correlations at other lags tend to be in the same direction—more evidence that these are not chance results. The correlations in table 8.2, between the external series we have retained and Harvard III summary categories, tell a surprisingly consistent story. With the exception of the wage-price ratio, our measure of prosperity, the correlations are almost all in the same direction. There are consistent negative correlations between literary references to collectivities—organized social groups—and innovation, sensate emphasis, illegitimacy, industrial productivity, and war. These variables tend to be positively related to references to Persons—because, in almost all cases, of high usage of the subcategory Self (references such as "I," "me," "mine"). This finding certainly suggests an emphasis on individualism. The other correlations are consistent with that interpretation. The variables are negatively related to cultural patterns (references to social norms) and social-emotional actions (the subcategories are "communicate," "approach," "guide," "control," "attack," "avoid," "follow"). In other words, there is an avoidance of references to norms and conformity to them. The positive relation to references to nature suggest that this is what the French structural anthropologist Claude Lévi-Strauss (1964) might call "raw" poetry: it is about the nonconforming or amoral self in a state of nature. All of the extraliterary variables have to do in one way or another with individualism, nonconformity, and freedom. Innovation by definition is a break with old—or current—conventions. Having an illegitimate child is to defy social and religious norms. Sensate philosophies also defy at least religious norms. Sorokin (1937) defined them as usually antireligious. Both Marxists and free-market economists will tell you that industrialists—but perhaps not workers—do best in an absolutely free market. What is good for industrialists is by definition good for industrial productivity. War is an act of the state, but the state needs people to start it and people to fight it. Indeed, the psychologist David McClelland (1975) has argued that wars become more likely when the people in a nation are more individualistic and concerned with power and less concerned with affiliation and other people.

Eras of prosperity produce poetry that tends to emphasize social collectivities and to avoid references to the self. References to cultural patterns

TABLE 8.2

Correlations between British Extraliterary Series and Harvard III Summary Categories[a]

			Series			
Category	Innovations	Sensate Emphasis	Illegitimacy	Industrial Productivity	War	Wage-Price Ratio
Social Realm	.36	.49		.69		
Persons	.49**	.60**	−.38			.58
Roles	−.37				−.31	
Cultural Realm						
Collectivities	−.76**	−.52*	−.54*	−.77*	−.40*	.73
Cultural object	−.45*	−.47*	−.72**			.50
Cultural setting		−.48*		−.77*		.47
Cultural pattern	−.47*	−.51*	−.72**		−.39*	.52
Natural Realm	.37	.48*	.40	.61		−.38
Psychological Processes	.46*	.53*				
Emotions			.38			
Thought	.62**	.68*			.34	
Evaluation		−.43				
Behavior						
Social-emotional	−.55**		−.63**			.41
Instrumental	.46*	.38	−.61**		−.42*	.62

[a]Largest correlation from lags of −1, 0, and 1. Correlations without superscripts are significant at $p < .10$.
*$p < .05$.
**$p < .01$.

and social-emotional acts are emphasized and references to nature de-emphasized: in other words, "cooked" rather than "raw" poetry. That poets are reflecting a general sense of social solidarity and conformity in the larger society certainly seems reasonable, but the data at hand do not assure us that this is the case.

The poetry of an era of innovation and illegitimacy is opposite to that of an era of prosperity. Intercorrelating our social indices should give us an idea whether prosperity squelches individualism and innovation. The wage-price ratio is negatively related, at least at a marginal significance level, to all of the other variables except war. If we factor-analyze the correlations, we find two main dimensions. The first opposes the wage-price ratio to productivity, innovation, illegitimacy, and sensate emphasis in philosophy; the latter set of variables all tend to be intercorrelated. The second dimension opposes war to the wage-price ratio and industrial productivity. The first dimension seems to be getting at individualism or social disorganization versus social solidarity. In several studies, Simonton (1984a) has found that rate of innovation is related to variables such as political fragmentation, which would seem to be related to social disorganization.

AMERICAN LITERARY CONTENT AND SOCIOCULTURAL VARIABLES

I turn to data from American literary content for more information on the relation between art and society. It is most profitable to examine the relationship between literary content and extraliterary factors in the sample of American short stories. Since this series was selected by date of composition rather than birth date of author, there is no uncertainty about how to align the literary and extraliterary series.

A set of historical statistics was drawn from the volumes compiled by the United States Bureau of the Census (1975a, 1975b, 1985). After examining a number of series, I retained several as most useful. Of course, this biases the case toward finding significant relationships. In most cases, however, I did not reject series because they were unrelated to literature. Rather, I rejected those that didn't seem to be comparable across time or to be measuring anything of interest. (For example, it was difficult to come up with a good measure of religious involvement: church membership figures should work but don't; denominations split up, recombine, and so on.) For each series, the value used was that for the midpoint (such as 1825 or 1835) of the period.

1. Consumer Price Index (Series E135 in United States Bureau of the Census, 1975*a*).
2. Balance of Trade: Exports (Series U1) per capita divided by Imports (Series U8) per capita.
3. Patent Index: Number of patents for inventions issued (Series U99) per capita.
4. Popular vote for National Republican, Whig, or Republican presidential candidate (Series Y83) in the year nearest the midpoint of each decade per capita.
5. Military personnel on active duty (Series Y904) per capita.

Before each variable was analyzed, the usual detrending was done. Most of the series showed strong secular trends, which have to be removed if one is to tell whether correlations are due to real relationships. Table 8.3 shows that military strength and political conservatism (as roughly measured by the Republican percentage) are almost perfectly correlated. In turn, these variables are negatively related to technological innovation (as measured by the Patent Index) and weakly but positively related to economic prosperity (as directly measured by the balance of trade and inversely measured by the Consumer Price Index).

TABLE 8.3
Intercorrelations of American Social Indices

Variable	CPI	TB	PI	RP	MS
Consumer Price Index (CPI)	1.00				
Trade Balance (TB)	−.42†	1.00			
Patent Index (PI)	.19	.00	1.00		
Republican Percentage (RP)	−.24	.43†	−.51*	1.00	
Military Strength (MS)	−.23	.35	−.57*	.93**	1.00

†p < .10.
*p < .05.
**p < .01.

Correlations between mean values for the stories in each period on the Harvard III Psychosociological Dictionary categories and the social indices are shown in table 8.4. Out of fifty-four independent correlations, we should expect about five to be significant at a probability of less than 1 in 10 purely by chance. This is what we find for the Patent Index. For the Consumer Price Index, only two correlations are significant at this level. Thus, we should regard with suspicion the correlations between these indices and literary content. Correlations with relevant dimensions from the other content-analysis dictionaries are shown in table 8.5.

In both tables 8.4 and 8.5, balance of trade, Republican percentage, and military strength correlate in the same directions with literary content. On the other hand, the Patent Index correlates in an opposite direction. It would seem that in eras of political conservatism and economic prosperity, American literary content tends to be concrete (as in the positive correlations with measures of concreteness of vocabulary, use of qualifiers, and references to cultural objects and cultural settings), to avoid reference to thought and emotion (as in the negative correlations with emotion, thought, evaluation, and cultural patterns), and have a static quality (as in the negative correlation with activity). Conversely, in eras of political liberalism and economic depression, literary content tends to be animated, abstract, and intraceptive.

We can compare the amount of total variability explained by evolutionary versus reflectionist causes. Because the social indices were not computed separately for each story, mean values for each of the multidimensional axes and for the evolutionary variables were computed for each period. Since it was not exactly clear how secular trends in the social indices should be corrected so as to avoid possible spurious correlations, several analyses were performed. In the end, the evolutionary and the reflectionist theories seemed to be about equally valid for this sample of stories. Each accounts for about 20 percent of total variation. Because the social indices and the evolutionary variables are not significantly correlated with each other, each explains largely independent portions of total variation. Remaining, unexplained variation is presumably due to a healthy dose of random error and to individual differences in personality and social circumstances of the authors.

TABLE 8.4

Harvard III Psychosociological Dictionary Summary Categories, Categories, Sample Words, and Correlations with American Social Indicators

Summary Category[a] / Category (Sample Words)	Consumer Price Index	Trade Balance	Patent Index	Republican Percentage	Military Strength
Persons					
Self (I, me, mine)					
Selves (we, us, ours)					
Others (you, yours, they)					
Roles					
Male role (actor, boy, brother)			.43†		
Female role (actress, aunt, bride)			−.49†		
Neuter role (baby, American, anybody)					
Job role (agent, author, captain)					
Collectivities					
Small group (agency, band, board)				.43†	
Large group (administration, army, church)				.43†	
Cultural Objects					
Food (bean, beer, candy)			−.46†		
Clothing (button, dress, fur)					
Tools (bag, automobile, ambulance)			−.51*	.47†	
Cultural Settings	−.42†	.59*		.59*	.56*
Social place (abroad, American, bedroom)	−.42†	.59*		.59*	.56*

TABLE 8.4 (Continued)

Summary Category[a] Category (Sample Words)	Consumer Price Index	Trade Balance	Patent Index	Republican Percentage	Military Strength
Cultural Patterns		−.76**		−.63**	−.60*
Ideal value (ability, able, beauty)					
Deviation (abnormal, blind, crazy)		.83**			
Action norm (agreement, business, commission)					
Message form (art, book, cash)		−.54*			
Thought form (abstraction, basic, contrast)		−.66**			
Nonspecific objects (affair, aspect, capital)		−.62**		−.61**	−.47*
Natural Realm					
Body part (arm, body, brain)		.55*			
Natural object (plant, animal, mineral)					
Natural world (air, beach, gulf)					
Qualifiers		.69**		.61**	48†
Sensory reference (aloud, black, fresh)		.48†		.59*	50*
Time reference (after, again, began)		.50*			
Quantity reference (add, any, big)					
Space reference (about, ahead, back)		.56*		.51*	49*
Emotions					
Arousal (attitude, awaken, felt)				−.47†	−.57*
Urge (dream, eager, incentive)					
Affection (admire, affection, charm)					
Pleasure (cheer, delight, funny)					
Distress (afraid, alarm, break)				−.49*	−.55*
Anger (angry, boil, burn)					

TABLE 8.4 *(Continued)*

Summary Category[a] Category (Sample Words)	Consumer Price Index	Trade Balance	Patent Index	Republican Percentage	Military Strength
Thought					
Sense (appear, attend, aware)				-.55*	-.46†
Think (assume, choice, doubt)			.42†	-.61**	-.47†
Equal (alike, same, consist)			.45†	-.55*	-.57*
Not (cannot, not, differ)					
Cause (affect, cause)					
Evaluation					
Good (admirable, clean, fair)		-.63**			
Bad (awful, bitter, cheap)		-.43†			
Ought (duty, ought, proper)	.50*	-.63**			
Social-Emotional Actions					
Communicate (address, admit, answer)					
Approach (arrive, attach, bring)					
Guide (aid, allow, benefit)					
Control (appoint, arrest, bind)					
Attack (annoy, attack, beat)					
Avoid (abandon, absent, conceal)					
Follow (agree, apology, consent)		-.46†			
Instrumental Actions					
Attempt (aim, apply, bid)				-.45†	
Work (adjust, construct, cook)					
Get (afford, attain, beg)					
Possess (belong, occupy)					
Expel (blew, cast, defecate)				-.45†	
Move (pull, put, run)		.61**		.46†	

[a]Each of the summary categories (e.g., "Persons") is the sum of the inset categories listed below it.

†$p < .10$.

*$p < .05$.

**$p < .01$.

TABLE 8.5
Correlations of Literary Variables with American Social Indicators

Dimension	Consumer Price Index	Trade Balance	Patent Index	Republican Percentage	Military Strength
Noun Concreteness	−.43†	.34	−.21	.28	.36
Verb Concreteness	−.39	.41	−.57*	.62**	.62**
Adjective Imagery	−.47†	.55*			
Evaluation					
Activity		−.32	.21	−.57*	−.50*
Potency		−.36		.22	.36
Composite Variability Index					
Primordial Content	−.31	.36			−.25

NOTE: Correlations less than ± .20 not shown.
†p < .10.
*p < .05.
**p < .01.

AMERICAN POPULAR MUSIC

Cynthia Kaplan (1975) gathered or constructed external social, economic, and cultural indices in order to investigate their relationship with lyrical content. Several measures were based on the National Bureau of Economic Research economic indicators (Moore and Shiskin 1967):

1. *Leading economic index.* These measures tend to precede economic fluctuations. Ten variables—such as corporate profits after taxes, stock market prices, and industrial materials prices—were standardized and added together to form the index.
2. *Concurrent economic index.* Composed of six variables, such as gross national product, personal income, and retail sales.
3. *Lagging economic index.* Composed of five variables such as expenditures on new plants and equipment, book value of manufacturing and trade inventories, and labor cost per unit of manufacturing output.
4. *Unemployment rate.* Supposed to be a concurrent economic index (Moore and Shiskin 1967) but was not highly correlated with other concurrent indices for the period under investigation.

    Three more measures were designed to assess degree of social disintegration. Factor analyses showed the components of each measure to be highly related to each other:

5. *Crime rate.* Per capita homicide, burglary, and robbery rate.
6. *Social disorder.* A composite measure of number of assassinations, riots, protest demonstrations, deaths from domestic violence, and police killed per capita.
7. *Anomie.* A composite of per capita rates for divorce, suicide, illegitimate births, arrests for drunkenness, and arrests for narcotics violations.

Three other indices tapped:

8. *Political conservatism.* As roughly measured by the number of Republican-held seats in the Senate and in the House of Representatives.
9. *Military strength.* The percentage of the U.S. population on active duty in the military services.

10. *Technological innovation.* As measured by the per capita patent index.

Two measures specific to the music industry were adapted (Peterson and Berger 1975):

11. *Music industry concentration.* A composite measure of the degree to which a few firms control the music industry.
12. *Change in music sales.* The yearly percentage change in record sales in constant dollars.

Unfortunately, the Harvard III dictionary wasn't applied to the lyrics. However, in contrast with what we have found up to now, some interesting correlations with primordial content turned up. The external indices as well as primordial content in lyrics were lagged from one through four years and intercorrelated, allowing us to see whether these indices predict primordial content in later years or vice versa. The indices were also correlated with primordial content for the same year. Table 8.6 shows concurrent correlations (the middle column) as well as lagged correlations. The first two columns on the left, giving correlations between the external

TABLE 8.6
Relationship of Primordial Content in American Musical Lyrics to Social and Economic Indices

	Lag (in Years)				
Index	−4	−3	0	+3	+4
Leading Economic Index	.04	.12	.47*	.39	.29
Concurrent Economic Index	−.10	−.08	−.39†	−.30	−.35
Lagging Economic Index	−.25	−.13	−.43†	−.26	−.49*
Unemployment	−.27	−.58*	.12	.51*	.56*
Crime Rate	.21	.16	−.29	−.80**	−.14
Social Disorder	−.13	.21	−.47†	−.10	−.26
Anomie	−.20	−.17	−.48*	−.21	−.04
Political Conservatism	.57*	.34	.33	−.04	−.00
Military Strength	.56*	.31	.42†	−.14	−.09
Technological Innovation	−.43†	−.10	.03	−.07	−.39†
Music Industry Concentration	.57*	.33	.45*	.11	−.06
Change in Music Sales	.49*	.60**	−.07	−.60**	−.46*

†p < .10.
*p < .05.
**p < .01.

indices lagged for four and three years, tell us the correlation between the values of the indices in earlier years and primordial content in a later year. The last two columns show correlations between primordial content and values of the external indices in later years: thus, they show how well musical content predicts the economic and social indices in later years. Correlations for lags of one and two years are generally in the same directions but—for whatever reason—usually not as high as the figures shown in the table.

Results for the economic indices are consistent. With the exception of unemployment, they do not predict lyric content as well as lyric content predicts them. Economic productivity (which the indices were designed to measure) is negatively correlated with primordial content. Conversely, hard times are positively related to primordial content. We could speculate that economic adversity leads people and artists to turn inward toward fantasy and away from harsh economic realities, thus causing an increase in primordial cognition. In other words, music is perhaps at least a substitute for "the opium of the people."

The indices of social disorganization are, for the most part, negatively related to primordial content. Primordial content is a good predictor of future crime rates: the correlations (not shown in the table) between primordial content and crime rate one year and two years later are $-.43$ and $-.56$. Because low levels of primordial content tend to coincide with stylistic change, we might conjecture that such change is easier or more likely in periods of social disorganization. This hypothesis is consistent with the positive relationship between political conservatism and military strength (which we might take as implying greater social control or organization) and primordial content: extensions of a style coincide with—and are preceded by—periods of military strength and political conservatism. Thus, stylistic change seems to be fostered by social fragmentation and retarded by social centralization or control.

If we take low levels of primordial content as indicating stylistic change, the figures for music industry concentration fall into place. Dominance of the industry by a few large corporations in the current or prior several years retarded stylistic change. This makes sense if we assume that large corporations are less likely to take risks with new styles. The sociologists Richard Peterson and David Berger took a similar view of the music industry: "oligopolistic concentration reduces innovation and makes for homogeneity of product" (1975, p.159). The figures for change in music sales are also consistent. Prior increases in sales predict high levels of primordial content; these may indicate that musicians retain current styles and merely work out their possibilities. If they do this long enough, several things are likely. First, some of the audience will tire of the old style and will not buy so much. Second, a stylistic change will become necessary— and will also alienate some of the audience, who will not buy so much. A combination of these two factors may be the reason that high levels of primordial content predict decreases in music sales after a lag of three to four years.

EXTRA-ARTISTIC FORCES AND PAINTING

I used measures similar to those for the study of British poetry to examine the impact of external conditions on British and French painting. Before the measures could be compared, detrending for long-term trends and autoregressive influences was, as usual, necessary. Because reflectionist theorists often argue that there may be some lag before art comes to reflect something (see Sorokin 1937), all variables were lagged both one and two periods. Finally, all relevant correlations at lags of 0, 1, and 2 were computed. Because we were operating with a few periods, correlations at even marginal levels of statistical significance were treated as significant.

According to some idealistic reflectionist positions, art should predict external social conditions. According to Marxist or materialistic reflectionism, the reverse should be the case. Lagged correlations give us an idea of the direction of causation. If we consider lags of one and two periods, there are seventy-two correlations between the four painting variables and the nine external variables. If we attempt to predict from painting to external conditions, only four of these correlations are even marginally significant—fewer than the seven significant correlations that would be expected on the basis of chance. This is a severe blow to the idealistic notion that artistic changes are a bellwether of social changes. On the other hand, social changes do seem to predict changes in art: twelve of the correlations from external conditions to art are, at least marginally, significant. They, along with correlations at a lag of zero, are shown in table 8.7. French battles, British prices, and British wages yielded no significant correlations and so are not shown. In the table, when a correlation for one nation is significant, its paired correlation from the other nation is also shown. Both primordial content and arousal potential show consistent negative relationships with sensate emphasis in philosophy and positive relationships with the extent of British war. It is not clear why British, but not French, war should be related to the content of both British and French painting. The relationship is consistent, but makes no sense for the French series. Painters who react to war should react more to it in their own than in a neighboring country. French internal disturbances are negatively related to primordial content in French painting. The latter is positively related to prosperity. Both correlations are consistent with Marxist predictions (a decline in primordial content coincides with stylistic change). There is, however, no such relationship for the British series. British internal disturbances are negatively related to the arousal potential of French paintings but not of British ones. The reason is not obvious. Nor is it obvious why European technological innovations should affect French but not British painting.

The fairly weak and inconsistent results are not caused by problems with the extra-artistic variables. Considering lags of 0, 1, and 2, there are 180 nonredundant correlations among these variables (the detrending procedure ensures that a variable cannot predict itself at any lag). Of these correlations, thirty-one are significant as opposed to the nine we should expect by chance. Furthermore, the correlations make sense. For example, wars in prior periods predict high prices in subsequent periods. When lagged correlations are examined, ideology (Sorokin's sensate emphasis in philosophy) seems to be caused by social conditions (French war and internal disturbances, technological innovations, British prices, and British prosperity) more than vice versa. Again, the data are more supportive of the materialistic, or Marxist, position than of the idealistic, or Hegelian, one.

In British history, there is a polarity between eras of prosperity and conformity, on the one hand, versus eras of individualism and freedom. The poetry of these eras differs markedly. In eras of prosperity, poetic content is rather complacent and oriented toward society and its rules. In eras of individualism, poetry is individualistic, asocial, and "lawless." This seems to be not a universal regularity but one specific to Britain. In the

TABLE 8.7

Correlations between Extra-Artistic Variables and British and French Painting Content[a]

	Primordial Content		Arousal Potential	
	British	French	British	French
British Battles	$.35_0$	$.43_0^\dagger$	$.59_0^*$	$.52_0^*$
British Internal Disturbances	$.51_1^*$	$.23_1$	$-.02_0$	$.72_0^{**}$
French Internal Disturbances	$-.25_1$	$-.57_1^*$	$-.18_2$	$-.48_2^\dagger$
Sensate Emphasis in Philosophy	$-.52_1^*$	$-.48_1^\dagger$	$-.37_2$	$-.62_2^*$
Technological Innovations	$-.13_2$	$.60_2^*$	$-.06_1$	$-.53_1^\dagger$
British Wages Relative to Prices	$.33$	$.45_2^\dagger$	$.41_1^\dagger$	$.26$

[a]Subscripts indicate number of periods for which the extra-artistic variable was lagged.
†p < .10.
*p < .05.
**p < .01.

case of American literature, prosperity has a somewhat different effect: it leads to a "thoughtless" approach which de-emphasizes emotion and thought and focuses upon concrete objects. In neither British poetry nor American short stories is primordial content related to much of anything in the external society. It tends, however, to be related to prosperity in the case of American popular music lyrics and English and French painting. We could say that decadence (as indicated by high levels of primordial content) is related to prosperity for these—but not other—art forms. The evolutionary laws governing art history seem to be fairly universal. On the other hand, the laws governing the relationship between art and society seem to be much more particularistic, varying from nation to nation and from time to time.

CHAPTER 9

The Artist
and the Work of Art

I HAVE argued that the effect of the pressure for novelty arises not so much from its strength as from its persistence. In the first part of this chapter, I investigate whether the pressure for novelty is strong enough to affect individual artists. Does the evolutionary theory help us understand only the great sweep of history, or can it shed light on stylistic development in the individual artist? Studies of creators as diverse as Beethoven and Grieg, Picasso and Rembrandt, and Dryden and Yeats suggest that the evolutionary theory is, indeed, relevant to the individual artist. At the end of the chapter, I report on some quantitative studies of nonevolutionary forces, such as temperament and psychopathology, that also shape the content of poets' verse. In the middle part of the chapter, I turn quantitative methods upon individual works of art, ranging from prose through poetry to music. We find coherent trends across the course of literary narratives—trends that arise, in part, from a need to keep the reader's attention but, in larger part, from what an author is trying to say. In fact, the type of trend we find sheds valuable light on what an author is—consciously or unconsciously—trying to say.

Though modern artists often espouse novelty as an explicit goal, this has not been the case with artists in general. As often as not, artists may see the pressure for novelty as a nuisance rather than a positive goal. Does this pressure for novelty operate in the individual? Do individual artists feel a need to surpass their own previous works as well as the works of their predecessors? If they try to outdo themselves, are they able to? And if they are, does the attempt involve deepening levels of regression and/or stylistic change? There is no single answer to these questions. Some artists, such as Picasso or Beethoven, clearly pass through a succession of styles, treating themselves as they treat their predecessors—as rivals to be outdone. Other artists seem not to operate under this compulsion. Swinburne's poetic style, for example, seems to have changed little in his lifetime.

MUSICAL MOVEMENT

Research by Simonton (1980b) provides a statistical answer to one of our questions. He studied the unpredictability or melodic originality of the first six notes from 15,618 themes by 1,479 Western composers, including all the most eminent composers and their most important compositions—essentially the entire corpus of Western music. Simonton computed two-note transitional probabilities for the entire set of 15,618 themes: that is, the probability of every possible note-to-note transition. Then he computed an improbability or melodic originality score for each theme: a theme consisting of very probable transitions would receive a low score; one consisting of very improbable transitions, a high score. Looking at melodic originality as a function of age, Simonton found that it tended to increase across most of a composer's lifetime. On average, melodic originality increased until the age of fifty-six and then showed a slight decline. Still, a composer's last works were much more original than the early ones. It would seem as if composers do, in fact, try to outdo themselves and tend—at least until late in their careers—to succeed. Thus, evolutionary pressures crucially shape not only the overall trends in art history but also the component trends in the life histories of individual creators.

Composers can increase melodic originality in several ways. By analogy with what I said in earlier chapters, it may be that artists engage in more and more primordial cognition across their lifetimes. On the other hand, they may do so for a while and then invent or adopt a stylistic change allowing them to increase originality with less primordial cognition. Or, a composer could increase melodic originality by pure "brain work." For example, melodic originality can be increased by *chromaticism:* that is, by including "accidental" notes from outside the key a piece is written in. For that matter, one can simply write increasingly in a minor key, since the transitions in minor keys are statistically less probable than analogous transitions in corresponding major keys (Simonton 1984*b*), there being fewer compositions in minor than in major keys. Thus, in the key of C, the minor transition—C to E-flat—is statistically less probable than the analogous C-to-E transition in C major. It is easy enough to do these things without regressing to a primordial state of mind or engaging in a thoroughgoing stylistic change. Owing to our success in assessing primordial content in music with rating-scale measures, we tried this method in studying the composers Beethoven, Chopin, and Grieg.

Beethoven

Simonton (1987) studied melodic originality in 103 compositions, including 593 separate themes, by Beethoven. In respect to individual themes, melodic originality increased across Beethoven's lifetime. The correlation ($r = .12$) is low but significant because of the large number of themes studied. When whole compositions were taken on the unit of analysis, the correlation is somewhat higher ($r = .25$). Melodic originality did not decrease in the later years of Beethoven's career, perhaps because he died when he was fifty-six.

To see whether the increases in Beethoven's melodic originality were accompanied by changes in primordial content, Rod Troyer and I had twenty-five subjects rate a set of his themes (Troyer and Martindale 1988). Using Barlow and Morgenstern's catalogue (1948) of the most important themes in classical music (generally they give from four to seven measures of each theme), we tried randomly to sample two of Beethoven's themes for each year from 1795 through 1826. Since this was not possible for all years, we ended with a sample of 56 themes. The melody or right-hand part of each theme was played on a piano and tape-recorded. We used only a piano to avoid the variety of effects inevitable with different instruments or with more than one. We wanted to study the basic themes, not the entire composition in which each was embedded. Subjects heard the themes in a random order and rated each of them on several scales. After determining that the subjects agreed in their ratings, we added the scales to form two composite measures. Arousal potential was defined as the sum of ratings on the scales Tense, Strong, Active, and Complex. Primordial content was defined as the sum of ratings on Otherworldly, Unnatural, Meaningless, and Dreamlike.

Computing two-note transitional probabilities for the themes, we found a correlation of .19 with year of composition—a finding similar to Simonton's and marginally significant. Rated arousal potential showed a highly significant decline with time (the correlation is −.51). Apparently, Beethoven chose themes that were structurally simpler across time. Presumably their contour was simpler, but the exact intervals involved were more improbable—something naïve listeners would be unlikely to notice.

It is well known that Beethoven's music themes tend in general to be simple—for example, the opening bars of his Third Symphony. Beethoven achieved some of his musical effects by elaborating and varying simple themes throughout a piece. Presumably, if we had played longer segments of each piece, naïve subjects would have responded differently. Although in the course of his career Beethoven worked with basic themes that strike naïve listeners as increasingly simple, he was at the same time moving toward ever more complex elaborations of these themes. His early work is fairly monophonic or "Mozartian"; his late work, fugal and polyphonic. The more complex his thematic transformations became, the simpler the themes he used—the reason being, I imagine, to avoid the overwhelming impact of a complex melody subjected to complex transformations. Though here I am extrapolating beyond our data, this hypothesis could be empirically tested.

Primordial content shows a significant inverted-U trend across Beethoven's lifetime. The data points in figure 9.1 have been smoothed, using a *two-year moving average:* that is, each data point is an average of values

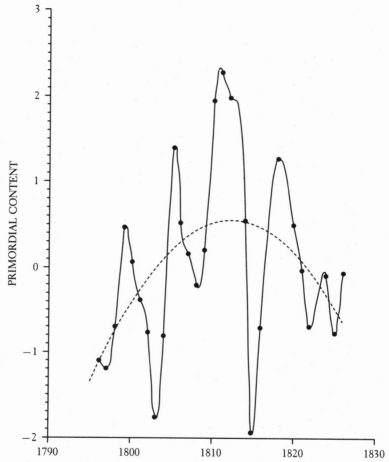

Figure 9.1 Average amount of primordial content in Ludwig van Beethoven's compositions for each year from 1795 through 1826 (two-year moving averages). The main
historical trend is shown by the dashed line. Oscillations around this trend are also
statistically significant *(see text)*.

for two successive years. This makes the main trends show up more clearly.
We are, after all, assessing each year on the basis of only one or two
themes. For the data shown in the figure, the inverted-U trend accounts
for 21 percent of the variation. The quasiperiodic oscillations around this
trend seem to be real: an autoregressive analysis shows a significant autocorrelation at a lag of two years. The autocorrelations account for 41

percent of the remaining variation. Combining the two components yields the equation

$$PC = -1.59 + .23t - .01t^2 + .58PC_{t-1} - .55PC_{t-2},$$

which accounts for 50 percent of the variation from year *(t)* to year. One has to be careful in dealing with smoothed data. The smoothing by its very nature introduces some autocorrelation because the score for one year is in part composed of the score for the prior year. However, autocorrelations introduced by smoothing are positive and decline regularly with increasing lags. That is not at all what we find in the case of Beethoven—or in other cases where I have used smoothed data. The smoothing is not creating correlations where none existed; it is magnifying patterns already in the data.

There is a correspondence between decreases in primordial content and Beethoven's stylistic changes. It is conventional to divide Beethoven's work into three styles: an early Mozartian period (1795–1802), a middle or romantic period (1802–16), and a late or postromantic period (1816–27). It is also conventional to point out that these divisions are rough, involving gradual rather than abrupt transitions. Our data do give indications of these three styles but also suggest a fine-grained periodization. The early period coincides with an increase and subsequent decrease in primordial content. The increase coincides with Beethoven's working out of the possibilities of the Mozartian style, while the decrease coincides with the stylistic change as he moved toward his own romantic style—a finding consistent with the judgments of music historians.

Our data suggest that Beethoven's middle period consists of two styles—the first culminating around 1805 and the second culminating around 1811. Over all, primordial content increases from 1803 to 1811 but clearly drops from 1811 to 1815, coincident with the beginning of Beethoven's later or postromantic style. Again, the data suggest dividing Beethoven's final style into two substyles. The results are satisfying in several respects. Beethoven seems to have left something of his state of mind in the themes of his compositions, a something—hypothetically the marks of differing degrees of primordial cognition—noticed by naïve listeners. In broad outline, our results conform with those of musical historians, if not exactly with conventional wisdom.

Chopin

It is usually thought that Chopin was a fairly good composer who did not change styles during his lifetime. Troyer and I did another study to find out whether his work shows any evidence of stylistic evolution. Though Chopin's compositions can't all be precisely dated, we obtained for our sample fifty-nine themes from at least nine or ten compositions from successive three-year periods between 1829 and 1846. Because these were all piano pieces, it was reasonable to present subjects with both the right- and the left-hand parts of each theme.

The overall measure of rated arousal potential increased, though not significantly, across time, as did note-to-note transitional improbability. Rated dissonance did show a significant increase ($r = .28$). Apparently, Chopin was increasing the impact of his music by increasing its dissonance, and thus more or less neglected other means of increasing arousal potential. Figure 9.2 presents data for primordial content in Chopin's compositions. Again, two-period moving averages were analyzed. Primordial content exhibited a statistically significant cubic trend, accounting for 63 percent of year-to-year variations in primordial content. It increased from 1829 to 1835 and then decreased until around 1843. We probably should not make much of the slight increase after 1843. This finding suggests that Chopin did go through a stylistic change. From 1829 to 1835, he worked out the possibilities of his initial style; afterward, stylistic innovation—or, perhaps, mere ingenuity—allowed him to engage in ever less primordial cognition.

The oscillations around the trend line are not random. As with Beethoven, a significant second-order autocorrelation accounts for 28 percent of the variation around the main trend. In this case, only the autocorrelation for a lag of two is significant. We could interpret these oscillations as indicating the working out of short-lived or minor *microstyles*. The trends in primordial content for Chopin and Beethoven are remarkably similar: the major trend is an inverted U; primordial content increases and then decreases; and quasiperiodic oscillations are superimposed on the main trend.

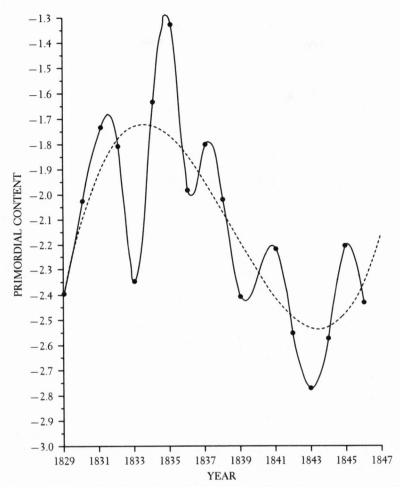

Figure 9.2 Average amount of primordial content in Frédéric Chopin's compositions for each year from 1829 through 1846 (two-year moving averages). The main trend is shown by the dashed line. Oscillations around this trend are also statistically significant *(see text).*

Grieg

Though no one would rank Edvard Grieg with Beethoven or Chopin, we studied him to find out whether the laws of stylistic evolution are general or apply only to the most eminent creators. Another reason to take an interest in Grieg is that his audience was different from that of Beethoven or Chopin. Immensely popular in Norway, Grieg responded to this popularity by writing music to enforce it. It is no criticism of anyone's taste in music to assume that music designed to be popular with any large group of people will not be particularly innovative. Grieg himself indicated that he probably would have been a better composer if he had left home and written "European" rather than Norwegian music.

Since Grieg occasionally let several years pass without writing any music, we took samples of his musical themes for successive three-year periods from 1865 to 1901 (nothing can be precisely dated to the period 1892–94); five to six themes from each period gave a total of sixty-five themes. The melodic line of each theme was played on a piano to sixteen subjects. The themes were, of course, presented in a random order. The measure of rated arousal potential declined significantly with time ($r = -.30$). Transitional improbability showed an insignificant decline. Rated dissonance, however, increased across time ($r = .25$). Like Chopin, Grieg apparently focused on dissonance in order to increase arousal potential. Unlike Chopin, he neglected other determinants of arousal potential so that they showed declines. This was a reasonable course: had he increased both dissonance and melodic complexity, he would probably have increased arousal potential too much.

Average ratings for primordial content in each period are shown in figure 9.3. Since the method of sampling had already averaged out random fluctuations in the data, we did not need to do it again by smoothing. Analysis of variance of ratings of the sixty-five themes indicates significant interperiod differences. The main historical trend is a quartic (M-shaped) one. An autoregressive analysis shows that oscillations around this trend are real rather than just due to chance. We could interpret the data as indicating the quick working out of an initial style (the increase from period 1 to period 2); slow development of a second style (the decrease from period 2 to period 8); quick exhaustion of this style (the increase from period 8 to period 9); and development of a third style (the decline after period 9). Though these don't seem to be massive stylistic changes, they are similar to the microstyles evident in both Beethoven and Chopin.

Though we cannot conclude much from studies of 3 composers, Simonton's study (1980b) of 1,479 is strong evidence that composers increase the melodic originality of their compositions across most of their lifetimes.

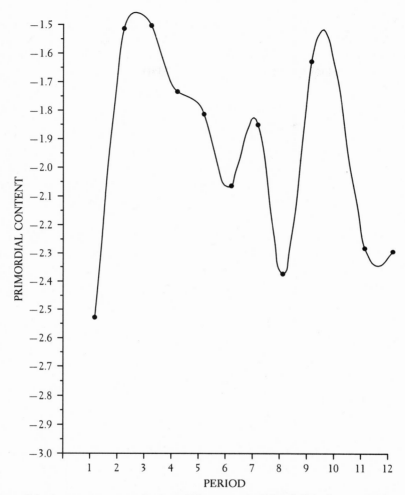

Figure 9.3 Average amount of primordial content in Edvard Grieg's compositions for consecutive three-year intervals from 1865 through 1901.

We cannot be sure that they do so because of the evolutionary pressure to increase arousal potential, but that seems the most parsimonious explanation. And I can think of no other plausible explanation for finding the same trend in composers working at a variety of times under a variety of individual circumstances. Our studies of Beethoven, Chopin, and Grieg suggest that composers increase arousal potential by alternately developing styles and working out their possibilities. The quasiperiodic oscillations in primordial content we found for each composer suggest that each developed and worked out a series of styles. The fact that these trends were not obscured by other forces suggests that more studies of trends in individual style would be fruitful.

LITERATURE

The only evolutionary study of individual development in literature is one that I did some years ago (Martindale 1975). In comparing poetic texts written before and after the midpoints of the careers of nineteen British and French poets, I found no significant trends in either arousal potential or primordial content. But the very design of this study may have made it unable to detect any trends: If the measures of interest rose during the first half of poets' careers and fell during the second half, the two trends would cancel each other. Later I used more fine-grained sampling methods on the poets Dryden, Shakespeare, Wordsworth, and Yeats. First, let me consider a poet who seems clearly to have changed styles during his lifetime.

Dryden

When John Dryden began writing, he was heavily influenced by the metaphysical poets, especially John Donne. Nonetheless, Dryden is as much as anyone else responsible for introducing the quite different neoclassic style. To trace this evolution with our measures, I drew random samples of about 300 words from Dryden's (1958) poetry for each year from 1659 through 1700, for a total sample of 11,958 words. As usual, translations and verse dramas were not included. When the Composite Variability Index was computed for these samples, I found a modest increase across time ($r = .23$). Primordial content (see figure 9.4) shows a significant U-shaped pattern. It apparently declined as Dryden perfected the neoclassic style. Once he had developed it as much as he wanted, primordial content began to rise. The deviations around the U-shaped trend can in part be accounted for by an autoregressive equation with a

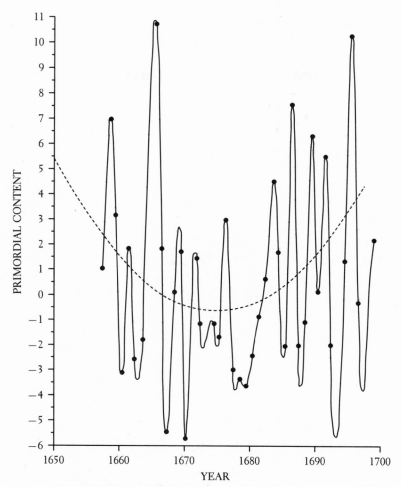

Figure 9.4 Average amount of primordial content in John Dryden's poetry for each year from 1659 through 1700. Both the U-shaped trend shown by the dashed line and the oscillations around it are statistically significant.

lag of two years. If ups and downs in primordial content indicate introduction and working out of new styles, the oscillations suggest a series of small-scale stylistic changes across the course of Dryden's career. If we put together the general trend and the autoregressive component, the best-fitting equation is

$$PC = 2.73 - .37t + .01t^2 - .32PC_{t-1} - .36PC_{t-2}.$$

The equation accounts for 22 percent of overall variation in primordial content.

Though their parameters are different, the equations for Dryden and for Beethoven are the same. Both equations have a quadratic component that describes the trend across the creator's lifetime. Of course, the grand trend is U-shaped for Dryden and has an inverted U-shape for Beethoven: Dryden began forging his own style from the start and worked out its possibilities in the second half of his career; Beethoven did the reverse, working out the possibilities of the neoclassic style during the first half of his career and forging a new style during the second half. For Beethoven, there were unexploited possibilities in the neoclassic or Mozartian style; whereas for Dryden, the school of Donne was over and done with, leaving nothing more to do in the metaphysical style. Dryden had perforce from the start to develop a new style. Of course, neither man's career was so simple: superimposed upon these grand trends, systematic oscillations indicate the discovery and exploitation of what I call microstyles.

Shakespeare

One reason to turn to Shakespeare's plays is that there is no special reason to expect the evolutionary theory to apply to him. He seems not to have gone through any decisive stylistic change. So far as we know, he was as interested in making money with his plays as in their literary value. So far as I know, critics have not suggested any systematic movements across his lifetime indicative of increasing arousal potential or primordial thought. Thus, he was under the usual pressure to outperform his own earlier work. The other reason to look at Shakespeare is that the data are at hand. Peter Derks of the College of William and Mary is doing a computer analysis of the First Folio edition of the plays. Since I've given him a hand on some computer technicalities, he has shared some preliminary results with me. To content-analyze the First Folio, one has either to program the computer to understand Elizabethan spelling or to modernize the texts. Derks did the latter. Some modernization can be done automatically. But, since spelling hasn't changed systematically, one eventually has to go through the texts word by word—a big job, involving about 790,000 words. At present, only the twelve tragedies have been completely modernized—or 276,283 words (excluding stage directions and the like).

In the tragedies, the Composite Variability Index increased with time. The correlations—.15 when an act is the unit of analysis, and .22 when a play is—are not statistically significant. Nonetheless, since we are dealing not with a sample but with the entire population, the upward trend is real. Statistics are designed to tell us about the probability that a sample is giving true estimates of a population. If you measure an entire population—all the words in all the plays in this case—you don't need statistics. Probability levels can, however, give us an idea of the strength of a trend even if we have measured the entire population. In this case, the trend is not strong. We'd know that even without probability levels. A correlation of .15 explains $.15^2$, or a negligible 2 percent of the variation. Shakespeare did increase some of the components of the Composite Variability Index to more than a negligible degree. The correlation of the hapax legomena percentage (percentage of words used only once in an act) with time is .50. The correlation of word length with time is .28. On the other hand, Shakespeare used less and less extreme or high-polarity words over time ($r = -.33$). This was my first use of the Composite Variability Index with drama; as was the case with prose, it is probably not the best measure of arousal potential for this genre.

The correlation between primordial content and time is a significant $-.42$. Deviations from this linear trend are not significant, so the only trend is a decline across time. I show mean values for each of the tragedies in figure 9.5. The fact that Shakespeare moved away from primordial toward conceptual cognition across time could mean that there was fairly continuous stylistic change throughout his career. It could also mean that—for reasons having nothing much to do with evolutionary pressures—he became more interested in concepts and less interested in concrete things and actions. Before accepting the hypothesis that the decline in primordial content indicates stylistic change, we would want further evidence. For example, percentage of words added and dropped across time should show trends indicative of style change. Poets always seem to lose interest in emotion, and Shakespeare was no exception. His use of emotional words declined significantly with time ($r = -.33$)—presumably as a byproduct of his movement from primordial toward conceptual cognition.

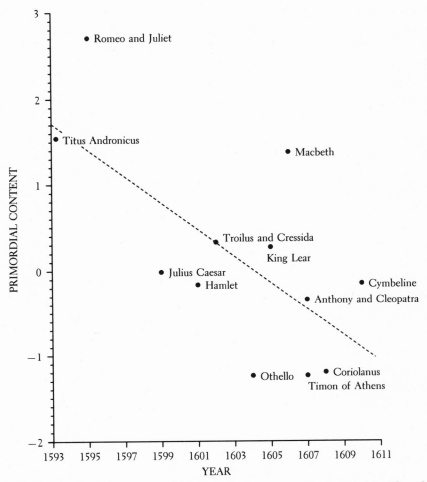

Figure 9.5   Primordial content in William Shakespeare's tragedies declined significantly with time.

The computer agrees with the critical consensus that Shakespeare became more pessimistic across time. The average evaluation rating of his words declined with time ($r = -.36$), and the average potency rating increased ($r = .57$). Compare the raging King Lear (c. 1605) with the defeated optimism of Romeo and Juliet (c. 1595). Thus, over time, he became more concerned with high-impact negative themes. Shakespeare does not seem to have made these changes to pander to his audience. If recent popularity as measured by Simonton (1986b) is close to popularity in Shakespeare's time, he was working against himself. The correlation between polarity and popularity is positive ($r = .35$) rather than negative. The correlation between word length and popularity is negative ($r = -.28$) rather than positive. The correlation between the Composite Variability Index and popularity is extremely significant ($r = .51$). On the other hand, primordial content and evaluation rating are unrelated to popularity, but potency is negatively ($r = -.40$) rather than positively related to it.

The trends I have been discussing do not seem to be particular to Shakespeare's tragedies. Preliminary results—the texts are not completely modernized—show that similar trends also occur in the histories and comedies. These seem to be general trends in Shakespeare's writing rather than genre-specific ones. What remains unclear is whether evolutionary pressures are in part responsible for these changes.

If we do an autoregressive analysis of means of the data shown in figure 9.5, we find nothing. If we smooth the data for all of the plays, we do get significant autocorrelations at lags of one and two years. In other words, there seems to have been a sequence of microstyles. The pattern of raw autocorrelations tells us that this could not be an artifact of smoothing. Shakespeare, like other creators, seems to have been propelled through a sequence of microstyles. Only the force of evolution could serve as the source of this propulsion.

Wordsworth

Although Wordsworth did not invent the romantic style, he had a big hand in it. He developed the aspect of romanticism devoted to finding the strange and poetic in the ordinary and familiar. Unlike many other British romantic poets, Wordsworth lived to an old age. It might have been rather better if he had not, since he ultimately became a part of the establishment that romanticism began by fighting against. Worse, his later poetry seems to lack the poetic power of his earlier verse. Let us take a quantitative look at him.

I selected sixteen lines of poetry for each of the years in which Wordsworth (1904) wrote anything, producing fifty-three samples from 1785 through 1847. The first three are from the 1780s when Wordsworth was in his (unprecocious) teens; then there is something from almost every year between 1795 and 1847. The sample totals 8,101 words. Figure 9.6, presenting values of the Composite Variability Index aggregated by decades, shows that Wordsworth did seem to fail poetically in his later years: the index rises until the 1810s and then declines—a significant inverted-U trend. I dealt with two-year moving averages of primordial

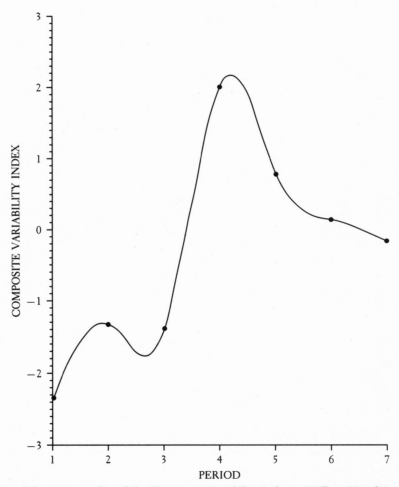

Figure 9.6 Average value of the Composite Variability Index in William Wordsworth's poetry for the decades from the 1780s through the 1840s.

content. Whether primordial content is analyzed by decades or by years, it shows a strong quartic trend, as shown in figure 9.7. Primordial content was initially high. Its decline from the 1790s to the 1800s corresponds to Wordsworth's developing his own uniquely "prosaic" style. This style was worked out, with a corresponding increase in primordial content over the next decades. Whether we ascribe the decline in primordial content in the 1830s and 1840s to development of a late style or to a collapse of

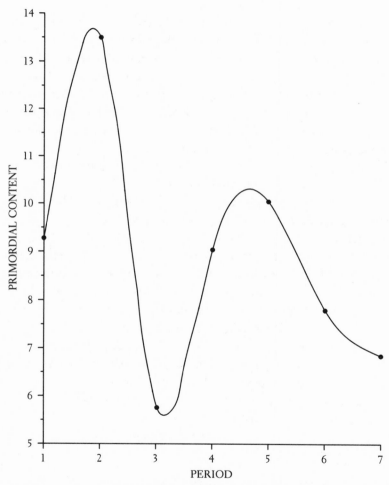

Figure 9.7   Average amount of primordial content in William Wordsworth's poetry for the decades from the 1780s through the 1840s.

Wordsworth's poetic vision is a matter of taste or charity. Just as with Dryden and Shakespeare, Wordsworth's poetry shows a series of microstyles. Autoregressive analysis turns up significant autocorrelations at lags of both one and two years, showing that the oscillations around the main trend line are real rather than just due to chance.

Yeats

William Butler Yeats began writing poetry in a symbolist or decadent style characteristic of the late nineteenth century. Early in the twentieth century, he developed his own unique neo-symbolist style. To study this progression, I drew ten samples of about ten lines each from Yeats's (1956) poetry for each of the decades from the 1880s through the 1930s. The samples average about 1,560 words per decade. Computing the Composite Variability Index, we find a correlation with decade of .01. We find the same correlation for incongruous juxtapositions. Now, the computer measures do not pick up the fact that Yeats's later poetry has more of what I call arousal potential than his early work, since the poetry delivers its impact through ideas rather than language. The style change was on the ideational rather than on the linguistic level.

The trend in primordial content is in conformity with expectations (see figure 9.8). Analysis of variance shows that the trend is highly significant. The increase from the 1880s to the 1890s is expected. During this time, Yeats was writing in a symbolist style and exploiting its possibilities. The decline in primordial content coincides with Yeats's break with the old style. After the break was complete, primordial content—as expected—began to increase again. Since I sampled the data by decades without getting yearly samples, it is not possible to see whether microstylistic oscillations are superimposed on this general trend. The reason the data were so sampled is that I did the study before I thought it would be profitable to look for year-to-year trends.

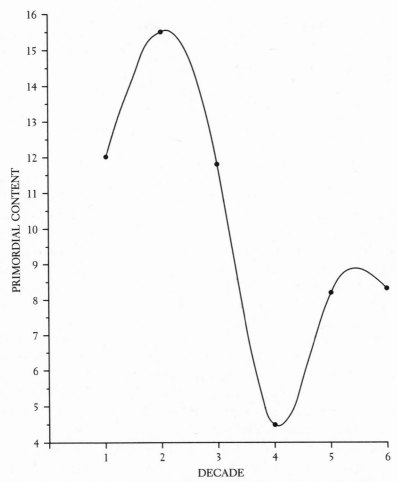

Figure 9.8 Average amount of primordial content in William Butler Yeats's poetry for consecutive decades from the 1880s through the 1930s.

PAINTING

The laws of individual stylistic evolution seem to be similar regardless of whether we are dealing with poetry or music. The arousal potential of creative works tends to increase across a creator's lifetime but may decline toward the end. Since artists produce arousal potential in different ways, a general measure does not always show the increase. A creator who went through a major stylistic shift tends not only to show a career-long nonlinear trend in primordial content but also to go through a sequence of microstyles. We should find the same trends in the visual arts.

Picasso

Critics agree that Picasso progressed through a sequence of discrete styles. To find out whether naïve observers agree with this judgment and whether the evolutionary theory could account for the progression, I sampled one painting per year from 1895 through 1972 from several collections (Duncan 1974, Elgar and Maitland 1955, Janis and Janis 1946, Schiff 1983, and Wertenbaker 1967), using where possible only paintings depicting people. For the few years where no reproduction was available, I included an extra one from the next year so as to end up with a sample of eighty paintings. For purposes of analysis, I wanted to be sure to have five paintings for each of the sixteen five-year periods beginning with 1895. I then asked twenty-one subjects to rate the paintings on scales designed to tap arousal potential (Tense, Strong, Complex, and Active) and primordial content (Otherworldly, Unnatural, Meaningless, Not Realistic, and Not Photographic). Eight of the twenty-one subjects correctly guessed that the paintings were by Picasso. The subjects' estimates of creation dates correlated with the actual dates; but the average estimated date of creation, 1797, made me reasonably sure that the subjects were not art experts. When I did separate analyses for subjects who did and did not know that the paintings were by Picasso, the results were about the same, so I present results for all of the subjects.

Analysis of variance of scores grouped into five-year periods showed significant interperiod differences in both arousal potential and primordial content. The trend in arousal potential is best accounted for by a simple linear increase—in conformity with theoretical expectations. On the other hand, variations in primordial content were not due simply to a monotonic increase, though this increase accounts for 65 percent of the variation in the means shown in figure 9.9. When this trend is removed, a significant autocorrelation at a lag of two periods accounts for 25 percent of the remaining variance. Thus, we again find microstylistic oscillations.

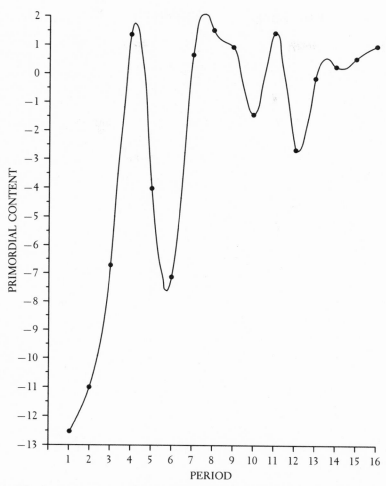

Figure 9.9 Average amount of primordial content in Pablo Picasso's paintings from sixteen consecutive five-year periods from 1895 through 1972.

The microstylistic oscillations correspond to fairly clear stylistic changes. The increase in primordial content culminating in period 4 (1910–14) corresponds to Picasso's initial cubist style. The subsequent decline corresponds to his movement toward a more realistic and modeled (see figure 9.10)—as opposed to flat and fragmented (see figure 9.11)—style. The trend in primordial content suggests that the former style was quickly worked through. Although it is not completely smooth, the trend

Figure 9.10 Pablo Picasso, *A Woman in White*, 1923 (The Metropolitan Museum of Art, New York. Rogers Fund, 1951. Acquired from the Museum of Modern Art, Lizzie P. Bliss Collection. 53.140.4)

Figure 9.11   Pablo Picasso, *Accordionist,* Summer, 1911 (Collection, The Solomon R. Guggenheim Museum, New York. Gift of Solomon R. Guggenheim, 1937. Photo: David Heald; Photo © 1990 The Solomon R. Guggenheim Foundation)

in primordial content goes down from period 7 (1925–29) until period 12 (1950–54) and up after that. This finding suggests that Picasso was gradually establishing a new style and then—after 1950–54—working out its possibilities. If we are to take him at his word, Picasso was learning to paint like a child during this time. A painting done while primordial content was decreasing (figure 9.12) and another done while it was increasing (figure 9.13) show that he did learn how to paint like a child. Furthermore, Picasso showed even more fine-grained "micro-micro" stylistic oscillations. For example, in this analysis I aggregated over or averaged out such short-lived styles as the rose period, the blue period, and so on.

Rembrandt

To study Rembrandt's stylistic evolution, I sampled five of his paintings from each of the successive five-year intervals from 1625 to 1664, using where possible one painting for each year. To control for content, only historical—that is, mythological or biblical—scenes were used. All of the paintings were taken from Gary Schwartz (1985), who presents a color reproduction of every painting known to be by Rembrandt or generally attributed to him. I showed slides of the paintings in a random order to twelve naïve subjects who rated them on the same scales as in the study of Picasso. When subjects were asked to guess who had done the paintings, none knew. While they agreed well on their other ratings, they did not agree when asked to estimate the date of each painting. Their estimated dates did not correlate with the actual date of creation: the correlation was .12; the average estimated date of creation, 1464.

The measure of arousal potential declined significantly with date of composition. The correlation of −.50 tells us several things. For one thing, I did not do a competent job of selecting appropriate scales to measure arousal potential. Since Rembrandt's main innovation was the handling of light and shadow, he was probably increasing arousal potential by increasing his use of chiaroscuro techniques. And he seems to have handled these techniques better and better across time. If I am correct, it is likely that the more Rembrandt used chiaroscuro, the

Figure 9.12   Pablo Picasso, *Girl Before A Mirror,* Boisgeloup, March 1932. Oil on canvas, 64 × 51¼" (Collection, The Museum of Modern Art, New York. Gift of Mrs. Simon Guggenheim)

Figure 9.13   Pablo Picasso, *La famille*, 1970 (MP. 222, Musée Picasso, Paris. Photo: Cliché des Musées Nationaux-Paris, Copyright 1990 ARS N.Y./Spadem)

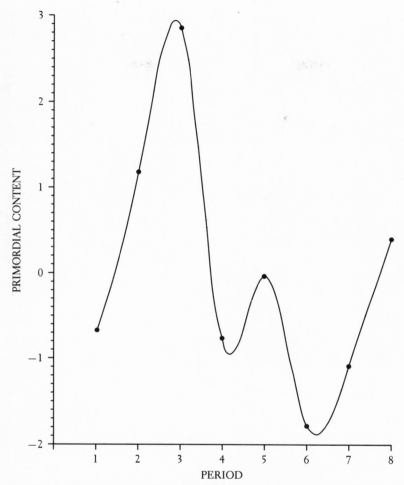

Figure 9.14 Average amount of primordial content in Rembrandt's paintings for consecutive five-year periods from 1625 through 1664.

more he decreased other determinants of arousal potential. Otherwise, overall arousal potential would have been pushed too high.

As may be seen in figure 9.14, primordial content shows a cubic trend across Rembrandt's career, which accounts for 15 percent of variation in primordial content among the forty paintings and for 72 percent of the variation among the mean values for each period. When I extracted this trend from the means shown in the figure and performed an autoregressive analysis, I found a significant autocorrelation at a lag of one period, which accounts for 53 percent of the remaining interperiod variation among the means shown in figure 9.14. When I analyzed the data by years rather than by periods, I found significant autocorrelations at lags of two and four years. In either case, I found a pattern that is becoming familiar: long-term trends in primordial content with superimposed oscillations suggestive of a series of microstyles.

The main cubic trend fits with what is known of Rembrandt's style. His early work is in a standard baroque idiom. The initial increase in primordial content corresponds to his working through this style. As Rembrandt developed his unique style—mainly based on chiaroscuro techniques—primordial content declined. After his style was fully developed, and he began to exploit its possibilities, primordial content began to increase again.

THE DEVELOPMENT OF A WORK OF ART

Aesthetic evolution shows a surprising *self-similarity* under magnification: when we examine the course of primordial content across centuries, we find long-term trends with superimposed oscillations. If we examine the course of primordial content across the career of an individual artist, we see exactly the same thing on a smaller time scale. Theoretically, these patterns are caused by the need to increase arousal potential. This need is caused by habituation: the audience—and the artist—tires of old forms and wants new ones. Habituation corresponds, as I have said, to building up a set of expectations. After these expectations are well developed, a work of art that conforms too closely to them will elicit neither interest nor pleasure. It is to avoid this sad fate that the artist must increase the arousal potential of his or her works.

We can apply the same line of reasoning to the individual work of art. For example, a work of literature that is too predictable will not be read through to its end. The author must obviously sustain interest steadily or increase it—a task that gets ever more difficult the further one is in a work. Consider a novel. As one reads it, one learns more about the characters and the "narrative world," and, in so doing, becomes able to predict to some extent what will happen. One is also becoming used to, or habituating, to the characters and their traits. To counter this habituation and sustain a reader's interest, the author uses narrative devices such as suspense and surprise. The study of ratings of suspense and surprise in American short stories (chapter 5) showed that arousal potential does in fact increase in the course of a work.

A writer must not only either increase depth of regression or change styles in order to increase incongruity, complexity, and the other devices that constitute arousal potential, but do so in an individual work of literature as well. Evidence for this hypothesis is hard to come by, a writer being likely to "erase" it during revision. A literary work does seem to reflect the psychic level at which it was created, in terms of the amount of primordial content evident. A work created at different psychic levels should reflect this by the differential distribution of primordial content throughout.

The psychoanalyst Anton Ehrenzweig (1967, p.171) argues that, no matter what else it is about, a work of art is always about its own creation. I have argued that creativity involves a movement from conceptual to primordial cognition and then a return to a conceptual state of mind. In the next section, I show that we can trace in a quantitative way just such a movement across the course of many literary narratives. In later sections, I show that other narratives exhibit other sorts of trends in primordial content as well as in other types of content. The sort of trend we find is a valuable hint about the symbolic meaning of a narrative. Hermeneutics, which is aimed at elucidating the meaning of a work of art, is usually done by philosophically minded literary critics in ponderous tomes that leave one more confused than enlightened. Hermeneutics can also be done in a quantitative manner that is, I think, more enlightening and more compelling. In the final section, I show that the same methods used to delineate trends in literary narratives can just as well be applied to music.

Night Journey Narratives

Some narratives show systematic trends in respect to primordial content (Martindale, 1978*b*, 1979, 1987). One type of such narrative concerns what the author Joseph Campbell (1949) called "the monomyth." This is probably the single most common plot in myth and literature. Typically, the plot begins with a hero who is confronted with difficulties or seemingly insoluble problems in the real world. He undertakes a journey to hell, the underworld, or some other distant and fabulous destination. On the way, usually guided by some sort of helping figure, the hero overcomes obstacles and undergoes various trials. Full-blown versions of the theme culminate in a victory over a dragon or another evil figure, which results in the hero's obtaining treasure, wisdom, knowledge, or the hand of a captive "persecuted maiden" whom he rescues. With varying degrees of difficulty, the hero then makes his way back to the real world where he often enjoys new knowledge or power gained by virtue of his journey. He reappears as someone who has been reborn or revitalized in some sense. A journey to hell is one of the standard features of Western literary epics. Aeneas' journey to hell in the *Aeneid* and Dante's in the *Inferno* come readily to mind. In Eastern literature, the *Tibetan Book of the Dead* consists of a guidebook for the forty-nine–day journey between death and rebirth. The symbolic texts produced by many alchemical writers also exhibit the night journey theme (Jung 1963). Theoretically, all of these seemingly diverse narratives really tell the same story.

Psychologically, the night journey theme has been interpreted by Jung (1963) and the Jungian analyst Erich Neumann (1954) as symbolizing descent into the unconscious, alteration in state of consciousness, or regression to archaic modes of thought. On the psychological level, the theme of the journey to hell and back hypothetically symbolizes a regression from the conceptual (abstract, analytic, reality-oriented) thought of waking consciousness to primordial (concrete, free-associative, autistic) thought and then a return to conceptual thought. Of course, the psychoanalyst Ernst Kris (1952) holds that any act of creation involves an initial stage of inspiration and a subsequent stage of elaboration. In the inspirational phase, there is a regression toward primordial thought, whereas in the subsequent elaboration stage there is a return to analytic thinking. The inspirational stage yields the "rough draft" of the creative product, whereas the elaboration stage involves logical, analytical thought in putting the product into final form. Thus, the theme of the night journey mirrors the psychological processes involved in the creation of art. Ehrenzweig (1967) argues that the minimal content of any aesthetic creation includes such "poemagogic" mirroring of the act of creation. Whatever else they are about, night journey narratives are about themselves, about their own creation. This is even more clear in romantic "crisis poems" (Bloom 1975), which I take to be subjective versions of the night journey theme.

The regression-and-return cycle can also be seen in the diurnal cycle of sleeping and waking (Rapaport 1957) and in mystical and religious experiences, both of which tend to involve subsequent feelings of rejuvenation. Jung (1959) dealt with personal growth under the rubric of individuation. In later stages of life, this process, too, involves attempts to regress and "bring back" beneficent aspects of "the unconscious" (primordial cognition). Many varieties of psychodynamic psychotherapy are based on the idea that the patient must first be made to regress in order to allow a later "progression" or movement toward mental health. Thus, renderings of the night journey theme might be seen as providing metaphorical maps pointing the way toward personal growth and creativity.

The psychological interpretation of the night journey theme is internally consistent, as can be shown by qualitative analyses. For example, in the *Inferno,* sexual sins are punished at a shallow level of hell; anal themes peak at middle levels; and oral themes, culminating in the image of Count Ugolino perpetually gnawing Archbishop Ruggieri's skull, are found only deep in hell. If descending into hell symbolizes a descent into the unconscious or a regression toward primordial cognition, then this sequence is consistent with what would be expected on the basis of psychoanalytic theory. The problem with most psychological analyses of literature—and, indeed, with literary criticism in general—has been that there have been no scientifically acceptable methods for deciding among alternative explanations of a text. Are the examples of the night journey mentioned here really similar? It might be argued that much literary criticism, whether psychologically oriented or not, involves imprecise, subjective, and qualitative content analysis. We can bring more objective and quantitative procedures to bear on the question.

If a narrative describing a journey to hell or a similar region symbolizes regression from a conceptual to a primordial state of consciousness and a subsequent return to a conceptual state, we might expect that words indicating primordial content would first increase and then decrease in the narrative. To test this idea, we can divide the narrative into segments, and measure the amount of primordial content in each. I do not mean to imply that an author necessarily has gone through an "inner voyage" to and back from primordial cognition while writing such a narrative. Rather, the narrative is *about* such an inner voyage that the author must at some time or another have taken.

As an example, let us consider book VI of Vergil's *Aeneid,* in which Aeneas descends into Hell, consults with its denizens, and returns. I divided the text (in English translation) into twenty-three segments of about four hundred words each. The primordial content for each of these segments (figure 9.15) clearly increases and then decreases as predicted. The inverted-U trend accounts for 42 percent of the variation. The quasiperiodic oscillations around this curve are not random but are, at least in part, caused by a marginally significant autocorrelation at a lag of five segments. When I put the two sources of variation together, I came up with this equation for the *Aeneid:*

$$PC_t = 10.53 + .80t - .04t^2 - .37PC_{t-5}.$$

Now this is exactly the sort of equation we found for art history and the careers of individual artists, showing that primordial content seems to unfold across history, careers, and individual works in parallel ways: there is a long-term coherent trend (of an inverted-U shape in this case) with systematic oscillations superimposed on it. As I suspected, another increase in magnification produces a self-similar pattern—a simple long-term trend in primordial content and a quasiperiodic oscillations weaving around it.

This is not an isolated instance. The best equation for Coleridge's "The Rime of the Ancient Mariner" is about the same as that for book VI of the *Aeneid,*

$$PC_t = 16.80 + .73t - .04t^2 - .36PC_{t-5}.$$

The degree of the autoregressive lag of five segments has to do with exactly how the poem is segmented. The crucial point is that the autocorrelation is there. The fact that in these poems primordial content shows clear trends across the course of the narrative must mean that the narrative is symbolically *about* alteration in state of consciousness. If it were not, primordial content should be distributed randomly. Of course this is not the only thing these two poems are about. A poem can have multiple

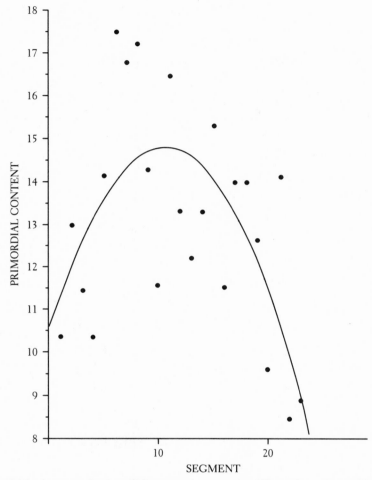

Figure 9.15   Amount of primordial content in successive 400-word segments of book VI of Virgil's *Aeneid.* The main trend in primordial content is shown by the solid line.

meanings. Indeed, references to good versus evil also show systematic trends in both texts.

The inverted-U trend can also be found in other night journey narratives. It shows up clearly in *The Tibetan Book of the Dead* and in the first part of Dante's *The Divine Comedy.* It is also present in two alchemical texts I have analyzed: *Aurora Consurgens* (von Franz 1966), which has been attributed to Saint Thomas Aquinas, and the anonymous parable given by the psychoanalyst Herbert Silberer (1917). We also find the same pattern in less obscure texts. Shakespeare's *Hamlet, King Lear,* and *Cymbeline* all show inverted-U patterns. In all of the texts showing this pattern, the hero is somehow transformed by the night journey: he is better off or at least more enlightened.

This approach will work only if an author is cooperative. For example, though H. Rider Haggard's *She* is a good example of the night journey plot, primordial content shows a linear increase across the course of the text. The reason is not far to find. Almost the entire book is devoted to getting to the mysterious land that She rules and what happens once there. The return is only briefly mentioned. The trend is really an inverted-U, but the peak is pushed very, very far to the right.

Real travel is supposed to broaden one's horizons. Anyone who has traveled to strange or exotic places would probably agree that such travel does induce an alteration in consciousness. After a few days in a culture where everything is upside down, backward, and strange, one becomes disoriented and confused. You don't think straight. You can't if for no other reason than that thinking in the usual way won't get you anywhere in an alien culture. As you head home, things gradually become more familiar and your thinking returns to normal. Presumably, though, you have become a bit wiser or at least more knowledgeable. Paul Theroux has traveled to some strange places and came back to tell about it. In *The Great Railway Bazaar* (1975), he tells of his journey from London through Asia and back again courtesy of the Trans-Siberian Railway. Bill McCormack and I fed samples of the book to the computer (McCormack and Martindale 1983) and found a nice inverted-U trend in primordial content.

Inverse Night Journeys

Rather than descending into the unconscious and coming back a better person, just the opposite can happen. You can start out there, try to escape, and get sucked back in and destroyed—more or less what D. H. Lawrence (1955 [1924]) said Melville's *Moby Dick* is about. Ahab represents consciousness. Moby Dick is the unconscious, the id, the body. Ahab wants to destroy the white whale. He wants to become pure consciousness, and for a while seems to be on the track of success. Then he gets sucked under, killed by the whale. We can translate that into the terms I've been using. The story is about trying to escape from a primordial state, making some progress at it, and lapsing back in. If this is true, primordial content should show a U-shaped trend across the course of *Moby Dick*. To find out, Nancy Hasenfus and I (Martindale 1979) took two hundred word samples from every fifth page of the book and came up with a highly significant U-shaped trend. It accounts for 10 percent of the overall variance (figure 9.16). The variation around the trend is not random; some of it is accounted for by oscillations produced by an autoregressive trend at a lag of four segments. The general equation is the same as always except for a change of sign and of crucial lag,

$$PC_t = 4.95 - .10t + .001t_2 - .22PC_{t-4}.$$

Shakespeare's *Romeo and Juliet* and *Troilus and Cressida* show the same U-shaped pattern. They don't seem to be the same story as *Moby Dick*, but in a sense they are.

Burial is an important theme in the stories of Edgar Allan Poe. Several of his tales—such as "The Fall of the House of Usher," "Ligeia," and "Berenice"—are about the unsuccessful attempt of a hero to bury another character. In these stories, the hero tends to grow in strength, energy, or sensitivity as the other character gradually weakens into a state of somnolence and is buried. Following the burial, this character begins to revive as the hero loses vitality in one way or another. Finally, the secondary character returns alive from the grave. On the basis of structural analyses, I suggested the hypothesis that these tales can be interpreted as symbolizing unsuccessful attempts at escape from a regressive state of consciousness (Martindale 1973c). These are stories about attempts to escape a primordial state of consciousness that fail. That is, they symbolize the following sequence: a beginning in a primordial state of consciousness, partial escape from this state into a more conceptual state (compare the gaining of strength of the central character and the burial—that is, repression—of the secondary character), and a final relapse into the regressive state (compare the return from the grave of the secondary character—that is, the "return of the repressed"—and the destruction or disintegration

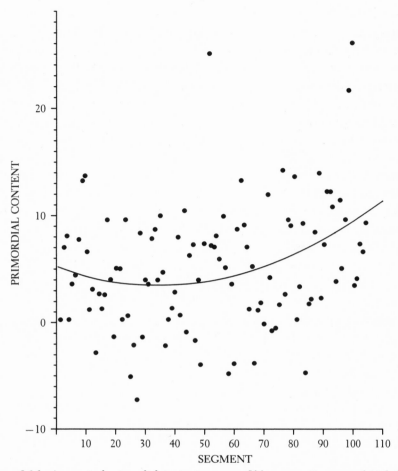

Figure 9.16 Amount of primordial content on every fifth consecutive page of Melville's *Moby Dick*. The solid line indicates the main trend.

of the central character). On the other hand, Poe's far less common tales concerning successful burial—such as "The Cask of Amontillado" and "Eleonora"—can be read as variants of the night journey theme. They symbolize a sequence of "descent into the unconscious," successful repression of negative aspects of the personality, and return to a normal state of consciousness.

One justification for a psychological "translation" of the two types of story is that the structure of the narrative is isomorphic with the psychological processes involved. For example, in the universe of Poe's tales, the quantity of vitality is constant (Martindale 1973c): that is, one character can only gain vitality or strength as another loses it. This is not a relation true of real people in the real world, but it is true (hypothetically) about the relationship between ego and id or "conscious" and "unconscious" in Freudian or Jungian theory. Another example is that people who are buried in Poe's tales behave not at all like people buried in the real world but like repressed ideas in psychoanalytic theory. Such arguments for the psychological interpretation are ones of internal consistency and the possibility of translation without remainder. This method of "proof" is subject to the obvious criticism that it is too subjective and might allow one to conclude almost anything one wants depending upon which aspects of a narrative one chooses to emphasize. The poet and literary critic Richard Wilbur (1967) used this method to argue that "The Fall of the House of Usher" is an example of what I have termed a successful night journey, while I used the very same method to argue just the reverse (Martindale 1972b). Let me do some counting to see who is on the right track. I analyzed five of Poe's stories: "The Fall of the House of Usher," "Berenice," "Ligeia," "The Cask of Amontillado," and "Eleonora." The first three, describing cases of unsuccessful burial, should exhibit the pattern of decreasing and then increasing primordial content. The second two, concerning successful burial, should exhibit the opposite pattern. Briefly, the plot of each narrative follows:

"The Fall of the House of Usher": Madeline Usher gradually weakens and falls into a trance. As she does, Roderick Usher gains in vitality. Madeline is believed dead and locked in a vault. Roderick now weakens as she revives in her crypt. Finally, she returns. The consequences of this return are less than pleasant.

"Berenice": Berenice sickens and falls into a trance. Seeming dead, she is buried. In a fugue state, the narrator exhumes her and extracts her teeth. It is discovered that she is not dead.

"Ligeia": Ligeia sickens and dies. The narrator remarries; and, as his new wife sickens, she is apparently transmuted into Ligeia.

"Eleonora": Eleonora, too, sickens and dies. Her spirit returns to haunt the narrator; but by what Poe explicitly calls a mysterious "dispensation" connected with his *perfect* love for Eleonora, the spirit departs forever.

"The Cask of Amontillado": The narrator entices his enemy, Fortunato, into his wine cellar, chains him in an alcove, and bricks him up in it. As if giving us a hint, Poe repeatedly emphasizes that the narrator's hatred for Fortunato is perfect and complete. The burial is successful and is not discovered.

Each story was divided into successive units of about 250 words each. So the stories would be comparable—and allow me to do some statistics— these units were grouped into five larger sequential segments. Figure 9.17 shows them to be as predicted. Analysis of variance tells us that the difference in trends is real, or statistically significant.

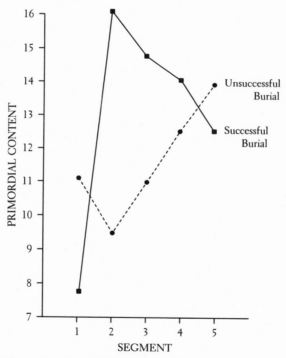

Figure 9.17 Amount of primordial content in consecutive segments of narratives by Edgar Allan Poe concerning successful burial ("The Cask of Amontillado" and "Eleonora") and unsuccessful burial ("The Fall of the House of Usher," "Berenice," and "Ligeia").

Thematics of the Soul

Some texts that seem to be night journey narratives do not show the expected trends in primordial content. Joseph Conrad's *Heart of Darkness* seems to be a perfect example of the type. Marlow, the hero, sets off from Brussels to find Kurtz. He travels up the Congo River and finds that Kurtz has sold his soul to the devil. He argues with Kurtz's soul without success and finally makes his way back to Brussels. Primordial content pervades the book, but does not change in an inverted-U fashion because there is no rebirth or rejuvenation in this story. Marlow was hired to find Kurtz. He finds him and returns home. He goes through a lot, but he doesn't change. He is the same person when he returns to Brussels to collect his money as when he left. The English poet Thomas Sackville's "The Induction" is similar: there is a journey to Hell but no personality change or enlightenment; and again, no overall trend in primordial content.

Narratives of Salvation

Salvation of the soul is not—at least on the surface—the hot topic for poets lately that it used to be. Narratives that tell you how to save your soul show a particular distribution of primordial content. Figure 9.18 shows the amount of primordial content in each of the one hundred cantos of Dante's *Divine Comedy.* The main trend takes the shape of an M with an extra up-flourish at the end—a trend that can be described by a quintic or fifth-order polynomial. This trend not only is present across the entirety of the *Divine Comedy* but is superimposed on the trend line in both *Inferno* and *Paradiso.* This is yet another case of self-similarity when magnification is increased. As Dante and Virgil descend into Hell, primordial content increases—as we would expect if the descent symbolizes one into a state of primordial cognition. In the first part of *Purgatorio,* as Dante and Virgil climb the mountain of purgatory, the primordial content decreases. At the top of the mountain of purgatory, they discover the Garden of Eden (cantos 27–33). As can be seen in the figure, primordial content increases dramatically in this last part of the *Purgatorio.* It

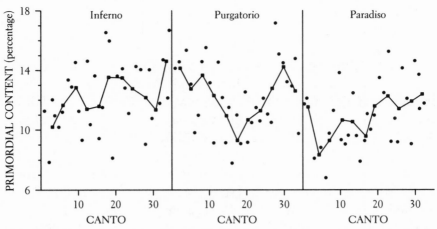

Figure 9.18   Amount of primordial content in the one hundred cantos of Dante's *Divine Comedy*. The solid line connects averages of each successive set of three cantos.

falls off rapidly and then increases throughout the *Paradiso,* which describes the ascent of Dante and Beatrice through the spheres of heaven.

This pattern seems to characterize narratives about religious salvation. There is a similar pattern in Flaubert's *Legend of Saint Julian the Hospitaler,* which is about the salvation of Saint Julian; and in both parts I and II of Goethe's *Faust.* A related pattern occurs in Joseph Beaumont's *Psyche,* which is explicitly about the salvation of the soul (Psyche). The first six cantos describe Psyche's (the soul's) degradation in the world of the senses and her repentance. Then follow ten cantos on the story of Christ, presented as a pattern for Psyche to follow. The final eight cantos of the poem describe Psyche's subsequent life. In respect to primordial content (figure 9.19), the inverted-U, or regression-and-return cycle, is found in the first six cantos (labeled Psyche 1 in figure 9.19). Thus, only the first six cantos, not the whole of the poem, is analogous to the rebirth texts discussed previously. As may be seen in the figure, the Christ section and *Psyche* 2 exhibit the same cubic (increasing, decreasing, and increasing) trend in primordial content. In the last part of the poem, Psyche follows the primordial content pattern set forth for her in the Christ section of the poem.

While the first sixty cantos of the *Divine Comedy* exhibit an inverted-U pattern of primordial content, the remaining forty cantos show

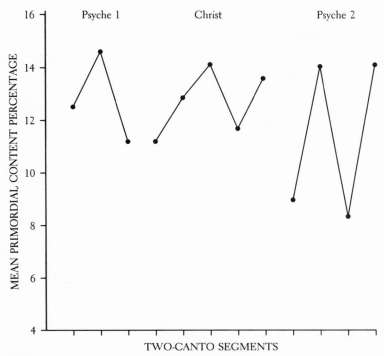

Figure 9.19   Average amount of primordial content in successive two-canto segments of Joseph Beaumont's *Psyche,* a narrative poem concerning salvation of the soul.

the same cubic (increase-decrease-increase) trend in primordial content as do the Psyche 2 and Christ segments of *Psyche.* Thus, Psyche 1 and the Christ segment (or Psyche 1 and Psyche 2) taken together present exactly the pattern that occurs in the whole of the *Divine Comedy.* In both cases, two regression-and-return cycles are followed by a final regression. It makes some sense to argue that the first regression-and-return cycle involves an overcoming of the tendency to use primordial thought for sensual purposes; and the second, an overcoming of the tendency to use it for personally relevant or socially oriented purposes. Only after these tendencies have been overcome, can primordial thought be used to operate on neutral, spiritual, or abstract contents. Presumably, the final regression in both the *Divine Comedy* and *Psyche* represent this sort of spiritualized regression. Most people use primordial thought in fantasies and reveries concerning wish fulfillment. Kris's (1952) notion of "regression in the service of the ego" refers to a type of cognition where primordial thought is used on neutral or abstract contents. It is hypothetically this sort of cognition that is involved in creativity, religious experience, and other nonpathological regression.

The trends in primordial content found in the *Divine Comedy* and *Psyche* fit well with the five stages of mystical experience proposed by Evelyn Underhill (1911). On the basis of studies of the lives of a number of mystics—such as Saint Theresa, Saint John of the Cross, and Jacob Boehme—Underhill proposed that full-blown mystical experiences consist of five sequential stages: awakening, purgation, illumination, the dark night of the soul, and the unitive life. Although not using the terms *regression* or *primordial cognition*, Claire Owens (1975) explicitly diagrammed these five stages with two inverted Us and a final upward-moving line—a diagram exactly predicting the patterns we have found in narratives about salvation. Table 9.1 sets forth in schematic form the hypothetical correspondences between Underhill's stages and our findings. The farthest left-hand column of the table lists each of Underhill's stages. The second column gives a prediction about whether the stage involves regression (movement toward a primordial state of consciousness) or progression (movement away from a primordial state of consciousness) based on Underhill's descriptions. If a stage involves regression, primordial content should increase in a text describing that stage. If a stage

TABLE 9.1
Stages of Mystical Experience
Predicted Trend in Primordial Content of Texts Describing Each Stage, and Episodes in the
Divine Comedy and *Psyche* Corresponding to Each Stage

Stage of Mystical Experience	Primordial Content Trend	Episode	
		Divine Comedy	Psyche[a]
awakening	increasing	descent into hell	degradation in the world of the senses
purgation	decreasing	ascent of the mountain of Purgatory	repentance
illumination	increasing	Garden of Eden segment	life up to the crucifixion
dark night of the soul	decreasing	transition to Paradise	burial
unitive life	increasing	ascent to heaven	resurrection

[a]Psyche 1 and Christ segments.

326

involves a decrease in regression, primordial content should decline in a narrative describing the stage. The last two columns list episodes of the *Divine Comedy* and *Psyche* corresponding to each of the stages. Each of these episodes shows a trend in primordial content in the predicted direction.

Fortunately, we have one more bit of evidence. The psychologist Alan West is doing content-analytic studies of the King James version of the Bible. Primordial content throughout the Bible shows exactly the quintic trend I have been discussing, and it accounts for around 40 percent of the variation in primordial content. Thus, this strange quintic trend seems to be the signature of narratives dealing with salvation.

The Wasteland

No one is sure what T. S. Eliot's *The Wasteland* is about. Eliot did not know himself. It is certainly not about salvation of the soul. Among other things, it does seem to be about despair that such salvation is not possible. There are plenty of references to myths about salvation and rebirth, but the overall tone is one of despair rather than hope. The trend in primordial content (figure 9.20) looks like the pattern found in salvation narratives, except that the final increase in primordial content is not present. The M-shaped trend is significant. This is a highly structured poem, at least if you ignore Eliot's divisions and segment it into 250-word sections as in this analysis. (The muse seems to dictate in 250-word breaths. The divisions authors impose often obscure things.) The variation around the trend is not random, as shown by the fact that part of it is captured by a significant autocorrelation at a lag of two segments.

Multiple Interpretations

Not all narratives show coherent trends in primordial content; nor is this the only sort of content that shows coherent trends. One can use the approach I have described to investigate any type of content. I have, for example, looked at trends in the average evaluative connotations (good versus bad) of words in the texts I have discussed. For example, the words

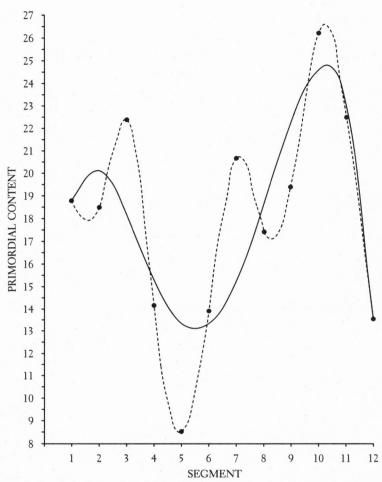

Figure 9.20 Primordial content in consecutive 250-word segments of T. S. Eliot's *The Wasteland*. The main trend in primordial content is shown by the solid line, but some of the oscillation around this trend line is also statistically significant.

in "The Rime of the Ancient Mariner" move from good connotations to bad and back to good ones. The trend accounts for 47 percent of the variation in evaluative connotation. Several autoregressive components account for some of the remaining variation. From this, I draw the hardly surprising conclusion that the poem has to do with meeting and overcoming evil. Thus, it is *both* about alteration in consciousness and about good and evil. A poem can mean more than one thing. Indeed, one aspect of literary quality seems to be such polyvalence or susceptibility to multiple interpretation. There are also coherent trends in the evaluative connotations of words in book VI of the *Aeneid* and in the *Divine Comedy.*

We can use coherence of trends to decipher what a narrative is about: that is, if a narrative is about overcoming evil, the trend in evaluative connotation should be stronger than the trend in primordial content. If a narrative is about alteration in consciousness, the reverse should be the case. The *Tibetan Book of the Dead,* for example, shows a clear trend in primordial content but no trend at all in the use of good versus bad words: it must be about alteration in consciousness rather than good versus evil. This conclusion conforms with what a Tibetan Buddhist would probably tell you. The descent into Hell in book II of Homer's *Odyssey* is more about good and evil than about alteration in consciousness, though it seems to be about both. In this case, the trend indicates that Hell is a better place than earth, and is consistent with pagan conceptions of the afterlife. The Babylonian *Ishtar's Descent into the Underworld* shows the same pattern as book II of the Odyssey: the connotations of words move from negative to positive and then back to negative. *Ishtar's Descent* doesn't seem to have a thing to do with alteration in consciousness at least on the level of its plot. Primordial content shows no coherent trends. We find the reverse with *Moby Dick,* which doesn't have much to do with ethics but does seem to symbolize alteration in consciousness. Ethics and consciousness certainly don't exhaust the possibilities, though most narratives I have analyzed do show some oscillation in primordial content or evaluative connotation. Lewis Carroll's *Alice in Wonderland* is an exception: it has no trends at all in either evaluation or primordial content. The story is about something else.

More Musical Movement

We can analyze music in the same way we have analyzed narratives. Where in narratives I looked at primordial content, I could have used the same techniques on any content—even on word length, or number of vowels per word, or anything measurable. The most obvious thing to measure in music is the sequence of notes in a melody. For a graph of

Bach's *Minuet in G* (figure 9.21), I simply transformed the notes into numbers—1 for the lowest note and so on. The graph looks quite like the graphs depicting the content of literary works.

This similarity should not really be surprising. A piece of music has an overall pattern. In this case, part of the pattern is captured by the fifth-order polynomial trend shown in the figure. The trend accounts for 20 percent of the variance of the notes. I imagine that we could classify

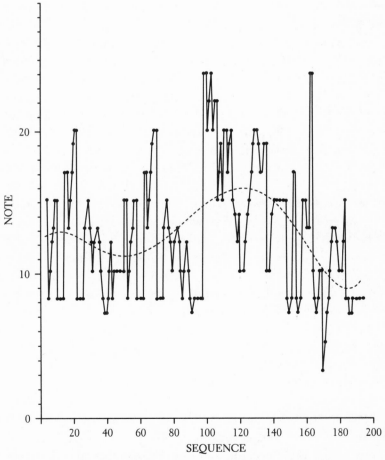

Figure 9.21 Johann Sebastian Bach's *Minuet in G* in graphic form. The main trend is shown by the dashed line. Unsurprisingly, the oscillations around this trend are statistically significant rather than random.

pieces of music according to their overall trends. We do know that some trends have different emotional impacts. Rising cadences are rated as happier, whereas falling cadences are rated as sadder (Kreitler and Kreitler 1972). Pieces with a wider dynamic range give rise to agitation. It is certainly reasonable that each possible polynomial trend tends to be associated with a particular type of feeling tone. I have never looked into the matter.

That the oscillations around the polynomial trend are not random should not be surprising either. If they were random, it would be easy to write music. We can perform the sort of autoregressive analysis that I used on literary works. It is not surprising that we came out with several significant autocorrelations. Autocorrelations at lags from 1 to 8 account for 56 percent of the variation around the polynomial curve. At this point we have a polynomial equation with significant autoregressive components.

The deviations from the trend described by this equation seem to be random. Maybe they are. Maybe Bach's brain combined a few trends to get the outlines of the piece, and then threw in some random noise. That doesn't sound right. The alternative is that our sequence of leftover notes looks random but really is not. Some perfectly deterministic equations can produce sequences that seem to be random but really are not. Mathematicians call this sort of sequence chaotic rather than random. An everyday example is water dripping from a faucet. Although successive drips seem to be spaced in a random manner, the water's behavior is governed by deterministic laws—gravity, surface tension, and so on. The physicist Robert Shaw (1984) showed that the dripping is not at all random, but seems to be because the factors governing it interact in a complicated way. The same must be true of our leftover notes. One of the interesting features of certain chaos equations is that they are self-similar under magnification (Mandelbrot 1977). Self-similarity is exactly what got me into this whole discussion of trends within works of art.

Though I don't know the equation for Bach's *Minuet*, I think it is knowable. Either the notes are random or they are not. If not, there are equations to describe their sequence. There is no place in the discussion for a third possibility: incoherent and rambling effusions about the spirit of man, or about Bach's genius or the delicacy of the spirit. You can talk about music that way, but it doesn't lead anywhere. It is neither enlightening nor interesting. I agree with the physicist Stephen Hawking (1988) that we are on the verge of discovering some deep principles about why the universe is the way it is and not some other way. If we can figure out things like that, then we should be able to figure out why Bach put some notes together in one way rather than another.

PERSONALITY AND ARTISTIC CONTENT

Where discovering what a work tells us about its creator used to be one of the main goals of criticism, the main point of twentieth-century literary studies has been to find out something about literary texts irrespective of the personalities of their creators. However valid this change in emphasis, the critics' logic is askew. As I have suggested in the last few chapters, knowledge about states of consciousness does shed light on literary content and style. The state of mind a creator is in when a work is written determines in large part what its content will be. If we didn't know or guess this, it would never have occurred to us to measure primordial content. If we hadn't measured primordial content, we wouldn't have seen the profound regularity in literary history. The main axis of literary or artistic style is isomorphic with the main axis of cognition. Maybe other axes of artistic style are isomorphic with other important psychological dimensions. On the level of personality, temperament and mental health spring immediately to mind.

Temperament

Unless we consider the personality of the author, we are not likely to discover whether other axes of style are isomorphic with the main axes of personality or individual differences. Though it is not usually made explicit, modern thinking about the basic dimensions of temperament is about the same as ancient thinking on the matter. A psychologist, asked about how people vary, is likely to explain with some variant of the theory of the four temperaments (Eysenck 1953; Hogan 1983; Martindale and

Martindale 1988). The names will be different, but the idea is the same. Since Galen's theory of the temperaments was good enough for Kant, Wundt, and Pavlov, I'll just use the old terms. The idea of temperament theory is that people differ along two dimensions: sanguine (optimistic and happy) versus melancholic (pessimistic and anxious) and choleric (active and quick to anger) versus phlegmatic (calm and passive).

Galen connected the temperaments with bodily fluids which were seen in turn as expressions of the four elements: air versus earth and fire versus water. A nice theory, but it turned out to be wrong on the level of physiology and physics. Maybe, though, the connection between elements and temperaments is right on the psychic level. Gaston Bachelard (1964 [1938], 1983 [1942], 1943, 1948) has made this argument in his analyses of literature. His ideas were clearly foreshadowed by Leonard Lessius:

> [T]he Affections of the Mind follow (as is well known in Philosophy) the Apprehension of the Fancy. Now the Apprehension of the Fancy is conformable to the Disposition of the Body, and to the Humors therein predominant. And hence it comes to pass that Men are presented in their Dreams with various illusions, or Spectres, either more or less agreeable, or more or less terrifying and amazing. Thus some, who are choleric, are chiefly affected in their sleep with the imaginary Appearances of either Fire or Burnings, Wars or Slaughters: Others, of more melancholy Dispositions, are often disturbed with dismal Prospects of either Funerals, or Sepulchres, or some dark and doleful Apparitions: The Phlegmatick dream more frequently of Rains, Lakes, Rivers, Inundations, Drownings, Shipwrecks; and the Sanguine abound in different Kinds of Pleasantries, such as Flyings, Courses, Banquets, Songs, and amorous Sports. Now Dreams are nothing else but the Apprehension of the Fancy, when the Senses are asleep. Whereupon it follows, that as in Sleep, so likewise in Waking, the Fancy of the most part apprehends Things agreeable to the Humour and Quality then prevalent; and especially upon the first Approach, or Presentment of the Object, till it be corrected and otherwise directed by Reason.
>
> (Lessius 1743 [1634], p.71)

At least in states of fantasy and reverie, there is a correspondence between temperaments and elements. As the literary critic Northrup Frye put it, "earth, air, water, and fire are still the four elements of imaginative experience, and always will be" (Bachelard 1964, p. vii [1938]).

Anne Martindale and I showed that modern-day subjects seem to agree with Frye's comment (Martindale and Martindale 1988). When asked to sort words describing the four elements and the four temperaments, they made the "correct" element-temperament pairings at a level far beyond chance. Furthermore, an analysis of the way they sorted these words shows that they implicitly saw air/sanguine versus earth/melancholic words as forming one axis and fire/choleric versus water/phlegmatic words as forming an orthogonal axis—exactly as Lessius and Bachelard would have predicted.

This finding led us to try a quantitative study of Bachelard's ideas as they apply to poetry. Anne Martindale constructed a content-analysis dictionary that measures references to the four temperaments and to the four elements (examples of the words in each category are shown in table 9.2). We applied it to the twenty-one French poets discussed in chapter 3. To get indices indicating relative amount of emphasis, we calculated difference scores between theoretically opposite categories: fire — water (that is, fire minus water), air — earth, choleric — phlegmatic, and sanguinic — melancholic. A positive score on, say, fire — water indicates that a poet emphasizes references to fire as compared with references to water. A negative score indicates emphasis on references to water. These

TABLE 9.2
Element and Temperament Words

Element Categories			
Earth	*Air*	*Fire*	*Water*
cave	air	burn	drench
crystal	atmosphere	fire	flood
gravel	breeze	flame	fountain
mineral	heavens	hearth	lake
ore	sky	smolder	ocean
stone	wind	torch	water

Temperament Categories			
Melancholic	*Sanguinic*	*Choleric*	*Phlegmatic*
anxious	carefree	active	apathetic
pessimistic	contented	ambitious	calm
serious	enthusiastic	greedy	controlled
suspicious	hopeful	impulsive	inactive
uneasy	playful	irritable	reasonable
worried	sociable	proud	unemotional

scores allowed us to assess whether a relative emphasis on fire is accompanied by a relative emphasis on choleric traits, and so on. A factor analysis indicated that this was in fact the case.

I show the position of each poet in the factor space in figure 9.22. If you know much about the poets in question, you will agree that the arrangement makes a lot of sense. Since, however, data usually make sense after one sees what they are, I contacted four recognized experts on nineteenth- and twentieth-century French poetry. Without telling them what we had found, I asked each to classify the poets as to dominant emotional tone (happy, sad, lethargic, or angry). Though I usually got a preliminary lecture about why this was an impossible or senseless task, the

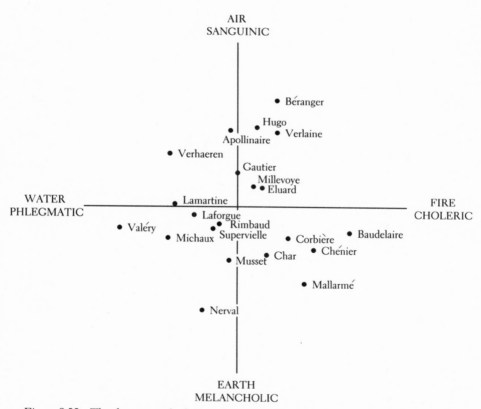

Figure 9.22 The degree to which French poets use words referring to the four temperaments and the four elements. Poets who make a lot of references to fire do also to choleric traits and so on—in accord with the predictions made by Gaston Bachelard.

experts did the task and, indeed, agreed very well with each other. In the main, they also agreed with the computer classification.

The positions occupied by the poets with extreme scores on the factors generally conform with what would be expected from qualitative reading of their work. In discussing Nerval, the most extreme earth-melancholic poet, the literary historian Louis Cazamian (1955)—with no thought at all of Bachelard—quoted seven lines of his verse. The lines from "El Desdichado" are melancholy indeed:

> I am the shadow, the widower, the unconsoled,
> The prince of Aquitaine with the ruined tower:
> My only star is dead,—and my star-strewn lute
> Bears the black sun of Melancholy.

Earth imagery is also clear in the concluding lines of "Vers dorés":

> Often in the dark being dwells a hidden God:
> And like an eye born covered by its lids,
> A pure spirit grows beneath the rind of stones!

Three of the four experts classified Nerval as sad, and one classified him as lethargic—nicely conforming with the content-analytic results in figure 9.22. Also in agreement with the content analysis, Mallarmé was classified as sad by three of the four expert raters.

Béranger, the most sanguine of the poets, was a popular early nineteenth-century writer. His verse is sentimental and optimistic. Cazamian (1955) remarked on his humor as he did on the "airy" quality of Verlaine's poetry. The two most sanguinic poets, Béranger and Hugo, were classified as happy by all four of the raters. Apollinaire was, in contrast, seen as happy by only one judge and as sad by the other three. However, as one expert pointed out to me, "since he was manic-depressive, either happy or sad would be about equally correct."

Baudelaire, the most extreme fire-choleric poet, was described by Cazamian (1955, pp.342–43) as "bitter," "cynical," "insolent," "brutal," "vitriolic," and "imperious." Recall that Baudelaire addressed *Les Fleurs du Mal* to the "hypocrite reader"—hardly a jovial way of beginning a book. Both fire imagery and choleric temperament are evident in the well-known lines from "Le Voyage":

> Pour us your poison to comfort us!
> We want, so much this fire burns our brains,
> To plunge to the depths of the abyss, Hell
>   or Heaven, what does it matter?
> To the depth of the unknown to find something
>   *new!*

Two judges rated Baudelaire as angry, but the other two saw him as lethargic—perhaps because several of his best poems do indeed stand out as languid and placid. Chénier and Corbière were seen as either angry or sad by all of the experts. This estimate conforms with their fairly high scores on both the choleric and melancholic factors.

The poets with extreme scores on the water-phlegmatic end of the continuum contrast markedly with Baudelaire, Chénier, and Corbière. Cazamian remarked that Valéry was "too resolutely intelligent to cater for emotion of any kind" (1955, p.422). It is notable that one of Valéry's best-known poems is "Le Cimetière marin," and one of Lamartine's best-known is "Le Lac." Both, of course, are full of references to water, and their emotional tone is placid and phlegmatic. Agreement was not especially good, either among experts, or between experts and factor scores, for the hypothetically phlegmatic poets. Part of the difficulty—pointed out gently by two of the judges—was that the term *lethargic* was not a good choice. Two of the judges classified Valéry as sad, and two as happy. Lamartine and Laforgue were both classed as lethargic by two experts and as sad by the other two.

Psychopathology

Neurosis and psychosis are theoretically connected with primordial cognition (Fenichel 1945; Werner 1948). It has long been held that creativity and insanity are related—as in Dryden's contention, in "Absalom and Achitophel," that "great wits are sure to madness near allied."

Several recent studies have shown high rates of mental disorder in highly creative people (Andreason and Cantor 1974).

By systematically searching biographical sources, I studied the incidence of psychopathology in twenty British and twenty French poets (Martindale 1972*a*). The poets were a subsample of those discussed in chapters 3 and 4: the three most eminent British poets born in each of the seven twenty-year periods from 1670 to 1809 and the three most eminent French poets born in the seven twenty-year periods from 1770 to 1909. Two of the poets had to be omitted because I could not find sufficient biographical information on them. A poet was counted as showing signs of psychopathology if he was psychotic or had clear symptoms such as mental "breakdowns," drug or alcohol abuse, or suicide attempts. Fifty-five percent of the English and 40 percent of the French poets showed symptoms of psychopathology. Fifteen percent (William Blake, William Collins, William Cowper, Gérard de Nerval, Christopher Smart, and John Clare) were either certainly or probably psychotic; only Blake may not have been psychotic. Though Baudelaire was psychotic when he died from general paresis, he wrote no poetry while he was overtly psychotic. The rate of psychopathology is far above the base rate for the normal population. If we correlate primordial content with presence of psychiatric symptoms, we find a significant correlation of .53.

I hope that I have, in this chapter, convinced readers that the evolutionary theory and the quantitative methods I have used shed light not only on the main trends in art history but also upon the individual artist and the individual work of art. It has always been known that at least some artists change style across the course of their careers. Quantitative methods give us a way of describing such changes. They also show us something more surprising. As well as long-term stylistic changes, artists tend to progress through a series of what I have called microstyles. I have argued that at least one of the causes of such changes is the universal and constant pressure for novelty. Given this, it is perhaps not surprising that almost identical equations describe trends in the works of creators as diverse as Dryden and Beethoven. It is also well known that personality shapes an artist's works. Quantitative methods show us that this influence is subtle as well as direct. Thus, for example, Baudelaire uses fire imagery while Hugo speaks of air and open spaces not by chance but probably because of their temperaments.

Literary narratives are coherent. Were they not, they would make no sense. Mathematics is the best tool we have for describing coherence and order. It should not be surprising, then, that we can use some simple equations to delineate the plots of such narratives. The equations do more than describe, though. I have argued that they can help unlock the hidden or symbolic meaning of a narrative. Narratives have more than one meaning. We do not need to leave it to the whimsy of the reader to decide which interpretation is most important. We can examine the coherence or orderliness of trends in the usage of different types of words to make an objective decision. For example, book VI of the *Aeneid* and Coleridge's "The Rime of the Ancient Mariner" are both about alteration of consciousness and about confronting and overcoming evil. On the other hand, book II of the *Odyssey* is only about the latter, and the *Tibetan Book of the Dead,* only about the former.

CHAPTER 10

Science and Art History

U P to now, I have focused upon quantitative descriptions of what actually happened in a variety of artistic traditions. In this final chapter, I up the stakes. In the first part, I argue that art history can be not only an empirical science but a genuinely experimental one. Furthermore, I describe experiments showing that we can indeed do experimental simulations of art history that both test the evolutionary theory and illuminate what must happen in art history. The pressure for novelty falls not only on the shoulders of the artist; it bears down upon all of us. In the second part of the chapter, I describe how it shapes the writing of both scientists and literary critics.

ART HISTORY AS AN EXPERIMENTAL SCIENCE

A genuine science aims to be not only empirical but also experimental. Although we can describe empirical regularities and make good guesses at what caused them, the world is complex, and even the simplest things have a thousand causes. In an experiment, we try to hold everything constant and vary one thing at a time in order to find out what is important and what is not. If any area of history can aspire to becoming an experimental science, it is art history. In fact, experiments on art history have been carried out for about a century.

Simulating the History of Taste

In the study of Italian painting I described in chapter 6, the slides were shown in random order. There was a significant order effect on the Dislike-Like scale: the later in the experiment a painting was shown, the less well it was liked. Presumably, this effect was due to habituation and, if the evolutionary theory is correct, should disappear if the paintings were shown in their correct chronological sequence. In this case, each successive painting would tend to have more arousal potential than prior paintings, canceling out the habituation effect. Thus, we should be able to duplicate in the course of an hour in the laboratory a process that occurred over several hundred years in Italian painting. On the other hand, if the paintings were shown in reverse chronological order, the decline in liking should be even greater than was the case with a random order of presentation, because decreasing arousal potential and habituation would cumulate.

To test these predictions, I had eighteen subjects rate their liking for the Italian paintings shown in chronological order and seventeen subjects rate them when shown in reverse chronological order (Martindale 1986a). To disguise the real purpose of the experiments, the Like-Dislike scale was embedded in a set of seven other scales. Since subjects showed highly significant agreement in their preferences, a mean preference rating was computed for each painting in both experiments. As predicted, the correlation of liking with order was insignificant for the chronological group. On the other hand, it was strongly negative—much more so than when the paintings were shown in a random order—for the reverse-chronological group. The correlation was −.45.

Simulating Art History

In a serial reproduction study, the first subject copies a design, the second subject makes a copy of this copy, the third subject copies the copy of the second copy, and so on. Each person gets to look for a few moments at the design to be copied, and then makes a copy. Though subjects are instructed to make an exact copy, that is hardly the end result. Such experiments have been done, though not in great numbers, for around one hundred years. Change always arises no matter how exact people try to be. The usual result of such a study is a movement toward simplification, rarely toward greater complexity (Haddon 1907). Another general finding is that some details of a design become amplified at the expense of others. Finally, especially if the original figure is an unfamiliar one, it is often assimilated to a more familiar one. The psychologist Sir Frederic Bartlett (1932) got the same results when he used verbal narratives rather than visual designs. Thus, the effect is a general one. The main cause of these trends seems to be the simplifying or schematizing properties of memory. Our memories are simplified records of what we have actually experienced. Of course, lack of skill in drawing also plays a role. An example of what happens with serial reproductions is shown in figure 10.1. The original stimulus is shown in the upper left.

Henry Balfour (1893) and Alfred Haddon (1907) argued that many changes in primitive art forms seem to be captured in serial reproduction experiments. More recently, T.H.G. Ward (1949) was able to simulate aspects of change in early British coins in the laboratory. He started out with a Roman original. After several reproductions, the drawing resembled the coins used in Gaul. After several more, they looked like early British coins. Cumulative errors in copying, he argued, could account for the historical changes.

Serial reproduction experiments give us a straightforward method for putting art history on an experimental basis. If any area of history can become a genuine science that is not only empirical but also experimental, it is certainly art history. But, it is generally objected, most artists do not aim to make exact copies. True enough, but we can change the instruc-

Figure 10.1 A Serial Reproduction Experiment. An example of what happens to a stimulus when it is repeatedly copied (From F. C. Bartlett, *Remembering* [Cambridge, England: Cambridge University Press, 1932.] Reprinted by permission)

tions in a serial reproduction study so that they mimic what the experimenter believes to be the driving force in art history.

Roger Frey at the University of Maine has gathered a large number of serial reproductions. He and I took nine series of ten reproductions and asked some subjects to rate them on scales that I have used in the study of art history. Everyone agrees that serial reproductions tend to become simpler across trials, but no one has ever looked at what I have called primordial content. Each of the series began with the original shown in the upper left of figure 10.1.

A factor analysis showed that the rating scales were getting at two dimensions: arousal potential and primordial content. The arousal potential factor had high loadings on the scales Complex, Tense, Active, and Strong. The primordial content factor had high loadings on the scales Unrealistic, Nonphotographic, Otherworldly, and Meaningless. When we looked at changes in factor scores across trials, we found that arousal potential decreased. On the other hand, primordial content increased to a significant degree—due mainly to declines in ratings of the degree to which drawings were natural and photographic. This finding suggests that the primordial content of art can change even without any pressure for novelty.

Should we conclude from the changes in primordial content that the later drawings were made in more primordial states of mind? This is a possible but not necessary conclusion. The most parsimonious explanation would probably be that the later drawings are less realistic because of the cumulation of simplifying memory effects and lack of skill. It is reasonable, though, to expect variations in the degree to which thought is primordial even in a laboratory situation. Primordial cognition does not mean only extreme states such as dreams and delirium, which are in fact not conducive to artistic production. Our thoughts are always varying to a slight degree along the conceptual-primordial axis (Klinger 1978; Singer 1978). It is exactly such slight variations that I have been talking about whenever I have claimed that artists are creating in an altered state of consciousness. A poet's reverie may be more primordial than the thought of someone in an experiment, but this is a difference in degree rather than in kind.

As in the case of art history, we can ask how much overall variation the theoretical variables account for. To find out, we need to know how much overall variation there is in the first place. We had another group of people sort the original drawing and the ninety reproductions. On the basis of how people sorted the drawings, we found that the main trend of movement across trials seemed to concern changes in arousal potential and primordial content.

In a different serial reproduction study, people were told to copy the drawing they were shown but to make their copy more original. I made it clear that it wasn't fair to achieve originality by changing subject matter altogether. For example, a subject who was shown a duck had to draw a more original duck rather than a rocket ship or something totally different. I meant to simulate what happens in an artistic tradition in which subject matter is not changed. As a control, a second group of subjects were instructed to make exact copies of the same drawings. Three types of drawings were used to start each series: four fairly simple geometric designs (for example, a triangle within a triangle), three realistic drawings (for example, a wine glass), and three ambiguous drawings (outlines of Rorschach inkblots). I used two groups of ten women as subjects. On the first trial, each reproduced one of the ten designs. On the second trial, each reproduced the first reproduction, and so on. One group worked under the originality constraint, and the other worked under the constraint for veridical copying.

Other subjects rated the resulting drawings on scales designed to measure the two theoretical variables. A factor analysis showed that the scales did so. Collapsing across all types of drawings, the originality group increased arousal potential. The correlation with trial was .57. The copying group did the reverse. In this case, the correlation was −.21.

There were no general trends for primordial content. We can see why if we break down the designs into geometric, realistic, and ambiguous. Results for the group told to make veridical copies are straightforward. Nothing much happens in the case of the fairly simple geometrical designs. If we extrapolate to art history, we would expect that—if there even *were* artists who wanted only to copy what prior artists had done—the tradition would be stable if it started out with geometric motifs. The result would be different if the tradition began with realistic motifs, which would become less realistic or more primordial in their content across time and eventually result in ambiguous designs. What would happen then? The results suggest that the art would then tend to become more realistic. I am piecing together the results for what the copying group did to realistic and ambiguous designs. To find out whether this interpretation is right, we would need to do experiments in which twenty or thirty rather than only ten trials were run.

The drawings made by the group under the constraint to produce original designs should give us a closer simulation of what occurs in most artistic traditions. Arousal potential increased significantly across trials no matter what sort of design was being reproduced. However, trends in primordial content depended upon type of design. Primordial content decreased with geometric designs: they tended to become more realistic across trials. It increased across trials with realistic designs: these tended to become more distorted and unrealistic. Results for the ambiguous stimuli were mixed. The least ambiguous of these, which looks like a bat, became less realistic across trials. The other ambiguous stimuli, which don't look like much of anything, became more realistic across trials. The two trends cancel each other if we average them together. These results do seem to conform with what has happened in a number of artistic traditions. Realistic art tends to become unrealistic: for example, the idealized depictions of renaissance painting were transmuted into the contortions of mannerist painting. On the other hand, unrealistic art tends to become realistic: mannerism gave way to the baroque style, which is more realistic than mannerism albeit in a different way than renaissance painting. A clearer example is the recent replacement of abstract expressionism by photographic realism.

Simulating Literary History

Trends of the sort I have described can also be produced in the laboratory if we have subjects play the role of literary creators. I conducted three experimental simulations to assess the effects of need for novelty on literary change (Martindale 1973b). Ten highly creative subjects were asked to compose series of similes with restricted and with unrestricted lengths and a series of fantasy stories, all with instructions that each had to be more original than all previous compositions. In each case, the first subject composed a simile or a story, the second made a response that was supposed to be more original, and so on, until all ten subjects had made a response. In these studies, each subject got to see all previous responses. Subjects were in fact able to increase the originality of their responses across trials—as I assessed by having judges rank the similes and stories in respect to originality. Where length of response was restricted or a higher need for novelty was induced, initial increases in primordial content were followed by evidence of stylistic change. Where length of response was unrestricted or a lower need for novelty was induced, primordial content increased continually across trials with no evidence of stylistic change. The results closely paralleled the pattern of results of the content-analytic studies of actual poetic texts reported in chapters 3–5.

The series of responses to the sentence stem "A table is like _____" shows remarkable parallelism with what has occurred in French poetry since 1800. In order, the responses were:

1. the sea, quiet
2. a horizontal wall
3. a formicaed [*sic*] bed
4. the platonic form
5. a dead tree
6. a listening board
7. versatile friendship
8. vanquished forest
9. a seasoned man
10. two chairs

The first three responses are based upon the flatness of the surface of a table. The fourth response mediates between these and the next two, which refer to the material composition of tables. All of these similes are clearly "appropriate," suggesting a high level of stylistic elaboration: irrelevant responses were being filtered out. This filtering is discarded with the seventh response. The ninth and tenth responses clearly indicate a new, less elaborated "style." The ninth response may be mediated by the word "seasoned," which is transferred from wood to man: man and wood share a common attribute, although in a completely different sense; therefore they are compared. The tenth response is based upon the close associative connection between table and chair. Associative contiguity overrides objective dissimilarity—exactly as happened in twentieth-century French poetry. Presumably, subjects in the later trials could continue to increase originality only by lowering level of elaboration, by applying less stringent stylistic rules to their responses.

Where length of responses was not curtailed, stylistic change was not

required so quickly—as in the series of responses to "A pencil is like
_____":

1. a yellow cigarette, spreading its cancer on paper
2. the headwaters of a river, flowing from the mind to the world
3. a black light on nothing
4. a stiletto, piercing truth
5. an artist's brush, painting paper
6. an ice scraper, unfreezing one's view of the world
7. the scratchy fingers of an insomniac
8. a grenade: useful, destructive, yet often self-destructive
9. the neck of an hourglass
10. God micturating upon the cosmos

Several of the later responses at first appear arbitrary, but the ninth and
tenth responses parallel the second. All are based upon the image of
something flowing between two poles—mind and world, God and cosmos,
upper and lower halves of an hourglass. The last two responses can be read
as physiognomic or concrete expression of the idea expressed more con-
ceptually in the earlier responses. All express the reasonable idea that a
pencil is used for communication. In this case, we seem to have an
experimental replication of what happens to the expression of a single idea
across the course of a single style.

In another part of the experiment, five successive subjects were asked
to write increasingly original Thematic Apperception Test stories. The
following stories in response to a picture of a boy looking at a violin shows
the sort of stylistic change that tended to occur when subjects wrote under
high pressure for originality.

1. Yes, violin, someday we will create for the world, you and I—
together—some day soon. They will look at us curiously—those people—
yes, *they* will stare and wonder at our remarkable progress. *They* will say
how young and precocious we are—*they* will smile, applaud, and leave
us.—Yes, leave you with me—you fragile piece of wood—you artifact of
man—like me. (Primordial content score, based on ranks: 70.0.)
2. Every birthday it's either a tie or a shirt from my grandmother, but

this year is different. I get a real, live violin, whatever a violin is. I wonder what the strings are for? I never saw a bow and arrow set with so few arrows and so many bows before but I guess it'll do. But wait. I think I've seen one of these before on television. I remember, you can make music with them, that's it. I remember a bald fellow with glasses playing one. Oh boy, mister violin, you and me can be another real live Jack Benny. (Primordial content score: 69.5.)

3. The house was quiet. Not long ago there was clip-clops of high heels and cigar smoke, pocketbook snap and keys jingle. Now he tried to imagine the music in his mind. It wasn't a picture of a concert hall, it wasn't a tuxedo, it was the music. Little ribbons floating in the air, falling down, bursting up. Some of them popped, others twisted and twisted and caught others. They swam around in a circle like a merry-go-round, some up, some down. It was all so very pretty. But thought of his last attempt kept squirming trying to enter, until all he could see was hairy ropes, and stones and cymbals and automobiles. (Primordial content score: 195.0.)

4. "Good God, life is miserable when you're a 467-year-old midget who can't do a goddam thing but play the violin. And can't even do that right either, after all, normal people use these frigging things to make music. All I can do is dress up like one." "Oh well, maybe tomorrow I'll be able to get a role as a kumquat." "Shit, if they'd only let me into the Guild I's sure I could play kettledrums beautifully." (Primordial content score: 109.5.)

5. "I don't care if you are Liz Taylor disguised as a violin," said Samual Mousetrd. "I mean why should I kiss you? I don't imagine it's very satisfying to kiss a hunk of wood. I'd probably get sawdust in my mouth. What do you mean—stick you under my chin and you'll turn into a beautiful woman? I'd rather you'd turn into a side street and escape the police or something. What's that? You want me to run that long thin stick across those strings above the hole? Why should I do that? One of the strings might break and the stick ram inside and if you really are Liz Taylor, nobody, much less me, would want a pregnant violin that thought it was Liz Taylor. (Primordial content score: 147.0.)

The first story is rather obvious and maudlin. The second introduces a sense of whimsy but continues the same theme. The theme of a boy dreaming in front of his violin is continued in the third story, but here we are given not conceptual ideas of ambition or curiosity but a dreamy reverie of physiognomic perception: the connotations are regressive and dreamlike. There is an abrupt shift with the fourth story to the level of the absurd. The tone, in contrast to the preceding stories, is brash, cynical, and comic. A decrease in the level of elaboration is suggested by the entrance of taboo words and references to drives. These trends are continued in the fifth story. Here drive references (most of which are not picked up by the computer scoring) increase within the confines of the new, absurd style. The new style is characterized by a breakdown of defensive propriety, lessened connection of the stories with the stimulus, and an absurd and comic style. In contrast, the first three stories are more closely related to the stimulus picture both in content and in manner. Within each style regression tends to increase. Since it is possible to produce such theoretically predicted trends in a laboratory simulation where external social and cultural changes are obviously held constant, these results strongly support the evolutionary theory.

APPLYING THE EVOLUTIONARY THEORY TO SCIENCE

The task of a scientist is to produce ideas. That wouldn't be hard if it weren't for the constraints. One of the most severe of these is that the ideas have to be true. More exactly, the ideas cannot be contradicted by empirical evidence. Furthermore, this constraint cannot be evaded by producing ideas that cannot in principle be tested against reality. Scientific ideas have to be falsifiable (Popper 1959). They have to be susceptible of being shown to be incorrect. This selection pressure is common to all scientific disciplines. Scientists are in the position of poets before the twentieth century, who had to produce realistic similes. Why don't scientists discard this constraint and produce surrealistic science? In fact, this is just what mathematics has done. In its early stages, mathematics was an empirical science. The constraint for realism has long since been abandoned, so that mathematicians produce "theories" that do not necessarily correspond to any empirical reality. While it may later turn out that a theory does describe some aspect of reality, this is not the concern or goal of the pure mathematician.

Science in general is far less concerned with everyday reality than most people realize. Consider a scientific experiment. When we do an experiment, we have some notion that *if* such and such were done then this or that would be the result. For example, if I drop something in a vacuum, then I hope that it will fall at 32 feet/sec². When we do an experiment, we are not doing so because such and such is usually the state of affairs or even because it could *ever* be the case. In fact, if our "such and such" were the normal state of affairs, we would not bother to do the experiment. We do the experiment precisely because such and such is *never* the normal state of affairs. There are no vacuums to be found outside the laboratory.

Pure science is more like art for art's sake than anything else. I would say that it is much closer to art than it is to practical or applied science. It has no utilitarian point. It is aimed at the production of what scientists themselves will tell you are beautiful theories. Of course, the beauty is of a somewhat different sort than that sought by the poet or artist. C. P. Snow's (1959) two cultures have probably arisen more from confusion and miscommunication than from any real antithesis. The person in the street—who ultimately pays the bills for our inquiries—is under the misapprehension that there is some practical use for science: that the ultimate purpose of biology is to cure cancer, or of physics, to produce cheap electricity and other nice things like that. Of course, this is to confuse science with technology.

Pure science is also similar to art in having no external audience. Even more than poets, scientists write for other scientists and for no one else. Pure mathematics is by far the most extreme case. The nonmathematician cannot understand the questions—let alone the answers—with which mathematicians deal. As Einstein remarked, a book on physics is incomprehensible after the first page, but a book on mathematics is incomprehensible after the first sentence. If you can't understand something, you can't very well control it. We might expect that science should show even clearer evolutionary trends than do the arts. It is scarcely worth mentioning that external social upheavals should have little effect on science. The laws of nature do not, after all, fluctuate with the economy. I am aware that some historians and philosophers with nothing better to do have tried to make the case that science serves or reflects political and other ideologies. In the main, this is silly. There may be a grain of truth in such notions so far as the less developed sciences—certainly including psychology—are concerned. Political ideologies can temporarily retard science and set up a pseudo science in its place. Hitler did try to rid the Third Reich of "Jewish physics." Since there is no such thing, there was no way to accomplish this absurd goal. Getting rid of physicists who happened to be Jewish did not change what Heisenberg thought about physics.

Many ideas are not contradicted by reality, but few of them qualify as scientific. For example, if I see John talking with Mary, I can assert that John and Mary are talking. This is certainly a falsifiable idea, but it is not a scientific one. One reason is that scientific ideas must be general or abstract: that is, there is a selection pressure for generality. This means that my idea about John and Mary would not survive in scientific circles. If I myself did not reject it, other scientists certainly would, and it would be ignored. Being ignored, it would die. Thus, scientific ideas are subject to two seemingly contradictory selection pressures. On the one hand, they must be concrete and perceptual: they must be related to and not contradicted by at least experimental reality. On the other hand, they must be abstract and general. These two selection pressures are not really contradictory at all. Conceptual thinking involves both perceptual and conceptual analysis. Thus, there are not two contradictory pressures operating on science. There is one consistent pressure for conceptual thinking and against primordial thinking.

Scientific laws cannot be tested directly because they refer to classes of phenomena. We can never do one single experiment in which we test the law that rewarding a behavior leads to its being performed more often. The units of the law—behavior, reward, and performance—refer to a host of things. A behavior can be anything from writing a poem to pecking a key. A reward can be anything from water to being elected president. This is why we can never prove scientific laws. Each of the component units can be realized in a virtually infinite number of ways.

Not every conceptual idea qualifies as a scientific one. Rather than asserting that John and Mary are talking, I could propose a more conceptual formulation: people sometimes talk to one another. This idea is not likely to win me any accolades in scientific circles either. Everyone knows it already. The idea is not novel. To be accepted, a scientific idea has got to be novel. To be more precise, in order to generate any excitement, interest, or liking on the part of other scientists, an idea has to be novel. But not just any novel idea will do.

It seems reasonable to say that the reaction of a scientist to an idea must follow the Wundt curve (see figure 2.1, page 42). Liking for a scientific idea should be determined by the same sorts of factors that determine liking for anything else. Ideas having medium arousal potential should be preferred. What determines the arousal potential of a scientific idea? One factor is certainly novelty. In science, just as in art, ideas must be new or they count for nothing. Thus, one way an idea could have essentially no arousal potential is if it were exactly the same as a previously proposed idea. The Wundt curve would lead us to expect that scientists should prefer ideas with a medium degree of novelty or incongruity. These would be ideas that are novel but not so novel that they clash violently with other currently held ideas. When first suggested, the idea that the earth orbits around the sun rather than the reverse was rather too novel. As a consequence, it engendered a good deal of displeasure. Scientists take particular pleasure in theories that produce counterintuitive predictions, predictions that are not obvious on the basis of common sense. Generally, such predictions do not fly in the face of common sense either. They must have a medium degree of novelty or incongruity. The idea about the earth going around the sun does fly in the face of everyday experience. If it were moving, we certainly should have noticed this motion.

At any point in time, one might assume that ideas that were conceptual to a medium degree should be preferred. These would be ideas with a medium degree of abstractness or a medium degree of fit with reality. Scientists should prefer ideas with a medium degree of fit with reality. Ideas that are extremely incongruous with reality are disliked. Why should a perfect fit not be preferred most? This is, after all, presumably the ultimate goal of science. The most important reason is that if an idea completely explained whatever it was supposed to explain, it would die. There would be nothing left to do. Scientists would have no further problems to solve. Other researchers would not refer to or cite the idea, because they would turn their efforts toward ideas still offering some problems. In evolutionary terms, this means that the idea would become an extinct museum piece—as happened to physical optics in the nineteenth century. Scientists should also prefer ideas with medium levels of complexity. A very simple idea is trivial, whereas an extremely complex one requires too much effort to think about.

I trace change in art to habituation of arousal potential. Because stimuli lose their arousal potential with repeated exposure, successive artists have to produce art with more and more arousal potential and, in so doing, have to engage in more and more primordial cognition. Can we make an analogous argument for science? I think that we can, but the pressure to increase arousal potential in science must lead in an opposite direction: toward less rather than more primordial thought. Broadly speaking, a poet's task is to create ideas of the form "x is like y" where x and y are coordinate terms or concepts on the same level. Habituation of arousal potential forces successive poets to draw x and y from ever more distant domains. They seem to do this by engaging in ever more primordial thought over time. Scientists, on the other hand, have to produce statements of the form "x is related to y," where x and y are on different levels. X is conceptual, while y is an observable percept, a subordinate of x. The pressure on a scientist should, then, be to expand the distance between x and y in a vertical direction: that is, scientists should engage in more and more conceptual or analytic thought over time (see figure 10.2.)

In the case of poetry, the amount of primordial thought does not go straight up over time, but increases in an oscillating fashion. This is because there are two ways of increasing the arousal potential of poetry: regressing more or elaborating less. When further regression becomes difficult, troublesome, or impossible, poets elaborate less: that is, they engage in some sort of stylistic change. It would seem that analogous oscillating increases and decreases in primordial thought are found in science. In general, successive scientists increase the arousal potential of their ideas by engaging in more and more conceptual cognition. When this becomes particularly difficult, they may bring about what Thomas Kuhn (1962) calls a paradigm change, which allows arousal potential to keep on increasing while degree of conceptual thinking temporarily declines.

Although they are usually intermingled, there are two types of scientific thought: devising general laws and making deductions from these laws. The deductive aspect of scientific thought is clearly conceptual in nature. On the other hand, scientists often seem to conceive of general laws by

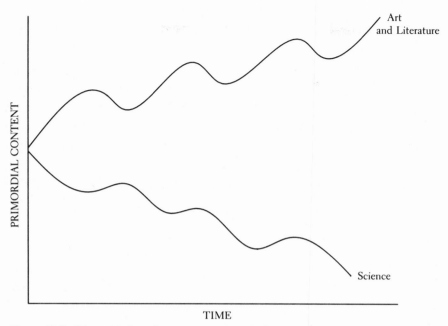

Figure 10.2 Theoretical predictions concerning historical trends in the primordial content of scientific prose versus art and literature.

means of primordial thought: that is, the inspiration or insight upon which the general law is based occurs in a primordial state (Ghiselin 1964 [1952]). This really has to be the case. The most purely conceptual type of thought is logic. Since logic doesn't tell you anything that you didn't at least implicitly know in the first place, it cannot by its very nature produce creative or novel ideas. The final formulation of a scientific idea, of course, requires a good bit of conceptual thought. Scientific thought is usually deductive. During periods of paradigm change, there tends to be more theorizing than deducing, though. This is the reason for hypothesizing that the amount of primordial thought increases during periods of paradigm change.

Scientific ideas tend to be clustered into sets of theories rather than being isolated propositions such as the one used in my example about people talking to one another. These theories are further organized into what Kuhn (1962) calls paradigms. A paradigm is a general way of attacking the problems of a scientific discipline. It consists of a set of theories, methods, and beliefs or goals. Kuhn stresses that paradigms are rather amorphous. Often they are best defined as consisting of a prototypical set of model problems and solutions to them. Examples of successive paradigms would be Newtonian physics versus Einsteinian physics or Ptolemaic astronomy versus Copernican astronomy.

Kuhn (1962) says that there are two types of science. Normal science operates within the confines of a more or less universally accepted paradigm that defines its problems and provides its methods. It consists of routine testing of hypotheses derived from established theories. These hypotheses are logically deduced from theories, and the scientist has every reason to expect that experiments based upon them will yield positive results. Kuhn equates normal science with puzzle solving. Its primary interests are increased precision of measurement, testing of obvious theoretical predictions, and minor elaboration of the paradigmatic theory. "Normal science does not aim at novelties of fact or theory and, when successful, finds none" (Kuhn 1962, p.52). The scientists likely to be engaged in such an enterprise do not sound creative, and usually are not. They rationally or logically deduce hypotheses and do not seek novelty. There is nothing at all creative about this sort of science. There is not supposed to be.

Over time, normal science produces more and more confirmations of theoretical hypotheses and more and more precise measurements. When unsuccessful, normal science also produces anomalies—results not in conformity with theoretical predictions. What happens then? Usually nothing, Kuhn says. A lot of anomalies must accumulate before change is likely. Any single anomaly can be attributed to a variety of causes—for example, the experiment was performed incorrectly, the theory was not interpreted correctly in selecting measurements, and so on. The most likely reaction to anomaly—if there is any reaction at all—is a minor revision in the theory.

On the other hand, according to Kuhn, revolutionary science has to do with a completely new paradigm, which is initially looser and more intuitive than the old one it replaces. If the new paradigm is accepted by other scientists, normal science resumes under its umbrella. Kuhn calls the replacement of one paradigm by another a paradigm shift. The distinction between normal and revolutionary science is never as extreme as this summary suggests (Lakatos 1978). Normal science itself involves activities that sound like revolutionary science (for example, modifying the general laws)—as Kuhn (1970) himself admits. Revolutionary science might be redefined to mean modifying general laws that are crucial for a variety of theories within a paradigm. It involves changing the laws upon which the whole paradigm rests—as the Copernican revolution in astronomy replaced the Ptolemaic theory that the sun and planets revolve in a circular fashion around the earth.

Kuhn's idea is that the history of science is not simply an accumulation of more and more knowledge. Rather, it consists of a series of paradigms. Within any one paradigm, normal science is carried out. Then a period of revolutionary science occurs and brings about a paradigm change. Normal science resumes under the guidance of the new paradigm. This sounds rather like the history of poetry with its series of styles: Within any one style, one could say that normal poetry is carried out. Then a period of revolutionary poetry brings about a new style. Kuhn himself remarked that the resemblance is hardly coincidental: he patterned his theory after theories of artistic change. Another similarity concerns the cumulation of knowledge. The general belief is that scientific knowledge cumulates or progresses, but artistic knowledge does neither. Kuhn, though, argued that scientific knowledge does not cumulate as much as is commonly believed. The history of science is not completely cumulative because a new paradigm generally destroys many of the "facts" produced by the old paradigm. For example, in modern chemistry things are defined in terms of compounds and elements. From the viewpoint of this paradigm, earlier experiments that used not pure compounds or elements but naturally occurring substances—wood or mud, for example—are completely pointless. In other cases, the facts and laws of the old paradigm are severely restricted in their range or rendered only approximately valid. From the perspective of modern physics, the laws of classical Newtonian physics are only approximations that hold only in medium ranges of space and time.

The Life Cycle of a Scientific Paradigm

Diana Crane (1972) has argued that scientific paradigms have a typical life cycle. When a paradigm first appears, it is espoused by a small group of scientists. These people formulate the general laws and develop the basic methods that define the paradigm. After the paradigm is established, normal science begins. Normal science is carried out by the members of what Crane calls an invisible college—a group of people who interact with each other and share the same goals and values. In the late stages of a paradigm, most major problems have been solved. This leads scientists to specialize on increasingly specific problems. This is necessary in order to extract the remaining ideas. In this stage, anomalies may also appear. In the final stage, there is exhaustion or crisis. The paradigm offers few possibilities and many problems or anomalies. As a consequence, members defect and are not replaced by new adherents. Very much the same thing happens in art and literature. A style gathers recruits who tend to know and interact with each other. There is excitement at first; but eventually the possibilities of the style are exhausted, and it becomes stale and decadent. Crane (1987) has analyzed the recent history of American painting in a manner analogous to her earlier analysis of science.

A paradigm can die for two reasons. There can be exhaustion without anomaly: that is, the paradigm has succeeded too well, and there are no problems left to be solved, as happened to Euclidean geometry. After the time of Euclid, there was nothing left to be done. The fit with reality had become perfect. Although Crane does not put it in these terms, we could say that arousal potential fell to zero, and the field elicited no further interest at least in the sense of scientists wanting to work in the area. In the case of exhaustion with anomaly, a different set of affairs exists. The exhaustion is not perceived as such. What is perceived is that a fit with reality can be obtained only with very complex theories. Further, new ideas can be generated only with considerable effort. In addition, there are undeniable anomalies or incongruities. Complexity, effort, and incongruity are likely to cause negative affect. In contrast, a new paradigm—if it is to be successful—will be more attractive: the fit with reality is not perfect, but neither are anomalies present as in an old paradigm. Anticipated payoff in relation to effort is much higher.

The new paradigm usually wins by default. The old paradigm does not die. Its adherents die. Because they have not been able to recruit new disciples, the paradigm dies with them. Once this happens, the new paradigm becomes dominant, and the process begins anew.

What goes wrong with normal science so that it is overthrown by revolutionary science? We can see what happens to normal science by looking at the life cycle of scientific specialty areas. The physicist and historian of science Gerald Holton (1973) compares a scientific specialty to exploring for gold. The task is to discover all of the gold in an area. The gold corresponds to interesting scientific ideas. A prospector confronted with the task knows that gold is discovered by walking around looking for it, which takes time. Over time, more and more gold will be discovered. On the other hand, the more time that has passed, the less gold there will be left to discover. To make matters worse, as soon as some gold is discovered, a lot of people will rush in to help find the rest of it. The consequence is that most of the gold will be discovered quickly. The amount left to be discovered will drop off quickly with time. Holton argues that this happens with specialized areas in science. They are quickly mined out.

Holton (1973) points out that the gold-mining analogy has to be complicated in one important respect. Ideas are not simply removed from the pool of potential ideas waiting to be discovered. Already discovered ideas can be recombined to form new ideas. Thus, discovery of an idea can add to, rather than subtract from, the pool of ideas waiting to be discovered. This tendency of ideas to propagate other ideas expands the range of possibilities for a specialty area but does not open up limitless possibilities. It merely postpones the inevitable time when there are no longer any interesting ideas left to be found.

Primordial Content in Psychological Journals

Later workers in a specialty area should have to engage in more conceptual thought than earlier ones do. Less deduction should be required to discover earlier ideas than later ones. This is only another way of saying that the earlier ideas are more obvious. If more deduction is needed over time, more and more conceptual thought will be required. Data from several studies support this hypothesis. Since its inception not much over one hundred years ago, experimental psychology has gone through three paradigms. The first paradigm, established by Wundt and his followers, is generally called introspectionism. Structuralism is really a better term, because introspection really constituted a very small portion of what early psychologists did. The structuralists defined psychology as the scientific study of mind. Mental life as we casually observe it is made up of what Wundt called psychical compounds, such as the perception of a tree or the idea of liberty. According to Wundt, such compounds are made up of psychical elements: that is, basic sensory attributes such as redness, roughness, and so on. The goal of psychology for the structuralists was to discover the laws of "mental chemistry"—that is, to enumerate the basic elements, find out the laws governing their combination, and so on. Structuralism was the dominant paradigm at least until the 1920s. By the end of the 1930s, it had pretty much died out. More precisely, most of the structuralist psychologists had died.

The next paradigm, behaviorism, was introduced primarily by J. B. Watson (1913). Watson's argument is that mental events cannot be directly observed and thus cannot be studied scientifically. Psychology, he argued, should be the scientific study of behavior. Its goal should be the formulation of laws governing behavior. These laws, furthermore, should be formulated in terms not of mental causes but of observable external stimuli. This was a wildly radical proposal. Many structuralists weren't really adverse to Watson's idea. They merely observed that he should call his new science something other than psychology, which is by definition the study of mind. The behaviorist idea is rather like saying that the proper subject matter of the historical study of Chinese poetry is English prose. After all, the latter is susceptible to study and discussion because it is written in a language we can understand. Radical and silly or not, behaviorism established itself as the dominant paradigm.

By the 1960s, a lot of psychologists were ready for a change. Behaviorism had not lived up to its promise. There were anomalies. For example, the behaviorist explanation of language was absurdly implausible. Having been at least an observer of the demise of behaviorism, it seems to me that one of the main reasons for the emergence of cognitive psychology, the third and current paradigm, was purely hedonic. The behaviorists really had only one explanation for everything. Whatever you asked about, the answer was that it was learned. If you asked about interesting things such as ideas and emotions, you were told that these were taboo topics. Behaviorism didn't have the allure of novelty. Quite the contrary. It had some very complicated explanations for some very boring phenomena—rats lost in mazes, for example—and no explanations for anything interesting. The perception was that it was a sinking ship. Cognitive psychology, on the other hand, was new and exciting. Cognitive psychologists argued that psychology is the scientific study of mind, which can't be directly observed but can after all be studied by indirect but quite objective methods. (It has turned out, of course, that behaviorism was not so bad as we thought, and cognitive psychology not nearly so wonderful as we had hoped.)

Now, what do we find if we treat scientific prose as we have treated poetry? Philosophers would have us believe that much of scientific writing is rhetoric, and for once they are probably right. So we have not really changed direction. We are still studying art, albeit a strange form of it. If poets leave the marks of the creative process in their works, it is reasonable to expect that scientists would, too. The stylistic rules of scientific writing aim to abolish these marks, but so, too, do the stylistic rules of poetry. The latter are exquisite and extensive, whereas the former are crude and primitive. They should fail to abolish all marks of origin just as poetic rules so fail.

The *American Journal of Psychology,* founded in 1887 by G. Stanley Hall, is the oldest American journal devoted to psychology. Beginning with 1887, I selected ten articles at random for each fifth year. The first twenty lines—up to the first end of sentence—was taken from each, giving around 200 words per article, for a total of 47,996 words. In this and the other studies of scientific prose, I left out brief notes, obituaries, book reviews, and things of that sort. I treated the samples as poetry and computed the Composite Variability Index. The large and significant differences among the twenty-one years in the sample are due to the fact that the Composite Variability Index has declined across time—a decline that has speeded up across time (see figure 10.3). It is reasonable to suppose that the prose has simplified as the ideas to be communicated have become more complex. The layman would find many of the earlier articles good reading—not merely because they are by writers such as William James, but mainly because the cognitive load is light and the topics are interesting. The later articles are difficult going. They are written for specialists. The topics are still interesting, but the layman can't even figure out what they are. The authors assume that you know stuff you don't know. The style, though, is extremely simple.

What about primordial content? Unsurprisingly, there is a lot less of it in scientific prose than in poetry. Surprisingly, it shows significant

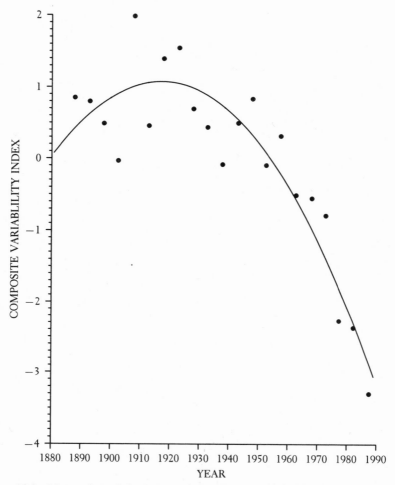

Figure 10.3 Mean values of the Composite Variability Index for articles in the *American Journal of Psychology* for every fifth year from 1887 through 1987. Scientific prose tends to simplify as the ideas conveyed become more complex.

interyear differences (see figure 10.4). Primordial content declines while the structuralist paradigm is dominant, and begins to rise as the behaviorist paradigm is introduced. After reaching a peak in the 1930s, it declines again, corresponding to the elaboration of behaviorist ideas. We don't see an increase in primordial content coinciding with the introduction of the

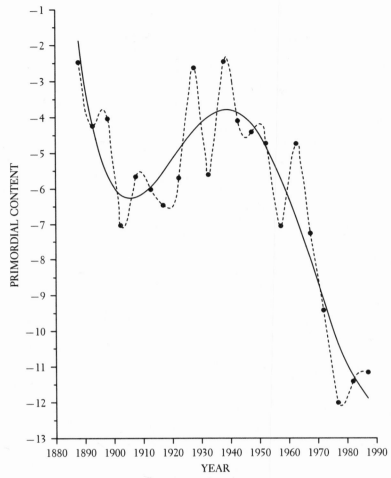

Figure 10.4 Average amount of primordial content in articles in the *American Journal of Psychology* for every fifth year from 1887 through 1987. Primordial content increased during the behaviorist paradigm shift and declined once the paradigm was established.

cognitive paradigm. This is not because the journal was not publishing material by cognitive psychologists: the Harvard III categories grouped under Psychological Processes show a sharp rise in the last several decades. (We can also—not so scientifically—establish, by just reading them or noting who wrote them, that the articles were about cognitive psychology.) The reason for no increase in primordial content may be that the articles on cognitive psychology are aimed at testing rather elaborate and already well worked out ideas.

I turned to the *Psychological Review*, which has been, at least recently, the main outlet for theoretical work in psychology. I sampled ten articles at random for each fifth year beginning with 1895, again to get about two hundred words per article, for a sample of 37,677 words. Exactly how many lines were used varied a bit because of changes in print size and format. The Composite Variability Index again declined with time. There were significant interyear differences in primordial content, due to the cubic trend shown in figure 10.5. I didn't find changes in primordial content coinciding with the shift from structuralism to behaviorism— probably because the type of article being published was also changing across the crucial years. In the early years, the *Psychological Review* contained a mix of empirical research reports and theoretical articles. It is only later that really concerns us. By the 1930s, the empirical articles were gone. We find a decline in primordial content as the behaviorist paradigm was elaborated, and an increase in primordial content beginning in 1965, when the cognitive paradigm was first being introduced.

An interesting subspecies, operant psychology, is a radical form of behaviorism introduced by B. F. Skinner. Skinner and his early followers were radical about a number of things. The most well known was their extreme anti-mentalism. Other behaviorists tended to sneak things such as motives or even expectations in between stimulus and response. Not Skinner. He wanted to stick purely to stimuli and responses. He had no truck with theory either: one shouldn't make up theories; rather, one should just report hard data. An example would be how a pigeon pecks a key given such and such a schedule of reinforcement. Skinner was even against using statistics to average across pigeons: you should just report what each pigeon does. At least until recently, operant psychology had little to do with the rest of experimental psychology. There were several reasons for this, a big one being that no one except an operant psychologist had the slightest interest in what specific pigeons did in specific Skinner boxes given specific schedules of reinforcement. The result was that operant psychologists published their work in their own journal, the *Journal of the Experimental Analysis of Behavior*. They didn't cite work in other psychology journals very much, and psychologists writing in other

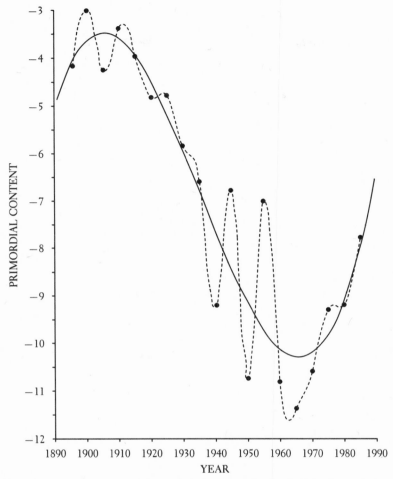

Figure 10.5   Average amount of primordial content in the *Psychological Review* for every fifth year from 1895 through 1985. Primordial content fell throughout the behaviorist era and began to rise with the introduction of the cognitive paradigm.

journals returned the favor (Krantz, 1971). Thus, this journal contains a nice record of a fairly closed scientific group that is essentially as autonomous from any external audience as French poets.

I selected ten articles at random from every second year from 1958, when the journal began, to 1986, when I got tired of accumulating samples. For each article, the first and also the last twenty lines were used.

The last twenty lines are from the discussion section. That gives about 276 words per article for a total of 41,449 words. The results for primordial content are in figure 10.6. Interyear differences among the samples are significant and arise from the trend shown in the figure. The statistics tell us to ignore the oscillations around the trend line. I think they are real,

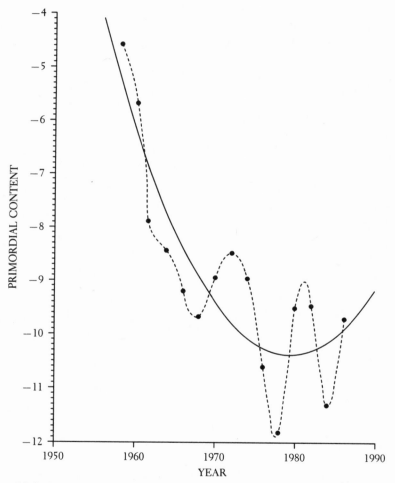

Figure 10.6 Average amount of primordial content in the *Journal of the Experimental Analysis of Behavior* for every other year from 1958 through 1986. Primordial content declined during the atheoretical paradigm and began to increase with the shift to the theoretical paradigm.

but we'd need a more extensive sample to be sure. The trend line shows a decrease in primordial content until 1978 and an increase since then.

In 1958, operant psychology was more or less focused on one question: How is rate of response related to schedule of reinforcement? There are only a few schedules of reinforcement; and by 1958, Skinner and other researchers had already answered the obvious questions for the obvious schedules. What to do? You can—and people did—check whether other organisms respond the way pigeons and laboratory rats do. How about muskrats, for example? Fortunately or unfortunately, such a line of inquiry is not very profitable. The general tendency was to investigate more and more complex combinations of schedules of reinforcement. For example, with a concurrent schedule, a pigeon is faced with one schedule of reinforcement if it pecks at one key and another schedule if it pecks another key. There are also compound and crossover schedules: the pigeon pecks at one key under one schedule so as to have the chance to peck at another one under another schedule, or something like that. It's all very complicated. This sounds like normal sciences run completely amuck. Perhaps it was, but some profound regularities emerged from this seemingly pointless data gathering.

When I analyzed the first data for this study in the mid-1970s, I didn't know much of anything about operant psychology. I expected primordial content to go straight down across time. Stanley Pliskoff was the editor of the *Journal of the Experimental Analysis of Behavior* during the period after 1968 when primordial content shows its first increase after a sustained decline from 1958. His office is down the hall from mine so, graph in hand, I went calling and demanded an explanation of why he had accepted articles that messed up my data. Perhaps he had encouraged a lyrical turn? No, he replied, the data probably indicated a theoretical turn, one for which he modestly disavowed any credit. Around this time, operant psychologists had begun to be much less atheoretical, and the general movement of operant psychology away from pure observation toward general theory (still connected, of course, with careful observation) is by now clear.

For the moment, the operant psychologists have the last laugh. Operant psychology and the latest version of cognitive psychology are in some aspects pretty much the same thing stated in vastly different ways (Rachlin et al. 1986; Rescorla 1988). Operant psychology isn't really about pigeons in boxes. It is about what Skinner said it is about—the behavior of organisms. Now, poets are organisms, so operant psychology should describe their behavior. As the operant psychologist A. Charles Catania (1976) pointed out, my 1975 theory of literary change could just as well have been stated in operant terms. The same is even more true of the theory as I have put it in this book. Rather than talking about pleasure and boredom, I could really just as well have talked about reinforcement and choice behavior. Primordial and conceptual thought doesn't sound distinctly behavioral, but one can make them so. For example, another psychologist, Eric Klinger (1971), called them respondent and operant thinking.

HUMANISTIC DISCOURSE

Science and poetry are not as different as most people imagine. Both the scientist and the poet try to tell us something about eternal or universal realities. The latter should not change, but poetic and scientific discourse change radically over time. I have, of course, argued that much of this change is due to a "clockwork" set up by pressure for novelty.

Literary critics attempt to tell us what poetry and other types of literature mean. The works they discuss stay the same, but their interpretations change drastically across time. I conclude by asking whether some of this change may not be due to the constant pressure to say something new and different—a pressure that bears down upon anyone who wants to say anything at all.

Since we have found trends in poetic and scientific discourse that are mirror images of each other, what may we find in the language of literary criticism? The latter makes no claim to being science, though it does at times claim to be poetry (Bloom 1975). I took samples at ten-year intervals, beginning in 1885, from ten randomly selected articles in the *Publications of the Modern Language Association*. The samples were taken from the beginning of each article and omitted any quotations. The aim of a sample of about two hundred words per article was closely met, so that total sample size was 24,058 words. There were no trends in Incongruous Juxtapositions or in the Composite Variability Index. If I was right in attributing decreases in the latter in scientific prose to increased conceptual complexity, then the complexity of humanistic discourse has apparently not changed across the last century.

Primordial content does show significant differences among years. The means for each year are shown in figure 10.7. There is a general increase

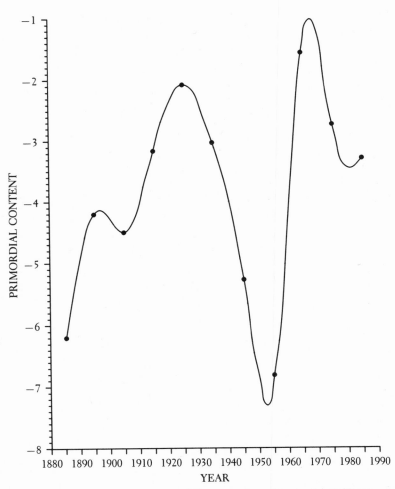

Figure 10.7 Average amount of primordial content in articles in the *Publications of the Modern Language Association* for every tenth year from 1885 through 1985. Primordial content increased with the paradigm shift to the new criticism and again with the paradigm shift to structuralism.

from 1885 to 1925. In part, critics seem to have become more lyrical. In part, the increase is due to a deletion of articles that are not specifically literary criticism. Some such articles appear in the early years. The decline in primordial content after 1925 makes sense. Its beginning corresponds to the introduction of the "new criticism," which emphasized close reading and an objective approach to literature. The more new criticism developed, the lower primordial content fell. The large increase in primordial content in 1965 corresponds to a paradigm shift from new criticism to structuralism. Of course, structuralism per se lasted for a short time and bore within it from the first the delirious seeds of deconstructionism and poststructuralism.

The data do not bear good news for those of us who find annoying the sentimental effusions of many literary critics. Rather than decreasing, as in poetry, references to emotions increased significantly across the last century. The figure for 1975 was 4.3 percent—more than double that of contemporary poetry. Literary criticism does seem to go through paradigms or styles—though to what end is not clear. It has not become more abstract or, apparently, more complex across the last century. It is like poetry and pure science in that it is useless. It is unlike them, though, in that those who write it do not seem to know this.

References

Alcina Franch, J. 1983. *Pre-Columbian Art*. New York: Harry Abrams.

Acland, J. H. 1972. *Medieval Structure: The Gothic Vault*. Toronto: University of Toronto Press.

Alland, A. 1983. *Playing with Form: Children Draw in Six Cultures*. New York: Columbia University Press.

Allport, G. W.; and Postman, L. 1947. *The Psychology of Rumor*. New York: Henry Holt.

Andreason, N. C.; and Cantor, A. 1974. "The Creative Writer: Psychiatric Symptoms and Family History." *Comprehensive Psychiatry* 15: 123–31.

Apollinaire, G. 1918. "L'Esprit nouveau et les poètes." In *Selected Writings*. New York: New Directions, 1948.

Ariès, P. 1981. *The Hour of Our Death*. New York: Alfred A. Knopf.

Arnold, M. 1889. "Emerson." In *Discourses in America*. London: Macmillan.

Bachelard, G. 1964 [1938]. *The Psychoanalysis of Fire*. Boston: Beacon Press.

———. 1983 [1942]. *Water and Dreams*. Dallas, Tex.: Pegasus Foundation.

———. 1943. *L'Air et les songes: Essai sur l'imagination du mouvement*. Paris: Librairie José Corti.

———. 1948. *La Terre et les rêveries de la volunté*. Paris: Librairie José Corti.

371

References

BALFOUR, H. 1893. *The Evolution of Decorative Art*. London: Rivington, Percival.

BARLOW, H.; and MORGENSTERN, S. 1948. *A Dictionary of Musical Themes*. New York: Crown.

BARRON, F.; and WELSH, G. S. 1952. "Perception as a Possible Factor in Personality Style: Its Measurement by a Figure Preference Test." *Journal of Psychology* 33: 199–207.

BARTLETT, F. C. 1932. *Remembering*. Cambridge: Cambridge University Press.

BAUDELAIRE, C. 1961 [1855–62]. Fusées. In *Oeuvres complètes*. Paris: Nouvelle Revue Française.

BEAUGRANDE, R. DE. 1980. *Text, Discourse, and Process*. Norwood, N.J.: Ablex.

BEGUIN, S.; et al. 1964. *Dictionary of Italian Painting*. New York: Tudor.

BELZ, C. 1969. *The Story of Rock*. New York: Oxford University Press.

BENJAMIN, W. 1968. "The Task of the Translator." In W. Benjamin, *Illuminations*. New York: Schocken.

BENNETT, H. S. 1947. *Chaucer and the Fifteenth Century*. Oxford: Oxford University Press.

BERLYNE, D. E. 1965. *Structure and Direction in Thinking*. New York: John Wiley.

———. 1967. "Arousal and Reinforcement." In D. Levine, ed., *Nebraska Symposium on Motivation*, vol. 15. Lincoln: University of Nebraska Press.

———. 1970. "Novelty, Complexity and Hedonic Value." *Perception and Psychophysics* 8: 279–86.

———. 1971. *Aesthetics and Psychobiology*. New York: Appleton-Century-Crofts.

BERLYNE, D. E., ed. 1974. *Studies in the New Experimental Aesthetics: Steps toward an Objective Psychology of Aesthetic Appreciation*. Washington, D.C.: Hemisphere.

BERLYNE, D. E.; and CROZIER, J. 1971. "Effects of Complexity and Prechoice Stimulation on Exploratory Choice." *Perception and Psychophysics* 10: 242–46.

BERLYNE, D. E.; KOENIG, J.; and HIROTA, T. 1966. "Novelty, Arousal, and the Reinforcement of Diversive Exploration in the Rat." *Journal of Comparative and Physiological Psychology* 62: 222–26.

BERNARD, O., ed. and trans. 1966. *Rimbaud*. London: Penguin.

BERRIAN, R. W.; et al. 1979. "Estimates of Imagery, Ease of Definition, and Animateness for 328 Adjectives." *Journal of Experimental Psychology: Human Learning and Memory* 5: 435–47.

Best American Short Stories. 1970–85. Boston: Houghton Mifflin.

BLATT, S. J. 1984. *Continuity and Change in Art: The Development of Modes of Representation*. Hillsdale, N.J.: Lawrence Erlbaum.

BLEULER, E. 1966 [1911]. *Dementia Praecox; or, The Group of Schizophrenias*. New York: International Universities Press.

BLOOM, H. 1973. *The Anxiety of Influence: A Theory of Poetry*. New York: Oxford University Press.

———. 1975. *A Map of Misreading*. New York: Oxford University Press.

BOND, F. 1913. *An Introduction to English Church Architecture: From the Eleventh to the Sixteenth Century*, 2 vols. London: Milford.

BONY, J. 1983. *French Gothic Architecture of the Twelfth and Thirteenth Centuries*. Berkeley: University of California Press.

BRANSFORD, J. D.; and FRANKS, J. J. 1971. "The Abstraction of Linguistic Ideas." *Cognitive Psychology* 2: 231–50.

BRETON, A. 1924. "Manifeste du surréalisme." In *Manifestes du surréalisme*. Paris: Gallimard, 1963.

———. 1929. "Second manifeste du surréalisme." In A. Breton, *Manifestes du surréalisme*. Paris: Gallimard, 1963.

BRETT-SMITH, S. C. 1984. "Speech Made Visible: The Irregular as a System of Meaning." *Empirical Studies of the Arts* 2: 127–47.

BREWER, W.; and OHTSUKA, K. 1988. "Story Structure and Reader Affect in American and Hungarian Short Stories." In C. Martindale, ed., *Psychological Approaches to the Study of Literary Narratives*. Hamburg, Germany: Buske.

BRINTON, C. 1960 [1949]. *The Anatomy of Revolution*. New York: Vintage.

BROOKS, C. 1947. *The Well Wrought Urn*. New York: Harcourt Brace.

BURCKHARDT, J. 1950 [1860]. *The Civilization of the Renaissance in Italy*. London: Phaidon.

BURKE, K. 1957. *Counter-statement*. Chicago: University of Chicago Press.

BUSCHOR, E. 1921. *Greek Vase-Painting*. London: Chatto & Windus.

BUSH, D. 1962. *English Literature in the Earlier Seventeenth Century: 1600–1660*. London: Oxford University Press.

CAMPBELL, D. T. 1974. "Evolutionary Epistemology." In P. A. Schilpp, ed., *The Philosophy of Karl Popper*. LaSalle, Ill.: Open Court.

———. 1965. "Variation and Selective Retention in Sociocultural Evolution." In H. R. Barringer, G. I. Blanksten, and R. W. Mack, eds., *Social Change in Developing Areas: A Reinterpretation of Evolutionary Theory*. Cambridge, Mass.: Schenkman.

CAMPBELL, J. 1949. *The Hero with a Thousand Faces*. Princeton, N.J.: Princeton University Press.

References

CANNON, B. C.; JOHNSON, A. H.; and WAITE, A. B. 1960. *The Art of Music: A Short History of Musical Styles and Ideas.* New York: Thomas Y. Crowell.

CATANIA, A. C. 1976. "On Attending at the 'Having' of Reviews." *Journal of the Experimental Analysis of Behavior* 26: 317–20.

CAUDWELL, C. 1937. *Illusion and Reality.* London: Macmillan.

CAVALLI-SFORZA, L. L.; and FELDMAN, M. W. 1981. *Cultural Transmission and Evolution: A Quantitative Approach.* Princeton, N.J.: Princeton University Press.

CAZAMIAN, L. 1955. *A History of French Literature.* Oxford: Oxford University Press.

CERULO, K. A. 1984. "Social Disruption and Its Effects on Music." *Social Forces* 62: 885–904.

CHAMBERS, E. K., ed. 1932. *The Oxford Book of Sixteenth Century Verse.* London: Oxford University Press.

CHAMBERS, F. 1928. *Cycles of Taste.* Cambridge: Cambridge University.

CHASTEL, A. 1963. *Italian Art: Architecture, Painting and Sculpture from the Early Christian Period to the Present Day.* New York: Harper & Row.

COHEN, J. 1966. *Structure du langage poétique.* Paris: Flammarion.

COLLINGWOOD, R. G. 1946. *The Idea of History.* Oxford: Oxford University Press.

COMEAU, H.; and FARTHING, G. W. 1985. "An Examination of Language Content for Manifestations of Primary and Secondary Process during the Hypnotic and Awake States." Unpublished paper, University of Maine.

COMTE, A. 1830. *Cours de philosophie positive.* Paris: Bachelier.

COURTHOPE, W. J. 1906–10. *A History of English Poetry,* 6 vols. London: Macmillan.

CRANE, D. 1972. *Invisible Colleges: Diffusion of Knowledge in Scientific Communities.* Chicago: University of Chicago Press.

———. 1987. *The Transformation of the Avant-Garde: The New York Art World, 1940–1985.* Chicago: University of Chicago Press.

DARWIN, C. 1859. *On the Origin of Species.* London: Watts.

———. 1896 [1871]. *The Descent of Man and Selection in Relation to Sex.* New York: D. Appleton.

DAVIES, N. M.; and GARDINER, A. H. 1936. *Ancient Egyptian Paintings.* Chicago: University of Chicago Press.

DAY, H. I. 1967. "Evaluation of Subjective Complexity, Pleasingness and Interestingness for a Series of Random Polygons Varying in Complexity." *Perception and Psychophysics* 2: 281–86.

DELPHENDAHL, R.; and MARTINDALE, C. 1985. Eine Computer gestützte Inhaltsanalyse von Goethes Faust in Bezug auf Primär- und Sekundärprozesse. Colloquium, Universität Ulm, Ulm, F.R.G.

DEONNA, W. 1912. *L'Archéologie, sa valeur, ses méthodes,* 3 vols. Paris: H. Laurens.

DERRIDA, J. 1967. *De la grammatologie.* Paris: Editions de Minuit.

DICKIE, G. 1971. *Aesthetics: An Introduction.* Indianapolis: Pegasus.

DICKINSON, E. 1924 [1870]. Letter to T. W. Higginson. In M. G. D. Bianchi, *The Life and Letters of Emily Dickinson.* Boston: Houghton Mifflin.

DILTHEY, W. 1894. *Ideen über eine beschreibende und zergliedernde Psychologie.* Leipzig: G. B. Teubner.

DISSELHOFF, H. D.; and LINNÉ, S. 1961. *The Art of Ancient America: Civilizations of Central and South America.* New York: Crown.

DOBZHANSKY, T. 1973. "Nothing in Biology Makes Sense Except in the Light of Evolution." *American Biology Teacher* 35: 125–29.

DOLEŽEL, L. 1972. "From Motifemes to Motifs." *Poetics* 4: 65–90.

DRYDEN, J. 1958. *The Poems of John Dryden,* J. Kinsley, ed., 4 vols. Oxford: Oxford University Press.

DUNCAN, D. D. 1974. *Goodbye Picasso.* New York: Grosset & Dunlap.

EAGLETON, T. 1976. *Marxism and Literary Criticism.* Berkeley: University of California Press.

EHRENZWEIG, A. 1954. *The Psycho-analysis of Artistic Vision and Hearing.* New York: Braziller.

———. 1971 [1967]. *The Hidden Order of Art.* Berkeley: University of California Press.

ELGAR, F.; and MAITLAND, R. 1955. *Picasso.* Paris: Fernand Hazan.

ELIOT, T. S. 1927. "The Silurist." *The Dial* 83: 259–63.

———. 1932. *Selected Essays, 1917–1932.* New York: Harcourt Brace.

ELLIOTT, E. 1988. "General Introduction." In E. Elliott, ed., *Columbia Literary History of the United States.* New York: Columbia University Press.

ELLMANN, R. 1976. *The New Oxford Book of American Verse.* New York: Oxford University Press.

EMPSON, W. 1930. *Seven Types of Ambiguity.* London: New Directions.

EVANS, D. R. 1969. *Conceptual Complexity, Arousal and Epistemic Behavior.* Unpublished Ph.D. dissertation, University of Toronto.

EYSENCK, H. J. 1953. *Uses and Abuses of Psychology.* Baltimore, Md.: Penguin.

FELTON, H. 1957. *A Portrait of English Cathedrals.* London: B. T. Batford.

FENICHEL, O. 1945. *The Psychoanalytic Theory of Neurosis.* New York: W. W. Norton.

References

FIEDLER, K. 1949. *On Judging Works of Visual Art*. Berkeley: University of California Press.

FIEDLER, L. A. 1964. *Waiting for the End*. New York: Stein & Day.

FINDLAY, C. S.; and LUMSDEN, C. J. 1988. "The Creative Mind: Toward an Evolutionary Theory of Discovery and Innovation." *Journal of Social and Biological Structures* 11: 3–55.

FISCHER, J. L. 1961. "Art Styles as Cultural Cognitive Maps." *American Anthropologist* 63: 79–93.

FISH, S. 1980. *Is There a Text in This Class?* Cambridge, Mass.: Harvard University Press.

FOCILLON, H. 1942. *The Life of Forms in Art*. London: Wittenborn.

FOLEY, M., ed. 1965. *Fifty Best American Short Stories: 1915–1965*. Boston: Houghton Mifflin.

———. 1975. *200 Years of Great American Short Stories*. Boston: Houghton Mifflin.

FORBES, H. M. 1927. *Gravestones of Early New England and the Men Who Made Them*. Boston: Houghton Mifflin.

FOWLIE, W. 1962 [1953]. *Mallarmé*. Chicago: University of Chicago Press.

———. 1967. *Climate of Violence: The French Literary Tradition from Baudelaire to the Present*. New York: Macmillan.

FOWLIE, W., ed. and trans. 1955. *Mid-century French Poets*. New York: Twayne.

FRANKL, P. 1962. *Gothic Architecture*. Baltimore: Penguin.

FRANZ, M. L. VON. 1966. *Aurora Consurgens: A Document Attributed to Thomas Aguinas on the Problem of Opposites in Alchemy*. Princeton: Princeton University Press.

FREUD, S. 1938 [1900]. *The Interpretation of Dreams*. In A. A. Brill, ed., *Basic Writings of Sigmund Freud*. New York: Modern Library.

———. 1959 [1910]. "The Antithetical Sense of Primal Words." In S. Freud, *Collected Papers*, vol. 4. New York: Basic Books.

FROMM, E. 1978. "Primary and Secondary Process in Waking and in Altered States of Consciousness." *Journal of Altered States of Consciousness* 4: 115–28.

GABLIK, S. 1976. *Progress in Art*. London: Thames & Hudson.

GARDNER, H. 1972. "Style Sensitivity in Children." *Human Development* 15: 325–38.

GAUTIER, T. 1955 [1835]. *Mademoiselle de Maupin*. Paris: Editions Garnier Frères.

GHISELIN, B., ed. 1964 [1952]. *The Creative Process*. New York: Mentor.

GILBERT, K. E.; and KUHN, H. 1939. *A History of Esthetics*. Bloomington: Indiana University Press.

GILLETT, C. 1972. *The Sound of the City: The Rise of Rock and Roll*. New York: Dell.

GLEICK, J. 1987. *Chaos: Making a New Science*. New York: Viking.

GODFREY, F. M. 1965. *History of Italian Painting: 1250 to 1800*. New York: Taplinger.

GÖLLER, A. 1888. *Entstehung der architektonischen Stilformen*. Stuttgart: K. Wittwer.

GOMBRICH, E. H. 1953. Review of *Social History of Art* by A. Hauser, *Art Bulletin* 35: 79–84.

———. 1956. "Psychoanalysis and the History of Art." In B. Nelson, ed., *Freud and the Twentieth Century*. New York: Meridian.

———. 1969. *In Search of Cultural History*. London: Oxford University Press.

———. 1979. *The Sense of Order: A Study in the Psychology of Visual Art*. Ithaca, N.Y.: Cornell University Press.

GOTTMAN, J. M. 1981. *Time Series Analysis: A Comprehensive Introduction for Social Scientists*. Cambridge, England: Cambridge University Press.

GRIERSON, H. J. C.; and BULLOUGH, C., eds. 1934. *The Oxford Book of Seventeenth Century Verse*. London: Oxford University Press.

HADDON, A. C. 1907. *Evolution in Art*. New York: Charles Scribner.

HAECKEL, E. H. 1899. *The History of Creation*. London: Kegan, Paul, Trench, Trubner.

HAMMOND, E. P. 1927. *English Verse between Chaucer and Surrey*. Durham, N.C.: Duke University Press.

HANSON, H. M. 1959. "Effects of Discrimination Training on Stimulus Generalization." *Journal of Experimental Psychology* 58: 321–34.

HARTLEY, A., ed. 1965. *Mallarmé*. London: Penguin.

HARVEY, J. 1961. *A Portrait of English Cathedrals*. London: B. T. Batford.

HASENFUS, N.; MARTINDALE, C.; and BIRNBAUM, D. 1983. "Psychological Reality of Cross-Media Artistic Styles." *Journal of Experimental Psychology: Human Perception and Performance* 9: 841–63.

HAUGH, L. D. 1976. "Checking the Independence of Two Covariance Stationary Time Series: A Univariate Residual Cross-correlation Approach." *Journal of the American Statistical Association* 71: 378–85.

HAUSER, A. 1951. *The Social History of Art*. London: Routledge & Kegan Paul.

———. 1963 [1958]. *The Philosophy of Art History*. Cleveland: World Publishing.

377

References

HAWKING, S. W. 1988. *A Brief History of Time: From the Big Bang to Black Holes.* New York: Bantam Books.

HAYWARD, J., ed. 1964. *The Oxford Book of Nineteenth Century English Verse.* London: Oxford University Press.

HEGEL, G. W. F. 1920 [1835]. *The Philosophy of Fine Art,* 4 vols. London: G. Bell.

HEISE, D. R. 1965. "Semantic Differential Profiles for 1000 Most Frequent English Words." *Psychological Monographs* 79: 1–31.

HERDAN, G. 1966. *The Advanced Theory of Language as Choice and Chance.* New York: Springer-Verlag.

HOBBES, T. 1840 [1650]. "The Answer to Sir William Davenant's Preface before 'Gondibert.' " In W. Molesworth, ed., *The English Works of Thomas Hobbes of Malmsbury,* vol IV. London: John Bohn.

HOGAN, R. 1983. "A Socioanalytic Theory of Personality." In M. Page, ed., *Personality—Current Theory and Research: Proceedings of the 1982 Nebraska Symposium on Motivation.* Lincoln: University of Nebraska Press.

HOGENRAAD, R.; and ORIANNE, E. 1986. "Imagery, Regressive Thinking, and Verbal Performance in Internal Monologue." *Imagination, Cognition, and Personality* 5: 127–45.

HOLTON, G. 1973. *Thematic Origins of Scientific Thought: Kepler to Einstein.* Cambridge, Mass.: Harvard University Press.

HOUSTON, J. P.; and MEDNICK, S. A. 1963. "Creativity and the Need for Novelty." *Journal of Abnormal and Social Psychology* 66: 137–41.

HUGHES, D. G. 1974. *A History of European Music.* New York: McGraw-Hill.

HUGO, V. 1963 [1827]. Préface à *Cromwell.* In *Théâtre complet de Victor Hugo,* vol. 1. Paris: Bibliothèque de la Pléiade.

HUIZINGA, J. 1924. *The Waning of the Middle Ages.* London: E. Arnold.

ILLING, R. 1963. *Pergamon Dictionary of Musicians and Music.* Oxford: Pergamon Press.

JAKOBSON, R. 1960. "Linguistics and Poetics." In T. Sebeok, ed., *Style in Language.* Cambridge, Mass.: MIT Press.

———. 1973. *Questions de poétique.* Paris: Seuil.

———. 1981. *Poetry of Grammar and Grammar of Poetry.* The Hague: Mouton.

JAMES, W. 1902. *The Varieties of Religious Experience.* New York: Collier, 1961.

JANIS, H.; and JANIS, S. 1946. *Picasso: The Recent Years 1939–1946.* Garden City, N.Y.: Doubleday.

JENKINS, G. M.; and WATTS, D. G. 1968. *Spectral Analysis and Its Applications.* San Francisco: Holden-Day.

References

JESSUP, A., ed. 1923. *Representative American Short Stories.* Boston: Allyn & Bacon.

JOHNSON, S. 1905 [1779]. Life of Cowley. In S. Johnson, *Lives of the English Poets,* vol. I. Oxford: Clarendon Press.

JONES, A.; WILKINSON, J. H.; and BRADEN, I. 1961. "Information Deprivation as a Motivational Variable." *Journal of Experimental Psychology* 62: 126–37.

JONES, W. T. 1961. *The Romantic Syndrome.* The Hague: Martinus Nijhoff.

JOWETT, B. 1937. *The Dialogues of Plato,* vol. I. New York: Random House.

JUNG, C. G. 1959. *The Archetypes and the Collective Unconscious.* In C. G. Jung, *Collected Works,* vol. 9, pt. 1. New York: Pantheon.

———. 1963. *Mysterium Coniunctionis: An Inquiry into the Seperation and Synthesis of Psychic Opposites in Alchemy.* New York: Bollingen.

KAHLER, E. 1968. *The Disintegration of Form in the Arts.* New York: Braziller.

KAMANN, R. 1963. "Verbal Complexity and Preferences in Poetry." *Journal of Verbal Learning and Verbal Behavior* 5: 536–40.

KAPLAN, C. S. 1975. *Psychosocial Determinants of Lyrical Change: A Content Analysis of Popular Music 1950–1972.* Unpublished M.S. thesis, University of Maine.

KAUTZSCH, R. 1917. *Der Begriff der Entwickelung in der Kunstgeschichte.* Frankfurt: Werner und Winter.

KAVOLIS, V. 1968. *Artistic Expression—A Sociological Analysis.* Ithaca, N.Y.: Cornell University Press.

KLEE, H.; and LEGGE, D. 1976. "Estimates of Concreteness and Other Indices for 200 Transitive Verbs." *Journal of Experimental Psychology: Human Learning and Memory* 2: 497–507.

KLINGER, E. 1971. *Structure and Function of Fantasy.* New York: John Wiley.

———. 1978. "Modes of Normal Conscious Flow." In K. S. Pope and J. L. Singer, eds., *The Stream of Consciousness: Scientific Investigations into the Flow of Human Experience.* New York: Plenum.

KRANTZ, D. L. 1971. "The Separate Worlds of Operant and Non-operant Psychology." *Journal of Applied Behavior Analysis* 4: 61–70.

KREITLER, H.; and KREITLER, S. 1972. *Psychology of the Arts.* Durham, N.C.: Duke University Press.

KRIS, E. 1952. *Psychoanalytic Explorations in Art.* New York: International Universities Press.

KROEBER, A. L. 1944. *Configurations of Cultural Growth.* Berkeley: University of California Press.

———. 1956. "Toward a Definition of Nazca Style." *University of California Publications in American Archaeology and Ethnology* 43: 327–432.

KRUSKAL, J. B. 1964. "Nonmetric Multidimensional Scaling." *Psychometrika* 29: 1–27, 115–29.

KRUSKAL, J. B.; and WISH, M. 1978. *Multidimensional Scaling.* Beverly Hills, Calif.: Sage.

KUBACH, H. E. 1975. *Romanesque Architecture.* New York: Harry N. Abrams.

KUBLER, G. 1962. *The Shape of Time: Remarks on the History of Things.* New Haven: Yale University Press.

KUHN, T. S. 1962. *The Structure of Scientific Revolutions.* Chicago: University of Chicago Press.

———. 1970. "Logic of Discovery or Psychology of Research." In I. Lakatos and A. Musgrave, eds., *Criticism and the Growth of Knowledge.* Cambridge, England: Cambridge University Press.

LAKATOS, I. 1978. *The Methodology of Scientific Research Programmes.* Cambridge, England: Cambridge University Press.

LANE, R. D. 1962. *Masters of the Japanese Print, Their World and Their Work.* Garden City, N.Y.: Doubleday.

LANGE, C. 1903. *Sinnesgenusse und Kunstgenuss.* Wiesbaden: J. F. Bergmann.

LARKIN, P., ed. 1973. *The Oxford Book of Twentieth Century English Verse.* London: Oxford University Press.

LASLETT, P.; and OOSTERVEEN, K. 1973. "Long Term Trends in Bastardy in England." *Population Studies* 27: 255–86.

LAVER, J. 1950. *Dress.* London: John Murray.

LAWRENCE, D. H. 1955 [1924]. "Studies in Classic American Literature." In E. Wilson, ed., *The Shock of Recognition.* New York: Farrar, Straus & Cudahy.

LESSING, G. E. 1962 [1766]. *Laocoön: An Essay on the Limits of Painting and Poetry.* Indianapolis, Ind.: Bobbs-Merrill.

LESSIUS, L. 1743 [1634]. *A Treatise of Health and Long Life.* London: Charles Hitch.

LÉVI-STRAUSS, C. 1963 [1958]. *Structural Anthropology.* New York: Basic Books.

———. 1962. *La Pensée sauvage.* Paris: Plon.

———. 1964. *Le Cru et le cuit.* Paris: Plon.

LINGOES, J. C. 1967. "An IBM-7090 Program for Guttman-Lingoes Configural Similarity-I." *Behavioral Science* 12: 502–3.

LOMAX, A. 1968. *Folk Song Style and Culture.* Washington, D. C.: American Association for the Advancement of Science.

———. 1972. "An Evolutionary Taxonomy of Culture." *Science* 177: 228–39.

LOMBROSO, C. 1895. *The Man of Genius.* London: Walter Scott.

LOTMAN, J. M. 1970. *Struktura xudozestvennogo teksta.* Moscow: Iskusstva.

References

LUCAS, ST. J.; and JONES, P. M., eds. 1957. *The Oxford Book of French Verse.* London: Oxford University Press.

LUDWIG, A. I. 1966. *Graven Images: New England Stonecarving and Its Symbols: 1650–1815.* Middletown, Conn.: Wesleyan University Press.

McCLELLAND, D. C. 1951. *Personality.* New York: Dryden.

———. 1975. *Power: The Inner Experience.* New York: Irvington.

McCORMACK, W.; and MARTINDALE, C. 1983. "The Great Railway Bazaar: The Analogy between Real and Mythical Travel." Paper presented at International Colloquium on Empirical Aesthetics, Cardiff, U.K.

MACHOTKA, P. 1966. "Aesthetic Criteria in Childhood: Justification of Preference." *Child Development* 37: 877–85.

MACHERY, P. 1966. *Pour une théorie de la production littéraire.* Paris: F. Maspero.

McKELLAR, P. 1957. *Imagination and Thinking.* New York: Basic Books.

MANDELBROT, B. 1977. *The Fractal Geometry of Nature.* New York: W. H. Freeman.

MANDLER, J. M.; and RITCHEY, G. H. 1977. "Long-term Memory for Pictures." *Journal of Experimental Psychology: Human Learning and Memory* 3: 386–96.

MARK, R. 1982. *Experiments in Gothic Structure.* Cambridge, Mass.: MIT Press.

MARKHAM, E. 1934. *The Book of American Poetry.* New York: Grosset & Dunlap.

MARKS, L. E. 1975. "On Colored-Hearing Synesthesia: Cross-Modal Translations of Sensory Dimensions." *Psychological Bulletin* 82: 303–31.

MARTINDALE, A.; and MARTINDALE, C. 1988. "Metaphorical Equivalence of Elements and Temperaments: Empirical Studies of Bachelard's Theory of Imagination." *Journal of Personality and Social Psychology* 55: 836–48.

———. 1989. "Stylistic Evolution of Medieval French Cathedrals." Paper presented at American Psychological Association convention, New Orleans.

MARTINDALE, C. 1969. *The Psychology of Literary Change.* Unpublished Ph.D. dissertation, Harvard University.

———. 1972a. "Father Absence, Psychopathology, and Poetic Eminence." *Psychological Reports* 31: 843–47.

———. 1972b. "The Parallelism of Archetype and Reality in 'The Fall of the House of Usher.'" *Poe Studies* 5: 9–11.

———. 1973a. "COUNT: A PL/I Program for Content Analysis of Natural Language" (abstract). *Behavioral Science* 18: 1948.

———. 1973b. "An Experimental Simulation of Literary Change." *Journal of Personality and Social Psychology* 25: 319–26.

———. 1973c. "Transformation and Transfusion of Vitality in the Narratives of Poe." *Semiotica* 7: 46–59.

———. 1974a. "LEXSTAT; A PL/I Program for Computation of Lexical Statistics" (abstract). *Behavior Research Methods and Instrumentation* 6: 571.

———. 1974b. "The Semantic Significance of Spatial Movement in Narrative Verse: Patterns of Regressive Imagery in the Divine Comedy." In L. Mitchell, ed., *Computers in the Humanities*. Edinburgh: Edinburgh University Press.

———. 1975. *Romantic Progression: The Psychology of Literary History*. Washington, D.C.: Hemisphere.

———. 1976a. "The Grammar of Altered States of Consciousness: A Semiotic Reinterpretation of Aspects of Psychoanalytic Theory." In D. Spence, ed., *Psychoanalysis and Contemporary Science*, vol. 4. New York: Macmillan.

———. 1976b. "Primitive Mentality and the Relationship between Art and Society." *Scientific Aesthetics* 1: 5–18.

———. 1977a. "Syntactic and Semantic Correlates of Verbal Tics in Gilles de la Tourette's Syndrome: A Quantitative Case Study." *Brain and Language* 4: 231–47.

———. 1977b. "The Psychology of Cultural Evolution: Studies of Change in Poetry, Painting, and Science." Paper presented at the New England Social Psychological Association meeting, Northampton, Massachusetts.

———. 1978a. "The Evolution of English Poetry." *Poetics* 7: 231–48.

———. 1978b. "A Quantitative Analysis of Diachronic Patterns in Some Narratives of Poe." *Semiotica* 22: 287–308.

———. 1979. "The Night Journey: Trends in the Content of Narratives Symbolizing Alteration of Consciousness." *Journal of Altered States of Consciousness* 4: 321–43.

———. 1981. *Cognition and Consciousness*. Homewood, Ill.: Dorsey.

———. 1984a. "The Evolution of Aesthetic Taste." In K. Gergen and M. Gergen, eds., *Historical Social Psychology*. Hillsdale, N.J.: Lawrence Erlbaum.

———. 1984b. "Evolutionary Trends in Poetic Style: The Case of English Metaphysical Poetry." *Computers and the Humanities* 18: 3–21.

———. 1986a. "The Evolution of Italian Painting: A Quantitative Investigation of Trends in Style and Content from the Gothic to Rococo Styles." *Leonardo* 19: 217–22.

———. 1986b. "On Hedonic Selection, Random Variation, and the Direction of Cultural Evolution." *Current Anthropology* 27: 50–51.

———. 1987. "Narrative Pattern Analysis: A Quantitative Method for Inferring the Symbolic Meaning of Narratives." In L. Halász, ed., *Literary Discourse: Aspects of Cognitive and Social Psychological Approaches*. Berlin: De Gruyter.

———. 1988a. "Innovation, Discovery, and Evolution." In E. O. Wilson, ed.,

"Special Issue on the Creative Mind: Toward an Evolutionary Theory of Discovery and Innovation." *Journal of Social and Biological Structures* 11: 120–22.

———. 1988*b*. "Positivism, Constructivism, and Poetics." *Siegener Periodicum zur internationalen empirischen Literaturwissenschaft* 7: 209–42.

———. 1989. "Stylistic Trends in British and French Painting: An Evolutionary Explanation." *Visual Arts Research* 15: 1–20.

MARTINDALE, C.; ABRAMS, L.; and HINES, D. 1974. "Creativity and Resistance to Cognitive Dissonance." *Journal of Social Psychology* 92: 317–18.

MARTINDALE, C.; COVELLO, E.; and WEST, A. 1986. "Primary Process Cognition and Hemispheric Asymmetry." *Journal of Genetic Psychology* 147: 79–87.

MARTINDALE, C.; and FISCHER, R. (1977). "The Effects of Psilocybin on Primary Process Content in Language." *Confinia Psychiatrica* 20: 195–202.

MARTINDALE, C.; and KEELEY, A. 1988. "Trends in the Content of Twentieth-Century Hungarian and American Short Stories." In C. Martindale, ed., *Psychological Approaches to the Study of Literary Narratives.* Hamburg, Germany: Buske.

MARTINDALE, C.; and MARTINDALE, A. 1988*a*. "Hedonic Selection, Least Effort, and English Gothic Rib Vaulting." Paper presented at International Colloquium on Empirical Aesthetics, Barcellona, Italy.

———. 1988*b*. "Historical Evolution of Content and Style in Nineteenth- and Twentieth-century American Short Stories." *Poetics* 17: 333–55.

MARTINDALE, C.; MOORE, K.; and BORKUM, J. 1990. "Aesthetic Preference: Anomalous Findings for Berlyne's Psychobiological Theory." *American Journal of Psychology* 103: 53–80.

MARTINDALE, C.; MOORE, K.; and WEST, A. 1987. "Relationship of Preference Judgments to Typicality, Novelty, and Mere Exposure." *Empirical Studies of the Arts* 6: 79–96.

MARTINDALE, C.; ROSS, M.; and MILLER, I. 1985. "Measurement of Primary Process Content in Paintings." *Empirical Studies of the Arts* 3: 171–77.

MARTINDALE, C.; and UEMURA, A. 1983. "Stylistic Evolution in European Music." *Leonardo* 16: 225–28.

MARX, K.; and ENGELS, F. 1947. *Literature and Art: Selections from Their Writings.* New York: International Publishers.

MASTERS, E. L. 1915. *Spoon River Anthology.* New York: Macmillan.

MATTE-BLANCO, I. 1959. "Expression in Symbolic Logic of the Characteristics of the System ucs. or the Logic of the System ucs. *International Journal of Psycho-Analysis* 40: 1–5.

MAYER-KRESS, G., ed. 1986. *Dimensions and Entropies in Chaotic Systems: Quantification of Complex Behavior.* Berlin: Springer-Verlag.

MEDNICK, S. A. 1958. "A Learning Theory Approach to Schizophrenia." *Psychological Bulletin* 55: 316–27.

MEKHITARIAN, A. 1978. *Egyptian Painting.* New York: Rizzoli.

MERRIMAN, J. D. 1972. "The Parallel of the Arts: Some Misgivings and a Faint Affirmation." *Journal of Aesthetics and Art Criticism* 31: 153–64, 309–21.

MEYER, L. B. 1956. *Emotion and Meaning in Music.* Chicago: University of Chicago Press.

MICHAUD, G. 1950. *Introduction à une science de la littérature.* Istanbul: Matbassi.

MILES, J. 1964. *Eras and Modes in English Poetry.* Berkeley: University of California Press.

MILLER, J. H. 1979. "The Critic as Host." In H. Bloom et al., *Deconstructionism and Criticism.* New York: Seabury.

MILLETT, K. 1978. *Sexual Politics.* New York: Ballantine.

MITCHELL, B. R. 1975. *European Historical Statistics 1750–1970.* New York: Columbia University Press.

MITCHELL, B. R.; and DEANE, P. (1962). *Abstract of British Historical Statistics.* Cambridge, England: Cambridge University Press.

MITCHELL, B. R.; and JONES, H. B. 1971. *Second Abstract of British Historical Statistics.* Cambridge, England: Cambridge University Press.

MOORE, G. H.; and SHISKIN, J. 1967. *Indicators of Business Expansions and Contractions.* New York: Columbia University Press.

MOSTELLER, F.; and WALLACE, D. L. 1964. *Inference and Disputed Authorship: The Federalist.* Reading, Mass.: Addison-Wesley.

MUKAŘOVSKÝ, J. 1976 [1940]. *On Poetic Language.* Lisse, The Netherlands: Peter de Ridder.

MUNRO, T. 1963. *Evolution in the Arts.* New York: Harry N. Abrams.

NEF, J. U. 1932. *The Rise of the British Coal Industry.* London: G. Routledge.

NEUER, R.; LIBERTSON, H.; and YOSHIDA, S. 1978. *Ukiyo-e: 250 Years of Japanese Art.* New York: Windward.

NEUMANN, E. 1954. *The Origins and History of Consciousness.* New York: Bollingen.

NIETZSCHE, F. 1872. "The Birth of Tragedy from the Spirit of Music." In *The Philosophy of Nietzsche.* New York: Modern Library, 1927.

NORDAU, M. 1895. *Degeneration,* 5th ed. London: William Heinemann.

OSGOOD, C. E.; SUCI, G.; and TANNENBAUM, P. H. 1957. *The Measurement of Meaning.* Urbana: University of Illinois Press.

References

OWENS, C. M. 1975. "Self Realization—Induced and Spontaneous." *Journal of Altered States of Consciousness* 2: 59–73.

PAIVIO, A.; YUILLE, J. C.; and MADIGAN, S. A. 1968. "Concreteness, Imagery, and Meaningfulness Values for 925 Nouns." *Journal of Experimental Psychology Monograph Supplement* 76: 1–25.

PANOFSKY, E. 1924–25. "Die Perspektive als 'symbolische Form.'" *Vorträge der Bibliothek Warburg* 4: 258–331.

PATTEN, W., ed. 1905. *Short Story Classics, American,* vol. 1. New York: P. F. Collier.

PECKHAM, M. 1965. *Man's Rage for Chaos.* Philadelphia: Chilton.

PETERFREUND, E. 1971. "Information, Systems, and Psychoanalysis." *Psychological Issues,* monograph no. 25/26. New York: International Universities Press.

PETERSON, I. 1989. "From Dust to Dust: A Unique Supercomputer Provides a Glimpse of How Galaxies Evolve." *Science News* 135: 24–25.

PETERSON, R. A.; and BERGER, D. G. 1975. "Cycles in Symbol Production: The Case of Popular Music." *American Sociological Review* 40: 158–73.

PEVSNER, N. 1960. *An Outline of European Architecture,* 6th ed. Harmondsworth, England: Penguin.

PHELPS BROWN, E. H.; and HOPKINS, S. V. 1955. "Seven Centuries of Building Wages." *Economica* 22: 195–206.

———. 1956. "Seven Centuries of the Prices of Consumables Compared with Builders' Wage-rates." *Economica* 23: 296–314.

PIERCE, D. A. 1977. "Relationship—and the Lack Thereof—between Economic Time Series, with Special Reference to Money and Interest Rates." *Journal of the American Statistical Association* 72: 11–26.

PLANCK, M. 1949. *Scientific Autobiography and Other Papers.* London: Philosophical Library.

PLEKHANOV, G. 1936 [1913]. *Art and Society.* New York: Critics Group.

PODRO, M. 1982. *The Critical Historians of Art.* New Haven: Yale University Press.

POE, E. A. 1955 [1842]. "Longfellow's Ballads." In E. Wilson, ed., *The Shock of Recognition.* New York: Farrar, Straus & Cudahy.

POPPER, K. R. 1959. *The Logic of Scientific Discovery.* New York: Basic Books.

POUND, E. 1934. *ABC of Reading.* London: Faber & Faber.

PRAZ, M. 1970. *Mnemosyne: The Parallel between Literature and the Visual Arts.* Princeton, N.J.: Princeton University Press.

PULLIAM, H. R.; and DUNFORD, C. 1980. *Programmed to Learn: An Essay on the Evolution of Culture.* New York: Columbia University Press.

RACHLIN, H.; et al. 1986. "Cognition and Behavior in Studies of Choice." *Psychological Review* 93: 33–45.

RANKE, L. VON. 1906 [1835]. *History of the Popes, Their Church and State.* London: G. Bell.

RAPAPORT, D. 1957. "Cognitive Structures." In J. E. Bruner et al., *Contemporary Approaches to Cognition.* Cambridge, Mass.: Harvard University Press.

RAYMOND, M. 1963 [1940]. *De Baudelaire au surréalisme.* Paris: Librairie José Corti.

REISS, T. J. 1982. *The Discourse of Modernism.* Ithaca, N.Y.: Cornell University Press.

REITLINGER, G. 1961. *The Economics of Taste: The Rise and Fall of the Picture Market, 1760–1960.* New York: Holt, Rinehart, & Winston.

————. 1965. *The Economics of Taste: The Rise and Fall of the Objets d'art Market since 1750.* New York: Holt, Rinehart, & Winston.

RENWICK, W. L.; and ORTON, H. 1939. *The Beginnings of English Literature to Skelton.* London: Cresset Press.

RESCORLA, R. A. 1988. "Pavlovian Conditioning: It's Not What You Think It Is." *American Psychologist* 43: 151–60.

REVERDY, P. 1926 [1918]. *Le Gant de crin.* Paris: Plon.

REYNES, R.; MARTINDALE, C.; and DAHL, H. (1984). "Lexical Differences between Working and Resistance Sessions in Psychoanalysis." *Journal of Clinical Psychology* 40: 733–37.

RICHARDSON, J.; and KROEBER, A. L. 1940. "Three Centuries of Women's Dress Fashions: A Quantitative Analysis." *Anthropological Records* 5: 111–53.

RIEGL, A. 1927 [1901]. *Spätrömische Kunstindustrie nach den Funden in Österreich-Ungarn.* Vienna: Staatsdruckerei.

RIMBAUD, J.-A. 1966 [1871]. Lettre à Paul Demeny. In O. Bernard, ed., *Collected Poems.* Harmondsworth, England: Penguin.

RINDOS, D. 1985. "Darwinian Selection, Symbolic Variation, and the Evolution of Culture." *Current Anthropology* 26: 65–77.

ROBERTSON, M. 1959. *Greek Painting.* Geneva: Skira.

ROSCH, E. 1975. "Cognitive Representations of Semantic Categories." *Journal of Experimental Psychology* 104: 192–233.

ROSEN, K.; MOORE, K.; and MARTINDALE, C. 1983. "Creativity and Rate of Habituation." Paper presented at Eighth International Colloquium on Empirical Aesthetics, Cardiff, Wales.

ROSNOW, R. L.; and FINE, G. A. 1976. *Rumor and Gossip.* New York: Elsevier/ North Holland.

References

ROTHENSTEIN, J., ed. 1970. *New International Illustrated Encyclopedia of Art,* 24 vols. New York: Greystone Press.

RUSCH, G. 1985. "The Theory of History, Literary History and Historiography." *Poetics* 14: 257–78.

RUSKIN, J. 1844. *Modern Painters.* London: Smith, Elder.

SACHS, C. 1946. *The Commonwealth of Art.* New York: W. W. Norton.

SAINTE-BEUVE, C. A. 1837. *Pensées d'août, poésies.* Paris: Eugène Renduel.

SCHIFF, G. 1983. *Picasso: The Last Years, 1963–1973.* New York: Braziller.

SCHMIDT, S. J. 1982. *Foundations for the Empirical Study of Literature.* Hamburg, Germany: Buske.

SCHNEIRLA, T. C. 1959. "An Evolutionary and Developmental Theory of Biphasic Processes Underlying Approach and Withdrawal." In M. R. Jones, ed., *Nebraska Symposium on Motivation,* vol. 7. Lincoln: University of Nebraska Press.

SCHOVE, D. J. 1961. "Solar Cycles and the Spectrum of Time since 200 B.C." *Annals of the New York Academy of Science* 95(1): 107–23.

SCHÜCKING. L. L. 1966 [1923]. *The Sociology of Literary Taste.* Chicago: University of Chicago Press.

SCHWARTZ, G. 1985. *Rembrandt: His Life, His Paintings.* New York: Viking.

SHARP, R. L. 1940. *From Donne to Dryden: The Revolt against Metaphysical Poetry.* Chapel Hill: University of North Carolina Press.

SHAW, R. 1984. *The Dripping Faucet as a Model Chaotic System.* Santa Cruz, Calif.: Aerial.

SHEPARD, R. N. 1967. "Recognition Memory for Words, Sentences, and Pictures." *Journal of Verbal Learning and Verbal Behavior* 6: 156–63.

SHKLOVSKY, V. 1972 [1919]. "The Connection between Devices of *Syuzhet* Construction and General Stylistic Devices." *Twentieth Century Studies* 7–8: 48–72.

SILBERER, H. 1917. *Problems of Mysticism and Its Symbolism.* New York: Moffat, Yard.

SIMONTON, D. K. 1980*a.* "Thematic Fame and Melodic Originality: A Multivariate Computer Content Analysis." *Journal of Personality* 48: 206–19.

————. 1980*b.* "Thematic Fame, Musical Originality, and Musical Zeitgeist: A Biographical and Transhistorical Content Analysis." *Journal of Personality and Social Psychology* 38: 972–83.

————. 1984*a. Genius, Creativity, and Leadership: Historiometric Inquiries.* Cambridge, Mass.: Harvard University Press.

————. 1984*b.* "Melodic Structure and Note Transition Probabilities: A Content Analysis of 15,618 Classical Themes." *Psychology of Music* 12: 3–16.

————. 1986*a*. "Aesthetic Success in Classical Music: A Computer Analysis of 1,935 Compositions." *Empirical Studies of the Arts* 4: 1–17.

————. 1986*b*. "Popularity, Content, and Context in 37 Shakespeare Plays." *Poetics* 15: 493–510.

————. 1987. "Musical Aesthetics and Creativity in Beethoven: A Computer Analysis of 105 Compositions." *Empirical Studies of the Arts* 5: 87–104.

SINGER, J. L. 1978. "Experimental Studies of Daydreaming and the Stream of Thought." In K. S. Pope and J. L. Singer, eds., *The Stream of Consciousness: Scientific Investigations into the Flow of Human Experience.* New York: Plenum.

SISAM, C.; and SISAM, K. 1970. *The Oxford Book of Medieval English Verse.* Oxford: Oxford University Press.

SKAIFE, A. M. 1967. *The Role of Complexity and Deviation in Changing Taste.* Unpublished Ph.D. dissertation, University of Oregon.

SMITH, D. N., ed. 1926. *The Oxford Book of Eighteenth Century English Verse.* London: Oxford University Press.

SNOW, C. P. 1959. *The Two Cultures and the Scientific Revolution.* New York: Cambridge University Press.

SOKOLOV, E. N. 1963. *Perception and the Conditioned Reflex.* New York: Macmillan.

SOROKIN, P. A. 1937. *Social and Cultural Dynamics,* 4 vols. New York: American Book Company.

SPENCER, H. 1910 [1892]. *Essays, Scientific, Political, and Speculative,* vol. 2. New York: D. Appleton.

SPENGLER, O. 1926–28. *The Decline of the West.* New York: Alfred A. Knopf.

STADDON, J. E. R. 1975. "A Note on the Evolutionary Significance of 'Supernormal' Stimuli." *American Naturalist* 109: 541–45.

STAËL, G. DE. 1964 [1800]. "Literature Considered in Its Relation to Social Institutions." In M. Bergen, ed., *Madame de Staël on Politics, Literature, and National Character.* Garden City, N.Y.: Doubleday.

STEVENS, S. S. 1975. *Psychophysics: Introduction to Its Perceptual, Neural, and Social Prospects.* New York: John Wiley.

STEWART, D.; and LOVE, W. 1968. "A General Canonical Correlation Index." *Psychological Bulletin* 70: 160–63.

STONE, P.; et al. 1966. *The General Inquirer: A Computer Approach to Content Analysis.* Cambridge, Mass.: MIT Press.

SYPHER, W. 1952. *Four Stages of Renaissance Style.* New York: Doubleday.

————. 1960. *Rococo to Cubism in Art and Literature.* New York: Random House.

TAINE, H. 1875. *Lectures on Art,* vol. 1. New York: H. Holt.

TAKAHASHI, S. 1972. *Traditional Woodblock Prints of Japan.* New York: Weatherhill.

THEROUX, P. 1975. *The Great Railway Bazaar: By Train Through Asia.* Boston: Houghton Mifflin.

THOMPSON, R. F.; et al. 1979. "Habituation and the Orienting Reflex: The Dual Process Theory Revisited." In H. D. Kimmel, E. H. van Olst, and J. F. Orlebeke, eds., *The Orienting Reflex in Humans.* Hillsdale, N.J.: Lawrence Erlbaum.

TOCQUEVILLE, A. DE. 1956 [1835]. *Democracy in America.* New York: New American Library.

TOGLIA, M. P., and BATTIG, W. F. 1978. *Handbook of Semantic Word Norms.* Hillsdale, N.J.: Lawrence Erlbaum.

"Topics of the Day: Landon, 1,293,699; Roosevelt, 972,897." 1936. *Literary Digest* 122(18): 5–6.

TROTSKY, L. 1968 [1925]. *Literature and Revolution.* Ann Arbor: University of Michigan Press.

TROWBRIDGE, J. T. 1903. *My Own Story, with Recollections of Noted Persons.* Boston: Houghton Mifflin.

TROYER, R.; and MARTINDALE, C. 1988. "Stylistic Evolution in the Works of Chopin, Grieg, Beethoven, and Wagner." Paper presented at American Psychological Association convention, Atlanta.

TYNJANOV, J. 1965 [1924]. "Das literarische Faktum." In J. Štriedter, ed., *Texte der russischen Formalisten.* Munich: Fink.

————. 1967 [1929]. *Archaisten und Neuerer.* Munich: Fink.

TYNJANOV, J.; and JAKOBSON, R. 1971 [1928]. "Problems in the Study of Literature and Language." In L. Matejka and K. Pomorska, eds., *Readings in Russian Poetics.* Cambridge, Mass.: MIT Press.

ULRICH, H.; and PISK, P. 1963. *A History of Music and Musical Style.* New York: Harcourt, Brace & World.

UNDERHILL, E. 1911. *Mysticism.* London: Methuen.

UNITED STATES BUREAU OF THE CENSUS. 1975a. *Historical Statistics of the United States, Colonial Times to 1970.* Washington, D.C.: U.S. Government Printing Office.

————. 1975b. *Statistical Abstract of the United States.* Washington, D.C.: U.S. Government Printing Office.

References

———. 1985. *Statistical Abstract of the United States.* Washington, D.C.: U.S. Government Printing Office.

UNTERMEYER, L. 1931. *American Poetry from the Beginning to Whitman.* New York: Harcourt, Brace.

VAN EECKHOUDT, C. 1981. "La regression comme concept et instrument au service de l'analyse du contenu." Unpublished M.A. thesis, Université Catholique de Louvain.

VENDLER, H. 1985. *The Harvard Book of Contemporary American Poetry.* Cambridge, Mass.: Harvard University Press.

VITZ, P. C. 1966. "Preference for Different Amounts of Visual Complexity." *Behavioral Science* 11: 105–14.

WAGGONER, H. H. 1968. *American Poets from the Puritans to the Present.* Boston: Houghton Mifflin.

WARD, T. H. G. 1949. "An Experiment on Serial Reproduction with Special Reference to Change in the Design of Early Coin Types." *British Journal of Psychology* 39: 142–47.

WATSON, G. 1974. *The New Cambridge Bibliography of English Literature,* vol. 1. Cambridge, England: Cambridge University Press.

WATSON, J. B. 1913. "Psychology as the Behaviorist Views It." *Psychological Review* 20: 158–77.

WELLEK, R.; and WARREN, A. 1942. *Theory of Literature.* New York: Harcourt, Brace & World.

WERNER, H. 1948. *Comparative Psychology of Mental Development.* New York: International Universities Press.

WERTENBAKER, L. 1967. *The World of Picasso.* New York: Time-Life Books.

WEST, A.; and MARTINDALE, C. 1988. "Primary Process Content in Paranoid Schizophrenic Speech." *Journal of Genetic Psychology* 149: 547–53.

WEST, A.; MARTINDALE, C.; and SUTTON-SMITH B. 1985. "Age Trends in Content and Lexical Characteristics of Children's Fantasy Narrative Productions." *Genetic, Social, and General Psychology Monographs* 111: 389–405.

WEST, A.; et al. 1983. "Marijuana-induced Primary Process Content in the TAT." *Journal of Personality Assessment* 47: 466–67.

WILBUR, R. 1967. "The House of Poe." In R. Regan, ed., *Poe: A Collection of Critical Essays.* Englewood Cliffs, N.J.: Prentice Hall.

WILLIAMSON, G. 1958 [1930]. *The Donne Tradition.* New York: Noonday Press.

WILSON, E., ed. 1955. *The Shock of Recognition.* New York: Farrar, Straus & Cudahy.

WITTGENSTEIN, L. 1953. *Philosophical Investigations.* New York: Macmillan.

WOLFE, T. 1975. *The Painted Word.* New York: Farrar, Straus & Giroux.

WÖLFFLIN, H. 1964 [1888]. *Renaissance and Baroque.* Ithaca, N.Y.: Cornell University Press.

————. n.d. [1915]. *Principles of Art History.* New York: Dover.

WORDSWORTH, W. 1904. *The Complete Poetical Works of William Wordsworth.* Boston: Houghton Mifflin.

WUNDT, W. 1896. *Lectures on Human and Animal Psychology.* New York: Macmillan.

————. 1904. *Völkerpsychologie.* Leipzig: W. Engelmann.

YEATS, W. B. 1956. *Collected Poems.* New York: Macmillan.

YEATS, W. B., ed. 1936. *The Oxford Book of Modern Verse.* New York: Oxford University Press.

YOUNG, F. W.; LEWYCKYJ, R.; and TAKANE, Y. 1983. "The ALSCAL Procedure." In *SUGI Supplemental Library User's Guide.* Cary, N.C.: SAS Institute.

ZELLMAN, M. D. 1987. *300 years of American Art.* Secaucus, N.J.: Wellfleet Press.

ZIPF, G. K. 1972 [1949]. *Human Behavior and the Principle of Least Effort: An Introduction to Human Ecology.* New York: Hafner.

Index